Logotherapy and Existential Analysis

Logotherapy and Existential Analysis: 100 Key Points and Techniques is a practical, inspiring guide to Viktor Frankl's meaning-centered approach.

In 100 concise, engaging chapters, it offers a clear roadmap for anyone navigating uncertainty, burnout, loss, loneliness, or the disorienting pace of modern life—whether in their personal journey or professional practice. Drawing from Frankl's timeless framework and contemporary research and clinical developments in the field, the book moves from foundational principles to hands-on techniques and real-world applications across a remarkable range of settings: therapy and counseling, healthcare, education, organizations, community, and beyond. What makes this volume distinctive is its integration of theory, evidence, and ready-to-use practices in one coherent, highly readable format. At a time when uncertainty, disconnection, and rapid change have made the search for meaning more urgent than ever, this book is an invaluable companion—insightful, motivating, and deeply human—for anyone who wants to live and work with greater purpose, courage, and direction.

Logotherapy and Existential Analysis: 100 Key Points and Techniques serves as an indispensable resource for psychotherapists, counsellors, and anyone seeking to integrate meaning-centered perspectives into their personal or professional lives.

Pninit Russo-Netzer, PhD, is an Associate Professor, author, speaker, practitioner, logotherapist, and a leading researcher in the field of meaning in life and logotherapy. She heads the Community, Meaning, and Healing (C.M.H.) Research and Development Institute as well as the Resilience and Optimal Development Lab at Achva Academic College. She is also the founder and director of the Compass Institute for the Study and Application of Meaning in Life, Founder and Director of the Academic Training Program in Logotherapy at Tel Aviv University and the co-author and co-editor of several books on the topics of meaning in life, resilience, and existential psychology.

100 Key Points

Series Editor: Windy Dryden

ALSO IN THIS SERIES:

Single-Session Therapy (SST): 100 Key Points and Techniques
Windy Dryden

Acceptance and Commitment Therapy: 100 Key Points and Techniques
Richard Bennett and Joseph E. Oliver

Gestalt Therapy: 100 Key Points and Techniques
Dave Mann

Single-Session Therapy (SST): 100 Key Points and Techniques 2nd Edition
Windy Dryden

Transactional Analysis: 100 Key Points and Techniques 2nd Edition
Mark Widdowson

Acceptance and Commitment Therapy: 100 Key Points and Techniques 2nd Edition
Richard Bennett and Joseph E. Oliver

Logotherapy and Existential Analysis: 100 Key Points and Techniques
Pninit Russo-Netzer

Logotherapy and Existential Analysis

100 Key Points and Techniques

Pninit Russo-Netzer

Routledge
Taylor & Francis Group
LONDON AND NEW YORK

First published 2027
by Routledge
4 Park Square, Milton Park, Abingdon, Oxon OX14 4RN

and by Routledge
605 Third Avenue, New York, NY 10158

Routledge is an imprint of the Taylor & Francis Group, an informa business

British Library Cataloguing-in-Publication Data
A catalogue record for this book is available from the British Library

Library of Congress Cataloging-in-Publication Data
A catalog record has been requested for this book

ISBN: 978-1-041-03599-2 (hbk)
ISBN: 978-1-041-03595-4 (pbk)
ISBN: 978-1-003-62441-7 (ebk)

DOI: 10.4324/9781003624417

Typeset in Times New Roman
by Taylor & Francis Books

"To live is the rarest thing in the world. Most people exist, that is all."

(Oscar Wilde)

For my parents, my partner Lior, and my daughters—Ariel, Shahaf, and Shir—who remind me, again and again, what it means not merely to exist, but to truly live: with love, wonder, and meaning.

Contents

Illustrations

Figures

Preface

The question of meaning has long occupied the human mind. It is among the most profound, complex, and distinctly human inquiries—an existential puzzle that civilizations across history have sought to unravel. From ancient myths and religious traditions to the creations of poets, artists, and philosophers, the search for meaning has been a guiding thread woven into the fabric of human culture. Myths offered symbolic narratives about origins and purpose; religions anchored meaning in transcendent frameworks; poets and artists gave voice to the ineffable longing for significance; and philosophy systematically wrestled with the ultimate questions of human life. Each of these avenues, in its own way, reflects humanity's enduring effort to grapple with the mystery of why we are here, and what gives life its weight and worth.

Over time, the inquiry into meaning moved from broad metaphysical speculation toward a more immediate existential concern, one that centers on the lived, personal experience of choosing, enduring, and becoming. The existentialist tradition sharpened this shift. Søren Kierkegaard framed the struggle for meaning as a deeply personal task grounded in authentic choice and commitment. Friedrich Nietzsche, in proclaiming the "death of God," challenged humanity to create meaning in a world stripped of absolute certainties, emphasizing values and self-overcoming. Martin Heidegger shifted the focus to the human condition of "being-in-the-world," where meaning is not an external object but emerges from situatedness and responsibility. Albert Camus confronted the absurd, arguing that even if life lacks inherent meaning, human beings can live with dignity and purpose through their revolt against meaninglessness. Paul Tillich, from a theological perspective, articulated the "courage to be" as a way of affirming meaning in the face of existential anxiety. This philosophical groundwork paved the way for Viktor Frankl, who uniquely brought the question of meaning into the realm of psychotherapy and clinical practice.

Through the development of logotherapy and Existential Analysis (LTEA; hereafter, logotherapy), Frankl reframed the question from "What is the meaning of life?"—a universal, metaphysical puzzle—to "What is the meaning in *my* life?"—a personal, existential task that must be answered anew by each individual in the concrete circumstances of their existence. This marked a profound turning point: meaning was no longer distant or speculative, but experiential and pragmatic, at the very heart of human survival and flourishing. Meaning, in this view, is not a luxury or abstraction, but a vital psychological and existential force. Its presence or absence can shape whether a person collapses into despair or finds inner resources to endure suffering, overcome adversity, and move toward self-transcendence. In this sense, meaning becomes both anchor and compass: it steadies us amid turbulence and directs us toward possibilities for growth, contribution, and fulfillment. By placing meaning at the center of psychotherapy and human development, logotherapy bridges ancient existential questions with modern efforts to understand, and support, human well-being.

The purpose of this book is not to be prescriptive or all-encompassing. Rather, it aims to serve as a bridge between the origins of logotherapy and its current—and future—developments. Each of these 100 chapters offers a condensed selection of insights and practices, inviting readers to notice what resonates most, reflect on it deeply, and use it as a starting point for further exploration of the rich landscape of logotherapy.

Part I

Foundations and historical context

1 What is logotherapy?

Logotherapy, often glossed as "therapy through meaning," places the *human capacity and obligation to discern meaning* at the center of psychological health. Its basic claim is neither sentimental nor naïve: whenever circumstances can be changed, one should work to change them; yet *even when they cannot*, a person can still choose a stance that confers direction and worth. In this sense, meaning functions as both stabilizer and navigator: it steadies agency through difficulty and orients it toward contribution, connection, and development.

Etymologically, *logo-therapy* joins two Greek roots: *logos*, which in classical usage ranges across meaning, reason, word, and ordering principle; and *therapeia*, care or treatment. Taken literally, it is "treatment by way of meaning." In practice, however, logotherapy is more than helping people "find a meaning" for life or for a particular situation. It is a comprehensive clinical orientation—a theory of the person and a set of methods—that treats meaning as a workable variable in assessment, formulation, and intervention. Logotherapy is rooted in the premise that human beings are capable of *self-distancing* and *self-transcendence*: we can take a perspective on our impulses and circumstances, and we can answer to values that reach beyond narrow self-interest.

Modern and postmodern conditions often loosen inherited structures—shared faith narratives, stable roles, and moral authorities—without clearly replacing them; Nietzsche's "God is dead"

DOI: 10.4324/9781003624417-1

is a classic shorthand for this loss of a taken-for-granted compass. Logotherapy offers a disciplined way to reconstruct orientation without moralizing and without collapsing into relativism. It invites persons to discover purposes that are *theirs to answer*, in their actual circumstances, by aligning capacities and commitments with what they judge to be needed and good.

2 Historical development and Viktor Frankl's journey

Frankl, the father of logotherapy, argued that the events of the 20th century, particularly the World Wars and the atrocities they brought—profoundly destabilized both religious faith and trust in humanity. In the past, including the modern era, individuals often perceived themselves as safeguarded by frameworks of belief and the existence of a higher power that provided coherence, purpose, and meaning to their lives. In the postmodern era, however, we have seen a decline in the belief in religious salvation and a weakening of traditions that once anchored human lives with moral guidance and a sense of direction. Hierarchies and structures that were once self-evident have lost their authority. The wisdom of ancestors and traditional figures of power no longer holds the same sway. Alongside this erosion, individuals experience fragmentation within familial and communal ties and a disconnect from deep cultural roots. This dissolution of traditional frameworks is accompanied by the rise of science, pluralistic values, and the emphasis on individual freedom. These values highlight the right of every person to form an independent stance on essential life questions and to live in accordance with their preferences. In such an age, the notion of a singular "grand narrative" or dominant ideology becomes unsettled. Universal laws give way to relative truths, the personal story takes center stage, and subjective perspectives replace the pursuit of objectivity.

Each individual is now compelled to navigate their path and choose the values that will guide their steps. This fragmentation of meaning-providing structures, which once offered stability and direction, has contributed to increasing feelings of uncertainty, instability, alienation, and meaninglessness for many. It has also fueled the rise of nihilism and hedonism, reflected in the frantic pursuit of comfort, pleasure, and the ideal of happiness.

Viktor Emil Frankl was born in Vienna on March 26, 1905 to Elsa and Gabriel Frankl. From an early age he grappled with the question of whether life's transient nature undermines its meaning, arriving at the conclusion that it does not. While still in secondary school, he began to formulate what would later become logotherapy. In response to a teacher who described the human being as "nothing more than an internal-combustion machine," Frankl protested that "a person must certainly be more than that." This resistance to reducing the human condition to chemistry and biology accompanied him into his medical studies.

Raised in Vienna, Frankl encountered psychoanalysis early and, while still in high school, began corresponding with Freud. At nineteen—at Freud's personal invitation—he published an article in the *International Journal of Psychoanalysis* (Frankl, 1924). Over time, however, Frankl became dissatisfied with Freud's tendency to reduce human behavior to repressed or frustrated sexuality, and he gravitated toward Alfred Adler's Individual Psychology (Hoffman, 1995). His second scholarly article appeared in 1925 in the *International Journal of Individual Psychology*. Even so, the relationship with Adler unraveled in 1927 after Frankl publicly argued that Individual Psychology should, among other aims, move beyond its "psychologism." He was expelled from the Society of Individual Psychology.

In a 1926 address to the Academic Society for Medical Psychology, he first used the term "logotherapy," emphasizing the centrality of life's meaning in the face of despair and emptiness that often arise when confronting tragic circumstances. Viewing suicide as the extreme expression of perceived meaninglessness, Frankl—then a young medical student—founded a suicide-prevention program that substantially reduced suicide rates, an outcome he attributed to restored meaning in life. He earned his M.D. in 1930 and later served as Professor of Neurology and Psychiatry at the University of Vienna's Medical School. In 1941 he married Tilly Grosser, who was later killed in the Holocaust.

In 1938, Germany invaded Austria. Although Frankl obtained a U.S. immigration visa in 1942, he struggled with the decision whether to emigrate to pursue his professional calling to advance logotherapy or to remain out of filial duty. Seeking guidance, he wandered the city and paused in a church during a concert but found no clear answer. Returning home, he noticed a large stone on the table, which his father had retrieved from the ruins of a synagogue destroyed by the Nazis. On it was the Hebrew letter kaf (⊠), indicating it came from the Tablets of the Law and marked the Fifth Commandment—"Honor your father and your mother." In that moment Frankl resolved to stay, and the next day he relinquished his U.S. visa. This decision determined the fate of Frankl and his family.

On September 25, 1942, Frankl, his wife, and his parents were deported to the Terezín (Theresienstadt) ghetto. He later worked there as a general physician until his psychotherapeutic expertise was recognized and he was asked to establish a special unit to help new arrivals cope with the initial shock. He also set up a unit to prevent suicides among prisoners. For most of his imprisonment, however, he lived as an ordinary inmate, registered as Jewish prisoner 119 104, and performed hard physical labor, such as excavation and laying railway tracks. On October 19, 1944, Frankl and his wife were transported to Auschwitz. They were soon separated, and Frankl later described how holding on to her image, and to the hope of seeing her again, without knowing whether she was alive, became a sustaining source of meaning. In March 1945 he was transferred to a subcamp affiliated with Dachau, where he continued to work as a physician until the camp's liberation on April 27, 1945. His parents, his brother, and his wife perished in the camps.

Within a year of the war's end, in 1946, Frankl published his seminal works, *Man's Search for Meaning: From the Concentration Camp to Existentialism* and *The Doctor and the Soul*. He remarried in 1947, to Eleonore Katharina Schwindt, and they had a daughter, Gabriele. Frankl completed a doctorate in philosophy and, from 1946 to 1970, directed the Neurological Outpatient Clinic in Vienna. Over the course of his career, he authored approximately thirty-nine books (translated into roughly forty-nine languages), received twenty-nine honorary doctorates from universities worldwide, and lectured at 209 universities across all five continents. Beyond his academic and clinical contributions, Frankl actively pursued goals and challenges in his personal life. He learned to fly, earned a mountain-climbing instructor's badge at an alpine club, and three climbing routes bear his name. In 1975 he was granted honorary citizenship by his native city of Vienna. He died there of heart failure on September 2, 1997, the same year his final book, *Man's Search for Ultimate Meaning*, appeared.

Elisabeth Lukas—his student and today one of the foremost exponents of his approach—recounts asking Frankl how his students, who had not endured war could credibly testify to what he taught. Frankl replied with grave seriousness: "Everyone has his or her own Auschwitz." This insight motivated Lukas to extend Frankl's legacy at both clinical and theoretical-conceptual levels. Today, dozens of logotherapy institutes operate worldwide, training practitioners, publishing empirical research that examines and validates the approach's principles and techniques, and convening international conferences.

3 The Vienna context and psychotherapy landscape

> In former days, people frustrated in their will to meaning would probably have turned to a pastor, priest, or rabbi. Today, they crowd clinics and offices. The psychiatrist, then, frequently finds himself in an embarrassing situation, for he now is confronted with human problems rather than with specific clinical symptoms. Man's search for a meaning is not pathological, but rather the surest sign of being truly human. Even if this search is frustrated, it cannot be considered a sign of disease. It is spiritual distress, not mental disease. How should the clinician respond to this challenge? Traditionally, he is not prepared to cope with this situation in any but medical terms. Thus he is forced to conceive of the problem as something pathological. Furthermore, he induces his patient to interpret his plight as a sickness to be cured rather than as a challenge to be met. By so doing, the doctor robs the patient of the potential fruits of his spiritual struggle.
>
> (Frankl, 1962, p. 93)

The state of affairs described in the excerpt above presents clinicians with a substantive challenge. Encounters that extend beyond conventional training in treating psychiatric symptoms often call for engagement with spiritual questions that arise when a person confronts unique, existential demands—the striving to discern purpose and meaning.

Logotherapy is known as the "third Viennese school" of psychotherapy, following Freud's psychoanalysis—centered, in Frankl's reading, on the pleasure principle—and Adler's Individual Psychology, which emphasized striving for superiority, agency, and independence. In contrast, logotherapy posits the will to meaning as the primary human motive. The pursuit of pleasure emerges when meaning is frustrated; the will to power is instrumental to a larger aim—living a meaningful life.

Frankl explicitly contrasted his view with psychoanalysis. Freud once wrote that "the moment a person asks about the meaning of life, he is ill." Frankl countered that such questioning is not a sign of illness but of humanity; to inquire into life's meaning is itself a human achievement. His broader project sought to overcome psychotherapeutic reductionism or "psychologism," which, by ignoring the spiritual dimension, diminishes the human person to instincts and drives. For Frankl, we lack a final, objective answer to life's ultimate meaning; the absence of a definitive answer does not nullify the question but heightens responsibility in pursuing it. Because human knowing is finite, we must bear the tension between our longing for meaning and the nonfinality of answers.

Recognizing that Western psychology had largely neglected this spiritual dimension, Frankl developed a theoretical and applied approach he termed "logotherapy" (therapy oriented toward *logos*, i.e., meaning) to address the human question of life's meaning. Logotherapy places meaning at the center of clinical practice and research in mental health and holds that doubt about the worthwhileness of life constitutes a form of spiritual distress. Such concerns should not be hastily pathologized as mental illness. Frankl further warned that treating phenomena whose roots are spiritual solely with techniques designed for psychic disorders risks burying or blunting existential despair under sedatives; the therapist's proper task is to help patients navigate developmental crises so they can harvest the potential fruits of spiritual struggle. Logotherapy links psychotherapy with meaning in life and offers a distinct account of human development, aims, and structure. It is an existential analysis and a philosophically informed, practical method for alleviating suffering by cultivating awareness of the spiritual (noölogical) dimension and connecting it to the will to meaning through goals, values, and ideals.

Rejecting reductionism, Frankl argued that the human being is more than an electro-chemical organism governed by fixed psychological patterns. He distinguished between drives that "push from below" (e.g., sexual or aggressive impulses) and meaning—and the values bound up with it—that "pull from above" (e.g., conscience, responsibility, commitment to a cause beyond the self). What most distinctly differentiates humans from animals is not, first and foremost, the gratification of drives or the restoration of inner equilibrium, the reduction of tension, or the pursuit of pleasure, but the need for meaning. Acknowledging the spiritual dimension unique to persons, logotherapy emphasizes the central influence of ideals and meaning on human functioning and maintains that strengthening the sense that life is meaningful can mitigate many symptoms.

Frankl viewed frustration of the will to meaning as a source of diverse symptoms that do not always fit standard clinical categories. He called these "noogenic (spiritual) neuroses," including restless risk-seeking, compulsive busyness, chronic skepticism, and at times despair—patterns that may culminate in familiar secondary pathologies such as depression, aggression, or addictions. In efforts to dull the pain of meaning-frustration, many turn to excessive reliance on psychotropic medication or to substance use. Yet the underlying disquiet warrants recognition: Is it not expectable that a person who lacks direction and life-orientation will feel anxiety when unable to find a path, or agonize over choices to the point of paralysis, or avoid commitment in favor of diversion and thrill? Prolonged meaning-frustration may understandably devolve into depression.

The suffering that accompanies crisis can obscure the yearning for meaning, and the empathic therapist may be drawn into the patient's despair and avoid confronting the ways the patient is choosing in relation to it. Logotherapy affirms empathic attunement as foundational to healing while also noting its possible risks when it inadvertently consolidates a stance that impedes growth. It distinguishes two forms of human suffering: (a) unavoidable suffering tied to an unalterable fate, and (b) suffering arising from one's response to circumstances—often unwittingly self-generated. Therapeutically, logotherapy concentrates on enlarging awareness of the person's freedom to shape an attitude toward the given situation in ways that illuminate core values. As individuals recognize their spiritual core and fashion their stance toward life conditions, pathways to meaning open—both in ordinary circumstances and within suffering. Logotherapy thus supports walking the various "paths of meaning" and transforming personal tragedy into human achievement.

Within his tripartite ontology—body, psyche, and spirit—Frankl reframed the unrest Freud linked to unsatisfied libido as an "existential vacuum," a non-pathological, common condition that expresses the human tendency to seek meaning. De-pathologizing both the quest for meaning and the despair that can accompany its frustration, Frankl proposed that the appropriate response is not merely pharmacological alleviation or analytic excavation of past conflicts, but an existential-spiritual intervention that reconnects the person with the path of meaning.

Importantly, Frankl presented logotherapy not as a replacement for existing psychotherapies, but as a complementary extension of them, "forming a picture of man in his wholeness" (Frankl, 1986, p. xvii). In this spirit, he invoked Stekel's image of "a dwarf standing on the shoulders of a giant" to acknowledge logotherapy's indebtedness to Freud and Adler while also arguing for a broader, more holistic anthropology (Frankl, 1986, p. 3).

Logotherapy retains psychoanalytic vocabulary while adding the spiritual dimension. Where Freud analyzed problems of the psychophysical sphere—instinctual tensions and repressed drives—Frankl directed analysis to the noölogical sphere, where values and a person's unique meaning reside. Conscience, values, love, and the religious sense are not merely sublimations of the id; the human being is originally a spiritual entity, subsequently layered by psychic and bodily strata that can at times occlude access to this core. Against the pleasure principle, Frankl set the principle of meaning: the "paradox of hedonism" entails that direct pursuit of pleasure defeats itself; like happiness, pleasure is a by-product of realizing worthy purposes. History repeatedly shows that people willingly forgo pleasure, and even embrace pain and sacrifice, for the sake of meaning.

Compared with psychoanalysis, logotherapy views human beings as primarily concerned with fulfilling meaning and realizing values, not solely with satisfying drives, reconciling id–ego–superego conflicts, or adapting to social demands. This stance calls into question deterministic accounts of behavior and distinguishes choices driven by impulse from choices guided by value; the latter make unconditional freedom, and responsibility, possible.

Frankl also engaged Adler's Individual Psychology. As a young medical student (1923–1927), after leaving the psychoanalytic society, he joined Adler's circle and was influenced by it, especially by Rudolf Allers and Oswald Schwarz (a founder of psychosomatic medicine). Adler attributed psychopathology largely to deficits in social interest and belonging, linking pathology to self-centeredness and struggles for superiority. Frankl appreciated the attention to social embeddedness but criticized reductive explanations. For example, the claim that secondary gains from illness suffice to explain neurotic behavior. In Frankl's view, symptoms are not merely instrumental means; they are expressions rooted in the uniquely human noö-spiritual dimension—the same source from which art, love, and meaning arise.

Both Adler and Frankl stressed meaning, yet they differed in scope and conceptualization. Adler limited his discussion to three life tasks—work, love, and community—and to their relational features. Frankl expanded the frame to include suffering, life, and death, with an explicitly existential emphasis. For Adler, meaning arises chiefly in social contexts—belonging, being valued, and contributing to others as expressions of striving for superiority. For Frankl, meaning is broader than relational experience and rests on experiential, creative, and attitudinal values; it is spiritual in origin and guided by conscience toward self-transcendence.

Adler's chief contribution lay in highlighting relationships and social connectedness, with wide implications for education and community practice. Frankl's distinctive contribution was to place meaning at the heart of psychotherapy and to treat the will to meaning as a fundamental human motive. Crucially, he maintained that meaning can be realized even in tragic, unchangeable circumstances—precisely where superiority cannot be attained. This gives logotherapy particular relevance for marginalized and severely burdened populations: individuals living with chronic medical or mental conditions or disabilities, survivors of trauma and post-traumatic stress, and those with histories of addiction or incarceration. For such populations, interventions premised on belonging and superiority may be difficult to implement or sustain. Meaning-centered work allows traumatic events to be reframed as ruptures in life continuity while encouraging the construction of a new, coherent narrative that can integrate the traumatic episode and restore personal flow with life's rhythm.

In sum, often called the "third Viennese school of psychotherapy," logotherapy both continues and critiques the traditions of Freud and Adler. Where psychoanalysis foregrounded pleasure (the pleasure principle) and individual psychology emphasized striving for superiority and power, logotherapy centers the will to meaning as the primary motivational force. Clinically, it resists reducing symptoms to mere drive expressions and instead interprets them through a uniquely human, noetic (spiritual) dimension, oriented to values, conscience, responsibility, and self-transcendence.

4 Logotherapy's place in contemporary therapy

Meaning has become a central clinical theme in contemporary psychotherapy, reflecting growing recognition that suffering often disrupts not only mood and functioning, but also direction, identity, and the sense that life matters. Logotherapy is positioned precisely at this intersection. It treats meaning as a fundamental human capacity, enacted through freedom of response, responsibility, and self-transcendence.

Within the broader evidence base, existential therapies—as a family of approaches—have been examined empirically, with meta-analytic findings indicating beneficial effects across psychological outcomes (e.g., Vos et al., 2015). Even when contemporary trials do not use the label "logotherapy," many of its central ideas are increasingly visible in meaning-centered interventions that explicitly target coherence, purpose, and significance following disruption. A meta-analysis of meaning-centered therapies found improvements in quality of life and reductions in psychological stress, with particularly clear relevance in contexts of serious illness and major life disruption (Vos & Vitali, 2018). As one concrete illustration, Meaning-Centered Group Psychotherapy has shown efficacy in a large randomized controlled trial with patients with advanced cancer, demonstrating improvements in existential/ spiritual distress-related outcomes compared to an active comparison condition (Breitbart et al., 2015). Taken together, this body of work supports one of logotherapy's contemporary contributions: offering a coherent clinical language for engaging existential concerns—meaninglessness, guilt, responsibility, and finitude—without collapsing them into symptom reduction alone (Frankl, 1959, 2006; Vos & Vitali, 2018). At the same time, locating logotherapy in contemporary therapy also requires situating it within the broader humanistic tradition from which it both emerged and distinctly diverged. This is especially evident in its dialogue with Maslow: where humanistic psychology often framed growth in terms of self-actualization, Frankl insisted that meaning is most reliably found through self-transcendence, an orientation beyond the self that reshapes how we understand motivation, suffering, and what it means to flourish (Frankl, 1988; Koltko-Rivera, 2006).

Logotherapy and Maslow's humanism: from self-actualization to self-transcendence

Another key approach responding to the dominance of psychoanalytic theory at the time was the emergence of humanistic psychology through the work of Abraham Maslow (1907–1970). While Logotherapy and Humanistic psychology share a humanistic emphasis, logotherapy diverges from the humanistic theory. Two concepts central to this divergence were self-actualization (i.e., a 'me'-focused striving to reach one's full potential central to humanistic theory) and self-transcendence (i.e., a 'we'-focused pursuit of meaning by being directed toward something greater than oneself). Frankl argued that self-actualization, like happiness, tends to function best as a *by-product*: it arises when a person dedicates themselves to a value, task, or person beyond the self. In his view, the direct pursuit of self-fulfillment can become a subtle form of hyper-intention, whereas meaning is discovered through self-transcendence and responsible engagement.

This position is not wholly at odds with humanistic thought. Maslow himself repeatedly emphasized that self-actualization is often expressed through commitment to work, calling, and values that matter. Yet Frankl's critique of Maslow's hierarchy is sharper at one decisive point: Maslow's classic model implies that higher needs come reliably *after* the satisfaction of more basic needs, whereas logotherapy insists that meaning can remain psychologically vital—even under severe deprivation. In contemporary terms, logotherapy treats meaning less as a "luxury variable" and more as a stabilizing orientation that can coexist with suffering and constraint.

Notably, Maslow's later work moved closer to this emphasis by adding self-transcendence beyond self-actualization—an extension that has been widely discussed as a "later" or revised hierarchy. In Maslow's late framing, self-transcendence involves stepping beyond self-referential concerns toward unity, service, or a larger frame of belonging and value—an axis that resonates strongly with Frankl's core claim that meaning is found "outward," not manufactured inwardly.

Frankl also challenged how peak experiences were sometimes treated as a single class of "highs." He argued that some intense experiences reflect self-transcendence and noetic depth, while others are better understood as momentary gratification. Maslow's later distinction between peak and plateau experiences can be read as a partial refinement along similar lines: peak experiences are often climactic and episodic, whereas plateau experiences involve a steadier "Being-cognition" marked by contemplative depth and sustained wideness of awareness. For logotherapy, this nuance matters clinically: meaning is not measured by intensity, but by *orientation*—what the experience calls the person to value, commit to, and live responsibly afterward.

This shift from intensity to orientation also provides a natural bridge from classic humanistic debates to contemporary therapeutic concerns. In a modern therapy culture that can sometimes idealize "feeling better" as the primary endpoint, logotherapy retains a different emphasis: meaning is not forced, and suffering is not romanticized. Instead, it clarifies a disciplined clinical distinction between the irreversible and the still-choosable—the choice of attitude, direction, and contribution within constraint

(Frankl, 1959, 2006). In this sense, logotherapy remains clinically relevant because it helps therapists work precisely at the seam between realism and agency: acknowledging what cannot be changed while recovering responsibility for what can still be lived.

Contemporary meaning science makes this stance increasingly legible in empirical terms. Current models commonly differentiate meaning into facets such as coherence (life makes sense), purpose (life has direction), and significance/mattering (life is worth living and counts)—a framing that parallels logotherapy's practical question, "for the sake of what?" while avoiding reduction to symptom management alone (Martela & Steger, 2016; George & Park, 2016). In a similar spirit, meaning-making research shows that distress intensifies when disruptive events violate global meanings and core assumptions, whereas adaptation is supported when coherence and purpose can be gradually reconstructed without premature reframing (Neimeyer, 2019; Park, 2010). Together, these developments help explain why many present-day clients—without necessarily meeting a single diagnostic prototype—arrive with experiences such as identity diffusion, loss of direction, moral injury, loneliness, and diminished mattering: phenomena that are clinically central yet diagnostically diffuse, and that require a language beyond symptom clusters.

One area where logotherapy's conceptual clarity has become increasingly relevant is existential distress in medical and palliative contexts. Constructs such as demoralization, marked by helplessness/hopelessness, loss of meaning and purpose, and subjective incompetence in coping, have been operationalized and measured, and are increasingly differentiated from depression in clinical research (Clarke & Kissane, 2002; Kissane et al., 2004). This is precisely logotherapy's historical terrain: supporting agency and dignity when life circumstances cannot be "fixed," and helping clients reconnect to responsibility, values, and relational significance (Frankl, 1959, 2006).

Consistent with this, meaning-centered psychotherapy protocols, strongly influenced by existential and logotherapeutic ideas, have demonstrated benefits for spiritual well-being, quality of life, and distress outcomes in rigorous trials (Breitbart et al., 2015). At a broader level, meta-analytic findings indicate that meaning-centered therapies tend to improve quality of life and reduce psychological stress, supporting the clinical claim that increases in meaning are associated with reductions in distress, especially in contexts of major life disruption (Vos & Vitali, 2018; Vos et al., 2015).

Taken together, logotherapy's place in contemporary therapy is best understood in three integrated layers: (1) as part of the existential–humanistic family, supported by a growing evidence base for existentially oriented therapies (Vos et al., 2015); (2) as a conceptual bridge between classic humanistic concerns (growth, authenticity, self-transcendence) and modern meaning science (coherence, purpose, significance/mattering) (Martela & Steger, 2016; George & Park, 2016); and (3) as a clinically disciplined stance for working with the irreversible—where dignity, responsibility, and self-transcendence remain available even when suffering cannot be removed (Frankl, 1959, 2006, 1988). In this way, logotherapy retains a distinctive voice in contemporary practice: not as an alternative to empirical psychotherapy, but as a precise framework for the human questions that persist across diagnoses, settings, and life stages.

1.1 Philosophical foundations

At its core, every form of psychotherapy rests on an implicit anthropology and philosophy of life that orient its aims—even when these assumptions are not explicitly articulated. Logotherapy, by contrast, makes its philosophical foundations explicit, drawing on two principal sources: the phenomenological tradition (the study of lived experience) and existential philosophy (the study of the conditions and challenges of existence). The former is concerned with the *how*—how we attend to the person and the world, adopting a stance that seeks to disclose the singularity of experience and bring the "taken-for-granted" to light. The latter is concerned with the *what*—the existential themes that contour human life, including death, isolation, freedom, and meaning.

5 The phenomenological foundation

Consider a melody. No single note is the melody, and yet without each note there would be nothing to hear. What we recognize unfolds in time: the present tone carries traces of the one that has just faded and leans toward the one not yet sounded. Its identity is neither a label on a score nor a fixed object but a lived configuration that appears only in the act of listening. Or consider a waterfall – in one instant the torrents rush over the lip; a moment later the very same waters are already elsewhere, carried downstream. If its elements are never identical from one moment to the next, where does the waterfall begin and end—and is it the label alone that confers its identity? The human person presents a comparable puzzle. We carry names, roles, and diagnoses that promise stability, yet we are continually in flux. As Heraclitus observed, one cannot step into the same river twice; the river changes, and so does the one who steps in. Phenomenology invites us to take this flux seriously. Rather than treating labels as the essence of what something is, it turns our attention to lived experience—the *how it is* to be who you are, *now*, in passing time. The person before us is a dynamic composition—intentions, memories, anticipations, and values coalescing and shifting in the flow of experience. Within the context of Logotherapy, meaning itself is also not a static essence waiting to be discovered in some abstract realm of ideas; rather, it is a dynamic, living, and evolving phenomenon that unfolds within the concrete circumstances of human life.

Phenomenology asks us to take that flow seriously. It is a disciplined way of attending to how the world and the self are given: how the body feels from within; how mood colors possibilities; how time thickens with past and future; how relationships and contexts contour what matters. Rather than explaining the person by subsuming them under prior theories, phenomenology "listens" for the phenomenon on its own terms, bringing the taken-for-granted into view and allowing meanings to show themselves before we translate them into concepts.

The term *phenomenology* derives from two Greek words: *phainomenon* (that which appears) and *logos* (account, meaning). As a philosophical orientation, it originates in the work of Edmund Husserl and was further developed by Heidegger, Sartre, and Merleau-Ponty. Phenomenology centers on describing and understanding the person's world—the *life-world* (*Lebenswelt*)—as it is disclosed in everyday *lived experience.* It arose as a corrective complement to the dominance of the natural sciences and marked a turn toward the human sciences. By privileging subjective experience, phenomenology stands in principled contrast to positivist–empiricist approaches that aim primarily to "observe and explain," rather than to interpret and understand human experience. It proceeds from the view that there is no single, context-free truth and that persons actively participate in the constitution of their experience and reality. Accordingly, the world cannot be gauged solely by laws external to human experience; our picture of the world is not fixed but continually re-formed in the interplay between observer and object.

Husserl's rallying cry—"back to the things themselves"—treats experience as the basic source of knowledge. Phenomenology, in his sense, is a rigorous, disciplined inquiry into the things as they show themselves, undertaken to reach a fundamental understanding of consciousness and human experience. Three core notions ground this method: *description, phenomenon*, and *intentionality*. The aim is to approach, as closely as possible, the structure of the lived experience of those who undergo it, rediscovering what is ordinarily taken for granted—"what it is like to be you," or "what success, love, or meaning is *for you*." This involves suspending prior assumptions and theoretical commitments and directing one's intentional awareness toward the phenomenon. For Husserl, every act of consciousness is intentional; phenomenological description concerns such directed acts.

Phenomenology distinguishes the *life-world* and *being-in-the-world*. The life-world names the world in which one lives daily from the *natural attitude; being-in-the-world* (Heidegger) articulates how human beings exist, act, and are involved in the world, emphasizing the active, dialogical, and dialectical reciprocity between person and world. Knowledge about experience arises from those situated within this life-world; meaning grows from personal autobiography. The notion of being-in-the-world thus portrays a mutual co-constitution—figure and ground continuously shifting with situational context. Because events are interpreted, what happens to a person entails not only pain but also *suffering*—the product of meaning-making. A traumatic episode may become a life-defining tragedy through the narrative the person constructs around it.

Within this frame, phenomenology often articulates three interwoven dimensions: the *Umwelt* (the surrounding world), the *Eigenwelt* (the world with oneself), and the *Mitwelt* (the world with others). These are not separate "worlds" but distinct modes of the one world in which the person exists, braided together.

- **Umwelt** refers to the environment—the natural and biological world of needs, drives, and instincts, the deterministic conditions into which one is thrown and to which one must adapt.
- **Eigenwelt** denotes the intimate relation one has with oneself—the ways one apprehends and experiences oneself. Although self-understanding shifts with each act of introspection, the self is ordinarily lived as relatively stable at any given moment.
- **Mitwelt** affirms that human existence is inherently social. The world is intersubjective rather than private; self-definition is relational, and the meanings ascribed to experience are co-authored in dialogue with others and with the world. In this sense, meaning is not housed solely in the subject, the object, or the other, but emerges from their interplay. Through the interpersonal relation, persons transcend themselves and may discover purpose or meaning—analogous, for some, to a religious orientation toward an absolute Other.

A central phenomenological construct is **intentionality**: consciousness is always "about" something—be it the real, the imagined, or the dreamed. This underscores the individual's unique, situated, and subjective mode of experiencing. Every conscious experience includes two inseparable poles: the *noema* (that which is intended or experienced) and the *noesis* (the manner of intending or experiencing it). One cannot address only "what happened" without also attending to *how* it was lived and interpreted. Attending holistically to both poles enriches understanding. **Reflexivity** enables persons to become aware of their experiences and thereby to constitute meaning; it is an ongoing process engaging cognitive and affective operations in which the "self," as subject rather than object, actively organizes life's significance. Because one cannot reflect in the very moment of pure immersion, reflection is necessarily retrospective. Phenomenology therefore differentiates **pre-reflective** and **reflective** modes: experience unfolds as a living stream pre-reflectively and acquires articulated meaning through subsequent reflection.

Language and meaning. Phenomenology regards language as a primary medium of meaning. Heidegger famously called language "the house of Being," signaling that our interpretations are always shaped, enabled, and delimited by linguistic forms. Language mediates between pre-reflective and reflective life, and between inner and outer realities; it both reflects and constructs the real, organizing and framing perception. Among the most powerful linguistic tools is **metaphor**, which carries us beyond literal content to what lies "behind the words." Metaphors give verbal form to patterns and structures of experience; they are woven into everyday thought and feeling and are used so habitually that they often go unnoticed. Attending to the metaphors and idioms patients use is therefore a vital avenue for discerning the meanings they attribute to their experiences.

Accessing phenomenological meaning: bracketing and epoché. Approaching the meaning or "phenomenological essence" of an experience requires a deliberate effort to minimize bias, presupposition, and hypothesis regarding the phenomenon under study. Two methodological strategies provide a foundation for logotherapeutic work:

- **Bracketing** (*Einklammerung*): to enter the patient's life-world and grasp the lived experience, the clinician "puts in parentheses" prior assumptions, judgments, and foreknowledge—a posture of methodical doubt ("I know that I do not know"). Bracketing demands continuous self-reflexivity about how one's history may color the therapeutic process and human interaction more broadly.
- **Epoché**: from the Greek "to refrain from judgment," epoché calls for a fresh way of looking—suspending the rush to objective, fact-seeking explanations and prior theoretical accounts. The therapist seeks descriptive access to the patient's life-world and postpones searches for hidden motives or causal attributions.

Beginning inquiry with how phenomena are *lived*, as they are experienced by persons themselves, is central to logotherapeutic practice. The logotherapist strives to approach the patient's experience as closely as possible, to rediscover the patient's "taken-for-granted," and to hear how the patient frames and understands the key terms of their life.

As a disciplined method for describing experience as it is given, prior to theoretical explanations, phenomenology constitutes a crucial philosophical and methodological grounding for understanding human experience, especially processes of meaning-seeking. Phenomenological listening helps the clinician bracket premature interpretations and hear the patient's distinctive motifs—their recurrent concerns and commitments, their horizons of significance—so that meaning can be discerned rather than imposed. Beginning inquiry with how phenomena are *lived*—as they are experienced by persons themselves—is central to logotherapeutic practice. The logotherapist strives to approach the patient's experience as closely as possible, to rediscover the patient's "taken-for-granted," and to hear how the client frames and understands the key terms of their life. What appears fixed-"the patient with X," "the caregiver," "the resilient one"-is, when described closely, a moving configuration of intentions, perceptions, and meanings unfolding across time. To understand the person is thus to ask: What is it like to be *you* here and now? How is the present saturated with memories, expectations, and values? Where is meaning tugging—toward what is cared about, feared, resisted, or longed for?

6 The existential dimension

Alongside this phenomenological foundation, existential philosophy furnishes a further scaffold by foregrounding the irreducibly existential dimensions of human being—death, isolation, freedom, and meaning—within which logotherapy discerns and strengthens the will to meaning.

Existential psychotherapy, of which logotherapy is a central strand, builds on a long philosophical lineage, from Heidegger and Sartre to Ernest Becker, alongside contemporary research inspired by existential psychology. It views the patient through the prism of a meeting between the person and the conditions of existence, a meeting saturated with dynamic existential concerns: the inevitability of death, the question of meaning in and of life, the fact of isolation, and the burden and gift of freedom. The therapist's task is to bring the person into contact with their freedom and with the meanings at the heart of their singular experience, while also acknowledging the loneliness and finitude that are always embedded in subjectivity.

Yalom (1980) argued that many psychological difficulties brought to treatment are secondary pathologies whose primary origins lie in these existential concerns; heightened therapist awareness of this level can therefore inform work across a wide range of clinical presentations. For example, the insight that "everything that suffers wants to live" can provide a therapeutic foothold for supporting renewed engagement with a life of meaning and satisfaction. In this spirit, the therapist's self is an essential instrument for reconnecting the patient to meaning, as the therapeutic relationship can model an actively engaged stance toward life. Authentic modeling can help patients move toward meaning and participation; however, if therapists are unaware of their own assumptions about the search for meaning, they may struggle to assist such a search—or avoid it for fear of amplifying anxiety in themselves or in the patient.

The existential concerns

In addressing the challenges of existence, existential philosophy and psychotherapy typically consider four core themes—death, isolation, freedom, and meaning—often termed the "existential concerns." These themes are regarded as universally characteristic of human beings and can provoke anxiety and pathology when insufficiently regulated or integrated.

Death anxiety. This concern centers on life's finitude. From the outset, human beings must reckon with their mortality and find ways to live alongside it. Philosophical questioning about meaning often arises as a response to this recognition; when such questioning is unanswered, psychic resources may be diverted into defensive constructions. The concern is sharpened in encounters with nothingness—the recognition that every experiential change entails some loss, and that no moment of life can be fully recovered. Ernest Becker's work and Terror Management Theory emphasize the paradox at the heart of human existence: the drive for self-preservation coexisting with awareness of transience. In the face of this destabilizing fact, people develop strategies such as denial and repression; adherence to religious or worldview commitments that reframe death; or the pursuit of symbolic immortality (e.g., through children, authorship, or commemorative projects). Under extreme stress, omnipotent defenses may appear, including hypomanic or manic reactions. Alongside such defenses, avoidance strategies—neuroses, addictions, compulsive sexual behavior, self-harm—offer temporary escape. In contrast, acceptance of mortality and finitude can become a catalyst for growth, enabling fuller and richer living because of this acknowledgment.

Existential isolation. We come into the world alone and depart alone; even the closest other cannot fully grasp our experience as we live it. The person stands at the center of their world and only they can decide the next act. Existential isolation can be felt intrapersonally (e.g., as a split or fragmented self, self-alienation) and interpersonally (e.g., difficulties sustaining intimacy). Defensive responses range from denial and excessive fusion with others (herd behavior, conformity, over-pleasing) to alienation and social withdrawal. As with death anxiety, authentic encounter with isolation—including the pain inherent in intimacy—opens the possibility for genuine closeness.

Freedom. Existential thought holds that human beings are always free to choose and thus responsible for making their lives worthy and of value. Because choosing one possibility forecloses others, freedom can evoke guilt. Defensive maneuvers include denial of freedom and responsibility, neurotic controls that create an illusion of mastery (defensive guilt, compulsivity, overeating, profligacy), or the adoption of fatalistic worldviews (e.g., superstition). Facing this anxiety authentically—owning responsibility for choices and their consequences—supports a fuller life marked by authorship of one's personal narrative and capacity for development.

Meaninglessness. This concern arises as a synthesis of the foregoing three. If one must die, chooses alone, and remains ultimately isolated, what significance can a finite, transient existence have? The concern with meaning is often the central existential issue and can permeate every layer of life. A deficit of meaning may yield boredom and anxiety, what Frankl termed the 'existential vacuum', manifesting as helplessness, emptiness, depression, and difficulties in functioning and adaptation. Defensive strategies range from apathy and indifference to an existential neurosis characterized by radicalism (e.g., fundamentalism or hedonism), narcissism, and even obsessive or delinquent behavior—attempts to fill the void left by lost meaning.

Seen through this lens, as the following sections will reveal, logotherapy brings these concerns into therapeutic focus, not to pathologize them but to clarify and cultivate the will to meaning as a primary human motivation. The clinician's role is to help patients discern where meaning already beckons, where despair has constricted possibilities, and how an attitudinal shift can transform suffering into purpose—work that is inherently existential and unavoidably human.

7 Freedom and responsibility

Existential thought locates meaning in the very exercise of freedom—the capacity to step beyond roles proposed by one's society and culture and to choose oneself authentically, moment by moment. Logotherapy concurs with the centrality of freedom yet insists that freedom must be coupled with responsibility; otherwise it devolves into arbitrariness. This distinction is especially salient today, when unprecedented freedoms often coexist with confusion amid cultural abundance. Seemingly freer than ever, individuals may preserve their liberty while simultaneously losing a sense of meaning and, with it, satisfaction in life. In Frankl's view, it is the assumption of responsibility—the willingness to inhabit a role or task—that confers meaning. Freedom is realized as each person enacts the role they have chosen, a role that, by its nature, entails commitment to others and to the world.

When confronted with fateful, unchangeable circumstances, logotherapy proposes two avenues: to alter the situation as far as possible, or to accept it as a challenge insofar as necessary. The approach does not deny what Frankl called "healthy determinism": human beings are not exempt from constraints arising from their biological, psychological, or sociological conditions. But it categorically rejects pan-determinism, which denies the human capacity for distancing, reflection, and self-transcendence. Thus, while a person is not "free from" determinants, they are always "free to": above all, free to choose and to take responsibility for the attitude they adopt toward life's events. Accordingly, a core therapeutic emphasis in Frankl's work is the cultivation of responsibility as response-ability—the freedom and readiness to respond.

Frankl draws here on Karl Jaspers, who characterized human existence as "existence based on decision": the human being does not simply exist but continually decides how to exist. Freedom, therefore, cannot be severed from responsibility. In this connection, logotherapy distinguishes fate from freedom. Fate names the domain in which we have no freedom; to this domain belongs the past—what has happened cannot be altered, except through learning from it and reshaping one's stance toward it. Logotherapy both recognizes freedom and educates toward responsibility, differentiating between two kinds of responsibility: (1) responsibility imposed externally by some authority or circumstance, and (2) responsibility freely assumed, taken up by choice. In the latter case we ask, "For what, and for whom, do I hold myself responsible?" and we are prepared to bear burdens or make sacrifices accordingly. According to logotherapy, responsibility exerts a paradoxical pull: one is simultaneously drawn to it and shrinks from it. This linguistic wisdom points to the inner cross-currents that can inhibit the taking up of responsibility. For Frankl, however, responsibility is precisely what enables a person to fulfill their unique task; hence, responsibility and meaning are intrinsically intertwined.

8 The role of values in logotherapy

> If you don't stand for something, you'll fall for anything.

In logotherapy, values are not decorative ideals or private preferences; they are pathways by which meaning becomes livable.

While a subjective condition is indeed required to *discern* particular values, it does not follow that those values are invented by the subject. In the logotherapeutic perspective, values are discovered in the demands and possibilities of concrete situations and are answered through responsible choice, thus binding freedom to responsibility and preserving the objectivity of what calls to be realized.

The stance individuals take toward their core commitments emerges as a determining element in their willingness to pursue meaningful action and their capacity for transformative change (Honka et al., 2019). Personal values operate as fundamental organizing principles, shaping how individuals interpret significance and directing their choices across both mundane decisions and pivotal life transitions (Sagiv et al., 2017). These deeply held convictions reflect what people regard as essential and worthy of pursuit (Schwartz et al., 2012), serving as expressions of underlying motivations, needs, and authentic preferences that influence daily conduct, major life decisions, and long-term subjective well-being (Lee & Kawachi, 2019; Schwartz & Sortheix, 2018).

Frankl described values as "to-be-realized meanings," encountered in the concrete demands of situations and answered through responsible choice. A distinctive contribution of logotherapy is its treatment of conscience as an organ of meaning-disclosure rather than merely a repository of social rules. Conscience "hears" the unique claim that a particular moment makes on a particular person—what Frankl called the *call of the situation*. Values, in this view, are not imposed abstractions but are *discovered* phenomenologically in the textures of lived life: in what compels our respect, awakens our care, or quietly insists "this is mine to do." The clinical task is to help patients discern these claims without substituting the therapist's values for their own.

The therapeutic cultivation of value-aligned living proves particularly powerful because authentic behavioral change depends fundamentally on consonance between outer actions and inner convictions. When individuals pursue goals that resonate with their genuine sense of self and fulfill intrinsic needs, these pursuits are more likely to be sustained and integrated into their identity (Ryan and Deci, 2000). This alignment between values and behavior creates a foundation for lasting transformation rather than superficial compliance. Research demonstrates that individuals become more receptive to challenging or potentially threatening information when they have recently reflected upon important personal values (Sherman and Cohen, 2006). This affirmation process appears to strengthen psychological resilience and reduce defensive responses to difficult truths. Brief interventions involving reflection on core values can mitigate the harmful effects of stress on performance and enhance achievement (Cohen and Garcia, 2008; Garcia and Cohen, 2013; Walton and Wilson, 2018) by reminding individuals of what truly matters, thereby protecting mental resources needed for effective self-regulation and coping (Creswell et al., 2005; Koole et al., 1999).

The gap between what individuals profess to value and how they actually live presents a significant therapeutic opportunity. While people experience greater well-being when their actions align with their values, the discrepancy between valued ideals and lived reality often creates internal conflict and diminished satisfaction (Sheldon and Krieger, 2014; Tessier et al., 2021). This suggests that individuals may benefit substantially from therapeutic support in actively pursuing goals connected to their authentic values (Bojanowska et al., 2022). In the logotherapeutic frame, values are the architecture through which meaning takes form—creative, experiential, and attitudinal routes by which a life becomes answerable to what it deems worthwhile. Empirical and theoretical accounts alike suggest that it is protective to cultivate multiple arenas of meaning through which values are expressed. Such diversification can operate as a psychological "shock absorber" when one channel is threatened or collapses. For example, when work—once a central source of meaning—comes under threat (e.g., impending job loss), additional sources such as family, friendship, study, or volunteering can partially compensate for the temporary loss of that channel. In the psychological literature this adaptive process is sometimes described as 'fluid compensation' (Heine et al., 2006), reflecting the capacity to reallocate value-expression across changing life conditions.

Within logotherapy, many contemporary presentations of distress are read as manifestations of a *value crisis*. When previously guiding commitments are eroded—by trauma, bereavement, displacement, moral injury (a wound to conscience after a profound moral violation), or rapid social change—persons can drift into what Frankl termed the existential vacuum, marked by boredom, apathy, and a sense that nothing is worth undertaking. These conditions often present under secondary forms (compulsivity, addictive patterns, diffuse anxiety, corrosive cynicism), yet their organizing principle is disorientation of value rather than symptomatology per se. Accordingly, value re-orientation is not an adjunct but a central therapeutic aim. Loss or distortion of value typically appears in three recognizably different ways: *value collapse* (what once mattered no longer seems credible or worthy), *value conflict* (competing goods paralyze choice and fragment agency), and *value occlusion* (meanings remain present but are obscured by pain, habit, or noise). Clarifying which of these signatures is operative guides the clinical task: not to install values from the outside, but to recover, differentiate, and enact the values already implicit in the client's life.

Overall, in the logotherapeutic frame, values function less as abstract ideals than as orienting demands that become concrete in creative work, receptive experience, and chosen attitude. When the compass of value is restored—whether from collapse, through conflict, or out of occlusion—clients regain direction even when conditions do not change. Put differently: symptom relief follows re-orientation, not the other way around: *What is this situation asking of me now, and how can I answer it?*

1.2 Core theoretical elements

9 The primary motivation: will to meaning

From the earliest stages of development, as language emerges, children's first inquiries revolve around the persistent question of "Why?," reflecting their bids to understand themselves and their place in a wider world. This natural orientation toward meaning is foundational for the consolidation of the self. It begins with felt capacities and grows into skills, aspirations, ideals, and values. In striving to master tasks they perceive as worthwhile—whether academic, social, or moral—children sketch the contours of identity. The question of "why" thus becomes both an epistemic tool and an existential compass.

Logotherapy situates itself precisely within this human impulse and motivation. As a meaning-centered psychotherapeutic approach, logotherapy posits the will to meaning as the primary human motivation. In doing so, it reorients the field beyond other influential traditions—psychoanalysis, individual psychology, and later humanistic approaches—by placing meaning, rather than pleasure, power, or self-expression per se, at the core of motivation. For Frankl, life does not "owe" us pleasure, control, or status. Rather, it offers us tasks and responsibilities in service of persons, purposes, and ideals that transcend the self. Echoing Kierkegaard's insight that "the door to happiness opens outward," logotherapy contends that human nature is not fulfilled by folding inward on itself, but by going beyond itself—self-transcendence.

When the call of meaning is muffled, attention collapses inward: not into authentic self-presence, but into self-enclosure—marked by hedonic pursuits, status comparison, and compulsive self-monitoring, with emptiness rising in their wake.

Modern life amplifies this tension. Many of us find ourselves negotiating between the demands of "what I should do" or "what is socially right" and the quieter pull of "what I truly want." The psychological needs for security, esteem, and belonging can easily entangle our choices in comparative hierarchies of what is "best" in the eyes of others rather than what is most fitting for our singular calling. Here it is crucial to distinguish "specialness" from "uniqueness." Specialness is comparative and often narcissistic, organized around being higher in rank or broader in achievement than others. Uniqueness is contributive and relational: it names the distinctive imprint from which only I can act and through which I can offer something the world would otherwise lack. Choices made from uniqueness do not chase the "best" in abstract terms; they converge on what is most congruent—what is mine to do.

Logotherapy begins from the assumption that, at the depth of our being, we awaken each day with more than the question, "What do I want to be?" We also awaken to the ethical-existential question, "For what, and for whom, am I to be?" The will to meaning is not an ornament added to a life otherwise complete;

it is the structuring motive that organizes agency, resilience, and responsibility. When people can locate a task, a value, or a relationship that calls them beyond themselves, they often find that vitality, courage, and even joy follow as by-products. When they cannot, symptoms frequently crowd in to fill the vacuum.

10 The existential vacuum

Never before has so much information, choice, and convenience been available in affluent societies, and yet rarely have so many felt unmoored. The menu expands while appetite wanes. The self turns to metrics and mirrors, chasing rank in lieu of purpose; diversions multiply even as vitality thins. These compensations—pleasure, comparison, reassurance—offer momentary relief but leave the deeper question unanswered: *to what end?*

Logotherapy reads this pattern not as a failure of motivation, but as a crisis of meaning. Clinically, it distinguishes two related conditions: **existential frustration** and the **existential vacuum**. Existential frustration is woven into the human condition. Our recognition of limits and death keeps the question of meaning on the horizon. When the *will to meaning* elicits no clear response, a chronic tension surfaces. The capacity to bear that tension, and to translate it into a concrete orientation, guards against more destructive sequelae.

Here logotherapy departs from views that place fear of death at the center of existential distress. For Frankl, the sharper threat, given our awareness of mortality, is the unanswered question *"To what end?"* When this question is credibly answered, death anxiety tends to diminish. Likewise, in contrast to classical psychoanalytic accounts that foreground sexual frustration or "castration anxiety," Frankl argued that such concerns become salient *when* the will to meaning is thwarted; they are secondary expressions of a more primary failure of meaning. When existential frustration remains unresolved over time, it may congeal into an **existential vacuum**. Unlike existential frustration, which is an inherent feature of human existence, the existential vacuum is a pathological development: it emerges when the search for meaning repeatedly fails and the will to meaning is chronically blocked.

Phenomenologically, the vacuum presents as boredom, alienation, and apathy, coupled with compensatory pursuits (hedonic distraction, status striving, compulsive comparison) that keep life occupied but not oriented and often unfulfilled.

Frankl traced the vulnerability to two historical losses bound up with becoming human. First, the loss of instinctual governance: unlike animals, we are not directed by fixed drives that unambiguously dictate aims (food, sex, shelter). Life within culture relocates us into a field of meanings that vary by place and epoch. We are tasked not only with meeting biological needs but also with enacting the ideals of our milieu; when these ideals fail to speak to us—or we fail to realize them—emptiness and despair can follow. Second, the gradual erosion of traditional frameworks—religion and inherited customs—that once supplied authoritative answers to questions of purpose. As their binding force weakens, many find themselves with neither instinct to tell them *what* they must do nor tradition to instruct them *how* to live. In this space, felt "emptiness" of listlessness, estrangement, and indifference become increasingly common.

11 Noögenic neurosis

Clinical science excels at explaining how behavior is initiated and regulated; it is less prepared to ask to what ends it is directed. Logotherapy restores this teleological question, locating disturbance in the noetic dimension where values, responsibility, and purpose are constituted. On paper, clients may "have it all": intact functioning, adequate resources, even impressive accomplishments. Yet what brings them to therapy is not simply anxiety or sadness but a more elusive complaint—*emptiness, pointlessness*, a sense that the machinery of life is running without a destination. Some respond with hyperactivity and relentless productivity; others chase novelty or certainty; still others drift into a flat, anergic apathy. The common denominator is not a shortage of energy but a shortage of *why*.

In logotherapy, this picture is interpreted as **noögenic distress**—suffering rooted primarily in the noetic (spiritual) dimension of human existence—rather than as a merely psychogenic or somatogenic disorder. Frankl estimated that in roughly one-fifth of clinical presentations a directly noögenic etiology can be identified, and that many additional cases involve noögenic factors indirectly. The point is not to deny bodily or psychological determinants, but to notice when meaning itself has become the site of disturbance. Frankl proposed that any neurotic phenomenon can be traced to four interwoven strata of human existence: it appears (1) as a **physical** occurrence, (2) as a **psychological** process, (3) within a **sociocultural** field, and (4) as a **mode of existence**—an existential-spiritual stance toward life. Only in the fourth stratum does existential analysis and logotherapy find its true point of departure.

When a person struggles to bear **existential frustration**—the ever-present tension generated by our awareness of finitude and our will to meaning—noögenic neuroses emerge, signaling that access to the spiritual/noetic dimension is blocked. Common noögenic presentations include the following:

1 **Compulsive Skepticism (Obsessional Doubt).**
   Skepticism is a natural posture in the face of existential limits; as a neurosis, however, doubt becomes pervasive and functionally impairing. Driven by a longing to discover *the* meaning and to avoid pangs of conscience, the person seeks endless reassurance—consulting authorities (parents, experts), conforming to majorities, or outsourcing judgment. Relief, when it arrives, is short-lived; indecision and, in severe cases, avoidance and paralysis follow. An extreme example could be OCD which may reflect, according to logotherapeutic view, an expression of hyperconsciousness of responsibility for one's life and a perfectionistic craving for certainty. Unable to tolerate the guilt inherent in consequential choices (career, partnership), the person displaces the demand for perfection onto trivial daily decisions and rituals (cleaning, checking, symmetry)—an overcompensation that soothes anxiety while narrowing life.
2 **Compulsive Adventurism (Novelty-Seeking Without Anchor).**
   At the neurotic level, adventure functions as refusal to accept existential limits—the not-knowing, the guilt bound up

with choosing one path over another. The compulsive adventurer cycles rapidly through careers, locales, and relationships, or clings to goals lacking authentic inner content. The style is energetic but restless, marked by risk-taking and vulnerability to behavioral and substance addictions.

3 **Compulsive Busyness (Doing Over Being).**
Here the person dodges existential tension and the guilt of choosing by perpetual *doing*, while avoiding states of *being*. As with adventurism, the activity level is high, but the aim is to outrun the disquiet that accompanies authentic meaning. Socially, this can earn praise—workaholism, round-the-clock availability, relentless tasking—yet it often coexists with anxiety about health, compulsive eating, excessive sexual behavior, and overuse of addictive substances.

4 **Vegetative Despair (Anergic Apathy).**
Unable to tolerate existential frustration, the individual dulls the longing for meaning itself, sinking into indifference and boredom—a kind of suspended animation. Some once had a meaningful direction but lost it; what previously felt significant now appears hollow. In adaptive cases, this recognition catalyzes a search for new orientation. Pathologically—especially where frustration has congealed into an existential vacuum—it yields resignation, depression, suicidality, violent acting out, and addictions. A stark cultural illustration is the so-called "27 Club," where wealth, fame, and success coexisted with profound inner emptiness.

The person who comes to therapy brings with them the full array of cultural discourses in which they are embedded: the historical background into which they were born, the ideals of the family, and the spirit of the age. These become internalized voices that accompany—and at times inundate—their being, heightening exposure to existential frustration. Against this backdrop the central questions surface: What is meaningful? How should one choose among these competing voices? In the therapeutic encounter, we listen for the stance the person adopts toward the tension between the longing for meaning and the inescapable uncertainty surrounding it, and we discern the shape of their noögenic neurosis in both the complaint and the manner of address. A certain client may present with compulsive skepticism, situating the therapist as the authority meant to dictate what is "right," whereas another may display a more compulsive adventurism orientation, narrating cycles of enthusiasm and suffering while seeking a steadying hand toward the equanimity they desire. A third may reflect compulsive busyness, filling the space with words and tasks that leave little room for authentic dialogue—an effort to avoid exposure to a terrifying sense of inner emptiness. Noögenic neurosis, in this light, discloses the constitutive uncertainty of life and at the same time affirms the importance of our freedom to choose within it. Help-seeking among those experiencing existential frustration can be read as a sign of strength and hope: they refuse to settle for generic, borrowed ideals and resist being absorbed by them. They remain with questions that can lead toward a distinctive meaning, yet often struggle to commit in the face of uncertainty—becoming tormented by a conflict that cannot be resolved until they find within themselves the capacity to take an existential stance. The therapeutic task is thus to help the person bear existential frustration by identifying the life-affirming impulse implicit within it and, through that recognition, to restore them to an authentic mode of existence—one that requires a decision about how their life will become worthy and meaningful.

12 The tragic triad

Human life is bounded by three non-negotiable facts: we are vulnerable, responsible, and finite. Where vulnerability enters, there is pain; where responsibility binds, there is guilt; where finitude asserts itself, there is loss (including death). Frankl named this constellation the *tragic triad*. Its elements are not pathologies in themselves but conditions of existence that can erode meaning—or deepen it—depending on the stance one takes. At this existential crossroads, logotherapy offers a distinct interpretation of the tragic, showing how suffering may be transformed into responsibility, value, and purpose.

Logotherapy distinguishes between the cause of suffering and its reason. A *cause* is always biological or physiological (including the concrete conditions under which a person lives); a *reason* is psychological or, in Frankl's terms, noetic, pertaining to the spiritual dimension of meaning and value. At the psychological level, maladaptive responses to existential frustration are often linked to a formative event, sometimes in early life and sometimes more recently. Such events frequently involve encounters with the tragic triad—guilt, loss and death, and pain—combined with the absence of orienting values for meeting them. In these circumstances, existential frustration is managed suboptimally and may shake a person's sense of meaning in the world.

Logotherapy offers a distinctive account of how to meet the tragic by specifying the constituents of suffering in human existence—what Frankl called *the tragic triad: pain, guilt, and loss*. No one escapes pain, or moments of guilt, and everyone loses someone or something of value. Later developments in logotherapy added injustice as a fourth element, yielding a "tragic diamond"; some treat injustice as the obverse of guilt, two sides of the same moral coin.

Loss

Frankl proposed that the very recognition of life's finitude can become a decisive awakening. The encounter with death and limits does not strip life of meaning; rather, it sharpens the responsibility to actualize meaning while life is still open. Drawing on the image of awakening from a dream, Frankl wrote that although we regard death as "something terrifying that happens to us," we "hardly suspect how well it is meant" (Frankl, 2010, pp. 175–176). Death renders life's transitions more vivid, highlights the unique and unrepeatable opportunities of our situation, and obliges us to assume responsibility for realizing them now. We also meet "death" in every transitional passage—an ending that precedes a beginning—and, of course, in parting from a beloved, retiring from work, or losing health. In logotherapy, loss—like death—can quicken fuller living and amplify meaning.

Guilt

Logotherapy differentiates three kinds of guilt:

1 *Neurotic guilt*—feeling guilty without having committed a wrong, for example because of a wish or thought.
2 *Actual (real) guilt*—guilt that follows from a concrete act (commission) or from a failure to act where responsibility was due (omission).
3 *Existential guilt*—a more diffuse restlessness and disquiet tied to underrealization of one's possibilities and responsibilities.

Elisabeth Lukas further distinguished justified and unjustified guilt, noting that each requires a different therapeutic response: we must separate guilt grounded in reality from guilt generated by imagination.

Neurotic guilt. Psychoanalysis traces this to unconscious childhood sources; in the Freudian structural model it reflects imbalances between id (drive) and superego (internalized moral authority). Here, even the *wish* to do wrong evokes guilt. Consider the adult daughter who tenderly cares for her dying father yet, at times, fleetingly wishes for release so she can return to her children and work; she may feel unworthy, despite acting responsibly every day. The logotherapeutic distinction is crucial: the psychophysical strata aim at pleasure and tension reduction, whereas the noetic (spiritual) dimension is where the person chooses in accordance with values—even at the cost of discomfort, pain, or higher tension. A person's spiritual core is not assessed by hidden wishes or passing thoughts but by the choices enacted in spite of them. Frankl also distinguished morality from conscience, and therefore did not treat neurotic guilt as suffering to be *endowed with meaning*; rather, it is suffering from which one should recover.

Actual guilt. Following Guttmann, actual guilt arises in two different situations: (a) *guilt by commission*, when one has performed a fundamentally wrongful act; and (b) *guilt by omission*, when one failed to do what responsibility required. In such cases there is a genuine basis for guilt; the therapeutic task is not to anesthetize it but to help the person assume responsibility in a manner consonant with their values.

Existential guilt. This refers to an interior unease—a pressure to act so as to silence it—that, when recognized and integrated, can propel a life of realized meaning. Guttmann notes that existential guilt often reveals *inattention* across three domains: to oneself (neglect of basic physical or intellectual–spiritual needs), to others (evading responsibilities toward loved ones or adopting a hardened, intolerant stance), and to the world (refusing responsibility toward nature and the broader environment).

Injustice

As noted, later logotherapeutic work expanded the triad to a **tragic diamond** by adding the experience of being wronged. Guilt and injustice can be viewed as two facets of the same moral field—harm done *by* the self and harm done *to* the self. Encounters with injustice often agitate those who seek redress and consolation—outcomes that may be beyond their control or, at times, impossible.

Pain and suffering

No one passes through life without pain. Authors in the logotherapeutic tradition describe a spectrum: from dental pain to chronic illness; psychological pain born of disappointment; the pain of interpersonal conflict and betrayal of trust; the pain of unrealized goals; the loss of valued work; and *spiritual pain*—doubt or loss of faith, wrestling with a former life, estrangement in relation to God, spiritual conflict, indifference, and loss of hope.

Logotherapy distinguishes three kinds of suffering: (1) suffering tied to an unchangeable fate; (2) suffering arising from emotionally painful experience; and (3) suffering produced by a lack of meaning.

1 ***Suffering bound to an unchangeable fate.*** If circumstances can be changed, they should be changed; only when fate is inalterable does the question of meaning in suffering become central—above all through the freedom to choose one's *attitude* toward the unavoidable. When change is impossible and suffering is inescapable, what remains unconditionally ours is

the freedom to transform our stance. Confronted with an unchangeable fate—an incurable illness, the death of a loved one—one is given the opportunity to realize the *highest* of values: the meaning of suffering. Frankl saw the supreme human achievement in meeting fate with courage. This does not deny pain, confusion, sadness, or anguish—these are real and powerful—but it affirms that the person, too, is powerful, and can choose a response to them.

2 ***Suffering arising from emotionally painful experience.*** Even here, meaning can be discovered. Suffering is not to be sought for its own sake, but its arrival can constitute an invitation to wrest from it a deeper meaning—one that reorients life.
3 ***Suffering from lack of meaning.*** The third kind is suffering generated by *existential frustration*—often felt as boredom or futility—which naturally provokes flight into activities that appear to justify life's worth. As elaborated elsewhere in this volume, existential frustration may crystallize into a range of pathological coping patterns and, diagnostically, often marks the starting point for meaning-centered analysis in logotherapeutic practice.

Taken together, the tragic triad delineates the terrain on which the central logotherapeutic question is posed: not only *what* causes suffering, but *to what end* it can be borne—what responsibility it summons, what values it discloses, and what singular meaning it invites a person to realize.

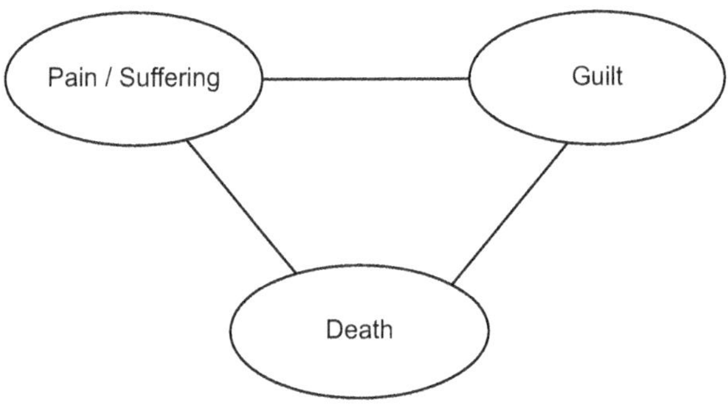

Figure 1.1 The Tragic Triad

13 Mass neurotic triad

Viewed at the population level, distress does not distribute at random—it clusters. Across settings and eras, when a society's shared sense of "why" thins, three compensatory patterns reliably swell: *aggression, addiction, and depression*. Frankl named this recurring configuration the *mass neurotic triad*. It is not a new diagnosis but a lens: these syndromes are read less as isolated disorders than as convergent responses to an existential vacuum—a lived absence of significance and direction.

Aggression

A compensatory attempt to mute the existential vacuum by escalating arousal and generating an illusory sense of control over existence. Aggression may be directed outward (hostility, anger, violence) or inward (risk-taking, self-harm, suicidality). In both directions, the surge of stimulation brings transient relief while leaving the underlying lack of meaning unaddressed.

Addiction

A strategy to anesthetize or override the existential vacuum either through numbing—dulling sensations, feelings, and thoughts to the point of self-loss and dissociation—or through the pursuit of artificial highs and ecstasy. Typical expressions include binge eating (or self-starvation), compulsive sexual behavior, overuse of alcohol and drugs, gambling, and related behavioral addictions. The common function is short-term regulation that displaces, rather than resolves, the question of meaning.

Depression

An attempt to quiet the existential vacuum by dampening the longing for meaning and consolidating an apathetic stance toward life. Clinically, one often observes diminished self-worth; a widening gap between the actual and ideal selves; and a disjunction between what is and what ought to be—all closely tied to a felt inability to occupy or fulfill the person's significant life roles. Here, the energy problem is secondary; the primary disturbance is teleological: direction has gone missing. Framed this way, the mass neurotic triad directs assessment beyond symptom clusters to questions of purpose and commitment: Where has meaning been eclipsed?

In clinical formulation, a noögenic (meaning-level) contribution is suggested when (a) the presenting syndrome functions chiefly as compensation for an absence of "why" (e.g., arousal seeking, numbing, resignation), (b) the patient's language centers on pointlessness, misalignment, or loss of direction rather than on sheer affective burden alone, and (c) symptom relief, when achieved, does not reliably restore orientation. Crucially, this lens supplements—rather than replaces—medical, psychological, and sociocultural determinants; standard differential diagnosis, risk assessment (including suicidality), and evidence-based treatments remain necessary and often synergize with logotherapeutic work.

14 Attitudes towards life

Clinical formulations often describe what people feel and do; logotherapy asks, in addition, *how they stand* toward life. An attitude is not merely a mood or trait but an orientation—a chosen stance toward facts that may be welcome, neutral, or irrevocably hard. Precisely because existential frustration and the sense of an inner

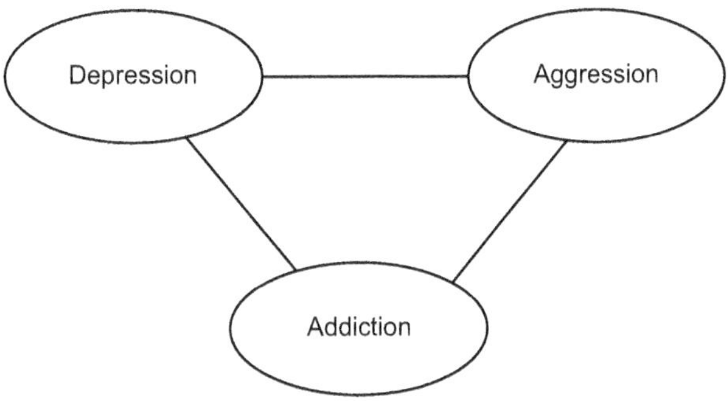

Figure 1.2 The Mass Neurotic Triad

vacuum are recurrent features of human life, the attitudinal domain becomes clinically decisive: when meaning is thin, people tend to adopt patterns of stance that organize experience, sometimes in ways that are protective, and sometimes in ways that are maladaptive. Against that backdrop, Frankl described four *non-adaptive* attitudes that commonly arise when the will to meaning is thwarted:

1 Fatalistic stance.

A worldview in which the person experiences life as bound to a fixed, pre-ordained order of events. This rigid determinism leaves little room for mystery or compassion and is expressed in cynical, pessimistic appraisals, difficulty with empathy, abdication of responsibility, passivity, a drive to secure control "at any cost," and reliance on superstition. The stance quiets anxiety by denying freedom—and with it, the possibility of meaning.

2 Hedonism.

A pattern of being moved almost exclusively by wishes and drives. Clinically it may present as indecision, absence of long-term goals and commitments, and an oscillation between short-lived satisfaction and bitterness about life, with a lingering sense of emptiness. Pleasure is pursued as a substitute for purpose; gratification rises while orientation erodes.

3 Conformist stance.

Adherence to majority opinion to the point of erasing individuality and personal responsibility. The person automatically identifies with prevailing social values, presuming the individual perspective to be less valid than that of "the many," and thus resolves questions of life-meaning by deference to the dominant view. Under existential pressure, direction is outsourced to the crowd.

4 Fanatical stance.

Here one's assumptions in the face of existential frustration are elevated to absolute truth. The person does not ask; they "know." A relative value is absolutized and idealized while other values are diminished. Life is organized around the chosen value, at times to the point of extreme action. As Lukas notes, this stance portends emotional crisis whenever that value is lost, since no other value is permitted to replace the idealized one.

In logotherapy, these attitudes are not reified as fixed traits but approached as modifiable orientations—habitual answers to the question "How shall I stand toward what is?" The clinical task is to help patients recognize and loosen non-adaptive stances while cultivating the attitudinal capacities at the heart of meaning-centered work: responsibility, courage, compassion, and the freedom to take a stance even when circumstances cannot be changed.

15 Dimensional ontology

Modern psychotherapy is rich in methods for regulating affect and behavior, yet it risks a categorical error if it overlooks *what kind of being* a person is. Logotherapy grounds clinical work in a *three-dimensional ontology*: body and psyche are necessary but not sufficient; an irreducible spiritual (noetic) dimension completes the picture. This dimension is not a metaphor for mood or morality. It names the field in which freedom, responsibility, conscience, love, imagination, and meaning are constituted—the very field in which a human life becomes *about* something. If we mistake *what sort of thing* a person is, we commit category errors in assessment and care. Each dimension discloses the person differently; none, taken alone, suffices. The task, therefore, is not to collapse higher meanings into lower mechanisms, but to understand how the dimensions relate—and how the noetic voice can be recovered when it is obscured.

Logotherapy conceives the person as an interwoven unity of **body, psyche, and spirit**. Frankl was deeply conversant with the Western intellectual tradition; even so, despite reasoned argument supported by research analogies, case vignettes, and dream analyses, his position remained marginal in his time. One reason, plausibly, was his insistence on describing the human **spiritual** dimension—partly hidden from the senses—during an era shaped by positivist thinking grounded in sensory data. Elisabeth Lukas, one of Frankl's closest collaborators, observed the challenge of validating this dimension. The **somatic**-biological domain can be measured directly; the **psychic** domain (emotions, drives) resists direct observation but can often be inferred from its effects. By contrast, the **noetic** domain—our zone of freedom—is so open-ended that it is unclear how far standard empirical methods can reach. Because a person can accept, ignore, or resist the constraints of body and psyche, empirical study here is necessarily limited.

Essentially, logotherapy rests on a **three-dimensional ontology** that differentiates the **somatogenic** (bodily), **psychogenic** (psychic), and **noetic** (spiritual) aspects of the person, and focuses clinically on the last.

Body (soma)

This may refer to the full sensory spectrum from pleasure to pain, acutely or chronically (e.g., arousal and sensory enjoyment, illness and injury). The body houses organic—biological and chemical—explanations for states and phenomena (hormonal, immune, neural activity). The bodily dimension also includes life conditions into which one is born that shape physical reality (e.g., race, origin, geography).

Psyche

Here we locate the spectrum of emotions—fear, sadness, anger—and socially inflected affects such as shame and embarrassment, typically evoked in relation to others. This layer also includes socio-cultural conditions that influence the expression of human phenomena such as love, conscience, and faith. Values formed here can be **inauthentic** when they echo sociology or zeitgeist alone. Clinically, this is the level at which we trace developmental traumas, family milieu, and difficult life events that contour the self.

Spirit (noetic)

From the Greek *noesis*—inner or intuitive knowing—the noetic layer is the deepest core of personhood. It spans the continuum from despair and emptiness to a sense of distinctive meaning, and includes capacities such as imagination, compassion, love, and responsibility. Authentic values live here; human phenomena such as love, conscience, and faith are not explained away by sociological explanations alone but express the person's **deep nature**.

Thus, love is not merely a biological instinct (somatic) or a social arrangement (psychic); it is also a longing for **self-transcendence**—for connection and unity beyond the self.

Using a geometric analogy, Frankl underscores two core features of the human as spiritual being: openness and uniqueness. Consider a cylinder and a cone. Viewed only through their projections (shadows), the cylinder may appear as a rectangle from the side and a circle from above or below. Looking solely at the base of either the cone or the cylinder, one might conclude both are simply circles. In each case, a two-dimensional silhouette conceals the volume and openness of the actual form, and conflates distinct objects when only their base is seen. Frankl's multi-dimensional ontology—body, psyche, and spirit—aims to restore the full picture: the cylinder has volume as well as openness; a cone is not a cylinder, even if both present as a circle from a certain angle; and each form is unique.

By the same token, the "closure" implied by reflex systems in biology or by reactive patterns in psychology does not contradict the human being's openness at the spiritual level—just as the cylinder's apparent closure from one vantage point does not negate its openness as a three-dimensional object. For this reason, Frankl warned that when a person is grasped only at one stratum—somatic, psychic, or spiritual—their unity is devalued or even denied. Each level manifests differently, and the observer tends to define the object according to the observer's vantage point. Hence a strictly two-dimensional view cannot "solve" the psychophysical problem posed since Descartes; given the limits of human cognition, we apprehend aspects of reality, not reality in its entirety.

Human reality as it is, not merely as it appears from a partial angle, is characterized by openness, which belongs to its very essence, and within which freedom of the will is disclosed. Frankl clarifies this by differentiating the dimensions: body and psyche operate as "closed systems" and can fall ill; the spirit (noetic) is an "open system," transcending the confines of time and space and cannot be damaged or diseased—it can only be obstructed or "buried alive." This claim highlights the unconditional freedom proper to the human spirit. Even when a person cannot change

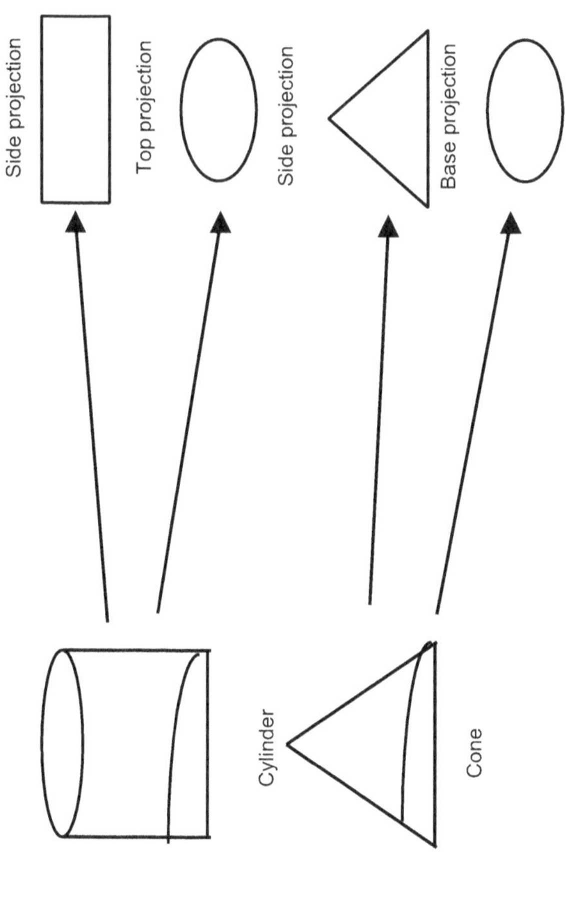

Figure 1.3 Geometric Analogy: Forms and their Projections

the conditions of life, they retain the capacity to choose their attitude toward those conditions, to discover values, and to realize meaning through uniquely human strengths such as courage, love, and compassion—resources available, in principle, up to one's last breath. In clinical terms, dimensional ontology guards against reductionism: it legitimizes medical and psychological interventions where appropriate, while preserving the noetic point of departure for meaning-centered work. It invites the therapist to ask, alongside diagnostic questions, where the open system of spirit is presently blocked, and how freedom and responsibility can be re-mobilized so that body, psyche, and spirit speak again in concert.

16 The spiritual (noetic) dimension

Frankl held that the human being is, in essence, spiritual (noetic), yet this spiritual essence is embedded within and expressed through psychic and somatic strata. The term *noetic* comes from the Greek *nous* (νοῦς), meaning mind or intellect, often used in philosophy to denote the *higher* human capacity for understanding, conscience, and insight. In Frankl's usage, the noetic points not to "religion" per se, but to the uniquely human dimension of freedom, responsibility, and meaning-orientation. While body and psyche function as closed and limited systems—especially under conditions of physical or mental illness—the noetic dimension is an open system situated at the deepest level of personhood and remains intact. Whereas body and psyche tend toward *self-satisfaction* (tension reduction, pleasure), the noetic dimension is oriented to *self-transcendence* (going beyond oneself). Psychotherapy addresses the psyche; logotherapy addresses the spirit. Accordingly, logotherapy links psychotherapy with meaning in life and proposes a distinct account of human development, aims, and structure. It is a form of existential analysis and a practical-philosophical therapy for suffering and distress that proceeds by cultivating awareness of the spiritual dimension and connecting it to the search for meaning through goals, values, and ideals.

Frankl rejected reductive accounts of the human being as merely electro-chemical matter propelled by fixed psychic patterns. He distinguished drives (e.g., sexual, aggressive), which push "from below," from meaning and values, which draw "from above." What distinguishes the human from the animal is that our primary concern is not drive satisfaction or internal equilibrium, tension reduction, and pleasure, but rather the need for meaning. Recognizing the specifically human spiritual dimension, logotherapy emphasizes the central influence of ideals and meaning; it therefore contends that treatment aimed at enhancing meaning can alleviate many symptoms.

In keeping with this three-dimensional ontology, both symptoms and their sources are examined with reference to body, psyche, and spirit. In the spiritual domain—already detailed earlier—the reason for symptoms is existential frustration, and the remedy is the discovery of unique meaning. The relative contribution of each domain varies by case, and advancing science has revealed the complexity of any given symptom, which typically implicates all three. For example, depression has bodily components (genetics, heritability), psychic components (developmental history), and spiritual components (philosophical, theological, or existential stance toward one's life and life as such). Consequently, logotherapy recommends replacing terminology that privileges one dimension in the essence of a symptom with terminology that clarifies the vantage point: one may adopt a bodily, psychic, or spiritual *perspective*. Illness can appear in any dimension and affect the others.

Lukas captures the interplay of dimensions with a musical analogy: imagine hearing a Beethoven sonata in a concert hall. A piano is required—without an instrument, the most exalted composition remains unheard. Yet the piano alone does not suffice. We also need a pianist who can play flawlessly. Still, a piano plus a pianist is not enough: without a *score*, randomly struck keys yield no coherent form. The pianist's technical facility mirrors the influence of *psychic* functions on the body; it has no higher content by itself. The *spiritual* dimension is the *composition* that unites instrument and performer, enabling the pianist to translate an idea into beautiful sound. When the final note fades, piano and pianist revert to separateness; the unity dissolves. The parable warns against *reductionism*—shrinking the person to the physical and psychic while ignoring the spiritual, which is integral to wholeness.

Within logotherapy, the spiritual dimension is the person's inner medicine chest, containing resources of self-transcendence: imagination, humor, creativity, compassion, love, freedom, responsibility, the defiant power of the human spirit, courage, and the drive to discover one's unique meaning. Equipped with these values and capacities, individuals can engage life events in ways that support change and spiritual growth. The spiritual dimension exists in all people, regardless of religion, spirituality, or value orientation.

Two capacities enable self-transcendence and an attitudinal stance toward existence:

1 ***Self-distancing (self-detachment).***
The ability to observe oneself and one's situation from the outside—to "zoom out" beyond the immediate state.
2 ***Self-transcendence.***

The ability to rise above circumstances and orient oneself toward someone or something beyond the self—an important task or a love for another person. This capacity runs counter to *homeostasis* (typically guiding body and psyche) and is governed by the spirit's drive toward *heterostasis* (constructive tension) in pursuit of worthy values or goals. In this connection, Frankl distinguishes *psychodynamics*—the balance and movement of forces in the psychic realm—from *noödynamics*—the distinctive way these forces are taken up and transformed in the spiritual realm. Clinically, this distinction protects against reductionism: we treat what is somatic and psychic as such, while restoring access to the noetic point of freedom and responsibility through which meaning can be discovered and enacted.

17 The role of conscience

The study of conscience has an expansive history in many disciplines, including those of psychology and philosophy. Over recent centuries, the focus has transitioned from philosophical introspection towards scientific neurological and psychological investigation. Key contributions have been offered by the likes of René Descartes, John Locke, William James, Sigmund Freud, Jean Piaget, and Carl Jung.

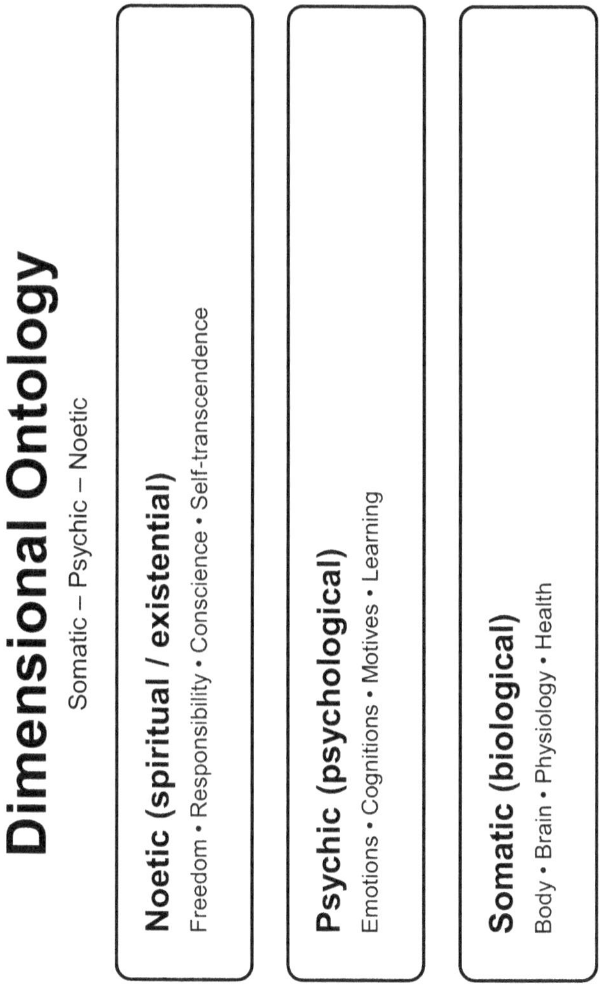

Figure 1.4 Dimensional Ontology

Psychoanalysis classically attributed conscience to the superego—an internalized paternal image that represents the norms of one's society and culture. In Freud's structural model, the psyche comprises id, ego, and superego, whose complex relations shape moral behavior. The superego functions as a quasi-conscience that develops through the introjection of social values, first via parents and later through teachers and other authorities. At first, the child conforms out of fear of punishment or loss of security and love; over time, through identification, external demands become self-demands, guiding conduct even without external pressure. A "weak" superego risks lax or pleasure-dominated living; an overly rigid superego risks asceticism and harsh self- and other-criticism regarding any gratification. This view, however, reduces value-directed life to derivatives of fear, dependency, and sublimated drives, treating morality as the by-product of conditioning.

Logotherapy shifts the center of gravity. Just as access to the instinctual unconscious in psychoanalysis reveals distinctive meanings in a life, existential analysis turns toward the spiritual (noetic) unconscious, where—Frankl argues—the primary instrument for discovering meaning resides: conscience. Conscience has an intuitive capacity to recognize the "pattern of meaning" latent in a given situation—to sense what is being asked of a person here. If we hastily collapse conscience into social conditioning, we imply that human morality is nothing more than compliance with cultural demands. For Frankl, acting "morally" merely to avoid sanction is inauthentic. Rules, by nature, are too rigid and too general to fit unique situations; received norms may guide, but they can also suffocate unless accepted in freedom and responsibility.

Norms are general; lives are singular. In practice, clients and therapists meet situations in which obligations collide, statutes underdetermine action, and two genuine goods compete. At such thresholds, the central question is not "Which rule applies?" but "What is being asked of me here?" Logotherapy names the faculty that answers this question *conscience*—a noetic capacity for situational discernment that detects the unique value latent in a concrete circumstance and summons freedom to respond. In logotherapy, thus, conscience is constitutive of being human rather than a product of learning, habit, or conditioning. It orients like a compass by way of personal values and helps us perceive the particular meaning we are called to realize in the unrepeatable situation before us. Thus conscience is the "organ of meaning" or "moral compass" that refines moral sensitivity and guides choices, great and small. From the perspective of the spiritual dimension, values are not merely reaction-formations to repressed drives; they are expressions of the human spirit. Accordingly, Frankl views conscience as a transcendent phenomenon: it is not reducible to an internalized external object.

The psychoanalytic reduction renders values subjective—dependent on personal stance alone. By contrast, for Frankl a given subjective state is the medium through which values are recognized; it does not create them. This rests on his three-dimensional ontology: body, psyche, and spirit function as prisms through which values are disclosed. On the psychic level one may describe social relations and prevailing ideals (for instance, a period's beauty standards) as shaping desire. On the spiritual level, however, we encounter **values themselves**—as when a person's beauty is apprehended even when it exceeds biological impulse or cultural canons. Openness to a given dimension becomes the medium for recognizing the value revealed there—somatic, psychic, or spiritual.

Logotherapy therefore distinguishes moral values that arise as reactive formations of drive-based dynamics from conscience-based values that are authentic expressions of the spirit. Frankl also distinguishes morality from conscience: morality rests on absolute or prevailing cultural codes that shift across epochs; conscience can surpass convention, expressing deeper, human, spiritual values that exceed the zeitgeist. At times, authentic spiritual values align with social morality; at other times, "morality," as the outgrowth of the instinctual unconscious or of conformist pressures, can mask unresolved inner conflicts. Conscience-values, by contrast, manifest the spiritual unconscious and thus carry an intrinsic authenticity.

This distinction may illuminate patterns behind historical atrocities: "morality" can be co-opted by totalitarianism and conformity, licensing actions deemed "moral" that nonetheless harm others. Conscience functions as an ethical instinct, preserving a decisive feature of the human as a moral being, and necessarily includes self-transcendence—rising above oneself for the good of the other. Clinically, when a person acts in line with authentic values, a clear, deep sense of meaning often follows. By contrast, a person who acts merely under the imperative of social morality frequently reports sacrifice tinged with depletion, tending toward existential emptiness in its various expressions. The moral demand may conflict both with drives and, at times, with one's authentic values. Acting from conscience, however, expresses one's interiority—not the psychophysical-instinctual unconscious, but the spiritual-axiological core. In that case, sacrifice is reinterpreted as self-transcendence—a realization of higher and deeper meaning rather than a drain on it.

For logotherapy, then, the clinical task is twofold: to help patients discern the voice of conscience amid the noise of drives and conventions, and to support commitment under uncertainty when conscience indicates a course that rules alone cannot specify. Conscience neither abolishes psychology nor law; it orients them—so that a human life can become answerable not only to what is permitted, but to what is meaningful.

18 Meaning in suffering

We are born into social worlds whose norms and expectations furnish a value system and an orienting compass. When the surrounding world renders life comprehensible—organizing experience into a coherent story—and affirms mattering—the sense of worth, visibility, and significance through beliefs, worldviews, symbols, and rituals—individuals can take a stance toward existential frustration, not merely confront it. In this way, culture and community function as a network of meaning that enables agency and coherence. Conversely, when these layers falter, people may lose their bearings. Traumatic life events can shatter basic assumptions and destabilize value structures. In the aftermath of trauma, if one cannot gradually reweave meaning into the ongoing narrative of life, existential frustration hardens, and the vacuum expands.

Logotherapy emphasizes the creative potentials latent in suffering. Unavoidable suffering becomes an opportunity to demonstrate the human capacity to rise above pain and to take warranted pride in that achievement. Frankl argued that in such conditions we are given a chance to discover inner richness despite outward failure; we can *mature through* suffering, grow with it, and thereby uncover new strengths. Most of us readily see how positive experiences deepen meaning. It is harder to recognize that suffering can do likewise—if we adopt the fitting stance toward it. Precisely then the opportunity arises to take a stand toward one's pain. Some logotherapists extend Frankl's view: not only the values of courage and dignity in facing an unchangeable fate confer meaning, but any experience of suffering through which we enact our deepest convictions and values may become a source of meaning.

Elisabeth Lukas has articulated several ways in which suffering can contribute to development:

- It guards against the hardening of the psyche and sharpens emotional awareness.
- It discloses our vulnerability and the fragility of life, compelling honest accountability.
- It enables repentance; lived repentance can undo the moral weight of the past by initiating a spiritual and ethical renewal, turning grief into a mission.
- It can inspire others: when people witness how suffering is borne with dignity, a deep sense of meaning is realized and shared.
- It refines freedom, since it forces a personal confrontation and a taking of responsibility.
- Ultimately, it can foster spiritual growth—through the work of enduring and emerging from suffering as a victor in the existential sense.

Where suffering is unavoidable, the question shifts from how to eliminate pain, to how to take a stance toward it so that it yields significance. It is no longer "How do we eliminate pain?" but "What stance can transform this pain into significance?" In Frankl's terms, this is the attitudinal jurisdiction of therapy: helping a person discern and commit to a meaning that can still be realized, precisely under constraint.

19 The search for ultimate meaning

Frankl drew a distinction between ultimate meaning, which seeks the reason for existence, and personal meaning, which concerns how people experience meaning in everyday life. Beyond the concrete meanings we enact in particular contexts, he also posits a further horizon—variously named super-meaning or ultimate meaning—anchored in the transcendent sphere of spirituality and, for many, religion. Ultimate meaning is not a riddle reason can settle; it is a reality that can be intimated but never exhausted. Access to this horizon typically proceeds through philosophical reflection, spiritual inquiry, and noetic intuition—forms of apprehension that outstrip strict rational analysis. It gathers a person's worldviews and first principles, religious convictions where present, and the larger narratives by which a life is situated. Because the ultimate, by definition, exceeds finite comprehension, the search is asymptotic: an ongoing orientation rather than a conclusion one can finally possess. Holding such a horizon in view does practical work: it furnishes a framework of intelligibility within which contingency and volatility can be borne without collapse, and within which suffering, responsibility, and choice can cohere.

Crucially, Frankl ties this horizon to the human capacity for self-transcendence. As beings whose spirit is structurally open, we are not sealed within our impulses or private interests; we are capable of reaching beyond ourselves to receive enduring values and fundamental truths as they are mediated from the encompassing dimension of ultimate meaning. In Frankl's terms, the person is constitutionally receptive and answerable to such meanings. This openness grounds what he describes as a basic, pre-theoretical confidence—a settled trust in the unconditional meaningfulness of life. That trust does not replace the task of discerning meaning in particular situations; it supports it, sustaining a sense of wholeness even when personal understanding is partial, and enabling individuals to respond to life's concrete calls with greater resilience and clarity.

Because, as finite beings, we cannot grasp the infinite nature of existence, Frankl proposed that, rather than prosecuting the grand question of *the* meaning of life, it is wiser to seek meaning in life—to ask what is personally meaningful and to focus one's resources on the question, "What is meaningful for me?" On this point, logotherapy proposes a Copernican reorientation: just as the Copernican revolution discovered that the earth is not the center around which the heavens revolve, but itself turns on its axis and around the sun, so too, instead of asking "What is the meaning of *my* life?" the person should ask, "What does life expect from me?"—and, upon discerning an answer, respond to it.

Given the limits of human cognition, the answer to the grand question of life's meaning does not lie within the reach of purely intellectual knowledge; it is, rather, a matter of faith and inner commitment. One can decide that there is meaning—or decide that there is none. At the base of logotherapy stands the working assumption that life is unconditionally meaningful. In other words, logotherapy operates with a presumption of meaning, holding it to be a superior way of life compared with its negation. The nihilist, who often presents as rigorously rational, presupposes that what cannot be known does not exist; in doing so, they overlook the limits of human knowledge—both their own and that of their age—and thereby deny values.

20 Collective meaning versus individual meaning

While logotherapy is often characterized as an individualistic approach that emphasizes personal responsibility for discovering one's unique meaning, recent scholarship reveals a more complex understanding that recognizes both the deeply personal nature of meaning discovery and the inherently social context within which such discovery occurs. Frankl observed that positive life purpose and meaning were associated with strong religious beliefs, membership in groups, dedication to a cause, life values, and clear goals, suggesting that individual meaning-seeking is profoundly influenced by collective frameworks and social belonging. Culture fundamentally shapes the meaning-making process through its provision of interpretive schemas, value systems, linguistic structures, and symbolic resources that individuals draw upon in their quest for existential purpose. This cultural embeddedness of meaning construction challenges the traditional view of logotherapy as purely individualistic, revealing instead a therapeutic approach that must navigate the intricate relationship between personal agency and collective meaning frameworks.

The dialectical relationship between individual and collective meaning is reflected in what Frankl termed the "collective neurosis" of contemporary society reveals another dimension of this tension. Frankl identified the twentieth-century collective neurosis as nihilism—the belief that life is meaningless—which he argued renders individuals susceptible to a "mass neurotic triad" of aggression, depression, and addiction when they experience an existential vacuum. This analysis suggests that while meaning must ultimately be discovered individually, the cultural and social context profoundly shapes both the obstacles to and opportunities for such discovery. The existential vacuum that characterizes modern society creates a shared predicament that requires both individual therapeutic intervention and collective cultural transformation.

21 Creative pathway to meaning in life

What creative gifts can you offer the world through your talents and strengths? Which tasks and goals do you judge to be valuable and meaningful? What genuinely stirs your enthusiasm?

The creative pathway to meaning anchors meaning in contribution, through the imprint of our work, service, and making on the communal sphere. Like fingerprints, no two contributions are the same; the recognition that there is a role only I can credibly fulfill sharpens a sense of irreplaceable responsibility and clarifies purpose. As Johann Wolfgang von Goethe reminds us, we come to know ourselves less by introspection than by action, answering the day's demands. In logotherapeutic terms, this path involves activity and engagement: authorship, caregiving, civic participation—any arena in which values take form through deeds. What confers meaning is the manner in which we take up our tasks. This is the person's signature imprint: a task or arc of contribution that, given one's capacities and circumstances, only this person can complete.

Three nuances are central here:

- *Uniqueness and non-substitutability.* Each life is singular and unrepeatable. What matters is not being "the best," but giving form to one's unique calling—something no one else can duplicate.
- *Situated variability.* Meaning varies across persons and across moments; what is fitting today may not be fitting tomorrow. Every moment is unrepeatable, calling for a fresh answer to the meaning of the moment.
- *Discovery-through-action.* Discovering meaning through the creative pathway is rarely knowable in advance; it is disclosed in the doing. Practice discloses significance: by committing to concrete tasks and letting reality answer back, we clarify what matters and refine our direction.

Contemporary research on longevity and well-being, such as for example, the "Blue Zones" project, consistently associates active lifestyle and value-connected engagement with better physical health, greater psychological resilience, and longer life expectancy. The mechanism is not merely "staying busy." Rather, goal-directed contribution appears to integrate daily effort, social bonds, and a sense of mattering—precisely the ingredients that logotherapy treats as meaning-bearing.

In practice, the creative pathway can be seen as an adaptive process—more rhythmic than linear—marked by continual movement among noticing, linking, and doing: (1) discern signature strengths, concerns, and sensibilities; (2) link them to real needs in one's immediate world; and (3) commit to bounded projects whose tasks, obligations, and beneficiaries are clear. In this way, a creative life becomes a sustained response to the day's demands. Meaning is realized as a living imprint—visible in the world and formative of the self—borne as a responsibility that, given one's particular capacities and circumstances, only one can credibly assume and bring to completion. It is enacted through the expression of one's uniqueness and through value-guided choices in real situations.

22 Experiential pathway to meaning in life

Which experiences and encounters with the world are most meaningful to you—for example, significant relationships, engagement with art, contact with nature, music, or inspiration drawn from a book or film?

Today's climate of time pressure, exhaustion, distraction, and the fear of missing out (FOMO) normalizes acceleration and multitasking, and attention, not time, has become the scarcest resource of modern life. In such conditions we skim rather than dwell; we *sample* experiences instead of *undergoing* them. The cost is subtle but real: we are not fully present, and so we overlook invitations to encounter life deeply. A moment that could bear significance—say, a child's embrace—can register as merely another waypoint on an overfull, distracted schedule unless we meet it with presence and awareness.

The experiential pathway reminds us that the potential for meaning is present in every moment, yet its apprehension depends on our orientation. When we pause to notice, allowing curiosity to replace automaticity—we begin to register moments whose significance would otherwise remain latent. Quieting the noise of borrowed expectations and constricting assumptions often opens space for discovery. Logotherapeutically, the stance is receptive rather than acquisitive. Frankl likened the process to listening to music: sound waves may fill the air, but they become music only where there is a receiver. So, too, life may be saturated with possible meanings, yet they become experience only where there is attentive presence. He also compared life to an image concealed within a puzzle: one must rotate the perspective until the pattern emerges. In practice, discerning the "meaning of the moment" requires conscious awareness and a willingness to respond. Experiential meaning rests on presence and participation, made possible by open, curious attention, consistent with Frankl's accounts of how moments of natural beauty, such as a sunsets, remained available as experiential meaning even under extreme deprivation. When we are attentive and know ourselves more accurately, we are better able to identify the meaning available in the present experience and to receive it as guidance for action.

Within this domain, a person finds meaning not in what is given to the world, but in what is received from it: in the contemplative experience of beauty in nature, in the resonance of music, in the encounter with works of art, and—above all—in significant relationships and a loving bond with another person. Refining the capacity to be present and mindfully attentive, and to savor one's everyday experiences, enables the recognition of the potential for meaning latent in any given moment. Savoring here denotes deliberate, felt appreciation—lingering with sensory, emotional, and relational textures, so that value becomes experientially available rather than conceptually inferred.

In other words, the experiential pathway to meaning requires an attentional shift: notice–dwell–be curious rather than defaulting to the taken-for-granted, habit, and distraction. These micro-practices counteract perceptual fatigue and re-enliven contact with beauty in nature, music, art, and—most centrally—significant relationships. Such awareness can also set the stage for new possibilities: when we adopt a stance of openness, flexibility, spontaneity, and receptivity to unanticipated opportunities, interruptions, and invitations, the seemingly ordinary becomes available as memorable and meaningful. This emphasis on attention accords with William James's claim that "my experience is what I agree to attend to" (1890/1950, p. 402). James illuminates a crucial point for the experiential pathway: meaning is not primarily the product of planning or inference; it is an encounter we consent to attend to. In Proust's terms, "the real voyage of discovery consists not in seeking new landscapes, but in having new eyes"—a disciplined receptivity that lets the whisper of meaning be heard in the unexpected.

Adopting a mindset of openness, flexibility, spontaneity, and receptivity to unexpected opportunities, interruptions, and invitations that can render an experience memorable and meaningful. Taken together, these dispositions—mindful presence, appreciative savoring, fresh seeing, and openness to serendipity—constitute the experiential pathway's craft. They shift meaning from a distant ideal to a lived encounter, allowing persons to receive what is good, true, or beautiful and to let it orient their lives in the here and now.

23 Attitudinal pathway to meaning in life

Which attitudinal values have you enacted when taking a stance toward challenge and crisis—e.g., courage, hope, humor? What, if anything, became newly possible as a result? What can be learned from a challenging person or a difficult relationship? In what way did the situation open an opportunity you had not previously seen?

In "Man's Search for Meaning", Frankl wrote, "If there is meaning in life at all, then there must be a meaning in suffering. Suffering is an ineradicable part of life, even as fate and death. Without suffering and death human life cannot be complete" (Frankl, 1959, 2006). This premise grounds the attitudinal pathway: when circumstances cannot be changed, meaning is realized in the stance we freely adopt toward them. Our responsibility, then, is to recognize the call of life embedded in each situation—*What am I being asked to be or do here?*—and to answer it with a value-guided attitude. From this follows *'tragic optimism'*: the capacity to transform tragedy into a specifically human achievement by changing ourselves when we cannot change the situation, answering fate with a value-guided attitude.

The attitudinal pathway is the third avenue to meaning: it concerns how we stand toward what befalls us. All three pathways—experiential (what we receive), creative (what we give), and attitudinal (how we respond)—embody self-transcendence by turning us outward beyond self-preoccupation. Among them, the attitudinal pathway is the most profound expression of self-transcendence, because it makes meaning available under any condition, including unavoidable suffering, through the deliberate adoption of a value-guided stance. Such a stance—marked by courage, hope, and even humor—safeguards spiritual freedom and orients action toward goods larger than the self.

In logotherapeutic terms, this is where freedom and responsibility are exercised at their most elemental: by adopting a value-guided attitude toward situations we cannot change. Our stance is especially consequential in conditions of crisis, challenge, and suffering. In such circumstances, a person can still find meaning by the *attitude* they assume toward their condition and their pain. A distinctive feature of attitudinal values is their universal availability: they can be enacted under any circumstance or limitation.

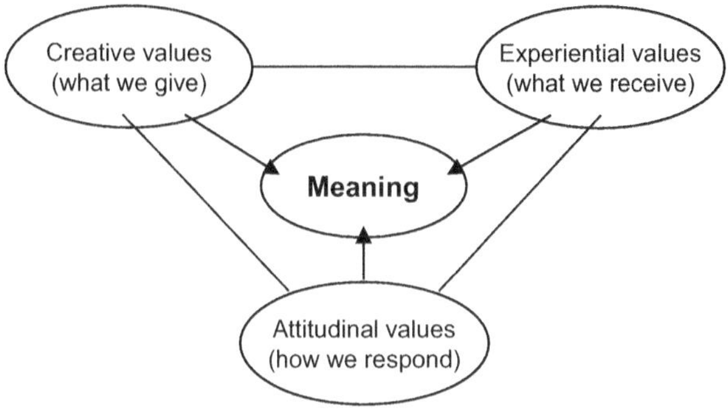

Figure 1.5 Three Pathways to Meaning

Clinically, this pathway invites a re-examination of priorities—a clarifying look at what truly matters now—and a disciplined shift of perspective that organizes coping ("How else might this be seen?"). Mobilizing tragic optimism—an acceptance of life's tragic elements joined to a steadfast conviction that meaning remains possible—often requires time and working-through; yet it can yield new insights, fresh opportunities for development, and the discovery of new meanings, culminating, put simply, in the transformation of personal tragedy into human triumph. The distinctive feature of attitudinal values is their universal availability: they can be enacted under any circumstance or limitation. In doing so, suffering is neither denied nor romanticized; it is answered in a way that confers direction, preserves dignity, and re-opens the field of meaning.

Part 2

Therapeutic framework and methods

2.1 Basic principles

24 The three pillars of logotherapy

Logotherapy is grounded in three mutually reinforcing premises concerning the human condition—which together define its therapeutic stance: the will to meaning, the unconditional meaningfulness of life, and the freedom of will.

Will to meaning. The first pillar is motivational: human agency is organized not only by drives or the search for equilibrium, but by a teleological orientation toward purposes judged worthy. Clinically, demoralization, apathy, and restless compensatory patterns (e.g., arousal seeking, avoidance) may be better understood as markers of thwarted or misdirected orientation rather than mere energy depletion.

Unconditional meaningfulness of life. The second pillar is ontological: life is meaningful in principle, even when meaning is not yet apprehended. Practically, this stance guards against two pitfalls: (1) collapsing value into social custom or personal taste, and (2) abandoning inquiry whenever immediate justification is absent. On this basis, therapy proceeds on the working hypothesis that meaning is discoverable—or can be fashioned—in situ: by realizing a value, receiving what is worthy, or adopting an attitude that confers significance. This working assumption does not predetermine the answer; it warrants the search.

DOI: 10.4324/9781003624417-2

Freedom of will. The third pillar is anthropological: human beings retain an irreducible capacity for freedom and responsibility. This is not freedom from conditions, but freedom in relation to them—the freedom to take a position and to answer with values. Logotherapy operationalizes this claim through (a) *self-distancing*—the capacity to step back from one's impulses, affects, and circumstances—and (b) *self-transcendence*—the capacity to orient action toward goods beyond the self. Freedom of will thus anchors the attitudinal pathway, while also empowering the creative and experiential pathways.

Taken together, the three pillars yield a coherent account of personhood. The will to meaning provides direction; the unconditional meaningfulness of life provides a moral horizon (a sense that life still calls for response); and freedom of will provides **agency** (the capacity to choose one's stance and next step). **Direction without horizon** can shrink into "whatever I feel like" goal-setting—short-term preferences or self-interest without ethical depth. **Horizon without agency** can slide into passivity or resignation: "meaning exists, but there is nothing I can do," so life is endured rather than engaged. **Agency without direction** often becomes motion without orientation—busy striving, chasing, or controlling, driven by tension rather than purpose. Integrated, the pillars resist reductionism (biological or psychologistic) by maintaining that even under constraint human beings can answer to values, and they avoid moralism by insisting that meaning is not imposed from without but discerned and realized in concrete situations. In practice, they can usefully be framed as three core questions:

Orientation (will to meaning): What is being asked here—what purpose could warrant commitment now?;

Horizon (unconditional meaningfulness): Within what larger frame can this situation be rendered intelligible?;

Agency (freedom of will): What stance, task, or encounter remains within the person's power?

Because meaning remains possible even when circumstances narrow, therapy can legitimately pursue creative, experiential, and attitudinal avenues of realization. Because freedom endures, responsibility can be calibrated to what is genuinely within reach. And because life is taken to be intelligible in principle, the search for significance remains justified even when outcomes are uncertain.

25 Freedom of will

At the turn of the 19th to the 20th century, influential accounts of the person were often framed in deterministic terms, bounded by biological drives, psychological conditioning, and social forces. Logotherapy resists that reduction. Human beings are not governed solely by the pleasure principle or driven passively by instinct (Freud, 1911/1958, 1920/1961), nor are they exhaustively explained by stimulus–response conditioning (Watson, 1913; Skinner, 1953). Rather, logotherapy foregrounds the noetic capacity for self-distancing and responsible choice even under constraint. The openness to discover meaning in one's circumstances does not presuppose a metaphysical or religious ideology; it requires an attitudinal posture that makes present a distinctly human endowment: the capacity to choose one's response.

As a theory and clinical practice, logotherapy rests on the conviction that the human spirit forms a preserved core of health and embodies this freedom. Biological, psychological, and sociocultural determinants are real; yet alongside them there is always the possibility of decision: to acquiesce to constraints or to rise above them by seeking meaning through them. Frankl emphasized

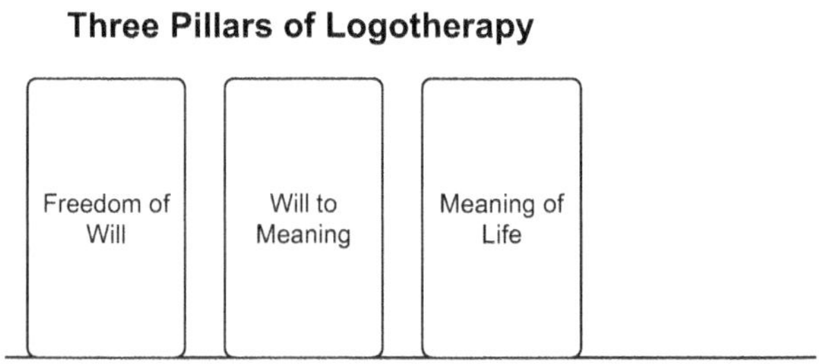

Figure 2.1 Three Pillars of Logotherapy

that such inner freedom could not be confiscated even under extreme coercion. Hence his distinction between "freedom from" (release from a condition) and "freedom to" (the power to decide how to relate to it). The latter shifts the axis of agency from outer circumstance to inner stance and highlights what Frankl called the "defiant power of the human spirit"—the ability not to capitulate to limitations or destructive impulses, but to take a stand toward life's situations. Logotherapy therefore focuses on the potential for freedom that remains available within any situation. It is not freedom from conditions, but freedom in relation to them: the capacity to take a stance and to answer with values. When external facts cannot be changed, one can still choose an attitude; that choice realizes value and constitutes a concrete exercise of freedom. Logotherapy further names a specific therapeutic dynamic: psycho-noetic resistance. Here, the noetic (spiritual) capacity counters psychological and physiological pressures—not necessarily by changing them, but by changing one's stance toward them.

From this orientation, the primary clinical task is to clarify the client's margin of freedom within constraint and translate it into responsible action. This involves helping the client (a) identify what is fixed versus still choosable, (b) practice self-distancing from automatic reactions and symptom-identification, and (c) choose an attitude and a value-guided next step that can be lived now. Understood in these terms, freedom of will is operational rather than theoretical: identifying one's sphere of freedom, choosing an attitude, assuming responsibility, and realizing values through concrete goals and tasks.

Thus, when a patient brings a sense of being trapped by circumstances ("Nothing can change") or defined by symptoms ("This is who I am"), the therapist supports a shift from outer control to inner stance: What can be decided here? What remains within your power? What value can be enacted even under limitation? Drawing on a nautical image, we cannot command the wind, but we can set the sails—and choose our tack. Practically, this orientation treats every situation as possibility-laden: alternatives can be generated; behavioral patterns are malleable; attention can shift from closed doors to those open—or openable; and purposes, tasks, and values specify what falls to us now. On this account, the human task is to exercise freedom in relation to conditions: to take a stance and to answer with values. Even when external facts cannot be changed, a person can still choose an attitude; that choice realizes value and constitutes a concrete exercise of freedom.

In sum, freedom of will grounds the attitudinal pathway and energizes the creative and experiential pathways, ensuring that meaning remains practicable even—and especially—when life is most constrained.

26 Will to meaning

Within logotherapy's basic principles, the will to meaning refers to a distinct motivational horizon: human striving is organized primarily by values to be realized, not merely by the discharge of instinct or the pursuit of equilibrium. Placing meaning first locates motive force in commitments to value; instinct and affect persist, yet are organized and at times constrained by purposive orientation. Motivation is toward ends, not merely toward relief. This value-orientation does more than energize action; it structures attention and choice. Clarifying what one is living for entails, at the same time, clarifying what one can de-prioritize. The will to meaning thus entails both goal focus and goal pruning: a movement toward tasks that instantiate one's commitments, and a disciplined release of pursuits that dilute them. The result is not asceticism for its own sake, but congruence—a tighter fit between daily effort and what one deems important.

Frankl contrasted biological homeostasis (tension reduction) with heterostasis or noetic tension—the productive tension that arises between what is and what ought to be. Far from being a symptom to be eliminated, this noetic tension is a sign of mental health: it signals that a person remains responsive to claims that transcend immediate comfort. Logotherapy therefore does not aim to tranquilize at all costs; it seeks to awaken and harness this tension so that it functions as a driving force. The task is calibration, not elimination: too little tension yields drift and apathy; too much, unmoored from values, devolves into agitation. Properly aligned, noetic tension is the felt vector of purpose. Importantly, logotherapy distinguishes noetic tension from pathological strain. Noetic tension arises from freely endorsed values; it is proportionate to meaningful aims and exerts a directional pull. Pathological strain, by contrast, is driven by avoidance, social comparison, or performance anxiety.

From this orientation, the primary clinical task is to clarify the client's value-claims and reframe "tension" as information: Is this tension pointing toward a meaningful task, or is it fueled by fear, avoidance, and social comparison? Clinically, the aim is to help clients name what matters, concentrate effort accordingly, and release pursuits that dilute commitment—so that inner pressure becomes a compass rather than a threat signal.

Thus, when a patient brings persistent stress, restlessness, or emptiness, the therapist explores what the person is living toward, and whether their daily effort fits that direction. If tension is value-aligned, it can be legitimized and harnessed as purposeful noetic tension. If strain is avoidance-driven, the work turns to loosening the avoidance cycle and reconnecting effort to freely chosen commitments. In this way, the clinical question is not merely how to dampen arousal, but which value-claim is being neglected or blocked, and how to realign life so that tension again points beyond the self toward a realizable good. On this account, the human task is to live toward ends that are worthy, allowing meaning to organize priorities, attention, and choice. The will to meaning supplies the non-coercive inner pressure that moves a person from intention to enactment.

In sum, the will to meaning orients life toward value and legitimizes noetic tension as a healthy signal. It reframes the aim of treatment: not the minimization of tension, but its purposeful calibration and use in the service of commitments that are worth a life.

27 Meaning in life

Logotherapy identifies tragic optimism as the ethically sound posture for engaging life as it is. On this view, one confronts the facts of life and chooses to respond with dignity and purpose, even when tragedy looms. Accordingly, no condition—however severe—can strip life of its worth or its claim to meaning, nor can it revoke the human freedom to enact values even within suffering. The boundary between meaningful and meaningless suffering, Frankl maintained, is drawn by the attitude one adopts; it is a personal decision and responsibility. Logotherapy maintains that even negative and tragic circumstances do not exhaust the field of significance: life's meaning is not conditional upon meeting particular milestones or upon the cessation of pain. By virtue of the stance we take toward them, constructive aspects can still be discerned, not by denying hardship, but by orienting freedom toward values that can be lived here and now.

From this orientation, the primary clinical task is to surface and scrutinize the assumptions that make meaning seem conditional, e.g., "Life is meaningful only if I achieve X," "only when the pain stops," or "only when others approve", and to support an epistemic shift toward unconditional meaning. As Frankl stated, "what our patients need is unconditional faith in unconditional meaning" (1969, p. 156). Clinically, this includes widening the field of attention so that the significance already latent in a situation can come into view, through both fine-grained engagement with the moment and a panoramic view of its horizon. Thus, when a patient brings demoralization, failure narratives, or a life organized around others' expectations, the therapist supports a shift from pleasing to willing: not calibrated to social approval, but to values one deems incumbent. Overreliance on the external gaze fosters avoidance—preferring to remain an "unrealized potential" rather than risk a "realized imperfection." Meaning-centered work strengthens fidelity to one's proper task, fitted to concrete circumstances. Meaning does not require grand achievement; it requires responsibility for what is asked now. In this frame, failure does not diminish worth; it can redirect the person toward a more fitting contribution or stance. Crises, too, may become sites of attainment when intention and process (not only result) are granted moral weight.

On this account, the human task is not to fabricate meaning ex nihilo, but to recognize and answer it. We move from the culture's success–failure axis to Frankl's meaning-of-effort axis. The former, governed by hedonic and comparative metrics, treats limitation as defect and adversity as sheer loss, predictably breeding frustration, demoralization, and withdrawal of effort. The latter evaluates a life by the values enacted in the manner of proceeding. On this view, both success and failure can be existentially fruitful—each a field for courage, fidelity, responsibility, and love. Illness and bereavement still hurt; their significance is shaped by the response they elicit.

In sum, unconditional meaning becomes operational through three questions: What is being asked here? Within what frame can this be rendered intelligible? What stance or act remains within the person's power? Practically, the work proceeds on three fronts: (1) delineate the person's margin of choice—what can be decided or influenced now; (2) shift attention from constraints to options that are available or can be created; (3) specify value-congruent goals and near-term tasks that are still doable. Within this frame, habits can be reshaped, options multiplied, and even error, failure, illness, and loss can be reworked into tasks of meaning.

28 The therapist's role

Companion of discernment. A logotherapist, as Frankl explains, is more like an eye doctor than a painter: "A painter tries to convey the world as he sees it, an eye specialist tries to enable us to see the world as it is" (Frankl, 1963). In other words, logotherapists aim at getting closer to the reality of the client, as they experience it uniquely and dynamically. Thus, the goal of the logotherapist is to tap into the unique human capacities of intentionality, responsibility, and freedom of choice and to broaden clients' perspectives to discover and actualize the meaning potentials in their lives (Ameli, 2016). In logotherapy, thus, the therapist is neither a dispenser of ready-made meanings nor a value-neutral technician. The logotherapist is best understood as a companion in discernment. The alliance is personal and person-to-person, formed to safeguard the patient's inviolable dignity while resisting psychologistic or biologistic reduction. In this work, philosophy and psychotherapy cooperate: questions of fate, freedom, conscience, responsibility, and meaning inform clinical method rather than compete with it. Practically, the therapist's task is to widen the horizon—to enlarge what can be noticed and considered—so that significance already latent in the situation may appear.

A helpful image is the two-legged stance. With one leg, the therapist stands inside the patient's lived experience—sometimes at the very edge of the abyss—listening phenomenologically and without premature explanation. With the other leg, the therapist stands in the space of possibility, choice, and meaning, holding open the field of alternative stances, tasks, and values that may still be enacted. This posture keeps the encounter simultaneously compassionate and purposive: faithful to what is suffered, yet oriented to what is still answerable.

Mutually reinforcing work. Elisabeth Lukas articulates the logotherapist's work in five mutually reinforcing functions. First, the therapist is a guardian of dignity, explicitly acknowledging the patient's spiritual/noetic dimension and treating the person never as a sum of symptoms but as a meaning-capable agent. Second, the therapist is a revealer of freedom, helping the patient identify a remaining area of choice—sometimes small but decisive—and translate it into concrete, value-guided tasks. Third, the therapist serves as a mediator of meaning, countering the existential vacuum by illuminating meaning-possibilities in the situation and orienting commitment "for someone or something" beyond self-preoccupation. Fourth, the therapist is a discriminator of guilt and fear, differentiating unjustified from justified guilt and treating fear as a call upon the human spirit, converting both—where appropriate—into responsibility and action. Finally, the therapist supports a movement from fate to freedom: symptoms and setbacks are consistently reframed within a horizon where constraints are acknowledged but do not annul the possibility of meaning.

In sum, the logotherapist can be seen as a midwife of meaning with a two-legged stance: firmly rooted in the patient's immediate reality and equally planted in the domain of possibility. In this spirit, the therapist "stands with" the patient in suffering while also "standing for" the claims of meaning, inviting decisions that restore authorship. By preserving dignity, revealing freedom, mediating meaning, and orienting responsibility, the therapist helps patients discover where they are still free, what remains worth doing, and how to answer life with values—so that, even under constraint, existence can become intelligible, directed, and humane.

29 The client's role

Co-author. In logotherapy, the client is an active co-author in a shared inquiry, assuming responsibility for discerning and realizing values under real constraints. According to Frankl's foundational principles, the client is viewed as the primary agent in discovering and creating meaning in their existence, rather than merely uncovering repressed material or correcting cognitive distortions (Frankl, 1963). The client's journey in logotherapy involves a conscious and deliberate engagement with existential questions that may have previously been avoided or suppressed. Unlike therapeutic modalities that focus primarily on symptom reduction or behavioral modification, logotherapy positions the client as an explorer of their own existential landscape, tasked with identifying values, purposes, and sources of meaning that can provide direction and resilience in the face of life's inevitable sufferings (Fabry, 1994). This process requires the client to move beyond a preoccupation with their psychological symptoms or life circumstances toward a broader perspective that encompasses their potential for growth, contribution, and transcendence.

Personal Responsibility. Central to the client's role in logotherapy is the cultivation of personal responsibility—not merely for one's actions, but for one's attitudes and responses to circumstances beyond their control. Frankl emphasized that while individuals cannot always choose their circumstances, they retain the fundamental freedom to choose their stance toward those circumstances (Frankl, 1946/2006). This perspective places significant responsibility on the client to recognize and exercise their capacity for self-determination, even within the constraints of their psychological, social, or physical limitations. The therapeutic process thus becomes a collaborative exploration of how the client can assume greater responsibility for their life's direction while simultaneously discovering meaning through self-transcendence.

Self-transcendence. A key concept in logotherapy is self-transcendence which requires the client to shift their focus from self-preoccupation toward engagement with something or someone beyond themselves. This might involve dedicating oneself to a cause, developing deeper relationships, or contributing to the welfare of others (Lukas, 1984). The client's role includes learning to identify opportunities for self-transcendence in their daily life and developing the courage to pursue meaningful activities even when they conflict with immediate desires for comfort or security. This process often involves confronting existential anxiety and the human tendency toward self-centeredness, requiring sustained effort and commitment from the client throughout the therapeutic journey.

Discovering Meaning. The client's engagement in the meaning-making process involves developing what Frankl termed "noö-dynamics"—the spiritual dimension of human existence that encompasses the capacity for self-awareness, choice, and responsibility. Through sustained reflection and dialogue, clients learn to access this dimension more consciously, enabling them to discover sources of meaning that may have been previously overlooked or undervalued. This process is neither mechanical nor prescriptive; instead, it requires the client's genuine participation in an ongoing exploration of their deepest values and aspirations, leading to insights that are both personally authentic and existentially significant.

30 Therapeutic relationship in logotherapy

Collaborative. The therapeutic relationship in logotherapy is characterized by a unique form of collaboration between therapist and client, where both parties are engaged in the process of meaning exploration, though with distinct roles and responsibilities. The client brings their lived experience, values, and personal history to the therapeutic encounter, while maintaining ultimate authority over the meanings they choose to embrace (Frankl, 1967). This collaborative dynamic requires the client to be an active participant in dialogue, willing to examine their assumptions, confront difficult questions, and consider alternative perspectives on their life circumstances.

Egalitarian. Essentially, logotherapy positions the therapist as a fellow human being who serves as a guide and catalyst in the client's search for meaning. Frankl conceptualized this relationship as fundamentally egalitarian, recognizing that both therapist and client share the universal human condition of seeking purpose and confronting existential challenges (Frankl, 1963). This perspective transforms the therapeutic encounter from a medical model of expert-patient interaction to an existential dialogue between two individuals engaged in the fundamental task of meaning-making.

Authentic and Vulnerable. Central to the logotherapeutic relationship is the concept of authentic encounter, which requires both therapist and client to engage with one another as whole persons rather than merely in their professional or patient roles. Frankl emphasized that genuine therapeutic change occurs through authentic human meeting, where the therapist's personal presence and genuine concern create a space for the client's authentic self-expression and exploration (Lukas, 1998). This authenticity demands that the therapist be willing to share in the existential vulnerability that characterizes the human search for meaning, while maintaining appropriate professional boundaries and therapeutic focus.

This requires the development of what Fabry (1994) described as "therapeutic empathy"—a deep understanding of the client's existential situation that goes beyond mere emotional resonance to encompass appreciation for their unique potential for growth and self-transcendence. Such empathy enables the therapist to perceive possibilities for meaning that may not be immediately apparent to the client, while respecting the client's fundamental freedom to choose their own path toward fulfillment. The therapist's role, thus, involves helping the client recognize both their capacity for choice and the responsibility that accompanies such freedom, while avoiding the temptation to direct the client toward particular meanings or values (Frankl, 1978). This requires a delicate balance between offering guidance and maintaining respect for the client's autonomy, recognizing that authentic meaning cannot be imposed from without but must be discovered or created by the individual themselves.

Safe and Stable. The relational context must also aspire to provide the safety necessary for clients to confront difficult existential realities, including the inevitability of suffering, death, and meaninglessness. The therapist's presence serves as a stabilizing force that enables clients to explore these challenging themes without becoming overwhelmed by existential anxiety or despair. Through consistent availability and genuine concern, the therapist demonstrates that it is possible to face life's fundamental uncertainties while maintaining hope and commitment to meaningful action, thereby modeling the very qualities that logotherapy seeks to cultivate in clients (Frankl, 1959).

A key skill that therapists must model in relation to this relates to setting boundaries. Each therapist must determine in what capacity they are able and willing to be available for their patients in a boundaried and clinically appropriate manner. For example, some clinicians may choose to leave themselves available to receiving and engaging in communication with their patients between sessions, some may welcome patients to write to them between sessions if this supports the client's self-reflective therapeutic journey, setting a clear boundary that the client will not receive a written reply but any reflections received can be explored during the next session, and others still may set the boundary that all communication other than administrative details should take place within sessions. Failure to determine clear boundaries will result in the collapse of safety and stability within the therapeutic relationship.

31 Assessment from a logotherapeutic perspective

Assessment in logotherapy fundamentally differs from traditional diagnostic approaches by prioritizing the exploration of meaning structures, value orientations, and existential resources rather than focusing primarily on symptomatology or pathological patterns. Frankl argued that conventional psychiatric assessment often overlooks the spiritual dimension of human existence, reducing complex existential struggles to mere psychological or biological dysfunction (Frankl, 1963). The logotherapeutic assessment process therefore seeks to understand the client's relationship to meaning, their capacity for self-transcendence, and their ability to exercise freedom and responsibility within their particular life circumstances.

This approach does not dismiss the importance of understanding psychological symptoms or behavioral patterns, but rather places them within a broader existential context that recognizes the human person's fundamental orientation toward meaning and value. The assessment process thus becomes an exploration of how the client's presenting concerns relate to their deeper existential needs, unfulfilled potentials, and blocked pathways to meaning (Lukas, 1991). Such an approach requires the therapist to develop sensitivity to existential themes that may underlie surface-level complaints, recognizing that depression, anxiety, or behavioral problems often mask more fundamental concerns about purpose, significance, and personal authenticity.

Central to logotherapeutic assessment is what Frankl termed "logo-analysis"—a systematic exploration of the client's meaning-making processes, value hierarchies, and existential attitudes. The assessment seeks to identify which meaning sources are currently accessible to the client and which may be blocked or underdeveloped. Logo-analysis also involves exploring the client's temporal orientation, examining how they relate to their past, present, and future in terms of meaning and possibility. This temporal assessment recognizes that meaning can be found in accepting one's past, engaging fully with present opportunities, or orienting oneself toward future goals and responsibilities (Fabry, 1994). The therapist pays particular attention to instances where the client may be trapped in regret about the past or anxiety about the future, preventing them from recognizing meaning possibilities in their immediate experience. This exploration often reveals patterns of existential avoidance or meaning-blocking that contribute to psychological distress. Related to this is the assessment of "noögenic disorders"—psychological disturbances that originate in the spiritual dimension of human existence rather than in the psychogenic or somatogenic spheres. These disorders are characterized by conflicts between competing values, moral distress, existential frustration, or spiritual crisis (Lukas, 1998). The logotherapeutic assessment seeks to differentiate between symptoms that may respond to traditional psychological interventions and those that require specifically existential approaches focused on meaning-discovery and value-clarification. This differential assessment is crucial for determining appropriate therapeutic interventions and avoiding the pathologization of essentially normal existential struggles.

Throughout the assessment interview, the therapist attends not only to areas of dysfunction in the client's life but equally to areas of continued strength, resilience, and sources of meaning. Accordingly, effective assessment questions extend beyond present realities to explore how past experiences and current circumstances might inform future possibilities for choice, value realization, and meaning discovery. Logotherapeutic assessment, thus, mainly focuses on careful attention to the client's language, metaphors, and narratives about their life experience. The therapist listens for indications of the client's value commitments, sources of fulfillment, and areas of existential frustration or blocking. This phenomenological approach to assessment recognizes that meaning is often embedded in the stories people tell about their lives and the language they use to describe their experiences. The assessment process thus becomes an opportunity for both therapist and client to discover meaning patterns that may not be immediately apparent through direct questioning or formal testing procedures. As the client's relationship to meaning is dynamic, therapy includes iterative reassessment of existential orientation, new discoveries of meaning possibilities, and emerging challenges to previously held values or purposes. This dynamic approach to assessment recognizes that meaning is not a static entity but an evolving aspect of human experience that requires continuous exploration and refinement throughout the therapeutic journey and beyond.

2.2 Core techniques

32 Paradoxical intention

Paradoxical intention is a logotherapeutic method that addresses anticipatory anxiety and the vicious circles it generates. Rather than striving to suppress a feared response, the client is invited—deliberately and playfully—to intend the very reaction that has been dreaded, sometimes even to exaggerate it. This counterintuitive move loosens the grip of hyper-intention and hyper-reflection: the fear of the feared response ceases to function as a performance demand, and a measure of freedom reappears. In practice, paradoxical intention helps clients step back from their symptoms, approach them with humor and courage, and act despite them—often discovering that the imagined catastrophe was inflated and that their agency is larger than presumed.

Historically, this is among the oldest techniques in logotherapy; Frankl applied it already in the late 1920s in the treatment of phobias and obsessive-compulsive presentations. Its rationale rests on two uniquely human, noetic capacities central to logotherapy: self-distancing (the ability to take a position toward one's own affects, impulses, and bodily states) and self-transcendence (the capacity to orient oneself to values and tasks beyond immediate self-concerns). By inviting the client to intend what is feared, the technique recruits these capacities: it creates distance from the symptom and re-orients action toward a value (courage, responsibility, humor) enacted in the very situation that formerly elicited avoidance.

Practically, paradoxical intention is especially pertinent where anticipatory anxiety fuels a self-perpetuating loop—e.g., in insomnia driven by the demand "I must fall asleep now," in fear of blushing or trembling, in public-speaking anxiety, in certain phobic avoidances, in stuttering under performance pressure, and in some obsessive–compulsive rituals. A classic insomnia application, for example, may involve asking the client to try to remain awake for as long as possible; when the paradoxical intention replaces the pressure to sleep, arousal decreases and natural sleep becomes more likely. In social anxiety, a client might be invited to aim to blush or to stutter on the first sentence; doing so often punctures the catastrophic expectancy and restores poise. Across such uses, the technique does not ridicule the person's suffering; it changes the relation to the symptom from compelled avoidance to voluntary encounter.

Paradoxical intention is not synonymous with flooding or with standard exposure, though it may overlap in behavioral effects. Its distinctive feature is the chosen paradoxical stance—the "I will it" that undercuts compulsive striving and breaks the fear-of-fear loop. It aims less at habituation to stimuli and more at liberating the person's stance toward self and situation. Clinical judgment remains crucial. The method is best introduced when there is a supportive alliance, adequate ego strength, and a shared understanding of the rationale. Empirical work has documented the utility of paradoxical intention across diverse presentations—including chronic insomnia, stuttering, anorexia nervosa, agoraphobia, and public-speaking anxiety. Its use, however, should be calibrated to the patient's support system and psychological context; preparatory psychoeducation about the rationale and graded practice in everyday life are often essential, so the maneuver can be deployed before the anticipatory-anxiety spiral tightens. Used judiciously, paradoxical intention can transform moments of symptom tyranny into opportunities for value realization—a lived exercise of freedom in precisely those scenarios that once felt least negotiable.

33 Dereflection

Dereflection is a core logotherapeutic method that mitigates excessive self-monitoring and self-preoccupation by re-orienting attention outward—toward activities, roles, and relationships that instantiate personally valued meanings. This outward turn is not a denial of inner life; it is a disciplined redirection that enables life to be lived more fully and purposefully. In doing so, dereflection fosters self-transcendence—the movement beyond narrow self-concerns in the service of something or someone that matters.

In contrast to traditional emphases on introspection and extended symptom talk, dereflection purposefully interrupts hyper-reflection, overthinking, and compulsive self-scrutiny that can entrench distress. Frankl argued that, particularly in the face of existential anxieties or unavoidable suffering, it is often unhelpful to intensify inward analysis of every reaction; the more fruitful course is to illuminate and mobilize the person's striving for meaning. Hence, rather than dwelling on symptoms, wishes, or discomforts in ways that tend to amplify them, the logotherapist helps the client to invest awareness and energy in concrete, value-laden tasks and in responsiveness to other people.

Frankl described two pathways into stuckness that dereflection addresses. The first is over-intentionality: concentrating all effort on achieving a specific internal state (e.g., "I must fall asleep now"), which paradoxically heightens tension and obstructs the very aim (sleep becomes less likely). The second is hyper-reflection: turning attention inward so obsessively that symptoms are magnified (e.g., ruminating about the consequences of not sleeping, thereby worsening arousal). Logotherapy treats the existential–spiritual dimension of such symptoms: focusing on an existential vacuum or on groundless dread does not dissolve it, because these belong to the human condition; but turning attention toward life, values, and responsibilities can loosen their grip.

Clinically, dereflection unfolds in two complementary movements. First, the therapist helps the client establish mindful distance from symptoms or worries—neither fusing with them nor organizing life around them. Instead of investing scarce attentional resources in the symptom, the client is encouraged to invest in values, ideals, tasks, and meanings that can, in fact, be enacted within present constraints. Second, throughout dialogue, the therapist repeatedly draws the client's gaze to zones of freedom that persist despite illness or limitation: (a) positives that remain alongside negatives—and sometimes even because of them; (b) future aims still attainable, rather than losses irretrievably tied to the past; and (c) aspects of the situation that fall within one's responsibility, rather than those that do not. In this process the therapist listens for "logo-hints"—keywords and narrative moments that reveal core values—and helps the client to name and embody them in the current context.

Frankl captured the spirit of dereflection by urging patients to look less into their inner chaos and more toward what life asks of them: identity is clarified not by circling the self, but by devotion to a task, a cause, or a person loved. For individuals facing an unchangeable fate or tragic circumstances, this meaning-oriented stance is especially vital: it anchors dignity and direction, highlights where agency remains, and preserves the taste of life under any condition. In this spirit, when a client enters a social setting braced for signs of panic and continually checks "How anxious am I now?", the therapist can invite a different stance: adopt a concrete, outward-looking purpose that expresses personal values. For example, at a work reception or parents' meeting, the client may choose two or three small, prosocial tasks—greet a newcomer and introduce them to the group, make sure someone has a seat and a drink, ask a quiet participant a question that brings them into the conversation. By doing so, attention is re-anchored in doing something that matters to someone else rather than monitoring internal sensations. The physiological arousal is no longer fed by hyper-reflection, and anxiety typically loosens as a secondary effect—not because it is suppressed, but because the person is engaged in meaningful, other-directed action.

In sum, dereflection counters the pitfalls of hyper-reflection by re-anchoring awareness in concrete meanings; through enacted values and self-transcendence, it opens paths to relief, responsibility, and renewal.

34 Socratic dialogue

Socratic dialogue in logotherapy is a disciplined, meaning-oriented conversation that invites clients to surface what already lives within their conscience and values rather than to receive ready-made answers. The therapist does not "supply" meaning; instead, they help the client recognize it by gently eliciting—through carefully shaped, open-ended questions—the beliefs, priorities, and invitations that the client's own life is presenting. In this sense, meaning is not transferred but disclosed. The method affirms human freedom and responsibility: even under constraint, one can still discern what is asked of them and choose a stance that embodies purpose.

Its philosophical pedigree lies in Socrates' maieutic practice, the "midwifery" of ideas. Learning, on this view, is not the delivery of content from expert to novice but the awakening of knowledge and orientation already present. Frankl adapted this stance to psychotherapy: rather than excavating drives and instinctual motives as in classical psychoanalysis, the logotherapeutic dialogue aims to unveil the noetic (spiritual) dimension—our pre-reflective yearnings for meaning, conscience, and ideals. The exchange therefore privileges questions that explore assumptions, clarify values, and bring to light possibilities for self-transcendence and responsibility.

In practice, the therapist listens for "logo-hints"—the client's own key words, repeated terms, metaphors, images, and turning points that point to core values—and uses them to pose open-ended, targeted questions. The inquiries are logos-directed—meaning and direction—rather than logic-oriented, designed to stretch perspective without severing contact with the client's lived phenomenology: one foot remains in the person's present experience, the other steps into a horizon of alternatives. Typical prompts invite appraisal and choice: *What, in this situation, is still within your sphere of responsibility? Which value is being tested here? Looking ahead, what is the next small action that would honor that value?* Such questioning helps clients differentiate what cannot be changed from where freedom persists, and to re-organize life around what matters.

Clinically, Socratic dialogue is especially useful when addressing the existential vacuum and noögenic conflicts, where confusion about purpose and value sits at the heart of distress. By shifting the focus from symptom preoccupation to meaning discernment, the dialogue regulates stance: it increases distance from automatic interpretations, strengthens "response-ability," and orients the client toward future-directed tasks. Rather than asking, "How do you feel about this?" the therapist might ask, "Given what you have learned, what does this situation call for from you?" or "Which values did this experience show to be non-negotiable for you?" In this way, insight is linked to commitment, and reflection culminates in enactment.

Effective use of the method depends on timing, tact, and authenticity.

Timing means choosing the right moment and pace for a question, tact refers to phrasing it with respectful, non-judgmental curiosity that stretches thinking without triggering shame or defensiveness, and authenticity implies the therapist's congruent, genuinely engaged presence—curiosity without pretense—rather than rote technique. Socratic questions differ from data-gathering or clarification prompts; they are not yes/no queries. They proceed from past or present toward the future, helping clients integrate prior turning points and achievements with emerging aims. Because the dialogue serves individuation and is improvised within a real relationship, it must remain flexible: sometimes the most therapeutic move is a well-placed silence that allows an intuition to ripen. When attuned and value-centered, Socratic dialogue becomes a reliable pathway through which clients rediscover purpose, reclaim agency, and align daily choices with a unique task that only they can fulfill.

35 Attitude modulation

Logotherapy's approach to human suffering fundamentally transforms the therapeutic encounter by empowering individuals to face inevitable hardship not through resignation but through purposeful engagement, thereby validating existence even amid its most challenging dimensions. This perspective enables clients to confront unavoidable suffering not with despair but with dignity, affirming life's worth even in its tragic aspects. Central to logotherapeutic practice stands the principle of freedom of will and the human capacity to select one's stance while maintaining the perpetual possibility of what Elisabeth Lukas termed "attitude modulation." This modulation occurs within the most profound core of human existence, where the liberty to respond remains intact despite external constraints. This dimension encompasses the realm of intentionality and relates to the value system according to which individuals choose to operate. Attitude modulation represents an expression of humanity's capacity to resist submission to objective environmental conditions, instead transcending them through responsive engagement and converting circumstances into opportunities for human growth.

The objective of attitude modulation involves disrupting the automatic chains of reaction (e.g., fear → avoidance → narrowing of life) and to open space for an inner dialogue that asks, *What is asked of me here?* This process recognizes that transformation occurs not merely through altered life circumstances but through the modified stance we adopt toward them. Within any given situation, we may experience loss—perhaps temporarily—of certain values. Simultaneously, however, we possess the capacity to actualize alternative values or even to realize spiritually, through our attitude toward the situation, those very values we have lost.

Consequently, in therapeutic work with clients confronting crisis, practitioners identify the motivating values that drive them and determine how their suffering might transform into opportunities for expressing these values in ways that endow their lives with meaning. It remains essential to remember that individuals demonstrate willingness to sacrifice their lives for their ideals; therefore, they will certainly prove willing to endure suffering for those same principles. The practice of attitude modulation in logotherapy facilitates a transformative process wherein clients discover their capacity to reframe their relationship with suffering.

This therapeutic approach recognizes that while we cannot always control what happens to us, we retain the power to determine our response, thereby converting even the most challenging experiences into opportunities to find meaning and foster personal growth.

36 Logo-anchor

In the darkest moments of human suffering, the mind's capacity to transcend present circumstances through imagination can become a lifeline to meaning and hope. Building on this insight, logotherapy formulates the *logo-anchor* method, which recruits temporal transcendence by directing attention to a specific, value-laden memory or a plausible, vividly imagined future moment, used as a stabilizing reference point during distress. Its roots lie in Viktor Frankl's personal experience within the Nazi concentration camps, where he discovered that his ability to imagine himself delivering a lecture in a conference hall in the future helped him endure the suffering he experienced in the present. What began as a spontaneous survival mechanism in an extreme situation has evolved into a sophisticated clinical tool that harnesses the human capacity for temporal transcendence in service of psychological healing and existential discovery. Subsequent clinicians, most notably Gerber, systematized the method, showing how patients can identify a personally resonant "anchor," elaborate it in rich sensory and value-laden detail. In this way the logo-anchor operationalizes two core noetic capacities—self-distancing and self-transcendence—by locating a standpoint outside the immediate crucible and orienting the person toward purposes that outlast the moment.

The logo-anchor technique (logoanchor or logohook) operates by focusing attention toward meaning-rich experiences in the past or future, utilizing imagination as a stabilizing anchor in the present moment. This intervention proves particularly effective in addressing depression, existential emptiness, and psychological withdrawal from life. According to Gerber, the technique's applications extend beyond individual therapy to include bridging communication gaps between couples in marital counseling and facilitating group work, consistently aiming to help patients rediscover motivation and life purpose.

The therapeutic process begins with systematic self-exploration designed to uncover personal meaning anchors. This exploration involves guiding the client toward identifying significant childhood memories and formative experiences, activities that previously generated energy and states of "flow," or moments that evoked a profound sense of authentic self-expression—times when individuals felt "most themselves." This excavation of meaningful past experiences serves multiple therapeutic functions: it reveals unrealized dreams and aspirations while simultaneously reminding patients that they have already encountered moments of transcendence that demonstrated, sometimes in revelatory flashes, life's inherent meaningfulness. Through this process, clients learn to identify the essential components of these peak experiences and integrate their transformative essence into present-day living. Once the therapist successfully assists the client in bringing such experiences "to the surface," these memories become material for creative exploration through drawing, journaling, or other expressive modalities. The goal is to engage as many sensory channels as possible that were originally involved in the anchor experience, creating a rich, multi-dimensional therapeutic encounter that strengthens the connection between past meaning and present possibility.

Gerber emphasizes that implementing this technique requires careful clinical judgment, demanding both psychological maturity and readiness from the client, as well as therapeutic sensitivity to recognize optimal timing for integration within the broader treatment process. She has developed a structured guided-imagery protocol to support this inner work; what follows is a general outline that can be adapted, refined, or culturally attuned to the client and setting:

> I invite you to sit comfortably in your chair. You may close your eyes if that feels right, and take several deep breaths, releasing the tension that has accumulated in your body. Now let's take another deep breath and release the emotional tension that has built up, the worries… let them dissolve… try as

> much as possible to be here and now… to be present in this moment in time. Continue breathing at your natural pace, your unique rhythm.
>
> Now, allow your consciousness to wander like day-dreaming. Let us walk together along the path of memories and search for an experience that filled you with a sense of wonder and awe. A moment or situation in which you felt full of life—vital and whole, where you felt a deep connection to your uniqueness and humanity. Perhaps there was a feeling of something transcendent… perhaps you felt expansion… or a moment when you felt love toward the world and what it contains… try to truly recreate that moment—how does it feel? In your body? What does this experience look like?
>
> Now try to bring this feeling forward to the present moment and actually try to feel it through your senses, to experience it anew. Try to embed this experience in conscious memory—to hear again the sounds that accompanied the experience, to sense the tastes, smells, bodily sensations, touch, emotions that accompanied the experience. Try to connect as many senses as possible to create a three-dimensional image of the experience and remember that it is part of you and that you can return to it at any moment you wish.

The session concludes with the therapist inviting the client to share their journey and the specific experience they identified as their personal "logo-anchor." Clients are then encouraged to represent this anchor through creative expression—whether through drawing, writing, or another chosen medium—creating a tangible reminder of their capacity to access meaning and transcendence even amid present difficulties. This creative artifact may serve as both a therapeutic tool and a concrete symbol of the person's inherent resilience and meaning-making capacity, bridging the gap between therapeutic insight and daily living.

37 Meaning-centered interventions

The contemporary landscape of meaning-centered interventions has evolved significantly following Frankl's original logotherapeutic framework, incorporating insights from positive psychology, narrative therapy, and existential-humanistic approaches. This expansion stems from two converging developments in contemporary psychotherapy: mounting research evidence demonstrating the effectiveness of meaning-oriented treatments, and the clinical understanding that questions of purpose, significance, and existential direction are not confined to specialized populations but rather emerge as underlying themes across the full spectrum of psychological difficulties. Consequently, modern therapeutic practice increasingly requires interventions capable of addressing these fundamental meaning-making processes within varied clinical presentations and diverse client populations.

Contemporary empirical research has demonstrated the efficacy of meaning-centered interventions across a remarkable range of clinical conditions, from trauma-related disorders to chronic illness adaptation. For example, Breitbart's Meaning-Centered Psychotherapy (MCP), originally developed for cancer patients, has shown significant improvements in spiritual well-being, sense of meaning, and quality of life while reducing anxiety and desire for hastened death. These findings have been replicated across multiple randomized controlled trials, with effect sizes comparable to or exceeding those of traditional cognitive-behavioral interventions for existential distress.

Recent comprehensive research has demonstrated the effectiveness of meaning-centered interventions across diverse populations and settings. Manco and Hamby's (2021) meta-analysis of meaning-in-life interventions revealed that these approaches produce meaningful therapeutic benefits, with mindfulness-based interventions showing particularly strong effects when compared to standard care, while narrative interventions proved most effective when implemented alongside other active treatments. Values-based interventions represent another crucial component of meaning-centered treatment approaches. These interventions utilize values clarification exercises and committed action planning to help clients align their behavior with their core principles, building on foundational research by Rokeach and Schwartz. Contemporary life crafting models (e.g., Napier et al., 2024; van Zyl et al., 2023) extend this work by integrating values exploration with narrative coherence building and self-concordant goal-setting, creating comprehensive frameworks that address the interconnected nature of purpose, coherence, and mattering in therapeutic practice. These integrated approaches demonstrate significant improvements in treatment engagement, behavioral change, and long-term psychological adjustment across diverse populations, making them valuable tools for practitioners working across various clinical contexts. Interventions targeting "mattering"—the sense that one's existence makes a difference to others—have also emerged as particularly powerful tools within comprehensive meaning-making frameworks (Flett, 2018; Kruglanski & Raviv, 2025). These interventions address multiple pathways to meaning by helping individuals clarify their values, construct coherent life narratives, and identify ways their lives can have positive impact on others.

The integration of meaning-centered approaches with current therapeutic modalities has also yielded particularly promising results. Acceptance and Commitment Therapy (ACT), for example, shares significant conceptual overlap with logotherapy in its emphasis on values-based living and psychological flexibility in the face of suffering, yet extends these principles through mindfulness-based interventions and behavioral activation strategies. A comprehensive 2020 meta-analysis examining 20 systematic reviews across 12,477 participants found that ACT's focus on committed action toward personally meaningful values showed efficacy across a broad range of clinical conditions, including anxiety, depression, substance use, chronic pain, and transdiagnostic presentations. Narrative therapy approaches, particularly those developed by White and Epston (1990), also offer another avenue for meaning-centered intervention through the systematic exploration and reconstruction of personal life stories. These approaches recognize that psychological distress often stems from dominant problem-saturated narratives that obscure individuals' preferred identities and values. Through practices such as unique outcome conversations and definitional ceremonies, narrative therapists help clients author alternative stories that highlight their agency, competence, and alignment with values.

38 Working with values

Values present us with a curious paradox. They are simultaneously the most personal aspects of human experience and the most universal. While the specific content of what we value varies dramatically across individuals and cultures, the structural necessity of having values—of caring about something beyond immediate pleasure or pain—appears to be a defining feature of human consciousness. Values shape what we notice, how we choose, what we are willing to sacrifice for, and what we refuse to betray. In this sense, values function as an organizing grammar of agency: they allocate attention and effort, justify commitments, and set limits on expediency. Values, thus, function as essential guiding principles in life, shaping individuals' perceptions of significance and influencing their decision-making and behavior (Sagiv & Roccas, 2017). As reflections of what individuals perceive as important and worth pursuing in life (Schwartz et al., 2012), values inherently mirror individuals' motives, needs, and preferences, significantly influencing their daily lives, as well as major life decisions, ultimately shaping their life trajectories and long-term subjective well-being (Lee & Kawachi, 2019; Schwartz & Sortheix, 2018). When people live in line with values they genuinely endorse, experience tends to cohere; when they live at odds with them, demoralization and fragmentation follow.

Within logotherapy, values are also carriers of meaning. Meaning is not secured by sentiment alone; it is realized through valued ends enacted in concrete situations—in what one gives (creative pathway), receives (experiential pathway), and how one stands when change is impossible (attitudinal pathway). Values generate noetic tension—the purposeful pull between *what is* and *what ought to be*—and thereby supply direction. The clinical task is to support clients to clarify which claims they recognize as binding, and to translate those claims into doable steps here and now.

Working with values, then, is a collaborative inquiry. It asks three linked questions:

1 *Orientation*: What is worth doing—*for you*—in this situation?
2 *Horizon*: Within what wider frame does that choice make sense?
3 *Agency:* What specific stance or task is within reach this week?

Discovering and implementing values in practice

The recognition that values serve as organizing principles of meaningful existence leads naturally to the question of how clinicians can help clients identify, clarify, and enact their authentic values. Unlike preferences or temporary interests, genuine values often require deliberate excavation—they may be obscured by societal expectations, family scripts, or the accumulated compromises of daily survival. The following framework suggests one possible systematic yet flexible approach to values work, recognizing that this rich domain offers myriad alternative methodologies for honoring both the phenomenological complexity of individual experience and the practical requirements of clinical progress.

Phase I: Eliciting personally owned values

Values clarification begins with creating multiple pathways for authentic self-discovery. Rather than relying on abstract philosophical inquiry, effective values work employs concrete narrative and experiential prompts that bypass intellectual defenses and access lived wisdom. This can involve narrative exploration methods:

- *Meaningful achievements*: Identify three significant accomplishments and explore what made them meaningful beyond external recognition
- *Admired figures*: Describe three people you respect and articulate the specific qualities that evoke your admiration
- *Character identification*: Recall a fictional character who captured your imagination and examine what drew you to their way of being
- *Peak experiences*: Reflect on moments of greatest happiness and identify which values were being expressed
- *Absence and longing*: Consider what feels importantly missing from your current life
- *Legacy questions*: Articulate the three values you would most want to transmit to a child
- *Non-negotiable elements*: Define values without which life would not feel genuinely yours

Counterfactual and threshold exercises

These prompts may help distinguish core values from peripheral preferences by exploring boundaries and limits:

- Which value would you refuse to compromise regardless of external pressure?
- What would you never accept as central to your identity or daily experience?
- Under what circumstances would you violate your stated principles, and what does this reveal about their relative importance?

The "wants and shoulds" inventory

1 Generating comprehensive lists of desired activities and perceived obligations
2 Clustering items into life domains (family, vocation, creativity, service, learning, relationships)
3 Identifying the implicit values underlying each cluster
4 Examining tensions between authentic desires and internalized expectations

Relational values mapping

The three-figures exercise provides rich material for values clarification:

- Select a fictional character, a formative caregiver, and a personally chosen influence
- For each figure, identify admired qualities, desired adoptions, experienced impacts, and missing elements
- Synthesize insights about what you value in others and wish to cultivate in yourself

Developmental values archaeology

The childhood-hero probe accesses early value formations:

- Describe a childhood hero in detail (appearance, impressive qualities, symbolic meaning)

- Identify which heroic qualities remain relevant and which you would now decline
- Explore how early admirations connect to current value commitments

Phase II: Convergence and distillation

Raw material from exploration exercises requires careful synthesis to identify core organizing principles:

Pattern Recognition: Review responses across exercises to identify recurring themes, even when expressed in different language or contexts.

Linguistic Refinement: Merge near-synonyms and clarify distinctions between related but separate values.

Strategic Reduction: Distill to four or five core values that capture the essential organizing principles of your authentic self.

Phase III: Translating values into practice

Values work gains therapeutic traction when it moves from declaration to enactment. A concise sequence may be helpful: (1) rank four–five core values by current importance; (2) rate present satisfaction with each on a 1–5 scale; (3) select one value for focused development over the next 2–4 weeks; (4) specify two or three observable actions to express that value this week. For example, to advance *generativity*, one might schedule a one-hour mentoring conversation with a junior colleague and send a brief, specific note of appreciation to someone whose growth one has witnessed.

Implementation Support Use if-then planning ("If I encounter X situation, then I will Y") and environmental design to reduce friction around values-based choices.

Strategic Elimination Values clarification illuminates not only what to embrace but what to release. Identify pursuits that dilute the target value and systematically postpone, delegate, or discontinue them where possible.

Experiential Feedback Loops After values-based actions, explore differences in affect, energy, and sense of coherence compared to values-inconsistent behavior. This strengthens the coupling between values awareness and behavioral choice through direct experiential learning.

The value inversion exercise

This intervention may be helpful to reframe deprivation as a prompt for contribution: (1) Identify values that were missing or insufficient in your formative years (security, appreciation, belonging, recognition). Rank these absent values by their impact on your development; (2) Commit to offering these very values to others this week. For example, if you find that safety was missing, create safety for someone through reliability and clear communication. If appreciation was scarce, actively recognize others' strengths and contributions. This exercise often generates immediate meaning-effects by converting grievance into generativity.

Alternatively, the therapist may invite reflection by posing thought-provoking questions:

- What does this value mean to you in your own words, beyond conventional definitions?
- What would honoring this value more fully require in practical terms?
- What price are you currently paying for its neglect?
- What barriers—practical, emotional, or social—impede fuller expression?
- Is this value conditionally held (dependent on external circumstances) or can it be expressed immediately at a smaller scale?
- What would constitute a credible first step this week?

Given the dynamic and evolving character of meaning in lived experience, values work can be approached as ongoing reassessment—attending to reorientation and new meaning-possibilities, monitoring strains on earlier commitments, and periodically reprioritizing values and updating satisfaction ratings—so that goals are reset in ways that keep tension purposeful rather than depleting. Overall, values work operates through evocation rather than prescription. The therapeutic aim is alignment with self-endorsed obligations, not conformity to external standards. Cultural, religious, and philosophical frameworks are engaged respectfully as contexts within which values are articulated and lived. This approach complements rather than replaces indicated medical or trauma-focused interventions. It guards against "spiritual bypassing" by consistently linking values to concrete, accountable behaviors in the present moment. Hence, values can be seen as serving simultaneously as compass and filter: they orient effort, justify sacrifice, and determine what is allowed to fall away. When lived creatively, experientially, and attitudinally, values do not merely describe a life—they actively generate its meaning.

39 The 'mountain range' exercise

The Mountain Range Exercise represents a powerful visual metaphor for exploring the relational dimensions of meaning-making. It draws on Frankl's metaphor of the mountain range in *The Doctor and the Soul* and was subsequently developed by Ernzen into a structured logotherapeutic activity (Ernzen, 1990; Frankl, 1986). This technique employs the symbolic landscape of mountain peaks to illuminate how significant relationships inform personal values and life direction, transforming abstract concepts of meaning into tangible, visually represented connections.

Grounded in existential and logotherapeutic principles, the exercise operationalizes Frankl's emphasis on self-transcendence and self-distancing. Meaning is not recovered by intensified introspection alone, but by stepping outside the press of the moment to apprehend a wider context. Adopting what might be called a 'helicopter perspective'—both temporally and spatially—shifts processing toward central features of events, reveals recurrent motifs rather than surface variability, and fosters choices more congruent with enduring values and longer-term goals.

The exercise methodology involves creating a visual representation of a mountain range, with each peak serving as a symbolic position for influential figures in the participant's life narrative. These individuals may span diverse categories—intimate family members, cherished friends, literary figures, artistic influences, spiritual guides, or mentors—united not by proximity but by their capacity to embody or inspire meaningful living. Through this cartographic process, participants externalize their internal network of meaning-bearing relationships, making visible the often unconscious ways in which others' values and purposes inform their own existential orientation.

The therapeutic inquiry extends beyond mere identification to explore patterns of resonance and aspiration. Participants examine the common threads that connect them with their chosen figures, uncovering shared values, parallel struggles, or complementary strengths that reveal their own emerging value system. This process of comparative reflection often illuminates previously unarticulated aspects of personal meaning, as individuals recognize recurring themes across their diverse influences. Equally significant is the forward-looking dimension: contemplating whose metaphorical peaks they aspire to join reverses the traditional focus from receiving inspiration to becoming a source of meaning for others.

The mountain range exercise unfolds in three linked movements: concrete visualization, interpretive insight, and practical application. First, the therapist invites the client to imagine life as a mountain range seen from altitude. Peaks and valleys are named: major accomplishments, moments of fulfillment, and periods of growth on the one hand; seasons of struggle, loss, or confusion on the other. Second, attention turns to linkage and causation: What "geological forces", such as values, commitments, ways of being, seem to generate the peaks? In what sense do valleys function as necessary traverses, periods of preparation or learning, or detours from an authentic path? Third, the client locates the present position within this terrain: ascending, traversing, or at a crossroads. This localization often clarifies whether current distress is a temporary descent within a meaningful trajectory or a signal that reorientation is warranted. The exercise concludes with a prospective phase: given the patterns already visible, which peaks lie on the horizon, and what passes must be traversed to reach them? In this way, abstract values are translated into concrete planning while remaining tethered to the client's authentic developmental arc.

Clinically, the technique is especially useful where existential myopia predominates—narrow focus on the immediate that obscures larger contours. It can counter both catastrophic construals (in which present pain eclipses all else) and manic inflation (in which a momentary rise is mistaken for permanent altitude). In transitional periods, the panorama frequently reveals that apparent disruptions—career changes, relational shifts, spiritual developments—are intelligible extensions of longstanding patterns once viewed from sufficient distance.

Contemporary applications have demonstrated the exercise's adaptability across various life domains. Pattakos (2004) pioneered its translation to professional contexts, where the mountain range becomes a map of career influences and workplace meaning. In this adaptation, participants populate their peaks with professional mentors, industry innovators, or colleagues whose work exemplifies meaningful engagement, subsequently exploring how these influences might inform their own vocational purpose and values-based decision-making within organizational settings. More specifically, the exercise lends itself to developmentally and clinically sensitive adaptation. With adolescents, emphasis can be placed on early peaks that suggest emerging identity themes, as demonstrated in group applications of the Mountain Range Exercise (Schulenberg, 2003). With older adults, the work often surfaces unifying threads that integrate diverse life phases. In serious illness, the method offers a frame for viewing the life-span as a meaningful whole while discerning which peaks remain attainable within real constraints. Delivery can be purely imaginal or augmented by drawing, icons, or brief written labels to increase accessibility.

The exercise's effectiveness lies in its capacity to render visible the intersubjective nature of meaning-making—the recognition that personal significance often emerges through relationship and identification with others who embody purposeful living. By transforming abstract questions about values and direction into concrete explorations of admired figures, the Mountain Range Exercise bridges the gap between conceptual understanding and felt experience, enabling participants to access their meaning-making processes through the more accessible pathway of relational connection and aspiration. Overall, the mountain range exercise embodies several core logotherapeutic insights. It privileges pattern recognition over moment-by-moment appraisal, cultivates the self-transcendent stance that enables meaning to be discerned, and respects the premise that meaning cannot be supplied from outside. The therapist offers the metaphor and facilitates the vantage point, but the topography is authored by the client: what counts as a peak or valley, which patterns matter, and which mountains beckon are judgments that arise from the client's own engagement with lived experience. As such, the visualization functions as both assessment and intervention, revealing existing meaning-structures while strengthening the capacity to adopt the temporal distance required for ongoing meaning-making. It exemplifies the logotherapeutic synthesis of phenomenological respect for the individual life-world with disciplined method aimed at enhancing existential clarity.

40 Prioritizing meaning

> I have spent my days stringing and unstringing my instrument, while the song I came to sing remains unsung.
>
> (Tagore, 1912, p. 7)

Rabindranath Tagore's reflection reveals a common therapeutic challenge: the gap between recognizing what holds meaning in our lives and actually living that meaning on a daily basis. Many clients entering therapy possess a clear intellectual understanding of their values—they know what matters to them—yet struggle to translate these insights into concrete action. Consider the parent who identifies family as their highest priority while remaining chronically absent from their children's lives, or the individual who speaks passionately about creative expression while their artistic tools remain untouched. These scenarios illustrate how intellectual awareness of meaning, while necessary, proves insufficient for psychological well-being when disconnected from lived experience. As Tagore suggests, we often become skilled at "preparing our instruments"—analyzing values, discussing priorities and goals—yet hesitate to take the vulnerable step of actually using these instruments to "sing our song." This preparation without performance creates a particular form of suffering: knowing who we wish to become while remaining trapped in contradictory patterns.

The importance of bridging this gap becomes evident when we consider how meaning unfolds in human existence. As Albert Camus observed, "Life is a sum of all your choices," while Annie Dillard adds, "How we spend our days is, of course, how we spend our lives." Meaning emerges not through grand gestures or isolated moments of significance, but through the accumulation of daily choices and actions that either align with or diverge from what we hold most valuable. When our lived reality consistently contradicts our stated values, we risk experiencing what logotherapy identifies as an 'existential vacuum'—a profound sense of meaninglessness despite intellectual awareness of what should matter to us. In contemporary life, where the rapid pace of obligations can eclipse the fundamental question of *why* we engage in various activities, prioritizing meaning becomes both therapeutic intervention and practical necessity. Rather than waiting for future circumstances to align with our values, logotherapy recognizes meaning-making as an active, present-moment practice. This involves cultivating the habit of regular self-inquiry—pausing to consider "What can I do today that will feel meaningful?"—and then following through with intentional action, however modest that action might be.

Prioritizing meaning, thus, refers to the extent to which individuals intentionally seek out activities and contexts—and make concrete choices—that are conducive to experiencing meaning in life (Russo-Netzer, 2018). In logotherapy, this emphasis operationalizes Frankl's claim that meaning is to be discovered and responded to rather than manufactured: the guiding question becomes what the situation is asking of the person now and how daily investments of time can honor that call. Daily behaviors are adaptable and subject to change (Gollwitzer, 1999), whereas time is finite; accordingly, the way people allocate their minutes effectively declares their priorities and reinforces their life goals (Csikszentmihalyi, 1997). Seen this way, *priorities* are enacted through the ways people invest their minutes and hours. The research program summarized here shows that meaning can be shaped and lived through quotidian choices about activities and interactions. Prioritizing meaning invites a proactive stance beyond post-hoc meaning *restoration* (cf. Steger, 2012), asking clients to take ownership of the cultivation of a meaningful life in real time.

Prioritizing meaning thus functions as a *micro-architecture* of eudaimonia: an ongoing process of discerning values, aligning choices with them, and refining those choices as contexts shift. It demands self-awareness (to clarify values), self-regulation (to translate values into plans), and reflection (to detect evolving "signals of meaning" and recalibrate accordingly). In the language of motivation science, it is closely allied with self-concordance—pursuing goals that genuinely express the self (Sheldon, 2014), and with processes that support authenticity and self-insight (Critcher & Dunning, 2015; Sedikides et al., 2017). Empirically, people who prioritize meaning through their actions tend to report a stronger sense of meaning in life and, in turn, less negative emotion and more positive emotion, gratitude, coherence (a felt sense of optimism and agency), happiness, and life satisfaction. In complementary work, aligning identified valued life domains with chosen actions has been associated with increased self-insight and sense of coherence and with reduced symptoms of psychopathology (e.g., Russo-Netzer, 2019; Russo-Netzer & Shoshani, 2020; Russo-Netzer & Atad, 2024). This pattern is consistent with the self-concordance model: acting in accordance with one's values appears to initiate a self-affirming loop in which implementing values clarifies and strengthens them (e.g., Sheldon, 2014; Sedikides et al., 2017).

To translate these insights into practice, the following brief, modular logotherapeutic protocol offers a structured intervention:

The Prioritizing Meaning Protocol (PMP)

Phase 1—Assess & Map (Discovery): The aim of this step is to clarify what matters and how time is currently spent.

1 *Values and Life-Domain Clarification*. Invite clients to identify their valued life domains (e.g., family, learning, contribution, creativity, faith/spirituality, health). Optionally administer a Prioritizing Meaning survey to index their baseline orientation (see Appendix).
2 *Time-Use Audit*. Review the last 24 hours and last 7 days. Where did time go? Which moments felt meaningful? Which felt depleting or empty?

3 *Coherence Check*. For each domain, rate (a) importance and (b) actual time/energy invested. Gaps signal opportunities for realignment.

The therapeutic emphasis here is on discovery, guiding clients to discern *where meaning is already calling* within their contexts.

Phase 2—Translate Values into Actions (Design): The aim of this step is to convert values into concrete, scheduled behaviors.

1 *Micro-acts and Macro-acts*. Create a portfolio of *meaning-aligned micro-acts*—brief, low-friction behaviors—and *macro-acts*—extended, recurring engagements—to guide implementation. Examples of micro-acts include a mindful pause before a difficult conversation or stepping outside to attend to beauty. Examples of macro-acts include a weekly volunteering shift.
2 *If-Then Planning*. Implementation intentions make chosen actions more automatic—if-then plans that link situational cues to value-congruent responses (Gollwitzer, 1999). For example: "*If* it is 8:30 a.m., *then* I will identify one value-aligned contribution for the day" (creative value).
3 *Schedule the Week*. Insert selected micro- and macro-acts into the calendar.

The therapeutic stance here is to keep changes small and tractable. The goal is repeatable wins that build momentum and testimony.

Phase 3—Prune, Protect, and Align (Decision): The aim of this step is to remove friction and protect what matters.

1 *Stop/Start/Modify*. Identify one activity to stop, one to start, and one to modify this week to better align with values.
2 *Boundary Rituals*. Create simple rituals that safeguard meaningful blocks (e.g., a "doorframe cue" to center before entering home).
3 *Communal Alignment*. Where relevant, surface shared values (family, classroom, team) and co-design small collective practices that embody them.

The therapeutic stance here is to frame alignment as selection and deselection in equal measure, attending to what must be stopped, constrained, or deferred alongside what is embraced.

Phase 4—Review & Refine (Discernment): The aim here is to consolidate insight and adjust to shifting calls of meaning. The therapist can use reflection prompts to support reflection, review and refinement. For example: *Looking back at the last 24 hours or week, which moments felt most meaningful? What made them so? Which meaningful activities or interactions will you prioritize in the next 24 hours? What could you remove or tweak this week to make space for what matters? How well did your to-do list reflect your values this week? Where did you notice a shift in what felt meaningful? Which one or two tiny acts of meaning will you schedule for tomorrow?*

Clinical considerations are important. First, meaning should be discovered rather than imposed; the clinician's role is to support discernment and response, not to prescribe what ought to matter. Second, special emphasis on attitudinal freedom helps clients locate their remaining latitude under constraint and craft concrete responses that honor dignity and responsibility. Third, vigilance is needed to prevent perfectionism from masquerading as "meaning"; coherence, not ceaseless achievement, is the therapeutic aim. Overall, this framework emphasizes gradual transformation through consistent micro-choices rather than dramatic life restructuring. By viewing each day as a canvas for meaningful action, we can systematically align our actual time investment with our authentic priorities, creating a daily rhythm that increasingly mirrors our core intentions rather than simply responding to external demands.

41 Biographical techniques

Biographical techniques in logotherapy recognize that the stories individuals construct about their lives profoundly influence their capacity to discover and experience meaning. These approaches operate on the fundamental premise that humans are meaning-making beings who continuously author and re-author their life narratives. The theoretical foundation for biographical techniques draws from Frankl's understanding of the temporal nature of human existence and the importance of connecting past experiences with present choices and future possibilities. This perspective aligns with contemporary research in narrative psychology, particularly McAdams' (2011, 2019) work on identity development through life story construction, which demonstrates that individuals who can integrate challenging experiences into coherent, growth-oriented narratives show greater psychological resilience and well-being.

One prominent example is the 'Life review' method (e.g., Haber, 2006) which extends beyond simple reminiscence to facilitate active meaning reconstruction. These interventions guide individuals through systematic exploration of significant life events, relationships, and turning points, with particular attention to moments of choice, growth, and value expression. Framed by logotherapy's three pathways to meaning, the review may enable clients to (a) trace creative contributions—work, caregiving, problem-solving, and initiatives that instantiate values in action; (b) recall experiential sources of meaning—love, beauty, belonging, awe, and gratitude that have nourished the self; and (c) recognize attitudinal achievements—stances of courage, dignity, and responsibility adopted in the face of constraints or suffering. Taken together, these lenses could support people to identify coherent patterns in how meaning has been found across the lifespan, to appreciate life achievements in each pathway, and to translate past insights into present purpose and future direction. More specifically, the 'Life Review' method adopts three interconnected therapeutic mechanisms that facilitate biographical exploration and narrative reconstruction (Maercker, 2002).

Equilibrium Restoration: This framework emphasizes the cultivation of psychological balance through systematic examination of life's contrasting experiences. Rather than allowing negative recollections to overshadow positive ones, the therapeutic process guides individuals toward recognizing and amplifying constructive memories—moments of resilience, achievement, and personal growth—while contextualizing difficult experiences within a broader life narrative that acknowledges both struggle and triumph.

Meaning-focused Process: The therapeutic work centers on helping individuals discover significance within their most challenging experiences through narrative reconstruction. Rather than minimizing the genuine pain of trauma or loss, this approach guides clients toward recognizing how difficult experiences may have fostered resilience, deepened compassion, or generated insights that would not have emerged otherwise. This aligns with contemporary research on post-traumatic growth (e.g., Calhoun & Tedeschi, 2014), guiding individuals in identifying specific ways their difficulties have shaped them positively—by strengthening their resilience, increasing their compassion for others, or helping them recognize what truly matters in life. As clients engage in this process, they construct a fuller understanding of their life story, one that frames adversity not merely as damage endured but as experiences that have fostered meaningful personal development and enhanced self-awareness.

Narrative Elaboration: Encouraging comprehensive and detailed memory exploration that transcends surface-level recall to develop nuanced, layered narratives. When addressing traumatic experiences, for example, disconnected memory fragments are systematically integrated into unified stories that incorporate the full spectrum of emotional, physical, and intellectual dimensions of lived experience.

The therapeutic process may also employ diverse creative modalities to facilitate memory access and narrative construction, such as visual documentation (e.g., personal photograph collections, creative collages, or scrapbook compilation) to serve as tangible anchors for memory exploration and life story organization. Material or auditory memory catalysts, such as childhood artifacts, family heirlooms, music, and other significant objects can unlock emotionally charged memories and may function as sensory gateways to forgotten or suppressed memories.

Contemporary applications of biographical techniques incorporate structured narrative interventions that have demonstrated empirical effectiveness. Research by Pennebaker and others (e.g., 2007, 2010) on expressive writing, for example, shows that when individuals write about significant life events with focus on meaning-making and emotional processing, they experience improvements in both psychological and physical health outcomes. Within the logotherapeutic framework, these writing exercises may be specifically designed to help clients recognize how their personal stories reflect their deepest values and contribute to their sense of life purpose. Through this process of active meaning-construction, clients may cultivate the capacity to maintain purpose and coherence when confronting future difficulties. This therapeutic goal reflects logotherapy's core aim: strengthening individuals' ability to transcend immediate circumstances through meaning-oriented living, utilizing their unique life experiences as the foundation for this transformative work.

42 Future orientation methods

The distinctively human ability to envision and mentally inhabit future scenarios—termed *prospection*—constitutes a core psychological capacity that enables individuals to transcend immediate circumstances and pursue long-term meaningful objectives (Baumeister et al., 2024; Seligman et al., 2013). This temporal flexibility allows people to evaluate potential consequences of current decisions, resist immediate impulses when they conflict with deeper purposes, and organize present behavior around future-oriented goals. Within the logotherapeutic framework, prospective thinking assumes particular importance as it enables individuals to engage in what Frankl identified as the essential human capacity for "self-transcendence"—the ability to move beyond immediate self-centered concerns toward future-oriented meaning realization.

The theoretical understanding of temporal self-evaluation is further enriched by Temporal Self-Appraisal Theory (Wilson & Ross, 2001, 2003), which posits that individuals continuously assess their temporal identity based on perceived advancement toward cherished objectives. This framework indicates that psychological proximity between current and future selves varies according to goal-related feedback, with meaningful progress fostering stronger identification with anticipated outcomes. From a logotherapeutic standpoint, this temporal coherence becomes crucial for sustaining what Frankl called "tragic optimism"—the maintenance of purpose-oriented hope even when confronting inevitable life challenges. A particularly significant aspect of prospective thinking involves *future self-continuity*—the extent to which individuals experience psychological, emotional, and ethical connection with their anticipated future selves (Hershfield & Bartels, 2018). Empirical evidence indicates that individuals who maintain stronger continuity with their future selves demonstrate greater likelihood of engaging in behaviors that support enduring well-being, including persistent goal pursuit, deferred gratification, and values-aligned decision-making (Bartels & Urminsky, 2011; Ersner-Hershfield et al., 2009). Contemporary research further suggests that future self-continuity enhances meaning in life through increased authenticity (Hong et al., 2024).

From a logotherapeutic perspective, future self-continuity reflects Frankl's understanding of responsible existence—the recognition that present choices determine not merely immediate outcomes but the entire arc of one's life trajectory. When clients cultivate strong psychological bonds with their future selves, they develop enhanced capacity for making choices that transcend momentary comfort or discomfort in service of enduring meaning fulfillment. This temporal integration supports what logotherapy identifies as the primary human drive: the search for meaning. Through imaginative engagement with future meaningful scenarios, individuals can access motivational resources that enable them to persist through present difficulties, drawing upon envisioned purpose fulfillment to sustain hope and directed action even when immediate conditions offer limited meaning opportunities.

While future-oriented methods can be powerful, practitioners should not assume that a client can readily "see a future." For many, especially following trauma, severe depression, bereavement, displacement, or moral injury—imagining any future may feel inaccessible, triggering, or heartbreakingly out of reach. It is crucial that clients are not implicitly pressured to produce a future narrative; even well-intended prompts can evoke shame ("something is wrong with me") or intensify despair when the future feels blank. In logotherapy, the ethical stance is to meet the person where they are: if the future is currently unavailable, this is not failure but meaningful clinical information. The task then becomes to widen the client's tolerance for a future horizon gradually, without forcing it, and to anchor work in the smallest livable next step.

Practically, integrating future orientation in logotherapeutic practice may include guiding clients through visualization exercises where they envision themselves five to ten years in the future, focusing on how they are living out core values and contributing to meaningful endeavors. However, this should be offered in graded form—beginning with the "nearest possible future" (e.g., later today, this week, the next small milestone) when longer horizons feel impossible. Clients can be encouraged to explore not just what they will be doing, but why these activities matter and how they connect to purpose. If imagery is difficult or overwhelming, the intervention can shift from visualization to gentle "as-if" questions ("If a future were possible, what might you want it to stand for?"), or to present-centered meaning ("What is being asked of you now, in this hour, given what you are carrying?"). Follow-up sessions may involve identifying specific present-moment actions aligned with these future-meaning scenarios. Alternative interventions emphasize connecting present challenges to future meaning by helping clients reframe current difficulties as developmental steps rather than meaningless obstacles, creating coherent narratives that link today's struggles with tomorrow's purpose fulfilment, but always with permission to pause when the exercise becomes activating or when grief about a lost future needs to be honored first.

Future orientation in logotherapy may also extend beyond individual prospection to encompass "generative prospection", envisioning how present actions contribute to meanings that transcend personal existence. This approach integrates narrative bridge-building between current struggles and future purpose with Frankl's emphasis on self-transcendence, recognizing that profound meaning often emerges through contributions to larger human purposes. In this spirit, clients may engage in structured exploration of how current choices might create enduring impact through family legacy, professional contribution, community service, or creative expression. Here too, generativity should be scaled to capacity: for some clients, the first "legacy" is simply surviving with dignity, repairing one relationship, or keeping one promise. Through guided reflection, clients may develop concrete plans for creating positive impact across generations, strengthening personal meaning and social connection. Practical applications include writing letters to future family members, designing mentorship based on lived growth, or initiating projects intended to outlast one's individual life—yet the clinician's task is to protect the client from performative futurity: the future is invited, not demanded.

Overall, prospection, future self-continuity, and temporal self-appraisal provide psychological scaffolding by which clients can "lean forward" without abandoning the present—sustaining tragic optimism while taking ownership of the next step. In logotherapeutic terms, the future is not a screen onto which one projects wishes, but a horizon that clarifies what is being asked now. When that horizon is blocked, logotherapy does not force a picture; it restores agency through the smallest faithful act in the actionable present. Over time, such acts can soften the "future blackout," allowing a modest horizon to reappear—first as a next step, then as a next chapter.

43 Working with dreams in logotherapy

Logotherapy approaches dreams as a profound gateway into the spiritual unconscious—the noetic dimension where values, conscience, and existential questions crystallize—offering access to spaces where transcendent meaning intersects with the concrete realities of lived experience. This perspective fundamentally reconceptualizes the psychoanalytic "royal road" to the unconscious: rather than treating dream images as mere drive residues, they become meaningful revelations through which the purpose-seeking self discloses its deepest concerns, value conflicts, and moral imperatives (e.g., Fabry, 1988; Marshall & Marshall, 2012). The spiritual unconscious emerges as a grounded construct bridging spirituality, existential meaning, and psychological well-being, suggesting that dream material exposes underlying value tensions and conscience calls that orient therapeutic work toward meaning-making rather than instinctual drive reduction (García-Alandete,

2024). This orientation aligns with the premise that dreams create metaphorically rich imagery that intensifies emotional themes, providing therapeutic material for exploring what is being cherished, threatened, or sought at the deepest levels of human concern.

The logotherapeutic approach to dreams begins with an existential-phenomenological stance, where the therapist suspends presuppositions (epoché) and encounters the dream as a disclosure of the dreamer's being-in-the-world. This process prioritizes description over explanation: As in psychoanalytic procedure (Freud, 2006), the dream is first rendered verbatim—word for word—to preserve its texture, sequencing, and linguistic nuances. The therapist explores recent experiences that may have influenced the imagery while utilizing classical transformations—condensation, displacement, symbolization, and inversion—as heuristic tools for understanding how affect is redistributed within the dream's manifest content.

The interpretive pivot, however, is distinctly noetic. Rather than seeking drive-based wish fulfillment, logotherapeutic questioning focuses on value tensions and meaning conflicts: Which values are in tension here? What questions of conscience does the dream raise? This value-centric approach reflects Frankl's understanding that the unconscious houses our ethical and spiritual orientations alongside instinctual material. Meanings emerge from within the dreamer's lifeworld rather than being imposed through prefabricated symbol systems, ensuring cultural humility while privileging the dreamer's authentic idiom (Moustakas, 1996).

Logotherapeutic dreamwork, thus, can be seen as unfolding through four interconnected movements, conducted as continuous dialogue rather than rigid sequence:

Phenomenological Elicitation involves obtaining the dream faithfully, capturing verbatim text, sensory qualities, and pivotal images, then gathering associations and day residues while allowing the dreamer to supply the initial web of meanings. This foundation ensures that subsequent interpretation remains grounded in the client's authentic experience. The therapist may use Socratic dialogue to test working hypotheses, and resists one-size-fits-all symbol dictionaries, maintaining cultural humility when spiritual or religious motifs appear.

Noetic Focusing identifies value tensions, moral questions, and intimations of conscience within the imagery. Opposing dream figures may crystallize conflicts between competing values like loyalty and truth, while blocked passages might dramatize experiences of externally imposed limitations on personal growth or authentic expression.

Existential Options formulate "calls to response" along logotherapy's three avenues of meaning: creative values (what to contribute or build), experiential values (what to receive or honor), and attitudinal values (what stance to adopt where external change proves impossible). These options transform dream insights into concrete possibilities for meaningful action.

Translation into Life distills one or two specific, value-aligned actions or stance practices to be enacted before the next session, with outcomes revisited to refine discernment rather than chase definitive interpretations. This movement ensures that dreamwork contributes to lived meaning-making rather than remaining purely intellectual.

This approach is congruent with empirical research and process-outcome findings on dreamwork, suggesting that therapist–client collaboration aimed at exploration, insight, and action ideas is associated with stronger session depth and perceived helpfulness (Hill & Knox, 2010). Throughout this process, essential guardrails maintain therapeutic integrity. Interpretations remain tentative and negotiated, with the dreamer's cultural idiom anchoring all meaning claims. Spiritual and religious contents are welcomed when they arise naturally, treated as potential resources for comprehensive understanding rather than imposed frameworks. When traumatic material surfaces, safety and stabilization take precedence, with any rescripting techniques integrated within broader trauma-informed care that respects the client's window of tolerance.

The logotherapeutic stance proves particularly valuable when trauma, guilt, or moral injury have shattered assumptive worlds. During such periods, when language may falter, dreams often carry fragments of suffering into symbolic spaces where coherence, agency, and dignity can begin reconstruction. Dream reflection links these images to enduring values, inviting attitudinal responses—patience coupled with courage, fidelity to truth, compassion with appropriate boundaries—and facilitating small, concrete enactments that rebuild meaning-oriented living, consistent with logotherapeutic approaches that emphasize existential reflection, responsibility, and action toward meaning (Lantz, 1998).

This approach reframes dreams not as puzzles requiring solution but as encounters demanding response. Dreams function as encounters to be answered rather than puzzles to be solved. These symbolic narratives reveal the meaning-seeking self's deepest concerns, loyalties, and fears—often in heightened or inverted form—providing living material for conscious choice-making in therapy. When therapists help clients move from the dream's manifest narrative to the value queries it intimates, then translate these insights into scheduled acts embodying those values, the result transcends symptom relief to strengthen what Frankl termed "tragic optimism"—credible hope oriented toward purposes that persist even under constraint.

Over repeated therapeutic cycles, clients learn to approach dreams as micro-dramas where the future-oriented, meaning-seeking self signals what requires protection, what calls for contribution, and where dignity remains possible despite adversity. This process facilitates the broader logotherapeutic goal of contracting the existential vacuum by moving from symbolic image to responsible action, ensuring that not only dream journals but also daily calendars bear witness to renewed purpose. Logotherapy's distinctive contribution to dreamwork lies in restoring dreams to their fundamental role as messengers from our deepest values, transforming symbolic insights into responsible waking actions that honor both the dream's wisdom and the dreamer's capacity for meaningful choice (Lantz, 1998; Pesant & Zadra, 2004). Through careful phenomenological exploration, noetic focusing, and translation into concrete action, this approach honors the dreamer's cultural idiom while facilitating the fundamental logotherapeutic process of recognizing meaning potentials and transforming them into lived purpose.

44 Metaphor and symbol

Human meaning-making operates fundamentally through symbolic and metaphorical processes that transform abstract experiences into comprehensible narratives. As Antoine de Saint-Exupéry beautifully suggested, "Behind all the things visible, there is something bigger; Everything is a path, a gate, or a window that opens up to something else." Contemporary research in cognitive linguistics supports this insight, demonstrating that metaphorical thinking is not merely decorative language but a primary cognitive mechanism through which human beings organize experience and construct meaning (Lakoff & Johnson, 2003). This resonates deeply with logotherapy's understanding of how individuals access and articulate their deepest values and purposes.

Within the logotherapeutic framework, metaphors and symbols serve as essential vehicles through which the spiritual unconscious communicates concerns that often resist direct articulation. When clients struggle to express their sense of purpose, metaphorical language frequently emerges as the primary means of authentic communication, suggesting that meaning itself may be fundamentally metaphorical in structure. Metaphors function as orienting devices that consolidate a person's concerns, values, and possibilities into actionable images. Rather than merely describing experience, they create frameworks for responsive engagement with life's challenges and opportunities. Similarly, symbols operate as living signs that derive meaning through situational encounter rather than fixed interpretation. They represent points of intersection where world and person meet, demanding responsible response rather than passive decoding. This dynamic understanding positions both metaphors and symbols as invitations to meaningful action within logotherapeutic practice. When a client describes feeling "stuck at a crossroads," the metaphor simultaneously reveals their current existential position and points toward necessary choice-making. The therapeutic work involves exploring what this crossroads represents in terms of values conflict and what movement forward might require, transforming metaphorical insight into concrete decision-making. The symbol's significance emerges through its connection to their particular life situation and values, creating opportunities for purposeful response rather than abstract contemplation.

This situational character of meaning can be clarified through an analogy Frankl often used: just as there is no universally "best" move in a board position, there is no abstract, general meaning of life apart from the concrete configuration one inhabits. What counts is reading *this* unique and unrepeatable position—its pressures, openings, and obligations—and selecting a move that fits. In the same spirit, the logotherapist's role resembles that of an optometrist more than a painter: the task is not to impose a picture but to refine the client's lenses so that the contours of their own life-world come into focus. Language, thus, is the medium of this calibration. Because human experience is intentional—always *of* or *about* something—words, images, and metaphors function as directed acts; they carry an intention from speaker to listener and from life toward the person. Therapeutically, we do not ask, "What does the symbol mean in general?" but, "What is being meant *here*, for *you*, now?"

A well-known episode Frankl recounts makes the point: a handwritten word was read by one person as a number and by another as the name of the divine—two radically different apprehensions of the same marks. The lesson is not to prefer one reading on doctrinal grounds but to recognize how prior commitments and concerns tune perception. For logotherapy, the crucial move is to turn from projection to intention: What question is the situation posing? What is life "asking" in and through this image? In that sense, meaning in life is akin to meaning in language: it is not fabricated by the interpreter but *found*—discovered, disclosed, or revealed—through careful attention to what is intended beneath experience, speech, and action. Such work requires disciplined openness: a readiness to bracket assumptions, to listen with mind and heart, and to admit the partiality of any given perspective on the complexity of existence.

Consequently, metaphors and symbols in therapy must be handled contextually and dialogically. The same image—a crossroads, a locked door—can call for different responses across persons and across moments in a single person's life. Meanings are particular, time-bound, and interpreter-dependent; they emerge where a person's values, constraints, and possibilities intersect. In practice, this means eliciting the client's own metaphors rather than importing prefabricated ones; clarifying what the image illuminates (and what it hides); testing its guidance against the three avenues of meaning (what to create or give, what to receive or honor, what stance to take where change is impossible); and translating the symbol's "call" into a concrete next step. The measure of a good interpretation is not theoretical accuracy but whether it sharpens sight and supports a value-congruent decision.

Logotherapeutic work with metaphors and symbols involves a process of capturing the client's exact image within its situational context, exploring what the metaphor reveals about underlying values or tensions, testing alternative images to refine understanding, and translating insights into concrete action. Through this progression, metaphors and symbols can become practical bridges between inner recognition and outer response, opening conversation toward meaningful action rather than closing it with interpretation.

The symbolic dimension becomes particularly significant when addressing the spiritual unconscious—that repository of values, conscience, and transcendent concerns operating beyond immediate awareness. Recent research on intuitive cognition suggests that symbolic processing may provide access to implicit knowledge systems that conscious deliberation alone cannot reach (Hodgkinson et al., 2009). Symbols carry emotional and spiritual resonance that transcends literal content, enabling individuals to access meaning experiences that rational discourse fails to capture. Furthermore, contemporary research on pattern recognition and meaning-making provides empirical grounding for understanding synchronicity experiences within logotherapeutic practice. Studies on apophenia—the tendency to perceive meaningful patterns in random stimuli—suggest that meaning-seeking consciousness naturally attunes itself to environmentally relevant information, particularly during periods of uncertainty or transition (Whitson & Galinsky, 2008). This research validates therapeutic attention to synchronistic experiences while maintaining scientific grounding. In this context, when clients report synchronicity experiences involving recurring symbols, the therapeutic work explores how these symbols connect to their deeper meaning-seeking processes. Rather than encouraging mystical interpretations, this approach recognizes how reflective attention to meaningful coincidences may support meaning-detection and life-narrative integration, potentially clarifying personally significant values and directions for action (Russo-Netzer & Icekson, 2023).

Practically, metaphors and symbols can be systematically integrated into logotherapeutic practice through structured techniques that transform clients' natural imagery into tools for meaning discovery and values clarification. These approaches recognize that clients often express their deepest concerns and aspirations through spontaneous metaphorical language that reveals more about their authentic values than direct questioning.

Metaphorical Values Clarification: Therapists access clients' authentic value systems through their spontaneous metaphorical language. Using prompts such as "My ideal life feels like…" or "When I imagine my purpose, I see…" clients generate imagery that reveals underlying meaning orientations more accurately than direct questioning. A client describing their purpose as "being a bridge between worlds" works with the therapist to unpack what bridge-building represents, perhaps values around connection, translation, and service, and then develops specific actions that embody these bridge-building qualities in daily life. This is consistent with meaning-oriented approaches that use personal metaphors and creative expressions to clarify deeply held values and support value-congruent action (e.g., Russo-Netzer, 2021).

Environmental Symbol Recognition: Clients cultivate awareness of recurring symbolic themes in their environment during periods of meaning exploration. Rather than mystical interpretation, this approach uses symbolic patterns as practical tools for values discovery. When clients notice repeated encounters with particular images, themes, or objects, such as frequent exposure to artistic expressions, the therapeutic work explores how these resonances might reflect emerging or suppressed values like creativity or aesthetic appreciation. These observations then inform concrete decisions about life direction and daily choices.

Metaphorical Reframing of Challenges: Difficult life circumstances receive metaphorical reconceptualization to support attitude development and meaning-making. Clients work with therapists to develop imagery that maintains dignity within limitation while opening possibilities for meaningful response. Rather than viewing unemployment as "being discarded," a client might explore metaphors of "transition seasons" or "preparing new ground," enabling shifts in perspective that precede behavioral change and renewed purpose engagement.

Overall, this approach transforms the therapeutic relationship from interpretation-focused dialogue to collaborative meaning-construction, where both therapist and client become co-explorers of the symbolic landscape within which purpose emerges. Through careful attention to the images that spontaneously emerge in therapeutic dialogue, logotherapy honors both the mysterious nature of meaning-making and the practical necessity of translating insight into action. The metaphors we live by become, ultimately, the meanings we enact.

45 Storytelling in therapy

> Tell me the facts and I'll learn. Tell me the truth and I'll believe. But tell me a story and it will live in my heart forever
>
> (Native American proverb)

Human beings possess a unique capacity among all species: the ability to create and communicate stories that transcend immediate experience. This fundamental characteristic lies at the heart of logotherapeutic practice, where the search for meaning unfolds through narrative construction and reconstruction. Narrative identity research shows that people link disparate events into coherent life stories, often through metaphorical frameworks that reveal how they construe self, others, and world (McAdams & McLean, 2013). First-person narratives are inherently socio-cultural: the language, images, and metaphors people draw upon are shaped by history, community, and moral worlds, and cannot be reduced to private cognition or biology alone. Attending to stories therefore reconnects therapy to the lifeworld—where values, hopes, and responsibilities take form—rather than to diagnostic abstractions alone. Words in stories and poems can access a client's lived meanings more directly than medicalized categories, especially when people feel life has lost significance; the challenge for clinicians is to recover a vocabulary that renders experience as it is lived and felt (Joranger, 2023).

Classic narrative theory helps clarify why storytelling is therapeutically potent. Bruner contends that personal stories create "impossible logic" (Bruner, 1990): they bind the exceptional to the ordinary so that anomalies, losses, or limit-situations can be *made sense of* within recognizable cultural plots and intentional states (what mattered, what was chosen, what was sacrificed). In this view, a story's inner logic binds fragmented and seemingly insignificant life episodes into a coherent whole, transforming them into a meaningful life history. In this way, the act of creating meaning restores a sense of wholeness—and to become whole is to be healed (Frankl, 1963). Thus, every human being is, by nature, a storyteller, regardless of whether the story resonates with others. As humans, we make sense of experience by casting events into a personal storyline. We appraise new accounts against stories forged by prior experience, asking whether they are faithful to what we take to be true and whether they cohere internally and with the wider world (Fisher, 1987), underscoring why therapeutic dialogue is most effective when it unfolds within the client's narrative and cultural grammar.

Recent empirical evidence provides compelling support for the narrative-meaning connection by transforming Campbell's (1949) abstract "Hero's Journey" into a practical intervention tool. Their operationalization translates this archetypal framework to seven measurable elements: protagonist, shift, quest, allies, challenge, transformation, and legacy. Their eight-study investigation reveals that individuals who perceive their life stories as following this archetypal pattern report significantly higher levels of meaning and enhanced resilience markers, including improved positive reappraisal and coping strategies, with evidence extending beyond correlational associations (Rogers et al., 2023). This intervention essentially prompts individuals to retell their life stories using the archetypal framework, enabling them to identify significant experiences and weave them into a culturally meaningful narrative. From a logotherapeutic standpoint, such frameworks reflect recognizing and articulating potentials for meaning. The Hero's Journey provides an accessible scaffold: *shift* helps locate crucibles and calls; *quest* clarifies chosen values; *allies* re-situate the person in community; *challenge* legitimizes suffering as integral to the path; *transformation* articulates growth and responsibility; and *legacy* orients beyond the self toward contribution. Applied with care, it can aid clients in discerning meaning without shoehorning their lives into a fixed storyline.

In logotherapeutic practice, storytelling serves as both a diagnostic tool and a therapeutic intervention. Clients' spontaneous narratives reveal their underlying metaphorical frameworks and meaning-making patterns, providing insight into how they organize their experiences and construct their identity. The therapist can identify where these narratives may be limiting the client's ability to discover meaning or where traumatic experiences have disrupted coherent story construction. Such processes may include practices such as metaphorical exploration, future-orientation and life review. The therapist thus becomes both witness and co-author, helping clients recognize that their personal narrative, however fractured by suffering, remains part of a larger meaningful whole. In this sense, every therapeutic story told is simultaneously personal and universal: it speaks to the individual's search for meaning while echoing the archetypal human journey from suffering through understanding to contribution.

46 Creative expression

Creative expression—whether through writing, drawing, music, movement, or craft—offers a distinctive and unrepeatable avenue for discovering and embodying meaning. Martha Graham's reflection that "there is a vitality, a life-force, an energy, a quickening, that is translated through you into action" (Graham, as cited in de Mille, 1991, p. 264), and that such expression is inherently unique, captures something essential about the creative path to meaning. In Frankl's terms, creativity constitutes one of the three primary avenues to meaning: through a deed or contribution, a person responds to life's question by bringing forth something that would not exist without them (Frankl, 1963). Within a logotherapeutic framework, this reflects an active response to the values, responsibilities, and tasks that life presents. Creative expression externalizes inner orientations—intentions, commitments, conscience—and renders them visible both to the creator and to others. Because creative media are rich in metaphor and symbol, they often disclose meanings that discursive language alone cannot fully capture, particularly when experience is pre-verbal, conflicted, or marked by ambivalence. In this way, creative work functions both diagnostically, by revealing value themes, strengths, and existential positions, and therapeutically, by clarifying direction, expanding freedom, and consolidating responsibility.

Crucially, any creative expression can become a site where values are enacted and shared. Creative making frequently elicits *flow*—an absorbed, autotelic state characterized by clear goals, immediate feedback, and a balanced match between challenge and skill (Csikszentmihalyi, 1990). Flow naturally "dereflects": it shifts attention away from hyper-self-focus and ruminative symptom monitoring toward a valued task. This attentional re-orientation aligns with logotherapy's dereflection technique: by engaging the person in meaningful doing for the sake of a real recipient or value, symptoms loosen their grip while agency and vitality can re-emerge. In this sense, even amid constraint, a person can answer life through creative micro-contributions that embody dignity and orientation toward the good. When suffering is unavoidable, creative expression also serves the *attitudinal* path: shaping a response that testifies to who one chooses to be in the face of fate. Thus, creative work can braid Frankl's three avenues—creative (what I give), experiential (what I receive and behold), and attitudinal (how I stand)—into a coherent pattern of meaning.

A structured therapeutic framework can guide creative expression without imposing predetermined outcomes. This approach begins when clients identify a single core value that life seems to be calling for—courage, justice, or compassion—and name a specific recipient: a person, community, place, or their future self. Clients then may create a modest artifact that embodies this value in an accessible medium: a letter, sketch, song lyric, collage, or brief prose piece. After creation, therapist and client together explore what has emerged and been recognized through the work. The process culminates by translating the artifact into concrete action—delivering, gifting, sharing, or installing it in the world. This may involve identifying an ally or witness, and when appropriate, addressing future recipients through a "legacy" note that articulates what one hopes to leave behind and how to begin now. Importantly, the therapeutic stance remains one of discovery and curiosity, with exercises framed as ways to recognize meanings already present in the client's situation. Social embeddedness proves essential: creative work becomes meaningful contribution when it addresses needs beyond the self. The approach requires avoiding aesthetic judgments, honoring sacred or cultural forms the client values, and securing clear consent before any sharing.

When creative expression is oriented by values, addressed to others, and anchored in freely chosen commitment, it transcends mere "self-expression" to become a profound response to life's questions. In Graham's terms, vitality translates uniquely through each person; creative expression is the channel of that translation, turning recognized meaning into lived practice.

47 Meditation and mindfulness

Meditation and mindfulness practices illuminate the extent to which present-moment awareness can open a person to life's meaning potential. As Jon Kabat-Zinn has observed, "The richness of present-moment experience is the richness of life itself." He further cautions that "too often we let our thinking and our beliefs about what we 'know' prevent us from seeing things as they really are" (Kabat-Zinn, 1990, p. 35). From this perspective, mindful awareness serves not merely as a therapeutic technique but as a fundamental orientation toward the meaning embedded in lived experience. The integration of mindfulness and meditation within logotherapeutic intervention represents a profound synthesis of contemplative wisdom and existential insight, offering clients systematic methods for cultivating what might be termed *meaning-sensitive awareness.* While Frankl emphasized the human capacity for self-transcendence and meaning-detection, mindfulness provides the attentional infrastructure through which these capacities can be systematically developed and refined. In this view, meaning-seeking entails sustained self-awareness for discerning personal values, aligning one's routines accordingly, and registering shifts in what life is asking—always from within ordinary experience. Mindful awareness has been defined as "a knowing and experiencing of life as it arises and passes away each moment… open, kind, and receptive" (Shapiro, Siegel, & Neff, 2018, p. 1694). The intentional stance that supports such awareness is often described through the triad of intention, attention, and attitude (IAA), which maps closely onto core processes of meaning-making (Shapiro et al., 2006). Intention corresponds to Frankl's emphasis on purposeful orientation toward values and meaning; attention aligns with the receptive awareness needed to discern what life is asking in each moment; and attitude reflects the accepting, non-judgmental stance that enables individuals to encounter life's circumstances, including suffering, with openness to their meaning potential. Taken together, this triadic framework offers a structured approach to cultivating what may be understood as *existential mindfulness*—an awareness specifically attuned to the meaning dimensions of experience.

Contemporary process models illuminate how mindful awareness facilitates meaning-making through specific psychological mechanisms. The Monitor-and-Acceptance Theory (MAT) demonstrates that combining attentional monitoring with acceptance reduces psychological reactivity while stabilizing the receptive awareness necessary for recognizing value-relevant affordances in daily experience (Lindsay & Creswell, 2017). From a logotherapeutic perspective, such receptive awareness may create favorable inner conditions for meaning-detection, enabling individuals to notice personally significant possibilities within their circumstances. The Mindfulness-to-Meaning Theory (MMT) further elucidates this pathway, proposing that decentering enables broader attention and more benign reappraisals, which promote positive affect and savoring, ultimately scaffolding eudaimonic outcomes such as purpose and coherence that are central to logotherapeutic goals. Empirically, scholars have suggested that mindfulness contributes to positive psychological outcomes in large part by enhancing a sense of meaning in life (Crego et al., 2020, 2021; Garland et al., 2015; Kashdan et al., 2015).

In practical application, the distinction between formal and informal mindfulness practice becomes crucial for meaning-centered work. Formal meditation practices—whether breath awareness, body scanning, or loving-kindness meditation—serve to stabilize attention and cultivate the accepting attitude necessary for meaning-detection. These practices function as training grounds where clients develop the capacity to remain present with whatever arises without immediately reacting or judging. However, it is through informal mindfulness that these capacities become integrated into the fabric of daily meaning-making. Informal mindfulness practice in logotherapy involves bringing contemplative awareness to ordinary activities—walking, eating, working, parenting—with specific attention to the meaning potential embedded within each moment. This approach transforms routine activities into opportunities for value realization and meaning-discovery. For instance, a client might practice mindful parenting not simply to reduce stress, but to cultivate awareness of how caring for their child expresses their deepest values and contributes to purposes larger than themselves. The practice of savoring becomes particularly significant in this context, involving not merely the appreciation of pleasant experiences but the recognition and lingering attention to moments of value alignment and meaning fulfillment.

The temporal dimensions of mindfulness practice extend naturally to logotherapy's emphasis on meaning across past, present, and future. Present-moment awareness enables the recognition of what Frankl called the "meaning of the moment"—the unique significance available within current circumstances. However, mindful reflection can also illuminate meaning patterns across time. Clients can practice mindful contemplative review of past experiences, using decentering to examine life events with less reactivity and greater perspective, identifying recurring values and meaning themes that might inform future choices. Similarly, mindful visualization of future scenarios, grounded in present-moment awareness rather than anxious projection, can support clients in envisioning concrete, value-consistent steps toward purpose and legacy.

The integration of mindfulness with logotherapy also addresses Frankl's emphasis that meaning can be found even in suffering. Mindfulness provides practical methods for maintaining open, accepting awareness when confronted with pain, loss, or limitation. Through practices such as mindful self-compassion and acceptance of impermanence, clients can develop the capacity to remain present with difficulty while simultaneously remaining receptive to whatever meanings might emerge from their struggles. This represents a crucial therapeutic capacity: the ability to hold space for both suffering and meaning, recognizing that they often arise together in human experience. Furthermore, the cultivation of meta-cognitive awareness through mindfulness supports clients in recognizing their own meaning-seeking processes as they unfold. By becoming aware of the patterns, obstacles, and turning points in one's existential path, self-awareness grows and the search for meaning shifts from an unconscious pull to a deliberate dialogue with life's circumstances. In Frankl's terms, the person becomes an active, responsible partner who discovers and embodies meaning rather than a passive recipient of predetermined ends.

The empirical evidence supporting mindfulness as a pathway to meaning provides additional validation for its integration with logotherapy. Meta-analytic evidence is consistent with this view: trait mindfulness was found to be associated with meaning, and randomized trials of mindfulness training yield gains in meaning, with change carried by decentering, authentic self-awareness, and attention to positive experience (e.g., Chu & Mak, 2020).

Ecological momentary assessment studies concurrently support the MMT pathway and show that savoring, positive affect, and well-being mutually reinforce one another in daily life. Reappraisal is more variable moment-to-moment and tends to register more clearly over longer timescales. These findings suggest that mindfulness operates not merely as an adjunctive technique but as a fundamental method for developing the psychological capacities that logotherapy aims to cultivate: the ability to transcend immediate circumstances, detect meaningful possibilities, and align daily choices with deeper values and purposes. The integration of mindfulness and logotherapy can be operationalized through several structured approaches. *Meaning-moment meditation* involves guiding clients to recall a recent experience of purpose or significance, then using mindful attention to explore the sensory, emotional, and cognitive elements that contributed to its meaningfulness. This practice develops sensitivity to the conditions under which meaning emerges, enabling clients to recognize similar opportunities in daily life.

Values-based body scanning expands traditional body awareness by inviting clients to notice how different values, such as compassion, creativity, or justice, manifest as felt sensations in the body, creating an embodied compass for value-aligned decision-making.

Mindful meaning dialogues structure therapeutic conversations around present-moment awareness of the client's search for and discovery of meaning. The therapist guides attention to immediate thoughts, feelings, and bodily sensations as the client explores struggles or aspirations, helping them notice how meaning is revealed—or briefly veiled—in real time. This approach shifts therapy from analyzing meaning to directly encountering its discovery.

Contemplative life review offers a structured practice for examining past experiences through the lens of meaning, using mindful attention to revisit significant life events while maintaining present-moment awareness, allowing new insights about enduring values and life direction to emerge.

Ultimately, through disciplined attention to what is actually present in the here and now—including our thoughts, feelings, circumstances, and the subtle promptings of conscience and calling—we develop the capacity to see past our habitual interpretations and limiting beliefs to encounter life as it truly summons us. In this convergence of contemplative practice and existential insight, mindfulness becomes not merely a technique for stress reduction or emotional regulation, but a pathway for discovering and living the meanings that make existence worthwhile. The present moment, fully inhabited through aware and accepting attention, reveals itself as the only place where meaning can actually be found and enacted—not as a concept to be grasped, but as a reality to be lived.

48 Journaling and self-reflection

Integrating journaling into logotherapy is a natural extension of Frankl's insight that human beings can choose a stance toward life and answer its call through deeds, encounters, and attitude. Reflective writing becomes more than documentation: it is a disciplined way of noticing what matters, creating reflective distance from experience, and discerning values that already glimmer within daily life. Contemporary meaning research helps structure this work. Across models, meaning comprises at least three facets (e.g., George & Park, 2016; Martela & Steger, 2016)—coherence (life makes sense), purpose (directedness toward goals), and mattering (one's existence has worth)—which journaling can systematically engage by asking: How does this episode fit? What does it direct me toward? Whom or what does it matter to (beyond myself)?

In self-reflexive writing, the person alternates between subject (immersed, feeling) and object (observing, evaluating) positions, cultivating meta-awareness and regulated distance—processes linked to reduced reactivity and clearer appraisal. Clinical and reflective-practice scholarship describes this as self-reflexivity: a dialectical stance through which clinicians examine both subjective and objective dimensions of self-awareness. In this view, journaling can function as a form of self-care and self-monitoring, supporting a mindfulness-based reflective practice that may help reduce vulnerability to burnout and compassion fatigue while strengthening clinicians' capacity for intentional presence in therapeutic work (e.g., Martin-Cuellar, 2018). Writing, re-reading, and responding to one's own words instantiate that oscillation, making internal states both felt and seen, and, crucially, actionable.

A parallel evidence base from expressive writing shows that giving language to experience—especially when cognitive (meaning) words increase over time—can improve psychological and even physiological outcomes, plausibly via exposure, cognitive change, and acceptance mechanisms. In practice, journaling that moves from immersion to observation, and back, invites precisely these shifts. Importantly, reflective writing is not only remedial; it can be directly growth promoting. Qualitative accounts of self-reflective journaling document increased self-understanding and acceptance, renewed creative engagement after periods of "resistance," and movement toward a more integrated or "ideal" self. These outcomes arise through metacognitive noticing, intentional "dialogue with the self," and iterative cycles of writing–re-reading–revising one's stance (Moses, 2019).

Practically, journaling can be integrated into the therapeutic process, both in session and in-between sessions. For example, the client can begin by naming a value as a short, free-form entry followed by describing a concrete episode from the day or week, followed immediately by a deliberate shift to observation: re-read the entry and annotate the margins through the three meaning lenses—coherence (what thread does this episode reveal in my larger story?), purpose (what directed step does it invite?), mattering (who or what is served?). Socratic questions can also be used as reflective prompts, such as "What is this situation asking of me?" "What contribution is mine to make here?" "What stance preserves dignity where I lack control?" The therapist and client then extract a mission, responsibility or a commitment (a deed, an encounter to receive, or an attitude to uphold) and identify a witness or recipient so that the insight becomes a lived answer. In subsequent sessions, clusters of entries are reviewed to surface repeating meaning moments (as a form of a "meaning catcher" journal), consolidating a personal pattern of values in action and sharpening "meaning sensitivity" in daily life.

Two safeguards strengthen the work. First, when material is highly charged, therapist and client titrate exposure by alternating immersive writing with observational re-reading and, if needed, shifting to present-focused anchors (sensory details, body posture) before returning to meaning questions—protecting against dysregulation while preserving freedom to choose a stance. Second, because reflective practice can tempt perfectionism, entries are kept deliberately brief and specific; the aim is fidelity to values, not literary polish. Through a disciplined alternation between immersion and observation, feeling and reflecting, journaling can become a systematic method for inhabiting and expanding the crucial space between stimulus and response. Each entry represents not merely a record of what happened, but a documentation of how one chose to respond—and more importantly, an opportunity to choose again. When clients write about their experiences, they simultaneously live them and rise above them, embodying the paradoxical stance of being both participant in and witness to their own existence. Perhaps most significantly, the practice of extracting missions, responsibilities, and commitments from journal entries bridges the gap between insight and action that plagues much therapeutic work. Frankl insisted that meaning could not be given but only found through engagement with life's concrete demands. Journaling becomes the bridge between recognition and response, between seeing what matters and living it out.

In a culture of velocity and distraction, journaling and self-reflection offer a quiet counter-practice: a deliberate slowing that turns experience into something we can see and answer. On the page, past, present, and future line up enough to reveal threads of coherence, point toward purpose, and remind us that our lives matter to someone beyond ourselves. The journal then becomes a small laboratory of freedom. We do not journal to escape life; we write to answer it—and in answering, we discover the meaning that was waiting there.

49 Ikigai and meaning in life

The Japanese concept of *ikigai*—often translated as "a reason for being" or "that which makes life worth living"—has gained increasing attention in recent years, both in scholarly and popular literature. From a logotherapeutic perspective, ikigai can be seen as a cultural articulation of the search for meaning that Frankl described as the primary human motivation.

Although often presented in the West as a simple formula for happiness, the construct is in fact complex, multidimensional, and deeply rooted in cultural context. It encompasses a profound alignment with one's values, purpose, and sense of worth (Kono & Walker, 2020; Kumano, 2018). In this sense, ikigai resonates with the broader psychological construct of meaning in life (MIL), especially in its eudaimonic dimension: living in accordance with one's authentic self, values, and commitments (e.g., Ryff & Singer, 2008). Empirical studies indicate that ikigai is positively associated with both physical and psychological well-being and has been linked, in longitudinal cohort studies, with lower mortality risk (Koizumi et al., 2008; Sone et al., 2008). Yet its significance goes beyond measurable outcomes: ikigai reflects a felt sense of vitality and direction, a deeply personal anchor that sustains individuals through challenges. Importantly, ikigai is experienced in diverse forms—relationships, nature, self-development, community contribution, creativity, or a sense of calling—making it both universal in essence and uniquely personal in expression.

Accordingly, a preliminary exploration of individuals' experiences and understanding of ikigai through metaphors, symbols, or images, suggests that creative methods may illuminate dimensions of meaning that are difficult to capture verbally (Russo-Netzer, 2021). This suggests that ikigai can be fruitfully explored through creative, experiential methods that move beyond traditional questionnaires and cognitive self-reports.

Integrating ikigai into therapeutic practice provides clinicians with a culturally rich and experientially grounded pathway to facilitate meaning discovery (phenomenological clarification) and cultivation (value-congruent enactment):

In the *discovery phase*, clients may be invited to reflect on and symbolically represent their ikigai—for example, through photographs, drawings, or metaphors—thereby externalizing and clarifying what matters most to them. This process often surfaces values, passions, and life anchors that words alone cannot fully articulate. Reflective prompts may include: *What does ikigai mean to you? If you had to find a metaphor for it, what would it be? Take time to reflect, then draw / take a picture / find an image that represents what ikigai means to you. Having found something, what title would you give this image that represents its meaning to you? Why did you choose this particular image to express your ikigai? What does it represent for you? How did you experience the process of taking/finding the image?*

In the cultivation phase, therapists help clients translate these representations into daily life by identifying concrete deeds, relationships, or attitudes that embody their ikigai. For example, a photo of a sunrise may become a reminder to embody light and hope in interactions; an image of a compass may guide decisions aligned with one's sense of mission. Taken together, ikigai offers a culturally resonant doorway closely aligned with the existential terrain long mapped by logotherapy: the human task of responding to life's call with values-congruent striving.

50 Sources of meaning in life

Sources of meaning in life may be understood as the domains in which worthwhile aims, values, and responsibilities become tangible. As Frankl (1963) wrote, "What man actually needs is not a tensionless state but rather the striving and struggling for a worthwhile goal" (p. 166). Within a logotherapeutic framework, such striving reflects the dynamic nature of human existence when oriented toward meaning, values, and responsibility. If meaning is discovered through responding to what life asks, then sources of meaning are the contexts in which that response takes shape—through creative deeds, experiential encounters, and attitudinal stances. They are the arenas in which values are enacted, commitments are embodied, and existential direction is sustained. Moreover, a diverse portfolio of meaning sources serves a protective function, helping preserve meaning when one significant source is threatened, interrupted, or lost.

Empirically, Schnell's Sources of Meaning and Meaning in Life Questionnaire (SoMe; Schnell, 2009) shows that people draw on a broad repertoire of meaning sources that cluster into four higher-order dimensions: self-transcendence (commitment beyond the self, both vertical—religious/spiritual—and horizontal—responsibility for others and nature), self-actualization (cultivating and using one's capacities), order (tradition, morality, practicality, reason), and well-being and relatedness (pleasure, care, community, love, harmony). Importantly, SoMe also distinguishes between the *presence* of meaningfulness and a *crisis of meaning* as independent dimensions rather than opposite ends of a single continuum—an empirical nuance that fits clinical experience: one can feel life is meaningful and still struggle, or feel empty without meeting full criteria for psychopathology.

Not all sources contribute in the same way or on the same timetable. For example, it was found that well-being and relatedness, and vertical self-transcendence are most consistently linked with higher positive mood and life satisfaction, whereas self-knowledge (a subcomponent of horizontal self-transcendence) can temporarily lower positive mood during active searching, even as it contributes to meaning. These patterns underscore a practical point: relationships and embeddedness matter, and "beyond-self" orientations often yield deeper, more durable meaning than purely self-focused pursuits.

A second principle is diversity and prominence of sources. A varied "portfolio" buffers meaning under stress: when one source is threatened (e.g., work), other sources (family, service, faith, beauty, place) can carry the load. This matches the 'fluid compensation model': threats to one meaning framework can prompt compensatory affirmation in another, preserving global meaning (Heine et al., 2006). This identification process, however, contains a paradoxical element whereby intense framework commitment can generate defensive and exclusionary responses when the framework encounters threat (Boucher et al., 2016). Practically, logotherapy aims for *breadth with depth*: cultivating multiple, value-true sources while guarding against "mono-source" identity that is brittle under change.

The theoretical understanding of meaning diversification as a protective factor naturally leads to the practical question: how can therapists systematically guide clients toward developing what we might call a "resilient meaning ecosystem"? This transition from conceptual framework to therapeutic intervention requires careful attention to both the discovery process—recognizing existing meaning sources—and the cultivation process—strengthening and diversifying these sources in sustainable ways. Such process may begin by mapping the person's sources across the four domains, using the client's language and examples (i.e., people, places, tasks, rituals), followed by identifying two sources in each domain and noting their prominence (how central) and access (how available). Then name one creative deed, one experiential encounter, and one attitudinal stance that enact these sources in the client's real context over the next few days. For example:

- Self-transcendence → deliver a concrete act of help to a neighbor (creative)
- Well-being and relatedness → schedule unhurried time with a family member and deliberately savor the encounter (experiential)

Another possible method may be creating a meaning-portfolio plan:

a confirm two primary anchors (e.g., family, service)
b develop two secondary buffers (e.g., nature, craft)
c draft one contingency for each.

Where the client shows over-reliance on a single source, broaden gently by linking it to adjacent sources (e.g., from achievement to generativity through mentoring). Throughout, keep the stance of discovery: we are not manufacturing significance but noticing and answering what life asks here and now.

Finally, review patterns over time. Invite brief weekly notes ("meaning moments") and, when needed, a Socratic check: "What is this situation asking of me?", "Who benefits if I answer?", "How can I stand when I cannot change the facts?" Use SoMe's distinctions to track two curves separately—meaningfulness and crisis—so that gains in one are not mistaken for losses in the other. When a crisis spikes, normalize it as a signal, widen the portfolio, and specify one small act in a beyond-self direction. In this way, the plurality of sources becomes a lived, renewable ecosystem of meaning enacted in everyday living.

51 Phases of the logotherapeutic process

The logotherapeutic process unfolds less like a straight line and more like a spiral through a series of movements that can be enacted in varying sequence and depth. Heuristically, the process can be distilled into three core phases:

(I) distancing from symptom and illuminating values
(II) re-shaping attitude and responsibility-taking
(III) orienting to meaning and consolidating forward maintenance.

These phases can be operationalized through four staged tasks widely described as differentiation from symptoms, attitude modification, symptom attenuation, and future-oriented maintenance (cf. Fabry, 1994; Lukas, 1979/1995).

Phase I Symptom decentering and value illumination

The therapeutic process begins by decentering the symptom and re-anchoring attention in the client's value horizon. The aim is to differentiate the person from the symptom, resisting any reduction of identity to a diagnosis: The client is not defined by symptoms;

they are a person oriented to meaning, with identity rooted in values that remain realizable under any condition. Alongside standard psychoeducation about symptom origins and course, logotherapy adds noö-education (spiritual/noetic education): clarifying maladaptive assumptions and replacing them with core principles—preference for meaning over pleasure, freedom to respond under all circumstances, and the unconditional meaningfulness of life. Two practices commonly guide the work at this stage: *1) Dereflection* (diagnostically and therapeutically) gently redirects attention from hyper-reflection on symptoms to values enactable here and now. Because many symptomatic states cloak a fracture in meaning, value-focused dialogue often reveals the roots of the "meaning crisis." *(2) Value illumination through logo-hints ("logocues")* helps the therapist identify value-laden words, images, metaphors, and stories in the client's language, and bring them forward as anchors—naming what matters, distinguishing it from symptom-driven avoidance, and translating it into small, concrete commitments that can be lived here and now.

Therapeutic dialogue repeatedly reorients along the temporal corridors of freedom, recovering what endures from the past (often not despite loss but because of it), delineating the present sphere of responsibility from what lies beyond it, and identifying future aims that remain realistically attainable. This temporal discipline becomes decisive when fate imposes non-negotiable limits (e.g., chronic illness, disability): where circumstances cannot be altered, attitudinal value constitutes the principal route by which dignity and worth are preserved.

Phase 2 Attitude reorientation and responsibility-taking

With the symptom decentered, clients can re-examine their basic stance toward self, others, and life. Symptoms are often maintained by tacit, maladaptive assumptions about life, frustration, and control. The therapeutic task is to surface these premises, make them explicit and examinable, and explore value-congruent alternatives. While situations constrain, they do not determine stance: attitude remains a matter of choice. Accordingly, this stage foregrounds freedom and responsibility—Frankl's *response-ability*—by helping clients recognize that their condition depends not on life circumstances but on their response to them. Through empathetic yet confrontational dialogue, the therapist guides clients to delineate the locus of responsibility—separating what lies within one's remit from what does not—surface and examine the foundational assumptions that maintain distress, and commit to chosen values through deliberate practice toward the unavoidable.

Meaning emerges through confronting suffering directly, not by avoiding it. Avoidance may propel existential vacuum where neurotic patterns flourish—addiction, violence, depression, suicidality, and spiritual neuroses. Key questions that may guide attitudinal reorientation include, *what prevents the client from accepting responsibility? What do they gain from avoiding it?* The therapist facilitates exploration of these defensive patterns while maintaining that authentic meaning-making requires direct engagement with the tragic triad rather than escape from it. By naming tragic experiences—guilt, loss, pain, or injustice—clients can reclaim inner freedom, adopt a conscious stance, and identify values whose realization enables spiritual growth. The therapist facilitates rather than imposes attitudinal shifts through empathetic dialogue, except when safety demands immediate intervention, such as with acute suicidality. This approach ensures that attitude reorientation aligns authentically with each client's personal value hierarchy (Fabry, 1994; Lukas, 1979/1995).

Phase 3 Meaning orientation and forward maintenance

As attitudinal reorientation consolidates, symptoms typically recede or become more manageable through the development of appropriate stance rather than symptom-focused interventions. Existential frustration and the anxiety arising from it become more containable and manageable, fostering freedom to choose diverse responses. This transformation relies upon the inexhaustible resources of the noetic dimension—creativity, hope, compassion, courage, humor, acceptance, trust, gratitude, the defiant power of the human spirit, and the capacity to say yes to life under all circumstances. The primary therapeutic vector flows from cultivating proper attitude to symptom management, grounded in noetic resources rather than conventional coping strategies. The therapeutic framework shifts from a success/failure paradigm to an axis of meaning, embodying the foundational principle that life has unconditional meaning—that existence remains meaningful under all conditions and circumstances. Every situation, whether pleasant or painful, contains potential for value actualization, transforming existential frustration and anxiety into manageable experiences that foster freedom to choose diverse responses. At this phase, the therapeutic consolidation operates through prospective, practice-based mechanisms: Clients enact values across logotherapy's three fundamental pathways: experiential (receiving life's offerings—relationships, nature, art, music), creative (contributing meaningful work—professional endeavors, caregiving, generative activities), and attitudinal (exercising freedom of stance toward unchangeable circumstances). They establish proximal goals while maintaining a diversified meaning portfolio to prevent over-dependence on any single domain.

Brief, periodic reviews (such as weekly "meaning moments") sustain awareness of available options and directional clarity, reinforcing that life remains answerable and worthy of engagement. Through this process, noetic resources are systematically cultivated—creativity, hope, compassion, acceptance, trust, gratitude, and the defiant power of human spirit—which collectively support sustained mental health within a logotherapeutic framework.

Overall, logotherapy's foundational premise spans all therapeutic stages: life possesses unconditional meaning, and lasting transformation flows from value discovery and enactment rather than tension elimination. Symptom amelioration emerges as a natural consequence of deeper identity shifts, from problem-focused to meaning-centered existence, from existential constriction to response-ability, and from symptom management to meaning actualization that remains viable regardless of circumstances.

Part 3

Clinical applications

3.1 Working with specific conditions

52 Meaninglessness

Meaninglessness in logotherapy is typically understood through Frankl's concept of the *existential vacuum*, a pervasive sense of emptiness, apathy, and despair that emerges when individuals are unable to fulfill their fundamental will to meaning. Ernesto Sabato's image of life as "nothing more than a sequence of anonymous screams in a desert of indifferent stars" captures the existential desolation that can accompany such a state. Within this framework, meaninglessness is not simply the absence of satisfaction, but a deeper erosion of direction, significance, and existential orientation. Frankl did not regard this struggle as pathological in itself, but rather as "a manifestation of intellectual sincerity and honesty" in facing life's ultimate questions (Frankl, 1969/1988, p. 91). The existential vacuum is often marked by two central features: feelings of emptiness, often expressed as apathy, and meaninglessness, often experienced as a loss of interest or direction. When prolonged, this condition may contribute to what Frankl termed the "mass neurotic triad" of aggression, depression, and addiction—maladaptive attempts to fill or escape the inner void. More broadly, the frustration of the need for meaningful goals may intensify aggression, addiction, depression, and suicidality, while also contributing to psychosomatic complaints and neurotic disturbances. Contemporary research further

DOI: 10.4324/9781003624417-3

suggests that burnout syndrome may be understood, at least in part, as a form of existential vacuum, with loss of life fulfillment and existential meaning as central features (e.g., Riethof & Bob, 2019). In this sense, meaninglessness extends beyond inner suffering to affect professional functioning, social engagement, and the person's overall capacity to remain vitally connected to life.

Building on this understanding, contemporary philosophical perspectives suggest that meaninglessness itself may serve a purpose in the human journey toward authentic meaning. DuBose (2016) articulates this view, arguing that meaninglessness should not be reduced to the mere absence of meaning or immediately corrected, but allowed to show itself "in its own way, as it is," requiring sensitivity to "the meaning of meaninglessness as meaninglessness" (p. 283). This expanded perspective emphasizes "being-with" clients in their experience of meaninglessness, a stance that deepens the core logotherapeutic principle of meeting clients where they are. Rather than rushing to transform meaninglessness, the therapist supports clients in exploring this experience as it naturally unfolds, recognizing that therapeutic work involves clarifying the lived experience and meaning of meaninglessness itself without privileging one existential state over another.

This approach requires integrating three interconnected dimensions (Vanhooren, 2019). The *micro-dimension* addresses the bodily felt sense, exploring how meaninglessness manifests somatically through sensations, symbols, or metaphors such as "heavy and dark" or "shrinking" sensations. The *meso-dimension* examines meaninglessness within relational and narrative contexts, exploring how it appears in life stories and relationships while avoiding purely intellectual analysis. The *macro-dimension* engages existential and transcendent concerns, addressing questions about life's meaning while helping clients discover what ultimately matters most to them. These dimensions operate dynamically rather than sequentially, with effective therapy moving fluidly between levels based on the client's readiness and capacity.

Logotherapy approaches meaninglessness as an existential challenge requiring collaborative exploration rather than symptom elimination. The therapeutic process sensitizes clients to meaning potentialities inherent in their lived experience—including the experience of meaninglessness itself—while avoiding the imposition of predetermined meanings. The logotherapist, thus, adopts a Socratic stance, supporting clients in detecting their own unique and individual meaning rather than persuading through logical reasoning. *Socratic Dialogue* involves deep, exploratory conversations using open-ended questions to uncover underlying values, beliefs, moments of past fulfillment, and sources of meaning. *Paradoxical Intention* helps clients confront meaninglessness directly by deliberately engaging with feelings of purposelessness for specified periods, using humor and exaggeration to reduce existential anxiety while recognizing that anxiety and intentionality cannot coexist simultaneously. Paradoxically, not attempting to transform meaninglessness can often become inherently transformative, aligning with logotherapy's principle that meaning emerges as a byproduct rather than a direct pursuit.

While these methods provide the foundation for therapeutic work with meaninglessness, their successful implementation depends on several considerations. Effective treatment requires differentiating between symptomatic depression and existential meaninglessness while establishing a therapeutic alliance based on existential partnership. The therapeutic relationship serves as a container where meaninglessness can be experienced safely through presence and shared exploration rather than solution-provision. Critically, therapists must avoid premature meaning-making—rushing to help clients "find meaning" before fully exploring meaninglessness itself. Such interventions can increase suffering by invalidating authentic experience. The therapeutic process involves creating space for authentic exploration of both meaning and meaninglessness rather than vacuum elimination. This approach honors client experience while maintaining that life has meaning under all circumstances, offering nuanced support that recognizes meaninglessness as both profound existential challenge and potentially meaningful experience.

53 Demoralization

Demoralization represents a distinct psychological condition characterized by "a persistent inability to cope", together with feelings of helplessness, hopelessness, meaninglessness, and diminished self-esteem (Grassi & Nanni, 2016). From a logotherapeutic perspective, demoralization can be understood as a crisis of meaning availability rather than meaning loss. The person experiencing demoralization typically retains their fundamental value system but faces a temporary disconnection from pathways through which these values can be actualized. This understanding aligns with Frankl's recognition that meaning frustration—the blocking of one's will to meaning—can lead to existential distress. The temporary inaccessibility can precipitate an existential crisis manifesting through panic reactions, loss of control, and helplessness, accompanied by despair and anxiety. At deeper levels, individuals may experience loss of personal identity, future vision, and life direction.

The fundamental distinction between demoralization and depression lies in the individual's response to potential pathways for action. In demoralization, once an actionable pathway is identified, the person remains open to pursue it. In depression, however, the individual may refuse such opportunities and withdraw from any offers of assistance. Furthermore, unlike depression, demoralized individuals typically do not report anhedonia—the loss of interest and inability to enjoy previously pleasurable activities.

The primary therapeutic task in demoralization involves helping clients reconnect with their existing values through alternative pathways. Unlike meaninglessness, where values themselves may be questioned, demoralization typically involves blocked access to value realization rather than value absence. The therapeutic work begins by identifying core values that remain important to the client, recognizing that these fundamental commitments typically persist even when pathways for their expression become blocked. The therapist then can explore specific barriers that prevent value expression and realization, examining both external obstacles and internal impediments. This exploration naturally leads to developing alternative pathways for value actualization, helping clients discover new routes through which meaningful values can be lived out despite current constraints. Throughout this process, it becomes essential to address the temporary nature of current limitations, distinguishing between permanent losses and situational challenges that may evolve over time. Finally, therapeutic attention focuses on strengthening coping resources and perceived competence, rebuilding the client's confidence in their ability to navigate difficulties and pursue meaningful engagement with life.

Using Socratic dialogue, therapists can help clients discover that their fundamental values remain intact while exploring new ways to express them. This process involves careful questioning that begins by examining which values feel temporarily inaccessible, helping clients articulate the specific nature of their blocked meaning pathways. The therapeutic inquiry then focuses on identifying what specific barriers prevent value expression, whether these obstacles are external circumstances, internal beliefs, or interpersonal dynamics that have shifted. From this understanding, the exploration moves toward discovering alternative contexts or methods for value realization, opening creative possibilities that may not have been previously considered. The dialogue draws strength from examining past examples of successful coping and adaptation, reminding clients of their proven resilience and problem-solving capabilities. Finally, this collaborative investigation identifies resources and strengths that remain available, helping clients recognize that while some pathways may be blocked, their fundamental capacities for meaningful living persist.

Demoralization often involves a constricted future perspective. Logotherapeutic intervention focuses on reopening future possibilities while acknowledging present constraints. In this framework, therapeutic work can begin by exploring realistic future scenarios where values can be expressed, helping clients envision concrete contexts in which their meaningful commitments might find new outlets. The process then moves to identifying incremental steps toward value realization, breaking down overwhelming future possibilities into manageable, actionable components that restore a sense of agency. Particular attention must be given to addressing catastrophic thinking about permanent limitation, challenging cognitive distortions that transform temporary setbacks into fixed beliefs about unchangeable futures. Hope is strengthened through concrete possibility identification rather than abstract reassurance, grounding optimism in realistic assessments of available opportunities and resources. Finally, the therapeutic work focuses on connecting present actions to future value fulfillment, helping clients understand how current choices and behaviors can serve as bridges toward meaningful engagement, even when the full realization of their values may require time and adaptation.

In general, the process begins with the establishment of a robust therapeutic alliance and felt safety, alongside a comprehensive assessment of the client's precipitating events and current stressors, available resources and supports, and differential diagnosis from mood and anxiety disorders that may warrant parallel or prior care. Once basic stability is secured, attention shifts to the client's core value system and primary sources of meaning. The task is twofold: (a) clarify values that currently feel inaccessible or blocked, and (b) design viable routes for their renewed expression. This work may include value archaeology—excavating the values once embodied in lost roles, relationships, or circumstances (e.g., care, mastery, belonging, service)—and rendering them explicit so they become available for alternative enactment in the present. For each salient value, therapist and client then map multiple pathways through which it can realistically be realized now, thereby reducing all-or-nothing appraisals. On this foundation, the therapist helps the client address cognitive and behavioral barriers (e.g., avoidance, perfectionism, global hopelessness) and strengthen problem-solving and adaptive capacities, so that value-aligned actions become feasible rather than merely aspirational. Clients are supported to take concrete steps toward value realization, monitor effects, and revise plans accordingly. Setbacks are anticipated and metabolized to preserve therapeutic momentum.

In sum, demoralization is a distinct clinical syndrome that warrants specialized attention. From a logotherapeutic standpoint, intervention prioritizes reconnection with existing values through alternative pathways, rather than constructing new meaning systems. This stance treats value inaccessibility as provisional, offering concrete methods to restore coping confidence and future orientation. By conceptualizing demoralization as a crisis of value accessibility, rather than value loss, therapists can create targeted, respectful care that honors real constraints while catalyzing renewed meaning discovery and enactment.

54 Depression

From a logotherapeutic perspective, depression is more than low mood or diminished pleasure. It is a *collapse of existential openness*: the person's inner world tightens, possibilities feel sealed off, and life no longer "calls" in a way that can be heard or answered. It is often experienced as a constriction of the person's capacity to sense value, direction, and aliveness, so the future looks blank, the self is appraised as depleted, burdensome, or without value, and even meaningful roles or relationships can lose their felt significance. In that narrowed field, the longing for meaning does not necessarily disappear, but is frequently numbed. What can emerge is a blunting of value-orientation: the person may still *care* at a deeper level, but can no longer *access* what matters, trust that it matters, or mobilize toward it. Accordingly, depression is expressed not only as sadness, but as a marked loss of motivation and initiative—apathy, social withdrawal, disconnection, and a diminished sense of agency. Contemporary meaning research helps clarify what is being impaired: meaning in life, which is commonly described through facets such as coherence (life makes sense), purpose (life has direction), and significance/mattering (life is worth living and counts) (Martela & Steger, 2016).

Clinically, it is crucial to distinguish depression from nearby existential states that may require a different therapeutic emphasis. Grief, for example, can involve profound sadness and reduced functioning while the person's value-world remains intact (they still *know* what mattered, even if it hurts). A related construct, *demoralization*, is characterized by distress along with a felt inability to act effectively, often an experience of being "stuck" because one cannot see a viable direction for action. In classic terms, demoralization is not primarily low mood, but distress marked by a felt inability to cope and action-guiding uncertainty ('I can't manage this, and I don't know what to do next'), reflecting a breakdown in perceived direction for action (de Figueiredo, 1993; Kissane et al., 2001; Tecuta et al., 2015). Depression, by contrast, is often marked by a depletion in the *magnitude* of motivation—initiative, energy, drive—so that motivational shutdown can persist even when the person can name a sensible direction, values, or next steps (de Figueiredo, 1993). Put differently, if motivation is viewed as having both *direction* and *strength*, demoralization is frequently a crisis of direction (and thus meaning/hope), whereas depression is frequently a crisis of strength (and thus follow-through). This distinction matters clinically for meaning-oriented work: demoralization may often benefit from relatively focused *remoralization*—clarifying what still matters, restoring a credible direction, and identifying concrete next steps that reduce uncertainty and rebuild hope, whereas depression usually requires the same value-clarity to be translated into small, scaffolded, energy-sensitive commitments, so engagement can be rebuilt gradually without triggering defeat or overwhelm (Kissane et al., 2001; Tecuta et al., 2015).

Empirically, the bridge between meaning and depression is well supported. Meta-analytic evidence indicates that higher purpose in life is robustly associated with lower depression and anxiety across diverse samples (Boreham & Schutte, 2023). More recently, an individual-participant meta-analysis across world regions similarly links higher purpose with fewer depressive symptoms at scale (Sutin et al., 2025). Beyond purpose, broader syntheses show that the presence of meaning is negatively associated with psychological distress, while the search for meaning can relate to distress in more complex, context-dependent ways (He et al., 2023). Meaning-making theory further suggests that when stressful events violate core beliefs or goals, suffering intensifies until some form of comprehension, reappraisal, or value-consistent adaptation becomes possible (Park, 2010). In depression, this adaptive work is often stalled by hopelessness, rumination, and a globalized sense of "nothing will change," which together flatten perceived possibilities.

Within clinical applications, logotherapy is best framed as a meaning-centered complement to evidence-based depression care, not a replacement, especially when depression is moderate-to-severe, chronic, psychotic, or comorbid. Major guidelines emphasize a stepped, individualized approach combining psychological treatments and/or medication depending on severity and patient context (National Institute for Health and Care Excellence [NICE], 2022/last reviewed 2026; World Health Organization, 2025). Measurement-based care and risk/safety assessment are also standard components in major clinical practice guidance (VA/DoD, 2022). A logotherapeutic stance can be integrated into these frameworks by helping clients recover value-orientation and "response-ability" in a way that respects the biological and psychological realities of depression (fatigue, slowed cognition, reduced reward responsiveness), and avoids moralizing ("you just need meaning") or premature uplift.

A coherent logotherapeutic pathway often begins after stabilization and alliance-building, when the client experiences sufficient safety to approach existential material without overwhelm. Here, *noö-education* (noetic/existential psychoeducation) can gently reopen the possibility that meaning is not fabricated by forced positivity but discovered in relation to life's concrete calls; that inner freedom of stance can coexist with constraints; and that meaning is not invalidated by suffering even when it is temporarily inaccessible. This orientation is strengthened by tracking meaning alongside symptom measures, explicitly treating them as related but non-identical curves over time. When clients observe that reductions in depressive symptoms and increases in felt meaning do not necessarily move in parallel from week to week, they often experience relief: the work is not "failing" simply because mood has not lifted yet. Tracking these as related but distinct trajectories can reduce shame, protect motivation, and support persistence, especially in phases when meaning begins to return before energy or pleasure does.

A particularly useful logotherapeutic move in depression is shifting from object-loss to value-loss. Depressive cognition tends to interpret loss as final and globally defining: if the relationship, role, capacity, community, health, or imagined future is gone, then "what mattered" is assumed to be gone with it. In this state, the lost object is experienced as the *only* viable carrier of the values it once embodied, so attention remains fixed on *who or what is missing*, while the value-level meaning of the bond or role remains unnamed. Grief can then become stuck, not because the person is unwilling to mourn, but because the loss is coded as the end of value itself, leading to further withdrawal and a shrinking of the lived world.

Logotherapeutic dialogue can help clients articulate the values that were expressed through what was lost and then explore how those values may still matter and can be honored in altered, realistic forms. This is not a forced "reframing", but a return to the deeper structure of attachment and identity, clarifying what mattered, why it mattered, and what forms of fidelity to those values remain possible now. Carefully paced Socratic questions can translate existential insight into feasible movement: "When you think of what you had with X, which values did that connection allow you to live?" "Which of those values still matter today?" and "What would a 1% expression of one value look like this week—small enough to be doable, but real enough to count?"

Once values are articulated, logotherapy works with carriers of meaning—new or revised pathways through which values can be realized under changed conditions. Frankl's meaning triad can be used as an organizing lens: creative values (what we give), experiential values (what we receive/encounter), and attitudinal values (the stance we take toward the unchangeable) (Frankl, 1963). Within depression, carriers must be energy-sensitive and "depression-realistic": small, time-bound actions with low activation barriers, supported by external scaffolding (scheduling, cues, accountability, social support). For example, if generativity had been expressed through a job now lost, a possible carrier might be one concrete act of contribution in a community context. If beauty and aliveness were expressed through travel that is now impossible, a carrier might be daily micro-experiential practices—light, music, texture, nature contact—chosen as experiential value realignment that rebuilds contact with the world.

Depression frequently maintains itself through attentional capture: ruminative loops, self-accusation, perfectionistic standards, and avoidance that masquerades as "protection." Here, logotherapy can integrate *dereflection*—shifting attention from self-monitoring toward task, relationship, and value—without invalidating pain. In practice, it means designing meaning tasks that are feasible and value-congruent, and then evaluating change across multiple domains, such as mood, dignity, vitality, connection, and agency. When circumstances cannot be changed, attitudinal values become central: the work is not to deny tragedy but to reclaim the freedom to choose one's stance within it—naming guilt, pain, and loss while refusing to let them be the final word. This is where clients may rediscover a form of grounded hope: not optimism about outcomes, but fidelity to values despite uncertainty.

Because depression is heterogeneous, it is also useful to integrate the broader evidence base on meaning-oriented therapies. A recent systematic review indicates emerging support for the usefulness of meaning-centered psychotherapies in depressed participants (outside of cancer/physical illness contexts), while also emphasizing the need for more rigorous trials and clearer mechanisms (Marco et al., 2024). Within logotherapy specifically, a meta-analysis of controlled studies found overall reductions in depressive symptoms following logotherapy-based interventions, while also highlighting considerable variability in effects across populations, settings, and study designs (Cornelius-White et al., 2025). Specific controlled trials, including group-based formats, also show increases in meaning alongside reductions in depression (e.g., Robatmili et al., 2015). Clinically, this pattern—meaning increasing while depression decreases—supports the logotherapeutic principle that symptom relief can follow as a byproduct of renewed orientation toward value and purpose, rather than as the sole target.

In sum, a coherent logotherapeutic approach to depression can be described as restoring access to what is worth living for, without forcing meaning, bypassing biology, or romanticizing suffering. The therapist helps the client (a) re-open the possibility of meaning when it feels absent, (b) differentiate object-loss from value-loss, (c) name the values that were expressed or embodied in the lost bond or role, (d) identify feasible carriers for those values across creative, experiential, and attitudinal routes, and (e) translate carriers into micro-actions supported by routines and relationships. Over time, the client's lived world may widen in small ways: apathy may ease into moments of direction, paralysis can give way to limited next-step capacity, and identity may slowly be re-centered around values that remain possible even under constraint.

55 Anxiety

Anxiety is a future-oriented state of heightened arousal and vigilance in which the mind treats uncertainty as if it were imminent danger. At its core, anxiety is not simply "feeling afraid," but living in sustained anticipation, scanning for threat, rehearsing what might go wrong, and attempting to secure certainty in an inherently uncertain world (Grupe & Nitschke, 2013). In clinical forms, this anticipatory mode can become self-reinforcing: ambiguous cues are appraised as risky, bodily sensations are interpreted as signs of impending harm, and the person's behavioral repertoire narrows to what feels safest right now, even when the cost is a shrinking life (Clark & Beck, 2010).

Across contemporary models, several well-supported maintenance processes converge. First, intolerance of uncertainty fuels worry and hypervigilance: when "not knowing" is experienced as unbearable, the mind keeps searching, checking, or mentally problem-solving in ways that paradoxically increase perceived threat (Dugas et al., 1998; Milne et al., 2019; Pepperdine et al., 2018). Second, avoidance and reassurance behaviors are negatively reinforced because they provide short-term relief, yet they also block corrective learning, leaving catastrophic predictions intact. This includes "safety behaviors" (i.e., subtle protective actions, self-monitoring, exit strategies, and reassurance seeking) that are intended to prevent disaster but have the secondary effect of preventing disconfirmation (Salkovskis et al., 1999; Wells et al., 1995). Third, exposure science increasingly emphasizes an inhibitory learning account: durable change is fostered less by waiting for fear to subside and more by repeatedly testing threat predictions and learning that the anticipated catastrophe does not occur, across varied contexts and without reliance on safety behaviors, so that new, non-threat associations become more likely to be retrieved when stress is high (Craske et al., 2014; Craske et al., 2022).

A logotherapeutic lens adds a distinct existential dimension that becomes clinically important when anxiety is entangled with responsibility, identity, and the "for-the-sake-of-which" of one's life. In Frankl's framework, human beings are not only threat-detection systems; they are meaning-responding beings. Anxiety often intensifies when life is organized around the immediate goal of eliminating discomfort, because the person's freedom is reduced to symptom control. Conversely, when the person reconnects to what calls them—values, commitments, relationships, contributions—anxiety can be met not only with regulation strategies, but with a chosen stance: "I cannot guarantee certainty, but I can choose my response in service of what matters" (Frankl, 1988).

This is not a romanticization of anxiety or a denial of psychopathology. It is a reframing that distinguishes between anxiety as a conditioned, threat-based response that benefits from evidence-based exposure and cognitive/behavioral change, and anxiety as a human signal of significance, arising when the future is open, and one's choices matter.

This meaning-based stance also clarifies a frequent clinical paradox: many clients are not primarily trying to "feel safe"; they are trying to live safely enough to avoid the risk of disappointment, shame, or failure. In logotherapeutic terms, anxiety can become a protection against existential exposure against the vulnerability inherent in loving, committing, creating, and showing up. The task is therefore not only reducing arousal, but widening the person's existential space so life is not organized around avoidance. Importantly, this "widening" is often gradual and energy-sensitive: clients learn to approach what matters in doses that are both feasible and dignifying, rather than in all-or-nothing challenges that reproduce defeat.

When used skillfully, logotherapy's two classic methods align closely with these contemporary mechanisms and can be integrated directly into modern anxiety treatment. *Paradoxical intention* is particularly useful when anticipatory anxiety is amplified by hyper-intention ("I must not feel anxious; I must control this perfectly"). By inviting the person to intentionally approach, exaggerate, or playfully "wish for" the feared symptom for a brief moment (e.g., "Let's try to shake even more for 10 seconds"), the therapy disrupts the control agenda, reduces catastrophic seriousness, and restores agency in the face of bodily arousal (Frankl, 2006). Although the strongest modern evidence base for paradoxical intention has been developed in specific domains such as insomnia, the underlying principle—undoing fear of fear by relinquishing coercive control, helps explain why the technique can be clinically potent in performance anxiety and anticipatory panic when applied carefully (Jansson-Fröjmark et al., 2022).

Dereflection complements this by targeting the attentional trap of anxiety: persistent self-monitoring ("How anxious am I? How do I look? Is my heart racing?") functions like a spotlight that magnifies threat and keeps the person fused with symptoms.

Dereflection is not distraction, but a purposeful re-orientation, shifting attention from the self as an object of surveillance toward a valued task, another person, or a meaningful contribution. This aligns closely with cognitive-behavioral findings that self-focused attention and safety behaviors maintain anxiety by increasing perceived threat and reducing corrective learning (Salkovskis et al., 1999; Wells et al., 1995). In logotherapy, the attentional shift is explicitly ethical and existential: it moves the person from preoccupation to self-transcendence, toward what (and whom) they are here for (Frankl, 1988, 2006).

Practically, these methods can be integrated with inhibitory-learning exposure into a meaning-anchored pathway that makes treatment both more tolerable and more sustainable. The sequence often begins with a meaning-centered case formulation: What responsibilities, relationships, and values has anxiety constrained? What has been postponed "until I feel better"? This is followed by crafting a concise stance sentence that affirms limited control and preserved freedom (e.g., "I cannot control the first wave of anxiety, but I can choose actions that serve my value of being present with my family"). Then, therapist and client build a value-graded exposure ladder in which every step includes (1) the prediction to be tested (the feared expectancy), and (2) the value it enables. For example: "Prediction: If I enter the elevator, I will panic and collapse. Value: reclaiming mobility and dignity." Exposure is then optimized using contemporary principles—varying contexts, reducing safety behaviors, approaching interoceptive cues when relevant, and explicitly attending to expectancy violation—while the meaning anchor answers the question: *Why is this worth doing even when it's hard?* (Buchholz et al., 2022; Craske et al., 2014; Craske et al., 2022).

Within sessions, paradoxical intention can be used as a brief "micro-move" to disarm hyper-intention right before, or during, exposure (10–20 seconds of intentional exaggeration), and dereflection can be deployed at peak arousal to shift attention toward the chosen meaning target (a person's face, a sentence to deliver, a concrete helpful act). Afterward, consolidation focuses not only on symptom metrics, but on the stance enacted: "What did you choose when you were uncomfortable?"—strengthening a narrative of courage and commitment rather than a narrative of fragile control. This emphasis converges with values-based behavioral approaches that aim to increase psychological flexibility: taking meaningful action in the presence of uncomfortable internal experiences (Twohig & Levin, 2017). It also matches what meaning research consistently suggests: stronger purpose/meaning is associated with lower anxiety and distress, even though this association is not a guarantee and does not eliminate the need for disorder-specific treatment when indicated (Boreham & Schutte, 2023; He et al., 2023).

Clinically, a small but important refinement is to track two curves in parallel: anxiety intensity and meaningful engagement (or dignity/agency/connection). These curves often do not move together week-to-week. Normalizing this divergence reduces demoralization and supports persistence: the client can see progress even when symptoms fluctuate. Over time, often gradually rather than inevitably, some clients experience a widening of their lived field: avoidance loosens, choices become more available, and life is reorganized less around "How do I stop anxiety?" and more around "What do I want to stand for, even with anxiety present?" This is the heart of logotherapeutic work with anxiety: not the promise of comfort, but the recovery of inner freedom and responsibility in the presence of uncertainty.

Finally, logotherapy can powerfully complement evidence-based care, but it does not replace medical assessment, pharmacotherapy, or structured psychotherapies (e.g., CBT and exposure-based protocols) when these are indicated by symptom severity, risk, or comorbidity. Meaning-centered work is most responsible when it is integrated into a shared, phased plan—first establishing stabilization and sound assessment, then targeting the cycles that maintain anxiety (avoidance, safety behaviors, reassurance seeking), and gradually reopening the person's relationship to the future by anchoring courageous, values-consistent action in what genuinely matters.

56 Addiction and substance abuse

Addiction and substance abuse may be understood as multidetermined conditions in which neurobehavioral learning, affect regulation, and social context converge around a progressively narrowed repertoire of choice and meaning. Frankl's observation that "when a person can't find a deep sense of meaning, they distract themselves with pleasure" captures an important existential dimension of this process: the attempt to fill, mute, or escape an inner void through immediate reward. At the same time, addiction cannot be reduced to a simple search for pleasure. Over time, a person's attention, motivation, time, and relationships may become increasingly organized around the substance or addictive behavior, not because pleasure is necessarily growing, but because the learned promise of relief or reward becomes more compelling and automatic than alternative sources of purpose, value, and connection (Volkow et al., 2016). Contemporary models help clarify this narrowing process. Incentive-sensitization theories propose that repeated use amplifies cue-reactivity and "wanting" (motivational pull) even when "liking" (hedonic payoff) plateaus or declines, making triggers feel urgent and disproportionately salient (Robinson & Berridge, 1993, 2025). Habit and compulsivity models describe a shift from intentional action to increasingly stimulus-driven routines, reinforced by changes in corticostriatal circuitry and weakened top-down inhibitory control, so behavior increasingly "runs itself," especially under stress or cue exposure (Everitt & Robbins, 2016). Allostatic perspectives highlight the accumulation of stress-system dysregulation and negative reinforcement, such that substance use becomes increasingly motivated by the need to relieve dysphoria, irritability, or withdrawal-like states, thereby strengthening long-term vulnerability through short-term relief (Koob & Schulkin, 2019).

Psychologically, many clients describe substance use less as the pursuit of pleasure and more as an increasingly practiced attempt to manage inner states, such as dampening shame, anxious arousal, traumatic activation, boredom, relational pain, or a felt sense of emptiness, and briefly restoring steadiness, self-worth, or connection. Self-medication and self-regulation formulations capture this clinical logic: particular substances tend to be selected and repeated because they reliably modify painful subjective states and compensate for vulnerabilities in affect regulation and self-experience (Khantzian, 1997, 2013, 2021). From a learning perspective, the relief that follows use functions as negative reinforcement: it strengthens avoidance of distress and accelerates the consolidation of a "quick-relief" routine, leaving fewer opportunities to develop and rehearse alternative coping routes such as relational repair, values-guided problem solving, tolerating uncertainty, or grief processing (Baker et al., 2004). Socially, stigma and anticipated judgment can further delay help-seeking and intensify concealment, which narrows recovery options and increases reliance on the substance-use routine (Earnshaw et al., 2025; Farhoudian et al., 2022). Social conditions shape both initiation and maintenance. Exposure to trauma, marginalization, isolation, and economic precarity can increase risk and reduce access to protective resources, while "recovery capital"—the internal, relational, and community resources that support change—predicts capacity to initiate and sustain recovery. Importantly, recovery capital can be positive (supportive relationships, stable housing, meaningful roles) or negative (barriers such as stigma, incarceration history, unsafe environments), and trajectories are rarely linear (Cloud & Granfield, 2008).

A logotherapeutic perspective complements these mechanisms by adding a noetic (existential) dimension: the human capacity for meaning, responsibility, and self-transcendence even under constraint (Frankl, 1963, 1969). From this vantage point, addiction often reflects not only dysregulated reward learning but also a constriction of meaning: diminished access to reasons-to-live-for, to valued roles, and to "for-the-sake-of-which" commitments that make restraint worthwhile. In an existential vacuum, the substance can become a substitute carrier of significance (I matter when I use), belonging (I'm connected when I use), agency (I can change my state when I use), or transcendence (I can escape myself when I use). The clinical goal, therefore, is not merely abstinence as a behavioral endpoint, but the restoration of freedom-of-stance and value-orientation so that abstinence/reduction becomes supported by a life that feels weighty, directional, and relationally anchored.

Meaning-anchored clinical formulation can be organized around three interlocking questions: *(1) function*: what pain is relieved or what "good" is pursued through use (e.g., soothing, energizing, belonging, numbing, daring); *(2) cost*: which values, relationships, and life roles are being eclipsed by the addictive routine; and *(3) context:* which environments (social, economic, cultural) constrict or expand access to purpose and support. Within this map, cravings can be reframed, carefully and non-romantically, not as "true needs," but as misdirected striving: energy and urgency attached to a narrow pathway that has been over-learned. This reframing reduces moralization and opens clinical curiosity: *If this urge is a learned route toward relief/meaning, what other routes can be built that are more faithful to the person's values and less destructive?*

In practice, several logotherapeutic levers integrate naturally with evidence-based addiction care (e.g., motivational interviewing, CBT, relapse-prevention, medication when indicated), while retaining a distinct existential stance. First, values clarification and commitment: through Socratic dialogue and narrative work, the client identifies concrete purposes larger than immediate relief—creative values (what I contribute), experiential values (what I receive and love), and attitudinal values (how I choose to stand in unavoidable suffering). These are translated into explicit "for-the-sake-of" statements that become clinically usable during high-risk moments (Frankl, 1969). Second, dereflection and attentional re-orientation: rather than amplifying the loop of "urge-monitoring → anxiety/shame → stronger urge," attention is redirected toward a valued task, relationship, or responsibility precisely when craving peaks, strengthening the capacity to move from self-absorption toward self-transcendence. Third, attitude modulation under distress: when discomfort cannot be eliminated, the client practices choosing a stance (honesty, courage, dignity, responsibility) and learns to treat suffering not as a command to escape, but as a moment in which response-ability can still be enacted. Fourth, meaning-anchored skills and exposure: standard relapse-prevention strategies (identifying high-risk cues, coping planning, "urge surfing," building alternatives) are embedded in identity and values, so skills become expressions of *who I am becoming* rather than merely acts of self-control (Witkiewitz & Marlatt, 2004). Motivational interviewing's spirit and method—evoking change talk, strengthening autonomy, aligning change with values—can be explicitly deepened by logotherapeutic "why" questions that connect ambivalence to responsibility and future-oriented meaning (Miller & Rollnick, 2013).

A practical micro-structure is to co-create "meaning tasks"—brief, concrete actions that remain feasible even when energy is low and craving is high, yet are value-dense enough to matter. Each task is explicitly linked to one chosen value and framed as a *small enactment* of identity (e.g., a two-minute repair text as fidelity, a brief act of service as generativity, a concrete health step as responsibility). Progress is then reviewed through dual tracking: not only shifts in symptoms (craving intensity, use episodes), but also shifts in meaning-relevant outcomes. This structure reduces shame when relief is slow and strengthens the logic of recovery: discomfort may persist, but values can still be enacted.

The growing empirical literature supports the clinical relevance of meaning and purpose in substance-related outcomes. Meaning in life is associated with lower harmful drinking, partly through mechanisms such as reduced alcohol valuation and greater self-control (Copeland et al., 2020), and experimental work suggests that brief meaning-in-life interventions may reduce the incentive salience of alcohol-related cues (Ostafin & Feyel, 2019). Sense of purpose prospectively predicts lower likelihood of later illicit drug use or prescription misuse (Kim et al., 2020), and purpose in life has been shown to predict treatment outcomes in cocaine dependence (Martin et al., 2011). Mutual-help pathways such as AA and 12-step facilitation, which often involve belonging, spiritual or existential meaning-making, and purposeful recovery practices, also show strong evidence for improving abstinence and remission in alcohol use disorder (Kelly et al., 2020). At the level of logotherapy-specific delivery, some studies report reductions in craving and relapse following logotherapy-based programs, warranting cautious optimism alongside the need for more rigorous replication across contexts and populations.

In sum, logotherapy contributes an integrative lens to addiction work: it holds the neurobehavioral realities of addiction while refusing to reduce the person to them or to blame them as morally deficient. Recovery is framed as the gradual re-opening of freedom within constraints, strengthening the capacity to choose responses, to endure discomfort in the service of what matters, and to rebuild life around values that can carry significance without substances.

57 Trauma and PTSD

Trauma, whether caused by interpersonal violence, natural disaster, war, or other overwhelming events, profoundly disrupts an individual's assumptive world. It can abruptly rupture a person's assumptive world—the largely implicit beliefs that life is reasonably safe, predictable, and intelligible, that others can be trusted, and that one has some capacity for agency and self-protection (Janoff-Bulman, 1992). When posttraumatic stress symptoms persist, converging cognitive models suggest that distress is maintained by a continuing sense of current threat, fueled by intrusive re-experiencing, avoidance of reminders, hyperarousal, and negative appraisals that keep the nervous system organized around danger (Ehlers & Clark, 2000). At the level of memory, traumatic experience may remain insufficiently integrated and contextualized, returning as vivid fragments, bodily states, or moments of "nowness" that are easily triggered under stress rather than remembered as safely past (Brewin, 2025).

A meaning-oriented perspective adds an additional depth of focus: trauma can also be a rupture in the person's meaning system. In meaning-making terms, traumatic events can create a sharp discrepancy between one's global meaning (core beliefs, values, and expectations) and situational meaning (what the event seems to say about life, self, others, and the future). The struggle is often not only "what happened," but "what does this mean now?"—about the world, about goodness, about identity, about what is worth living for (Park, 2022). In existential-humanistic language, trauma may be experienced as *existential shattering*: a destabilizing rupture in the person's lived sense of coherence and "being-at-home" in the world, leaving them unmoored from familiar sources of orientation, trust, and possibility (Hoffman & Vallejos, 2020). In that narrowed field, the longing for meaning does not necessarily vanish, but it may be overshadowed by survival-based constriction, numbness, or a sense that the future has collapsed into threat-management.

Within this landscape, logotherapy approaches meaning not as consolation, but as orientation—something that can be rediscovered through values and stance, without denying the wound, while re-opening the question of freedom of attitude—*how one stands in relation to what cannot be undone* (Frankl, 1969). This is not a promise that trauma will become "good," nor an expectation of growth. It is a clinical commitment to restoring response-ability in small, reality-based ways: helping the person regain access to values, relationships, and responsibilities that remain possible, even if life is now profoundly altered.

Practically, meaning-centered trauma work tends to be most responsible when it proceeds in a staged, grounded way. Early on, the priority is stabilization and felt safety: strengthening basic regulation (sleep, grounding, supportive connection, predictable routines) and reducing maintaining cycles such as avoidance, reassurance rituals, and hyper-monitoring—without invalidating the protective intelligence that created them. Only when the person has enough internal and relational safety does deeper narrative work become feasible: helping the survivor name what was broken (trust, agency, innocence, identity, moral order), and gradually weaving traumatic fragments into a broader life story that includes both injury and agency (Ehlers & Clark, 2000; Brewin, 2025). Logotherapy contributes here through *Socratic dialogue* that is careful, paced, and consent-based: not "Why did this happen?" but "What has this done to what you believe about life, and which of those beliefs do you want to keep, revise, or refuse?"; not "What is the meaning of this trauma?" but "What, if anything, feels worth protecting in you, despite this?"

A particularly helpful pivot in logotherapeutic work is moving from event-fixation to value-recovery, without bypassing grief. Survivors may initially feel that what was lost (a loved one, a home, a role, safety, bodily integrity, a future) was the sole "carrier" of what mattered. Meaning-oriented dialogue helps the client articulate the values and life-needs that were expressed through what was harmed or taken, for example, love, belonging, responsibility, protection, justice, vitality, faith, or creativity, and then explore whether those values still matter and can be honored in altered, realistic forms (Park, 2022). This is not about reframing for reassurance, but about reconnecting with the deeper structure of attachment and identity. Gentle prompts can include: "When you remember what was precious before the trauma, what did it allow you to live?" and "If that value still matters, what would a *small and safe* expression of it look like this week?" Over time, even limited enactments can widen the felt field: not necessarily by erasing symptoms, but by reintroducing direction, connection, and agency as lived experiences rather than abstract goals.

Logotherapeutic methods can be used with particular care in trauma contexts. *Dereflection* is often valuable when attention becomes trapped in threat-scanning or self-monitoring: it redirects focus, briefly and intentionally, toward a concrete task, relationship, or act of contribution that represents the client's chosen values. *Attitude modulation* supports the client in naming what is unchangeable while reclaiming a chosen stance toward it (e.g., dignity, honesty, tenderness toward oneself, courage to re-enter life gradually). *Paradoxical intention* may be helpful for specific secondary anxiety patterns (e.g., fear of fear, panic about symptoms), but it should be used judiciously and only when the client has enough stability that playful exaggeration will not be experienced as invalidation or re-exposure. A small but important clinical anchor is to track two lines of change: symptoms and meaning. When clients see that "less distress" and "more meaning" do not always rise together week to week, it can reduce shame, normalize nonlinearity, and support persistence (Fischer et al., 2020).

It is also worth situating logotherapy within the broader evidence base for PTSD care. Strong guidelines consistently recommend trauma-focused psychotherapies (including variants of CBT such as prolonged exposure and cognitive processing approaches), with additional treatments recommended conditionally depending on context and fit (Guideline Development Panel for the Treatment of PTSD in Adults, American Psychological Association, 2019; Watkins et al., 2018). Meaning-work can strengthen these approaches by clarifying the "for-the-sake-of": not simply *enduring* exposure or cognitive work, but reconnecting courageous action to what genuinely matters (parenting, love, faithfulness, justice, craft, community). In this integration, symptom reduction is not treated as the sole aim; it becomes part of restoring the person's relationship with the future—so that life can be approached again, not only survived.

Finally, the posttraumatic growth (PTG) literature suggests that some individuals may report positive changes that emerge *through the struggle* with profound disruption, often described across domains such as deeper relating to others, new possibilities, personal strength, spiritual/existential change, and appreciation of life (Tedeschi & Calhoun, 1996, 2004). Importantly, PTG is not the same as "silver lining," nor does it imply that the trauma was beneficial; it refers to changes that can occur alongside loss, grief, and a permanently altered life. Empirically, PTG and distress frequently coexist rather than replacing one another, and evidence suggests that the association between PTG and PTSD symptoms can be complex, including curvilinear patterns, underscoring that growth does not require the absence of pain (Helgeson et al., 2006; Kleim & Ehlers, 2009). Clinically, this matters because clients can feel pressured by an implicit cultural mandate to "grow," which may intensify shame or self-blame when they primarily feel shattered.

A logotherapeutic posture holds this tension respectfully: it refuses premature meaning and also refuses despair as the final word. Rather than aiming to produce PTG, meaning-centered work prioritizes restoring existential orientation, helping the survivor reconnect to values, relationship, contribution, and freedom of attitude in small, reality-based steps. When recovery unfolds, it may look less like a dramatic transformation and more like a gradual reopening of existential space: the person may regain access to choice within constraints, to relationship, to contribution, and to a sense that life can again carry weight and worth, even with the wound present (Frankl, 1969; Lantz, 1992).

58 Grief and loss

Grief is not only an emotional reaction to death or irrevocable loss, but also a crisis of meaning. Yalom's reflection that "mourning is the price we pay for having the courage to love others" captures the existential paradox at the heart of bereavement: the depth of sorrow reflects the depth of attachment. Loss can rupture the assumptive world ("this should not have happened"), identity ("who am I without them or it?"), and future orientation ("what is the point now?"), raising painful questions about justice, belonging, and purpose. Contemporary bereavement science underscores that adaptation to loss is rarely linear. Instead, people often move back and forth between loss-oriented experiences—such as yearning, sadness, and searching—and restoration-oriented efforts involving changed roles, altered routines, and the development of new capacities. The Dual Process Model understands this oscillation as a healthy and adaptive process, rather than a sign of avoidance or failure to cope (Stroebe & Schut, 1999, 2010). In parallel, research has increasingly emphasized that mourning does not necessarily culminate in detachment. Healthy grieving may include continuing bonds: an ongoing, evolving relationship with the deceased maintained through memory, inner dialogue, ritual, and legacy (Klass et al., 1996). At the same time, grief can become clinically impairing when intense acute reactions persist and significantly disrupt functioning over time. The inclusion of Prolonged Grief Disorder (PGD) in both the ICD-11 and DSM-5-TR reflects this recognition, offering a clinical framework for grief marked by enduring longing or preoccupation, together with symptoms such as identity disruption, difficulty accepting the death, and profound emotional pain beyond culturally expected patterns (American Psychiatric Association, 2022; Eisma, 2023).

A logotherapeutic formulation of grief

Logotherapy adds an existential-ethical stratum: The loss cannot be undone. Yet the client is not only a bearer of pain; they remain a person-in-relation, capable of stance, response, and self-transcendence. In practice, a logotherapeutic formulation in grief begins by holding two truths at once: the loss is irrevocable—the loss, the fact of missing, the non-negotiable pain of love—and yet the person is not reducible to what happened. What remains choosable is the response: how the bond is carried forward, how values are lived in altered form, how guilt and responsibility are related to ethically (repair rather than self-punishment), and how participation in life is re-entered despite sorrow. This is not a call to "find a silver lining," but an insistence on human freedom-of-stance in the face of the irreversible—an existential and ethical capacity that grief can obscure but not erase (Frankl, 1959).

Meaning-making research supports this two-level logic. Distress intensifies when the loss shatters global meanings (e.g., assumptions of safety, fairness, or control: "I can protect those I love"), whereas adaptation is facilitated when clients can gradually reconstruct coherence, purpose, and significance in ways that remain faithful to the reality of loss—without premature reframing or forced positivity (Park, 2010; Neimeyer, 2019).

From an evidence standpoint, bereavement interventions show their strongest effects when treatment is indicated, for example in Prolonged Grief Disorder, traumatic bereavement, or marked functional impairment—rather than delivered indiscriminately; meta-analytic findings suggest small-to-moderate average effects, with larger effects for targeted grief-focused approaches (Wittouck et al., 2011; Komischke-Konnerup et al., 2024). Within this landscape, logotherapy is best positioned as a clinical orientation and set of meaning practices that can be integrated with established grief treatments (e.g., grief-focused CBT, Complicated Grief Treatment) when severity warrants, so that exposure, re-engagement, and restoration tasks are continually tethered to "for-the-sake-of" reasons, and the client's grief is held with dignity while life is reopened (Shear et al., 2005; Bryant et al., 2014).

1 Meaning-centered assessment and "oscillation map": Begin with a concise collaborative map that includes **loss field:** the relationship, the circumstances, what is missed (roles, future, identity), **oscillation pattern:** where the client is pulled into loss-focus vs. restoration-focus, and where they feel "stuck," **meaning ruptures:** injustice, spiritual struggle, identity collapse, diminished mattering, and **existing anchors:** people, places, practices that still evoke connection, responsibility, or beauty. This assessment is also where clinical safeguards naturally belong: validate the pain first, screen for comorbidity (depression, PTSD, substance misuse), and, when needed, coordinate with medical/psychiatric care. The stance is explicit: meaning work is not a substitute for stabilization; it is what helps stabilization become *livable* and *worth sustaining*.
2 Continuing bonds as an experiential meaning pathway: A logotherapeutic frame legitimizes bonds as a source of

meaning rather than pathology—while keeping the bond flexible and reality-based (Klass et al., 1996). Practical methods include:

- **Letter-writing** or **"two-chair" dialogue** (when clinically appropriate): what remains unsaid, what the deceased gave, what the client wants to carry.
- **Rituals of presence:** lighting a candle, music, visiting a place, or a brief weekly remembrance practice that ends with a return-to-life step.
- **Legacy translation:** asking "What quality of theirs do you want to enact this week?" (e.g., kindness, courage, humor, fairness).

These practices often reduce the client's fear that "moving forward" equals betrayal—an existential barrier that can quietly maintain impairment.

3 Dereflection from grief-absorption to chosen engagement: In severe grief, attention can become narrowly organized around scanning, yearning, and repetitive "if only" loops. Dereflection does not deny longing; it gently redirects attention toward a chosen, doable act aligned with values, especially relational or contributive acts (Frankl, 1959/2006). For example, one supportive message to a friend, a micro-act of caregiving, creativity, or civic contribution.

Grief frequently includes guilt, sometimes realistic (an action one regrets), sometimes existential (the impossibility of saving), sometimes survivor guilt. Logotherapeutic dialogue distinguishes between responsibility (what I can learn, repair, or live differently now) and omnipotent blame (the fantasy that I could have controlled the uncontrollable). Here, Socratic questions are often more therapeutic than reassurance: "If your love could speak, what would it ask of you now?" "What would 'honoring them' look like in daily behavior, not in self-accusation?"

In sum, grief is the cost of attachment, and also a confrontation with finitude, freedom, and responsibility. Logotherapy does not ask clients to "find meaning" as a moral requirement; it helps them protect the dignity of grief while reopening life. When integrated with contemporary bereavement science, meaning work supports oscillation (not rigidity), continuing bonds (not denial), and purposeful participation (not premature closure). In that frame, adaptation is not forgetting; it is learning to live in faithful relationship to what was lost, through love enacted, values embodied, and a stance of human dignity in the face of the irreversible (Frankl, 1959; Neimeyer, 2019; Stroebe & Schut, 2010).

59 Chronic pain and physical injury

Chronic pain and acquired physical injury do not merely disrupt sensory processing and function; they also unsettle identity, agency, and one's sense of the future. As Frankl observed, "When we are no longer able to change a situation, we are challenged to change ourselves." This perspective is especially relevant in the context of chronic pain, where suffering cannot always be eliminated, yet one's way of understanding and responding to it can still change. Contemporary definitions frame pain as a biopsychosocial phenomenon—"an unpleasant sensory and emotional experience associated with, or resembling that associated with, actual or potential tissue damage," underscoring that lived meaning and context are integral to how pain is perceived and coped with (Raja et al., 2020). The ICD-11 classification further supports this multifaceted perspective by distinguishing chronic primary pain, in which pain is a condition in its own right, from chronic secondary pain, which is attributable to another disease process. This distinction reinforces the need for care that moves beyond nociception alone and addresses functioning, distress, and participation in life (Treede et al., 2019). In parallel, psychological models—especially the fear-avoidance framework—help explain how catastrophic interpretations, such as "movement will damage me" or "this will never improve," together with subsequent avoidance, may intensify disability over time even when such reactions are initially protective or understandable (Vlaeyen & Linton, 2000). Across clinical trials, psychosocial interventions appear to exert their most reliable effects on pain-related disability, interference, and emotional distress, while showing comparatively smaller effects on pain intensity itself—an important clinical reframing for individuals who equate recovery solely with the disappearance of pain (Williams et al., 2020). A logotherapeutic lens adds an existential dimension to this evidence: chronic pain and injury may narrow life's possibilities, yet they also intensify the question of what still calls the person forward. In practice, meaning-centered processes can help individuals re-author identity beyond lost functions, reduce pain-centrism—that is, the tendency for life to become organized around monitoring and managing symptoms—and cultivate a dignified stance toward unavoidable limitation without denying suffering or resorting to forced optimism. This position is consistent with contemporary meaning-making models, which understand adaptation as an ongoing effort to integrate difficult realities into a coherent life narrative and value system (Park, 2010).

A frequently cited case illustrates logotherapy's attitudinal pathway in the context of irreversible loss. As recounted by Long (1995), Klingberg (2001), and Levinson (2002), *Jerry Long*, a promising teenage pitcher, sustained a cervical spinal cord injury that left him quadriplegic. He recognized that an athletic career was no longer possible, yet he also discovered that freedom remained in other domains through which to actualize meaning. He completed high school, pursued university studies, earned a doctorate in clinical psychology, and practiced as a logotherapist—epitomizing the credo, "I broke my neck; it didn't break me." In logotherapeutic terms, this case demonstrates responsibility for the freedom that *remains*, and the disciplined cultivation of an attitudinal stance that allows life meaning to be pursued despite severe bodily constraint (Klingberg, 2001; Long, 1995; Levinson, 2002).

An evidence-informed logotherapeutic approach is most effective when integrated with contemporary pain science, especially the fear-avoidance cycle and the clinical shift from pain-intensity goals to participation- and values-based goals (Vlaeyen & Linton, 2000; Williams et al., 2020). The overarching aim is to help clients distinguish what cannot be changed from what can still be chosen, and to translate "remaining freedom" into small, repeatable, value-anchored actions that rebuild life space over time.

1 *Meaning-centered formulation aligned with pain processes*: Begin with a concise, collaborative map that links pain maintenance mechanisms to meaning disruptions and available choices. Identify:

- Maintaining loops (e.g., fear → avoidance → deconditioning/disability → increased fear).
- Meaning disruptions (identity/role loss, reduced mattering, narrowed future).
- Zones of choice (micro-participation, contribution, connection, stance—despite symptoms).

Then, the client can condense this map into a brief "for-the-sake-of" statement that organizes weekly choices across Frankl's three pathways of meaning—creative, experiential, and attitudinal values (Frankl, 1959). For example: "For the sake of being a present parent and a reliable colleague, I will take one value-aligned step daily, receive one moment of connection or beauty, and practice a steady stance when pain is unavoidable."

2 *Value-anchored pacing and graded exposure: testing fear predictions in the service of purpose:* Use pacing and graded exposure, while making the value link explicit at every step. Each step names: the prediction being tested ("If I walk 5 minutes, I'll spiral and lose control"), and the value it serves ("…so I can show up for family dinner / return to the team / care for my body without surrendering my life").

This structure targets fear-avoidance while restoring meaning to movement: activity is no longer "rehab compliance" but a chosen enactment of purpose. Exposure-based approaches have evidence for reducing pain-related fear and disability in chronic pain (e.g., Ariza-Mateos et al., 2019; Vlaeyen & Linton, 2000).

3 Dereflection: shifting from symptom surveillance to chosen engagement: When pain becomes an attentional magnet (constant scanning, checking, "How bad is it now?"), apply dereflection by redirecting attention toward a specific, doable act of

engagement or contribution within current capacity—for example: a supportive message to another patient, a short "project of the week," or a micro-act of caretaking, creativity, or civic contribution. Repeatable contribution strengthens agency and mattering even when symptoms persist—often a turning point for clients whose identity has collapsed into "patienthood" (Frankl, 1959, 2006; Schulenberg et al., 2008).

4 Meaning-centered group formats in multidisciplinary settings: In multidisciplinary pain clinics and post-injury rehabilitation programs, brief structured meaning groups can complement CBT/ACT and physiotherapy. Adaptations of meaning-centered protocols typically include identity continuity (life chapters; "what remains myself?"), creative sources (roles, responsibilities, realistic projects), experiential sources (relationship, nature, art, humor), and attitudinal sources (how one meets the unavoidable). Across conditions involving disruption and loss, meaning-centered therapies show reliable improvements in quality of life and reductions in psychological distress (Vos & Vitali, 2018).

5 Narrative reconstruction and legacy-in-miniature: Finally, support identity repair through narrative reconstruction: helping clients reweave the story from "a broken body" to "a person practicing courage, fidelity, and care under constraint." Use short life-review prompts ("When have you lived your values despite limitation?") and encourage legacy-in-miniature artifacts (a letter, audio note, recorded message). Longitudinal research in chronic pain suggests that presence of meaning predicts better psychological adjustment over time, making narrative work clinically consequential—not merely inspirational (Dezutter et al., 2015).

In sum, physical injury and chronic pain can narrow what a person can do—but meaning can expand what the person *is able to live for.* When pain science is integrated with logotherapy, clients are guided to act within what remains possible: to craft contributions, receive connection and beauty, and choose a dignified stance toward what cannot be changed. The goal is not only fewer symptoms, but a life re-oriented by purpose, participation, and responsibility (Breitbart et al., 2015; Frankl, 1959; Williams et al., 2020; Vlaeyen & Linton, 2012). Progress, therefore, should be tracked using outcomes that reflect lived recovery: participation, role re-engagement, emotional distress, and quality of life, rather than pain intensity alone, especially given that psychosocial approaches tend to show their strongest and most reliable effects on functioning and interference (Williams et al., 2020).

60 Eating disorders

Eating disorders (EDs), including anorexia nervosa, bulimia nervosa, binge-eating disorder, and related presentations, are multi-determined conditions shaped by neurobiological vulnerability, learning processes, personality features (e.g., perfectionism, harm avoidance), and sociocultural pressures that overvalue weight and shape. As the disorder progresses, physiological depletion and chronic threat-monitoring can narrow cognition, intensify rigidity, and destabilize interoceptive trust (i.e., confidence in internal bodily cues), pulling attention toward food, body, and control as if these were the central problems to solve (Khalsa et al., 2015).

Across contemporary models, several maintaining processes consistently recur: (a) overvaluation of weight/shape as a core metric of self-worth; (b) avoidance and safety behaviors that reduce distress short-term while preventing corrective learning; (c) intolerance of uncertainty supported by rigid rules and rituals; and (d) symptom-driven mood regulation, in which behaviors temporarily shift internal states and thereby strengthen the cycle (Fairburn et al., 2003). Because EDs can carry substantial medical risk, clinical work begins with medical and nutritional stabilization and proceeds within evidence-based protocols and multidisciplinary care. Current guidelines emphasize structured psychological treatments matched to diagnosis, age, and severity (e.g., CBT-E as a transdiagnostic approach; family-based treatment for many adolescent presentations; and specialist approaches for anorexia in adults such as MANTRA or SSCM where indicated) (NICE, 2017/2020; APA, 2023; Atwood & Friedman, 2020; Treasure & Schmidt, 2013).

A logotherapeutic lens complements these foundations by clarifying what the symptoms are attempting to secure at the level of identity and value. For many clients, ED symptoms operate as a narrowed "identity solution," offering a severe kind of order, purity, certainty, or belonging when life feels chaotic, empty, or morally threatening. In logotherapeutic terms, the clinical task is to help the client reclaim freedom within constraints and redirect it toward values that are genuinely life-giving, rather than toward the tyranny of self-evaluation (Frankl, 1959, 2006).

Meaning-centered formulation: from symptom function to value direction

A concise, clinically usable meaning-centered formulation can be built around three linked inquiries:

1 *Function:* What does each behavior accomplish *right now*? What distress does it mute, what uncertainty does it manage, what feared experience does it help the client avoid?
2 *Values captured by the illness:* What "good" is being pursued in distorted form (e.g., integrity, excellence, devotion, safety, belonging, care for others)?
3 *Values and roles eclipsed:* What domains of life have been displaced (relationships, learning, creativity, contribution, play, spirituality, service)?

This framing keeps meaning-work concrete: it locates values beneath symptoms without romanticizing the disorder, then asks where those values might be carried in healthier ways. One practical output is a brief *for-the-sake-of* statement that anchors treatment tasks in a life-direction beyond the body, for example: "I practice nourishment and flexibility for the sake of being present in my relationships and capable in my calling." This focus is especially important because EDs often constrict identity. Research increasingly links ED symptomatology with identity disturbance and shows that identity functioning can improve alongside symptom change during treatment (Verschueren et al., 2024).

Meaning-centered work does not deny the biology, learning processes, or sociocultural pressures involved in eating disorders; rather, it completes the clinical picture by naming what the illness has been falsely recruited to provide—identity, worth, certainty, control, or a sense of moral safety—and by helping clients reclaim these needs through life-giving pathways instead (Frankl, 1959, 2006). Empirical work increasingly supports the relevance of meaning-related constructs to ED presentations and comorbid internalizing symptoms, and meaning-centered interventions tailored to ED concerns show promising early effects in controlled trials (van Doornik et al., 2024; Schutzeichel et al., 2024). Clinically, the aim is that nourishment and behavioral change become livable because they are tethered to a reclaimed direction: recovery is not only symptom reduction, but a return to a life that is again worth inhabiting, through relationship, contribution, and responsibility. In practice, this stance can be operationalized through brief, repeatable "micro-interventions" that fit naturally inside evidence-based ED care (e.g., CBT-E, family-based approaches) and keep the client oriented toward *what recovery is for* at the very moments the disorder pulls attention inward (Fairburn et al., 2003; NICE, 2017/2020).

- *Dereflection at meals (attention re-orientation):* At meals, shift attention from self-surveillance to a simple outward meaning anchor—e.g., a conversation partner, a brief "purpose cue," or a concrete post-meal action connected to relationship or responsibility (Frankl, 1959, 2006).
- *Value-anchored exposure:* Structure each exposure step to specify both (a) the expectancy being tested and (b) the value served (e.g., "so I can participate in shared life without withdrawing"). This helps exposure remain purposeful rather than mere endurance, strengthening learning through direction (Atwood & Friedman, 2020; Fairburn et al., 2003).
- *Stance sentences (attitude modulation):* Prepare one or two short lines for predictable spikes (before meals, after sessions, social eating): "Discomfort is here; my response is chosen. I act for the sake of ___." The goal is not reassurance; it is orientation (Frankl, 1959/2006).

- *Responsibility cues (widening the relational field):* Identify who benefits when the client shows up more nourished and present (children, partner, students, patients, teammates). Use brief, non-shaming cues at decision points to support value-consistent choices.
- *Meaning-based body-image work:* Replace repetitive evaluation with time-limited prompts that reopen identity: "How do I want to be remembered—by a number, or by how I loved, created, and contributed?" Keep this grounded and bounded so it does not become another ritual.
- *Judicious paradoxical intention (selectively):* Not for weight/shape goals and not for symptom bargaining. Consider only where it reduces performance anxiety around social eating (e.g., fear of visible anxiety), loosening hyper-intention while remaining aligned with the treatment plan (Frankl, 1959, 2006).
- *Family as a meaning system (when indicated):* In adolescent work, caregivers can be framed as guardians of life and values rather than "body police," aligning meal support with steadiness, protection, and future-oriented love (NICE, 2017/2020).

In this framework, the treatment target expands from symptom reduction to directional living: each choice becomes a small, repeatable return to relationship, participation, and responsibility, until recovery feels coherent, not just possible.

61 Phobias

Phobias are best understood as learned, circumscribed fear networks in which a particular cue—whether an object, situation, bodily sensation, or social-evaluative context—becomes linked to catastrophic expectancies and a narrowed repertoire of escape and control. As Frankl observed, "A symptom evokes a phobia and the phobia provokes the symptom. The recurrence of the symptom then reinforces the phobia" (Frankl, 1969, p. 67). This formulation captures the self-perpetuating nature of phobic anxiety: anticipatory threat appraisals trigger arousal, the person relies on avoidance or subtle safety behaviors—such as exiting, checking, reassurance, distraction, positioning near exits, or carrying "just-in-case" items—and the short-term relief that follows negatively reinforces the pattern. Over time, the fear network may generalize, progressively shrinking the person's valued life space and narrowing the freedom to respond to life in ways aligned with meaning and value. From a logotherapeutic perspective, the cost of phobia lies not only in the persistence of fear but also in the gradual constriction of existential space, as life becomes increasingly organized around preventing anxiety rather than pursuing relationships, responsibilities, and meaningful possibilities. Exposure-based interventions therefore remain central in treatment, with robust evidence across specific phobias and related fear conditions (Choy et al., 2007; Wolitzky-Taylor et al., 2008). Contemporary exposure literature increasingly frames change through inhibitory learning and retrieval: progress is supported not by waiting for fear to fade, but by repeatedly learning, across varied contexts, that the predicted catastrophe does not occur, and by strengthening retrieval of these new non-threat associations under stress (Craske et al., 2014, 2022). For this reason, clinicians attend carefully to expectancy testing, the reduction of safety behaviors that block corrective learning, and contextual variability across places, times, postures, and social conditions in order to reduce relapse linked to context-bound learning. Experimental work further supports the clinical concern that safety-seeking may maintain anxiety by preventing disconfirmatory experience (Salkovskis et al., 1999). When in vivo access is constrained, virtual reality exposure can serve as a credible adjunct in some phobic presentations, with evidence suggesting that it is not necessarily inferior to in vivo exposure in specific phobia and agoraphobia (Wechsler et al., 2019).

A logotherapeutic contribution does not replace these mechanisms but aims to strengthen the motivational and existential conditions under which clients are willing to approach fear repeatedly. Phobic avoidance often reorganizes life around "not feeling anxious," which can quietly eclipse freedom, responsibility, and self-transcendence. Meaning-anchored exposure begins by articulating a concise for-the-sake-of: why facing this fear matters in the person's real life (e.g., parenting, partnership, vocation, faith, contribution). This shifts the decision point from "How anxious will I be?" to "What kind of life am I choosing?" and supports persistence when discomfort spikes. In Frankl's terms, exposure becomes a practice of choosing one's stance in the service of a value—creative (showing up to contribute), experiential (reclaiming connection, beauty, love), or attitudinal (dignity in the face of what cannot be controlled) (Frankl, 1959, 1969).

Within this integration, two classic logotherapeutic methods can be used with precision. *Paradoxical intention* can target anticipatory fear (especially performance and symptom-focused fears) by loosening the struggle for perfect control—inviting a brief, playful willingness toward the feared symptom to interrupt the vicious cycle of hyper-intention and escalating arousal (Frankl, 1959). *Dereflection* is useful when phobias are maintained by obsessive self-monitoring ("How am I coming across? How fast is my heart?"); attention is intentionally redirected from the self-as-threat to the task, person, or purpose at hand, which both reduces safety monitoring and supports valued engagement. The overall clinical aim becomes not only symptom reduction but reclaimed life space: a widening of action around what matters, so fear is no longer the organizing principle of the person's future.

In sum, phobias are often acquired and maintained through learning processes, and are therefore generally amenable to treatment—fear structures sustained by catastrophic predictions, avoidance, and subtle safety behaviors that prevent corrective learning. Evidence-based exposure remains the central mechanism of change, especially when it systematically tests expectancies, reduces safety behaviors, and varies contexts so that new non-threat learning can be retrieved under stress (Craske et al., 2014, 2022). Logotherapy strengthens this work by anchoring exposure in a clear "for-the-sake-of" orientation, linking practice to values, responsibility, and self-transcendence rather than to symptom control alone (Frankl, 1959, 1969). As clients repeatedly choose valued action in the presence of fear, avoidance gradually loosens, their behavioral world expands, and therapeutic success is indexed not only by reduced anxiety but by the deliberate reclamation of a fuller, more intentional life.

62 Life transitions

Life transitions—entering adulthood, shifting careers, becoming a parent, retirement, migration, widowhood, illness-related changes, or the gradual movement into later life—are not merely events, but profound reorganizations of identity, relationship, routine, and future orientation. As Elisabeth Kübler-Ross observed, "The most beautiful people we have known are those who have known defeat, known suffering, known struggle, known loss, and have found their way out of the depths [...] Beautiful people do not just happen" (Kübler-Ross, 1975, p. 96). Her words capture something essential about transitions: they are often forged through disruption, challenge, and reconstitution rather than simple movement from one stage to another. Transitions can also take the form of non-events—what was expected to happen but did not, such as a hoped-for promotion, partnership, pregnancy, recovery, or return to "normal." What makes such transitions psychologically consequential is not only the external change itself, but the way it alters the structure of everyday life and the self's orientation toward the future, rather than functioning as a simple milestone on the calendar (Schlossberg, 2011). Across life-course research, transitions are increasingly understood as processes rather than single points in time: socially shaped, uneven, and often prolonged. They may involve a liminal 'in-between' period in which an old identity is loosening while a new one has not yet fully stabilized; uncertainty, ambiguity, and heightened self-questioning are common in this phase (Stauber & Walther, 2022; Turner, 1969; van Gennep, 1960). From a clinical and existential perspective, what is often most shaken is the person's meaning structure—the sense of coherence, purpose, and significance—even when the transition itself is chosen, expected, or socially normative.

Meaning-making theory helps clarify why transitions can be both destabilizing and growth-promoting. When circumstances change, people often experience a mismatch between "global meaning" (core beliefs, values, identity commitments) and "situational meaning" (what this event seems to imply). Distress can intensify when the transition feels incoherent ("this shouldn't be happening"), purposeless ("I don't know what this is for"), or identity-threatening ("I don't recognize myself anymore").

Empirically, meaning-making processes are repeatedly linked to adjustment across stressful life events, while also showing important individual differences in what helps, when, and for whom (Park, 2010).

Logotherapy approaches transitions as existential turning points: moments that expose freedom and responsibility and invite renewed orientation to what is worth living for. Frankl's core propositions—freedom of will within constraints, the will to meaning, and the possibility of meaning under all conditions—do not deny grief, fear, or disorientation; they insist that even in flux, life continues to "ask" something of the person. Clinically, the task is to help clients recover value-orientation (what matters), translate it into credible direction (where to go next), and embody it in doable commitments (how to move, given current limits). Practically, a meaning-centered transition formulation can be built in a grounded way by integrating Schlossberg's "4 S" lens (Situation, Self, Supports, Strategies) with a logotherapeutic "values-in-motion" lens. The therapist first clarifies the transition landscape: what is changing (and what is irreversible), what is uncertain, what is chosen versus imposed, and which "old meanings" have been disrupted. Next, the therapist explores the self-in-transition: identity themes, narrative continuity, vulnerabilities (e.g., perfectionism, shame, intolerance of uncertainty), and strengths. The social ecology is then mapped: who provides practical and emotional support, what communities are lost or gained, and what cultural scripts shape the transition (especially relevant in migration, caregiving, retirement, and minority stress contexts). Finally, the focus moves beyond coping skills to the disciplined process of aligning value-based action with what the client can realistically manage at this point.

A particularly useful logotherapeutic framework for life transitions is shifting the focus from role-loss (or status-loss) to value-loss, and then to value-continuity. Many clients remain fixated on what ended ("my job," "my marriage," "my health," "my country," "my youth," "the future I expected"). That focus is human and often necessary early on; yet it can also conceal the deeper question: Which values were being lived through what was lost? For example, work may have carried contribution, mastery, usefulness, structure, status, or belonging; a partnership may have carried intimacy, protection, shared meaning, play, or devotion; a homeland may have carried identity, continuity, language, faith, and community. Naming these values clarifies what is truly at stake in the transition and enables the next responsible question: Do these values still matter, and if so, what new carriers might hold them now? Even when a pathway closes, a value can remain real and claimable.

This is where the task shifts from understanding to enactment: how to carry enduring commitments into a life that is now organized differently. Logotherapy can support this translation by drawing on narrative and developmental approaches that understand identity as an evolving life story. Narrative identity research shows that people sustain coherence by integrating a reconstructed past with an imagined future in a story that preserves continuity and purpose (McAdams & McLean, 2013). Possible-selves research likewise suggests that hoped-for and feared images of who one might become help organize motivation during uncertain periods (Markus & Nurius, 1986). Clinically, these ideas can be operationalized through "life chapter" work: (a) naming what has ended, (b) identifying what is being asked now, and (c) drafting a near-future chapter title that is value-consistent rather than symptom-driven. The clinician then helps the client distinguish constricting identity statements ("I'm no longer someone who matters") from opening responsibility statements ("Given what matters to me, what is the next small act that fits my strength today?").

Because transitions often come with depleted energy and heightened uncertainty, the size of commitments matters. Meaning-oriented work becomes clinically effective when it yields actions that are small enough to be feasible and significant enough to feel worth doing. A practical structure is to co-design a set of "micro-commitments" anchored in a chosen value—actions that can be completed even on low-capacity days, and that restore agency through repetition. For example: a five-minute contribution to a project that expresses responsibility; a short mentoring text that expresses generativity; one brave phone call that expresses fidelity to relationship; a brief walk that expresses stewardship of the body; a scheduled moment of beauty or prayer that expresses experiential meaning. Progress review then tracks two curves: symptoms (stress, anxiety, sadness) and meaning indicators (agency, connection, coherence, dignity). When clients see that symptom relief and meaning enactment do not always move in parallel week-to-week, persistence often becomes easier and self-judgment softens.

Transitions also require respectful attention to what cannot be controlled. Here logotherapy's attitudinal route becomes central, not as forced acceptance, but as the cultivation of a freely chosen way of meeting what is irreversible. Instead of "stance phrases," many clinicians find it more natural to work with brief inner commitments—compact statements that articulate dignity under constraint (e.g., "This hurts, and it is real; I will meet it with steadiness," "I cannot undo the loss; I can still live with integrity," "Fear is here; so is my responsibility"). In later-life transitions, this can integrate well with evidence-based meaning-oriented approaches such as life review (Butler, 1963) and dignity-based interventions that invite legacy themes, values, and relational messages (Chochinov et al., 2011). Finally, brief measures can help clarify which facet of meaning the transition is disrupting most—purpose, coherence, or mattering—and whether the client is primarily struggling with diminished meaning or with an intensified search. Qualitative assessment questions can guide formulation and planning, such as: "What feels threatened right now?" "What still feels sacred?" "Who needs you?" and "What would make the next month meaningful—realistically, given your current capacity?"

In sum, a logotherapeutic approach to life transitions treats transition as an encounter with uncertainty, finitude, and responsibility, while systematically helping clients restore orientation to values, rebuild continuity of identity, and translate meaning into feasible commitments. When this process is supported patiently—emotionally, socially, and behaviorally—clients often report that the transition becomes not only survivable, but also a period in which a more intentional life can begin to take shape, even if ambiguity remains.

3.2 Special applications

63 Group logotherapy

Logotherapy has developed not only as an individual approach but also as a robust framework for group psychotherapy, situated within the broader existential tradition (Frankl, 1988; Lukas, 1998). Existential group work typically pursues three aims: cultivating authenticity and honesty toward oneself, broadening perspectives on self and world, and identifying what gives life meaning in the present and future, within a group context that also draws on general therapeutic factors such as interpersonal learning, cohesion, and existential reflection (Schneider et al., 2015; Yalom & Leszcz, 2020). Logotherapy-based groups deepen these aims by placing meaning at the center of exploration and change, emphasizing freedom, responsibility, and self-transcendence as live possibilities in the here-and-now of the group encounter (Fabry, 1994; Frankl, 1988).

Meaning-centered and logotherapy-informed group formats have been applied across diverse clinical and developmental contexts, suggesting that both short psychoeducational formats and longer-term therapeutic groups may be useful when adapted to participants' needs and life circumstances (Lukas, 1998; Schulenberg et al., 2008). The general goals are twofold: (a) to expand participants' phenomenological field so they can recognize alternative interpretations that re-open engagement with life, and (b) to identify and reflect concrete pathways of meaning that express uniqueness, resources, strengths, and values (Fabry, 1994; Frankl, 1988).

Core processes and techniques

Group logotherapy employs distinctive methods. Facilitators and members attend to "logo-hooks"—recurring themes, metaphors, memories, shifts in tone, or emotional intensities that signal what is meaningful for a participant—and use them as anchors for further exploration (Fabry, 1994; Lukas, 1998). Socratic dialogue by both leader and peers fosters self-discovery, value clarification, motivation for change, recognition of freedom and responsibility, and articulation of meaningful goals (Frankl, 1988; Yalom & Leszcz, 2020). The group climate prioritizes trust and intimacy so members can carefully remove their "masks," sharing only what they choose, while orienting toward valued goals rather than merely gratifying immediate needs (Schneider et al., 2015; Yalom & Leszcz, 2020). Because logotherapy does not prescribe meanings but assumes that meaning is discoverable under all conditions, the group proceeds step-by-step to search for the meaning latent in each moment; the aim is authenticity, not conformity (Frankl, 1988; Lukas, 1998). Consistent with Fabry's stance, the facilitator serves less as a "healer" and more as a model of meaning-seeking, resonating with participants' stories and expanding their repertoire of value-based perspectives and coping options (Fabry, 1994).

Freedom, choice, and narrative integration

Group work highlights a core of freedom that remains even under physical, psychological, or social constraints; exercises often invite members to list choices still available in an adverse situation and to rehearse these choices via role-play or guided imagery (Frankl, 1988; Lukas, 1998). The past is reframed not only as a source of regret but also as a treasury of achievements and hard-won strengths that can ground responsibility in the present (Fabry, 1994). Groups also counter the sense of interchangeability common in existential emptiness by surfacing unique strengths and moments of contribution in relationships or creative activity (Schneider et al., 2015). Finally, the group underscores self-transcendence—living within the "healthy tension" between one's current reality and one's ideals—thus mobilizing growth, responsibility, and contribution (Frankl, 1988).

Group processes add therapeutic factors that amplify meaning work: universality, altruism, interpersonal learning, and existential learning nurture shared meaning construction and reduce isolation (Yalom & Leszcz, 2020). Contemporary meaning-centered group protocols informed by Wong's Meaning Management Theory systematically address purpose, understanding, responsible action, and enjoyment, showing gains in well-being and resilience across varied populations (Wong, 2016; see also Wong, 2023). Randomized and controlled studies of meaning-centered interventions report reductions in psychological distress, including depression, hopelessness, and desire for hastened death, alongside improvements in quality of life, spiritual well-being, and meaning-related outcomes (Breitbart et al., 2018; Vos et al., 2015). Evidence from clinical and community settings further suggests relevance for coping with physical symptoms and addictions, although the empirical base for these specific applications is less robust than the evidence in oncology and palliative-care settings supports meaning-focused groups for enhancing quality of life and coping with physical symptoms and addictions (Holmes, 1991; Henrion, 2002; Schulenberg et al., 2008; Vos et al., 2015).

Practical structure for group logotherapy

1 *Orientation and norms:* Clarify that neither leader nor peers can "prescribe" meaning; the group can only open gateways to discover it. Responsibility and choice remain with each participant (Frankl, 1988; Lukas, 1998).
2 *Logo-hook work*: Track metaphors, affect surges, and recurrent themes; use Socratic questioning to translate these signals into values, goals, and actionable experiments (Fabry, 1994; Yalom & Leszcz, 2020).
3 *Three pathways practice:* Design weekly acts across creative (contribution), experiential (relationships, art, nature), and attitudinal values (chosen stance toward constraints), with peer accountability (Frankl, 1988).
4 *Dereflection groups:* Shift focus from symptoms and ruminations to constructive, value-consistent activities that broaden perspective, loosen symptom centrality, and build courage and hope (Lukas, 1998).
5 *Choice lists and role rehearsal:* Generate menus of feasible choices in difficult contexts; rehearse them through role-play/guided imagery to strengthen agency and commitment (Frankl, 1988; Fabry, 1994).
6 *Integration and legacy:* Close each cycle by articulating how discovered meanings will be enacted beyond the group—in family, work, and community roles (Schneider et al., 2015).

In sum, group logotherapy leverages the unique forces of the group—universality, altruism, and shared inquiry—to widen the field of meaning, responsibility, and self-transcendence. It complements evidence-based group methods while preserving logotherapy's existential commitment to freedom and value realization under all conditions (Breitbart et al., 2018; Frankl, 1988; Yalom & Leszcz, 2020; Wong, 2016, 2023).

64 Family counselling and logotherapy

Families are not only systems of interaction but also systems of meaning, in which narratives, values, and responsibilities organize everyday life. Contemporary family science underscores that shared belief systems, rituals, and purposes are central to resilience, particularly in times of stress or crisis (Walsh, 2016). Systemic theories point to the way symptoms are embedded in interaction cycles and how change emerges when the system reorganizes its boundaries, alliances, and roles (Bowen, 1978; Minuchin, 1974). A logotherapeutic perspective adds an existential dimension: families do not merely regulate behavior, they transmit, negotiate, and enact meaning through creative contributions, experiential encounters, and attitudinal stances. Freedom and responsibility, in Frankl's terms, are thus practiced not in isolation but in the relational field (Frankl, 1988; Lukas, 1998).

From this standpoint, recurring family challenges, such as caregiver burnout, adolescent conflict, bereavement, or migration stress, often reflect a constriction of the family's meaning repertoire. Communication narrows to symptom control while the values and purposes that animate life recede into the background. Logotherapy reframes counseling aims: not only to alleviate distress but also to re-open access to what matters most, so that members can choose value-congruent responses under constraint (Frankl, 1988; Fabry, 1994). In practice, this means tracking "logo-hooks" in dialogue—emotional peaks, recurring metaphors, remembered moments—and using Socratic questioning to help families articulate what they stand for together, thereby re-orienting even difficult routines around purpose (Yalom & Leszcz, 2020).

Evidence increasingly supports these meaning-centered processes as clinically potent. A randomized trial with mothers of children with autism spectrum disorder demonstrated that group logotherapy significantly enhanced meaning in life, suggesting that existential reframing can help parents re-experience caregiving as a context for responsibility, love, and perseverance (Mihandoust et al., 2021). An online intervention for Chinese family caregivers of older adults with dementia reduced caregiver burden and increased hope, suggesting that even remote, group-based logotherapy can strengthen existential resilience under chronic strain (Yang et al., 2024). A systematic review of logotherapy and meaning-centered therapy among women with breast and gynecological cancer found reductions in depressive symptoms, anxiety, post-traumatic stress, and hopelessness, alongside improvements in meaning in life, quality of life, physical symptom perception, post-traumatic growth, and spiritual well-being (Aiello-Puchol et al., 2025). Likewise, a pilot study with older adults demonstrated that structured group logotherapy improved mental well-being and life satisfaction during late-life transitions (Humer et al., 2025). These findings converge with broader meta-analytic evidence showing that existential and meaning-centered interventions enhance resilience, coping, and life satisfaction across diverse contexts, including serious illness and family stress (Vos et al., 2015; Schulenberg & Yarbrough, 2021).

Several practice-oriented implications follow from this evidence. First, structured meaning-centered group and family processes, whether in-person or online, reduce isolation and normalize existential struggles, making them particularly suitable for families facing chronic illness, disability, or loss. Second, emphasizing the three pathways to meaning (creative, experiential, attitudinal) allows families to transform burdens into contributions, rituals of connection, and chosen stances toward what cannot be changed (Frankl, 1988). Third, peer dialogue and shared exploration of values are powerful antidotes to alienation; when family members collectively articulate and enact their "for-the-sake-of" commitments, daily routines regain significance. For example, caregiving tasks can be reframed as acts of fidelity to presence rather than mere symptom management; mealtimes can become rituals of connection rather than arenas of conflict; anniversaries of loss can be met with stance sentences—brief, shared reminders of dignity or gratitude—rather than avoidance or despair. Finally, choice lists and role rehearsals drawn from group logotherapy can be adapted for families: members generate possible choices in high-risk situations, support one another in selecting responsibility-bearing actions, and rehearse these choices through guided imagery or role-play (Lukas, 1998).

Overall, family counseling informed by logotherapy integrates systemic awareness of interactional patterns with existential commitment to meaning, freedom, and responsibility. By reconnecting families to shared values and by translating those values into concrete rituals and attitudes, symptoms lose their centrality not through denial but because life is reoriented toward purpose. Empirical evidence suggests that such approaches not only alleviate distress but also build resilience, restore dignity, and strengthen the family's capacity to live authentically, even under profound constraint. A meaning-centered family formulation maps four layers: functions of the symptom (what pain it organizes, what conflict it distracts from); values eclipsed by current cycles (e.g., loyalty, fairness, generativity, play); distribution of responsibility and freedom (where choices still exist, despite limits); contexts and constraints (illness, economic stress, cultural narratives) that shape enactment.

This yields a concise *for-the-sake-of* statement the family can endorse (e.g., "We manage diabetes in service of preserving presence, not fear; meals are for connection, not conflict").

Core methods adapted to families

- *Logo-hooks in dialogue:* Track recurring metaphors, remembered scenes, changes in tone, and peak affects that signal meaning ("When you say 'we used to sing on Fridays,' your voice softens"). These cues anchor exploration of values and losses (Fabry, 1994).
- *Socratic dialogue across members:* Questions elicit personal and shared values, reveal zones of choice, and surface responsibilities each member is willing to assume ("What would it look like to carry your part of courage this week?") (Frankl, 1988).
- *Dereflection as a family task:* When the system is absorbed by symptoms (checking, monitoring, ruminating), sessions redirect attention toward joint, value-consistent action (micro-rituals of care, service to others, shared play) to loosen symptom-centered gravity (Lukas, 1998).

- *Attitude modulation in caregiving:* Where suffering is unavoidable (advanced illness, grief), families practice a chosen stance—dignity, fidelity, humor—articulated as brief "stance sentences" for difficult moments ("We speak gently even when afraid").
- *Paradoxical intention, judiciously:* For anticipatory performance anxieties (first family gathering after loss; returning to school), playful permission to tremble/falter reduces hyperintention without trivializing pain (Frankl, 1988).
- *Three pathways as a family framework:*
    - Creative values: specific contributions each member will make for the whole (meal roles, logistics, care rotations).
    - Experiential values: scheduled moments of connection/beauty independent of the problem (music, nature, faith rituals).
    - Attitudinal values: commitments about "how we suffer together" (courtesy under stress, truth-telling with kindness).

In sum, Family counseling informed by logotherapy keeps the systemic focus on patterns while restoring the family's freedom to choose in service of shared values. When families reconnect daily tasks and difficult moments to creative, experiential, and attitudinal meanings, symptoms lose centrality, roles become fairer and more humane, and the home recovers its orientation as a place of responsibility, courage, and love.

65 Organizational applications

Organizations are not only systems of coordination and control; they are meaning-making environments in which people continually interpret why their work matters, how it connects to valued ends, and whether their effort is recognized as significant. Contemporary research converges on meaning as a multi-faceted experience that includes coherence/understanding ("my work makes sense"), purpose ("it serves valued goals"), and significance/mattering ("it is worthwhile and noticed") (George & Park, 2016; Martela & Steger, 2016). These facets are not merely "nice to have": a meta-analysis shows meaningful work relates strongly to work engagement, commitment, and job satisfaction, and—indirectly—to performance and reduced withdrawal intentions (Allan et al., 2019). A logotherapeutic lens adds two distinctive emphases. First, it frames meaning at work as an ethical-existential stance rooted in freedom and responsibility: even under real constraints, people can choose how to respond, what values to enact, and how to remain oriented toward contribution beyond the self (Frankl, 1988). Second, it treats self-transcendence as a practical organizational principle: meaning increases when work is connected to service, care, excellence, and accountability—not only to personal advancement.

Meaning as a resource in organizational life

Meaning can be usefully conceptualized as a psychological resource in organizations. Within Conservation of Resources theory, resources are things people strive to obtain, protect, and invest; stress intensifies when resources are threatened or lost, and resource loss can accelerate "spirals" of depletion (Hobfoll, 1989; Hobfoll et al., 2018). In this framing, meaning operates like a meta-resource: it supports sustained effort, buffers ambiguity and strain, and facilitates resource gain (e.g., social support, efficacy, vitality) when organizations create conditions in which meaning can accumulate and spread (Chen et al., 2015). Importantly, a meaning-centered approach must avoid becoming "meaning pressure" or organizational rhetoric used to compensate for poor conditions. The meaningful-work literature distinguishes authentic meaning-making from the *management of meaning* (i.e., manipulating purpose narratives while ignoring structural realities) (Lips-Wiersma & Morris, 2009). A logotherapeutic stance is explicit here: responsibility applies at both levels—individual freedom within constraint **and** organizational responsibility to provide decent, fair, and sustainable work conditions (Blustein et al., 2023).

Two complementary routes to cultivating meaning are especially practical and evidence-informed:

1 *Employee-driven job crafting*: adjusting tasks, relationships, and cognitive framing helps align daily work with strengths, values, and contribution (Wrzesniewski & Dutton, 2001). Job-crafting interventions show reliable positive effects on job crafting behaviors and typically small-to-moderate benefits for engagement and performance (Oprea et al., 2019).
2 *Meaning-mediating leadership (sensegiving)*: clarifies how everyday effort connects to shared purpose and human impact. A classic organizational example shows how leaders can increase experienced meaningfulness by translating abstract aspirations into concrete, shared objectives and milestones (Carton, 2018). This pathway aligns with evidence linking transformational leadership to perceived meaningfulness and well-being at work (Arnold et al., 2007).

Practice: meaning-centered organizational design

The practical task is not to design conditions in which employees can (a) understand what they do, (b) connect it to valued ends, and (c) experience mattering, while ensuring that meaning language is never used to mask overload, role drift, or unfairness. In logotherapeutic terms, organizations are called to scaffold freedom-within-constraint: supporting responsible choice at the individual level and ethical stewardship at the system level.

1 Diagnose meaning "channels" before prescribing solutions: Start with a brief meaning audit that combines validated measurement with targeted qualitative prompts. The Work and Meaning Inventory (WAMI) provides a practical baseline for tracking meaningful work across cycles (Steger et al., 2012). Pair it with three prompts aligned to coherence–purpose–significance, so the diagnosis immediately points to design levers: **Coherence:** "What about your work makes sense—and what feels disconnected or pointless?" **Purpose:** "Who benefits when your work goes well?" **Mattering:** "When do you feel noticed/needed/valued here—and when do you feel invisible?" This step prevents generic "purpose initiatives" and

clarifies *where* meaning is leaking (e.g., unclear contribution chains, weak recognition systems, or misaligned demands).

2 Convert diagnosis into agency: job-crafting cycles anchored in "for-the-sake-of": Next, translate findings into short job-crafting cycles where employees run micro-experiments in three domains—task, relational, and cognitive crafting—each explicitly anchored in a chosen value. For example, "for the sake of service/excellence/care/fairness, I will change one small thing in how I do X this week," "for the sake of contribution, I will strengthen one relationship that improves impact," "for the sake of responsibility, I will reframe one routine task by linking it to who benefits." Logotherapeutically, the anchor is not "what do I want?" but "what is asked of me here, and what is my responsible response?" (Frankl, 1988). Evidence supports job-crafting interventions as scalable methods for increasing engagement and performance-relevant outcomes (Oprea et al., 2019).

3 Strengthen meaningfulness by routinizing sensegiving: Job crafting strengthens employee agency from the ground up, while leadership provides the shared coherence that helps those efforts add up to a clear collective direction. Meaning becomes durable when leaders repeatedly translate strategy into human stakes and make the link between daily tasks and shared purpose visible in everyday rituals, such as short "impact stories" in team meetings (customer/patient/student outcomes), milestone maps ("where we are in the mission"), or explicit linking statements ("this report protects X / enables Y / reduces risk for Z"). Carton (2018) shows that sensegiving increases perceived meaningfulness precisely when it is concrete, shared, and repeated, rather than vague, episodic, or purely inspirational.

4 Build mattering as infrastructure: recognition, voice, and inclusion: If coherence and purpose answer "why," mattering answers "do I count here?" Mattering is built through predictable practices that make being "noticed/needed/valued" a reliable experience (George & Park, 2016), such as recognition tied to values enacted (not only outcomes), structured channels for voice that close the loop, or relational inclusion (peer

appreciation, mentoring, onboarding bonds). Without mattering, meaning erodes quickly, ven in high-purpose organizations, because the interpersonal substrate of significance is missing.

5 Protect the structural conditions that keep meaning ethical and sustainable: Meaning initiatives fail when employees experience them as compensation for poor design. Align meaning work with core levers of sustainable motivation and decent work: autonomy where possible, task significance, feedback that supports learning, and reasonable demands with fairness. When redesign is limited, logotherapy remains especially useful: it supports attitudinal values (dignity, courage, patience, integrity) and protects spaces for responsible choice. Yet this must be paired with organizational responsibility for conditions in which meaning can be lived without exploitation (Blustein et al., 2023; Hobfoll et al., 2018).

6 Crisis-ready meaning practices: prevent loss, then rebuild resources: During reorgs, overload, or ethical strain, prioritize loss prevention first: reduce ambiguity that severs task–mission links, clarify roles, stabilize communication. Then rebuild resources through visible micro-wins, peer support, and "return-to-purpose" check-ins that ask: "What is the most responsible, value-consistent next step—given reality?" This keeps meaning from becoming either denial ("be positive") or collapse ("nothing matters") and helps teams maintain agency under constraint.

Taken together, these practices operationalize a logotherapeutic approach at scale: diagnose how meaning is constructed (or eroded), expand employee agency through value-anchored crafting, stabilize coherence through sensegiving, embed significance through mattering, and protect ethics through fair and sustainable conditions, especially under crisis. In such intersection of design, relationships, and responsible choice, meaning becomes a cultivable organizational resource and an ethical commitment, not a rhetorical overlay (Allan et al., 2019; Hobfoll et al., 2018; Lips-Wiersma & Morris, 2009).

66 Educational settings

Educational settings have long been understood not only as sites for the transmission of knowledge, but also as formative spaces for cultivating values, identity, and purpose. Sydney J. Harris's observation that "the whole purpose of education is to turn mirrors into windows" captures this broader educational vision: education is not meant merely to reflect the self back to itself, but to open students toward wider horizons of meaning, responsibility, and possibility. Yet this vision stands in persistent tension with the dominant logic of contemporary schooling, which increasingly organizes itself around measurable outcomes, standardized assessments, and competitive achievement (Biesta, 2010). In systems structured around high-stakes testing and performance accountability, the inner life of students—their existential questions, their developing sense of self, and their search for meaning—is frequently displaced by the imperative to produce quantifiable results (Noddings, 2003). The cost of this displacement is not merely motivational but existential: as Frankl (1959, 2006) argued, when human beings are deprived not of resources but of meaning, the result is an *existential vacuum*—a pervasive experience of inner emptiness and purposelessness that cannot be addressed through achievement or positive affect alone. Empirical trends lend urgency to this concern: across contemporary societies, rates of depression, anxiety, loneliness, and disengagement among young people have risen markedly over recent decades (Twenge, 2017; OECD, 2023), pointing toward what may be understood as a collective meaning crisis that no amount of curricular innovation or well-being programming has yet adequately addressed.

In today's volatile, uncertain, complex, and ambiguous (VUCA) world, this role of education as a compass for meaning becomes even more urgent (Russo-Netzer, 2023). While positive education initiatives have rightly emphasized the importance of well-being alongside achievement (Seligman et al., 2009; White & Kern, 2018), critics have cautioned that some happiness- and well-being-oriented educational practices may risk narrowing education to techniques of emotional self-management unless they are embedded within broader ethical, relational, and meaning-oriented aims

(Reveley, 2015). This critique points to a deeper conceptual issue: the conflation of meaning with well-being, or the treatment of meaning as a mere correlate of positive emotion, risks obscuring the distinctive character of the meaning-seeking drive. As Frankl (1959) insisted, and as subsequent empirical research has confirmed, meaning and happiness are related but fundamentally distinct constructs (Baumeister et al., 2013; Steger, 2012). One may endure suffering and still find life deeply meaningful; conversely, one may report positive affect while remaining existentially adrift. Schools that focus exclusively on fostering pleasant emotional states may inadvertently cultivate what Frankl termed "the existential vacuum in disguise"—a superficially adjusted but internally purposeless orientation toward life. Logotherapy's foundational premise—that the search for meaning is a primary human motivation (Frankl, 1959)—offers an important corrective lens: education should aim not only to enhance students' well-being, but also to nurture an authentic inner compass that enables them to act in accordance with values and commitments that transcend immediate gratification (Russo-Netzer & Shoshani, 2020). From this perspective, schools are not merely sites of socialization or skill acquisition but *meaning-making ecosystems*—environments in which students are invited to encounter, explore, and respond to life's fundamental questions with growing depth, courage, and agency.

Recent conceptualizations of meaning in life emphasize three interrelated dimensions—coherence, purpose, and significance (George & Park, 2016; Martela & Steger, 2016). These dimensions are especially relevant for children and adolescents, who are in the midst of identity formation and value exploration (Damon, 2008; Erikson, 1968), and they map onto distinct developmental tasks across different stages of schooling. *Coherence*—the sense that one's life makes sense and follows an intelligible order—is particularly salient in early adolescence, a period marked by rapid cognitive, emotional, and social change that can disrupt previously taken-for-granted assumptions about the self and the world (Habermas & Bluck, 2000). When adolescents struggle to develop narrative coherence—the capacity to integrate past experiences, present commitments, and future aspirations into a more stable personal story—they may be more vulnerable to identity confusion and difficulties in sustaining a coherent sense of direction (McLean & Pasupathi, 2012). *Purpose*, the second dimension, refers to a stable and far-reaching intention to accomplish something that is both personally meaningful and of consequence to the world beyond the self (Damon, 2008). Unlike coherence, which is primarily retrospective and integrative, purpose is prospective and motivationally generative: it orients the individual toward the future and sustains effort in the face of obstacles. *Significance*—the sense that one's life matters and that one's existence is of value to others—has received growing empirical attention as a crucial buffer against feelings of marginalization, invisibility, and social exclusion that are particularly prevalent in school contexts (Flett, 2018). Importantly, these three dimensions develop along different timelines and require different educational conditions to flourish: coherence can be supported through narrative-based reflection from early childhood; purpose becomes developmentally accessible in mid-to-late adolescence; significance, by contrast, is relational in nature and dependent on environments that consistently affirm each student's inherent worth (Bronk, 2014; Damon, 2008).

Empirical studies show that meaning in life is associated with greater life satisfaction, resilience, and lower levels of maladaptive symptoms among youth (Brassai et al., 2012; Shoshani & Russo-Netzer, 2017). For example, having an authentic inner compass predicts adolescents' ability to pursue activities that enhance well-being and reduce behavioral difficulties (Russo-Netzer & Shoshani, 2020). Notably, these findings hold across diverse cultural and socioeconomic contexts, suggesting that the human need for meaning is not a privilege of advantaged populations but a universal developmental imperative (Steger et al., 2008b). Complementary insights from self-determination theory (Deci & Ryan, 2000; Ryan & Deci, 2017) reinforce these conclusions: the satisfaction of basic psychological needs for autonomy, competence, and relatedness within educational environments creates conditions that are conducive not only to intrinsic motivation but also to the emergence of meaningful engagement. Logotherapy and self-determination theory converge in their shared emphasis on the primacy of inner experience, value-driven behavior, and the necessity of supportive interpersonal conditions for human flourishing. Where self-determination theory highlights the motivational architecture underlying purposeful action, logotherapy adds an irreducibly existential layer: the insistence that students must ultimately discover meaning for themselves, and that no external incentive system can substitute for this first-person encounter with life's demands. Together, these frameworks suggest that the cultivation of meaning is not a supplementary concern for schools but a foundational one—a prerequisite for the kind of deep engagement, ethical development, and psychological resilience that education at its best is meant to foster. Such findings underscore the protective role of meaning as a buffer against existential emptiness, alienation, and risk-taking behaviors that often emerge during the school years (Reber, 2019).

Practical applications of logotherapy in educational settings may be structured around Frankl's three pathways to meaning—creative, experiential, and attitudinal (Frankl, 1959)—together with contemporary models of meaningful education. Interventions such as the 'Meaning Detectives Program' encourage students to identify meaning potentials in everyday experience through narrative, creative projects, and reflective journaling (Russo-Netzer, 2022). Similarly, activities that integrate purpose exploration (Bronk, 2011), classroom adaptations of job-crafting approaches (Wrzesniewski et al., 2013), and practices that enhance mattering (Flett, 2018) can strengthen students' sense of significance and agency. Empirical evidence further suggests that cultivating purpose in adolescence supports resilience, motivation, and academic persistence (Burrow & Hill, 2011; Damon, 2008), while interventions that focus explicitly on meaning can increase life satisfaction and reduce psychological distress (Steger et al., 2021).

From a logotherapeutic perspective, educators can act as facilitators of meaning rather than transmitters of knowledge. This involves guiding students to discern values expressed through challenges, encouraging self-transcendent commitments, and modeling attitudinal strength when circumstances cannot be changed. Practically, this may be done by integrating reflective exercises into curricula (e.g., life review, meaning portfolios), fostering social responsibility through service learning, and creating classroom rituals that affirm students' contributions and mattering within the community. In doing so, schools not only transmit knowledge but also fulfill their role as meaning-making ecosystems that prepare young people for both personal flourishing and responsible participation in society (Russo-Netzer, 2023; Steger et al., 2021).

67 Children

Across childhood, meaning functions as a developmental resource that organizes motivation, emotion, and behavior—not only a late adolescent or adult achievement. Contemporary models parse meaning into coherence/understanding ("my life makes sense"), purpose/goal-directedness, and significance/mattering; these facets scaffold self-regulation, resilience, and prosociality as children negotiate normative challenges (Martela & Steger, 2016; George & Park, 2016). A logotherapeutic lens complements this literature by framing children as *active discoverers* of meaning through Frankl's three pathways—creative (what I give), experiential (what I receive), and attitudinal (the stance I choose toward limits)—thereby locating freedom and responsibility within age-appropriate choices and relationships (Frankl, 1959).

Empirical work now substantiates the presence and importance of meaning in middle childhood. The Meaning in Life in Children Questionnaire (MIL-CQ), explicitly grounded in Frankl's "meaning triangle," demonstrated a robust three-factor structure (creative, experiential, attitudinal) in large samples of 9–12-year-olds, with good internal consistency and confirmatory fit indices (Shoshani & Russo-Netzer, 2017). Children's total meaning scores correlated positively with life satisfaction and positive affect and negatively with behavioral/emotional difficulties, indicating that meaning already operates as a protective factor at this stage (Shoshani & Russo-Netzer, 2017). Notably, the MIL-CQ operationalizes each pathway in concrete, child-friendly terms (e.g., helping others; savoring nature/relationships; adopting a constructive stance when things cannot be changed), enabling both assessment and intervention mapping in schools and clinics.

Developmentally, meaning processes align with shifting capacities. In late childhood, concrete operational thought and expanding social worlds make creative and experiential pathways especially tractable (e.g., contributions at home/school; friendships, play, nature), while attitudinal work can be coached through simple scripts ("I can't change X, but I can choose how to respond") (Piaget, 1952; Frankl, 1959). Purpose formation—linking valued ends to daily actions—emerges gradually and predicts well-being and adjustment (Damon, 2008; Burrow & Hill, 2011). Findings that children with higher meaning show fewer socio-emotional problems and greater prosocial behavior support positioning meaning as a *foundational competence* akin to emotion regulation or executive functions (Shoshani & Russo-Netzer, 2017).

Developmentally tailored, meaning-centered interventions

1 Meaning mapping with Frankl's three pathways. Use brief, concrete prompts to elicit one weekly act for each pathway: *creative* (a helpful deed or skill practice), *experiential* (notice/enjoy a moment of beauty, kindness, or learning), and *attitudinal* (choose a stance when a small frustration occurs). Tie each act to a "for-the-sake-of" statement (e.g., "I help at cleanup to be a good teammate"). This structure mirrors the MIL-CQ domains and targets mechanisms linked to well-being in children (Frankl, 1959; Shoshani & Russo-Netzer, 2017).
2 "Meaning detectives" routines in classrooms. Adapt evidence-informed programs that invite students to identify "meaning cues" in stories, science, nature, and peer interactions (e.g., What value is shown? Who benefits? How could *I* enact this value today?). Such routines can cultivate coherence (sense-making), purpose (goal setting), and mattering (feeling noticed/needed), which predict better academic persistence and emotional health (Martela & Steger, 2016; Steger, 2012; Brassai, Piko, & Steger, 2012).
3 Micro-practices for attitudinal strength. Teach brief stance sentences for common challenges ("I can breathe and try again," "I ask for help and keep going"), rehearsed during calm moments and cued by teachers/parents during stress.

This operationalizes the attitudinal pathway at a child's level and aligns with data linking meaning to fewer difficulties and greater positive affect (Frankl, 1959; Shoshani & Russo-Netzer, 2017).

4 Family–school partnerships around mattering and contribution. Establish simple "contribution contracts" (one weekly helpful action at home/school) and "mattering mirrors" (peers or caregivers name a concrete way the child made a difference). These practices reinforce significance and prosocial meaning, which co-vary with the MIL-CQ creative/experiential pathways and prosocial behavior (George & Park, 2016; Shoshani & Russo-Netzer, 2017).
5 Assessment and feedback loops. Where feasible, use brief meaning check-ins (e.g., three items aligned to creative/experiential/attitudinal pathways) or the full MIL-CQ for program evaluation, tracking gains alongside life satisfaction and behavior referrals. The MIL-CQ's age-appropriate phrasing and three-factor structure make it suitable for both screening and outcome monitoring (Shoshani & Russo-Netzer, 2017).

In sum, meaning-centered work with children should be developmentally grounded, relationally embedded, and culturally responsive. For younger children, meaning is best accessed through the concrete and the visible: visual anchors for the pathways to meaning (e.g., cards/icons), short stories and examples, role-play, and immediate opportunities to practice values in everyday moments (helping, sharing, persevering, noticing beauty). As children grow older, they can increasingly connect values to longer-horizon goals, sustained effort, and simple forms of contribution such as classroom responsibilities or age-appropriate community service (Damon, 2008; Steger, 2012). Because children's meaning is largely co-constructed in relationships, teachers and caregivers function less as "providers" of meaning and more as facilitators who help children *name what matters*, notice when they are already living it, and practice attitudinal freedom under constraint—showing, in child-friendly language, that we cannot always choose what happens, but we can often choose how we respond (Frankl, 1959). Finally, given evidence that meaning is associated with fewer emotional and behavioral difficulties even in the context of adversity, schools serving high-stress communities may prioritize attitudinal and experiential pathways—belonging, care, predictable connection, and moments of beauty—as daily buffers, while also inviting small creative contributions that foster competence and agency (Brassai et al., 2012; Shoshani & Russo-Netzer, 2017).

68 Adolescence

Adolescence is a pivotal period for identity consolidation in which young people experiment with values, goals, and social affiliations while negotiating rising autonomy and complex choice (Erikson, 1968; Steinberg & Morris, 2001). Contemporary meaning research parses meaning into three interlocking facets—coherence/understanding, purpose, and significance/mattering—that scaffold regulation, resilience, and prosociality across this stage (George & Park, 2016; Martela & Steger, 2016). A logotherapeutic lens complements these accounts by positioning adolescents not as passive recipients of meaning but as *active discoverers* who realize meaning through Frankl's three pathways: creative ("what I give"), experiential ("what I receive in love, beauty, learning"), and attitudinal ("the stance I choose toward limits") (Frankl, 1959). Developmentally, increasing cognitive flexibility and social perspective-taking enable adolescents to link abstract values to concrete choices, so that "who I want to be" can begin to organize "what I do next" (Damon, 2008).

Emerging evidence specifies mechanisms by which meaning supports adolescent well-being. The construct of an authentic inner compass (AIC)—a felt set of self-endorsed values, aspirations, interests, and goals that guide choices—predicts higher prioritization of meaning and positivity in daily life, which in turn relates to greater life satisfaction and fewer emotional/behavioral difficulties; structural equation models indicate both direct and indirect (mediated) pathways from AIC to subjective well-being (Russo-Netzer & Shoshani, 2020). These findings situate meaning not only as an outcome of identity work but as a *process resource* that channels attention and effort toward valued activities amid the volatility and choice overload characteristic of modern adolescence. Practically, cultivating AIC appears to buffer against rumination, deviant peer influence, and symptom burden by strengthening self-congruent decision-making and providing a stable reference point for action.

Logotherapy's emphasis on freedom and responsibility dovetails with this evidence: adolescents can rarely control context, but they can choose value-congruent responses within it. Purpose exploration and self-transcendent commitments (e.g., contributing to others) are associated with better adjustment and persistence, suggesting that meaning processes function as a developmental "organizer" of identity capital (Bronk, 2011; Burrow & Hill, 2011). At the same time, hedonic and eudaimonic orientations need not compete; prioritizing everyday positivity alongside meaning is linked to broader attentional scope and resource building, consistent with broaden-and-build dynamics (Fredrickson, 1998, 2001), and is observed empirically in the AIC pathways to well-being (Russo-Netzer & Shoshani, 2020).

Evidence-informed applications for adolescents

1 AIC-oriented formulation and micro-commitments. Begin by eliciting each adolescent's "for-the-sake-of" statement (two lines that name a value and its real-world beneficiary). Use *logo-hooks*—recurring metaphors, peak affects, remembered scenes—to surface implicit values, then translate them into one *creative*, one *experiential*, and one *attitudinal* weekly act (e.g., tutor a peer; savor time in nature with attention; use a stance sentence during setbacks). Link these acts to daily choice points to operationalize AIC into behavior (Frankl, 1959; Damon, 2008). Evidence that AIC strengthens prioritization of meaning/positivity justifies this micro-design at the level of routines.

2 Classroom "meaning routines" and choice architecture. Schools can embed short, repeatable routines that help students notice, articulate, and enact meaning in everyday learning. These may include *meaning detectives*, where students identify the value expressed in a story, lesson, or news item and reflect on who benefits and how; *mattering mirrors*, where

peers acknowledge one concrete way a classmate contributed or made a difference; and *goal notebooks*, where students link academic tasks to personally meaningful values, goals and commitments. These practices target coherence, purpose, and significance, and echo findings that AIC promotes intentional selection of meaningful/positive contexts with downstream gains in well-being (Steger, 2012; Martela & Steger, 2016; Russo-Netzer & Shoshani, 2020).

3 Autonomy-supportive adults as "meaning facilitators." Parents/educators act less as providers of ready-made meaning and more as facilitators of inner guidance: offering rationales, acknowledging feelings, and inviting value-consistent choice within limits (Assor, 2018; Soenens et al., 2017). The AIC findings imply that such facilitation strengthens adolescents' capacity to *prioritize* meaning/positivity in daily life, thereby amplifying subjective well-being (Russo-Netzer & Shoshani, 2020).

4 Monitoring and feedback. Use brief, developmentally appropriate check-ins (e.g., three items indexing creative/experiential/attitudinal acts each week) to give feedback on meaning enactment; where feasible, embed validated measures of well-being and difficulties to track change over time (Shoshani & Russo-Netzer, 2017).

In sum, developmentally, adolescence is a prime window for meaning-centered work. Integrating logotherapy's three pathways with AIC-informed mechanisms offers a coherent approach: help adolescents *name* what they stand for, *prioritize* contexts that evoke meaning and positivity, and *practice* chosen stances under constraint. The result is not mere symptom reduction but the construction of identity around freely endorsed values with tangible benefits for well-being and behavior.

69 Adulthood

Adulthood is marked by expanding and shifting roles—work, partnership, caregiving, community life—through which people negotiate identity, responsibility, and time horizons. Contemporary models describe meaningful living as comprising coherence/understanding, purpose, and significance/mattering; these facets organize motivation and well-being across adult decades (George & Park, 2016; Martela & Steger, 2016). Narrative identity research further shows that adults sustain meaning by constructing life stories that integrate challenges into redemptive or growth-oriented sequences, thereby linking "who I strive to be" with daily choices (McAdams & McLean, 2013). Logotherapy complements these accounts by framing adults as *agents* who realize meaning through creative (what I contribute), experiential (what I receive in love, beauty, and relationship), and attitudinal pathways (the stance I choose toward what cannot be changed) (Frankl, 1959). Developmentally, Erikson's generativity—care for and commitment to the next generation—functions as a central channel for meaning, with midlife often amplifying the call to serve beyond the self (Erikson, 1982; McAdams & de St. Aubin, 1992; Bauer & McAdams, 2010). Empirically, purpose in life is not merely uplifting; it predicts healthier behaviors, lower morbidity, and longevity in adulthood and later life (Boyle et al., 2009; Musich et al., 2018).

Adulthood also brings meaning stressors: career plateaus or pivots, partnership strain, parenting and eldercare demands, illness, and socio-economic volatility. Park's meaning-making framework helps explain how adults respond—by assimilating adversity into existing beliefs or accommodating beliefs to fit new realities, with outcomes depending on whether global meaning (values/goals) is restored (Park, 2010). In work contexts, meaningful work—captured by understanding, purpose, and significance—is associated with higher engagement and performance (Steger, 2012; Allan et al., 2019). Midlife studies likewise show that maintaining control beliefs and role clarity supports well-being when responsibilities peak (Lachman, 2015). Across these domains, a logotherapeutic stance emphasizes *freedom within constraint*: adults cannot always alter conditions, but they can choose value-congruent responses that re-anchor identity and action (Frankl, 1959; Wong, 2016).

Evidence-informed applications

1 Meaning-centered case formulation for adult roles. Map (a) the functions of the problem behavior or distress (what pain it avoids or regulates), (b) the values eclipsed by current routines (e.g., fairness at work, tenderness in partnership, generativity in caregiving), and (c) remaining zones of choice. Translate this into a two-line "for-the-sake-of" statement to organize weekly actions across Frankl's three pathways (Frankl, 1959; Park, 2010).

2 Job crafting aligned with values and strengths. Facilitate small changes to tasks, relationships, and cognitive framing to connect work with personal purpose and beneficiaries (Wrzesniewski & Dutton, 2001). Meta-analytic evidence shows job-crafting interventions increase engagement and performance, especially when anchored in valued ends (Oprea et al., 2019; Allan et al., 2019). Pair each crafting step with an explicit value (e.g., reliability, service, learning) to embody the **creative** pathway (Steger, 2012).

3 Generativity practices for midlife. Design "micro-generativity" roles—mentoring, community teaching, legacy projects—that translate identity commitments into weekly contributions; such roles are linked to eudaimonic growth and redemptive narratives (Bauer & McAdams, 2010; McAdams & McLean, 2013).

4 Attitudinal strength for non-negotiables. When constraints are immovable (chronic illness, caregiving limits), coach brief stance sentences (e.g., "I cannot change X; I can meet it with steadiness in service of Y"), operationalizing the attitudinal pathway and protecting well-being when control is low (Frankl, 1959; Lachman, 2015).

5 Experiential anchors for mattering and belonging. Schedule rituals that affirm significance—gratitude rounds in teams or families, impact check-ins that name who benefited from one's effort—because perceived mattering sustains the significance facet of meaning and counters burnout (George & Park, 2016; Steger, 2012).

6 Narrative reframing and meaning-making. Use Socratic dialogue and written "turning point" exercises to reinterpret

setbacks as value-tests or growth chapters, fostering coherence and purpose consistent with meaning-making models and narrative identity research (Park, 2010; McAdams & McLean, 2013).

In sum, in adulthood, meaning functions as both organizer (aligning identity with roles and choices) and resource (buffering stress, fueling engagement, and guiding ethical commitment). Logotherapy operationalizes this by turning values into small, repeatable behaviors—creative, experiential, and attitudinal—that restore purpose across work, love, and care. When adults practice freedom within constraint in service of what matters, they do more than relieve symptoms; they build a life that coherently *means* (Allan et al., 2019; McAdams & McLean, 2013; Martela & Steger, 2016).

70 Aging and elderly care

Late adulthood is a period of intensified confrontation with finitude and change—losses of roles, health, and peers—yet it is also a stage with distinctive capacities for meaning, perspective, and generativity. Carl Jung's observation that "the afternoon of life is just as full of meaning as the morning; only its meaning and purpose are different" captures this developmental shift: Aging does not signify the disappearance of meaning, but its transformation. Developmental and gerontological models accordingly emphasize that well-being in later life depends not only on health and functional capacity, but also on purpose, coherence, and significance, together with resources such as social integration and self-acceptance (George & Park, 2016; Martela & Steger, 2016; Ryff, 1995). Socioemotional selectivity theory further suggests that as time horizons contract, motivational priorities shift toward emotionally meaningful goals and relationships (Carstensen et al., 1999). Logotherapy adds an explicitly existential frame to this understanding: even under narrowing circumstances, older adults can continue to realize meaning through creative pathways of contribution, experiential pathways of relationship and appreciation, and attitudinal pathways that involve the stance one takes toward the unavoidable (Frankl, 1959). In this sense, purpose in life is not merely comforting, but consequential, predicting healthier aging trajectories, including reduced morbidity and longer survival (Boyle et al., 2009).

Recent empirical evidence supports the central role of meaning-focused interventions in aging and elderly care. Randomized, comparative, and quasi-experimental studies suggest that logotherapy can strengthen psychological and spiritual resources in later life, with findings pointing to improvements in existentially relevant capacities such as vitality, spiritual self-esteem, and aspects of mental well-being. These effects may be especially pronounced among older adults entering intervention with greater distress or lower well-being (Abdollahzadeh et al., 2024; Humer et al., 2025). Beyond logotherapy specifically, large-scale observational data continue to link purpose in life with reduced morbidity, healthier behavior, and greater longevity (Musich et al., 2018). A systematic review of purpose in later life spanning 44 studies similarly found that purpose is multidimensional—encompassing meaningful goals, inner strength, social relationships and mattering, and spirituality or religiousness—and is consistently associated with social integration, health, and psychosocial resources (AshaRani et al., 2022). Taken together, these findings suggest that meaning-oriented interventions, whether explicitly grounded in logotherapy or aligned with its principles, can support resilience, vitality, and well-being in late adulthood. They also indicate that the strongest effects are likely to emerge when interventions are tailored to older adults' clinical and existential profiles rather than delivered as uniform programs across highly heterogeneous populations.

Qualitative evidence on older adults' lived experience converges with these principles. In-depth interviews highlight recurrent existential concerns, including heightened awareness of death, fear of losing control, and loneliness—alongside active strategies that sustain meaningful living, such as establishing structured routines, contributing to others through volunteering, cultivating belonging and community, savoring beauty and learning, and practicing moderated, accepting attitudes (Russo-Netzer & Littman-Ovadia, 2019). These accounts portray meaning not as an abstraction, but as the daily organization of life: having something to wake up for, experiencing connection that affirms mattering, and adopting a stance that dignifies limitation without surrendering personhood. Importantly, participants described routine and contribution as antidotes to "dead hours," depressive drift, and isolation.

In sum, a meaning-centered developmental view of aging integrates evidence that purpose and coherence protect health and well-being, the gerontological insight that aging well must be defined in relation to what matters to older adults themselves, and logotherapy's claim that freedom and responsibility persist in the capacity to choose one's response and to serve beyond the self (Frankl, 1959; Rowe & Kahn, 1997; Russo-Netzer & Littman-Ovadia, 2019). These principles carry direct implications for both clinical and community-based practice in aging and elderly care.

Meaning-centered care for older adults

1. *Build "meaning routines" that operationalize the three pathways.* Co-create a weekly plan with one *creative* act (e.g., micro-volunteering, legacy project), one *experiential* practice (nature, art, spiritual ritual, relationship time), and one *attitudinal* commitment (a brief stance sentence for pain, fatigue, or uncertainty). These micro-structures counter emptiness, reinforce mattering, and mirror strategies spontaneously used by older adults to sustain purpose and mood (Frankl, 1959; Russo-Netzer & Littman-Ovadia, 2019).
2. Reframe care plans around purpose and contribution. Whether managing multimorbidity or rehabilitation, pair each health task with a "for-the-sake-of" statement (e.g., "daily walk in service of being present for great-grandchildren"), and identify at least one role that expresses generativity (phone support to a peer, community reading hour). This aligns with evidence that contribution and belonging function as core resources in late adulthood (Ryff, 1995; Carstensen et al., 1999; Russo-Netzer & Littman-Ovadia, 2019).
3. Design belonging and mattering as clinical targets. Routinely assess loneliness and perceived usefulness; add "mattering prescriptions": peer circles, place-based communities (faith, culture, interests), and recognition rituals that name concrete

ways the person makes a difference. Qualitative data show community as a stabilizing *anchor* that buffers fear, widens perspective, and re-animates daily life (Russo-Netzer & Littman-Ovadia, 2019).

4 Support attitudinal values. When change is no longer possible, later-life logotherapy places special emphasis on attitudinal values—the freedom to choose one's stance toward what cannot be undone. In older adulthood, irreversible losses such as bereavement, functional decline, or chronic illness can threaten dignity precisely because they resist "fixing." The therapeutic task, therefore, is to strengthen response-ability: to help clients experience that while they cannot always change what happens, they can still choose *how* to meet it—with steadiness, self-respect, and fidelity to what matters (Frankl, 1959). Clinically, this can be operationalized through brief, repeatable attitudinal commitments—simple, reality-based self-statements that anchor the person at moments of pain: "I cannot reverse this, but I can meet it with dignity and courage." These commitments may help widen the emotional field (sorrow alongside appreciation) and protect continuity of meaning even under constraint, consistent with logotherapy's attitudinal pathway (Frankl, 1959; Russo-Netzer & Littman-Ovadia, 2019).

5 Leverage strengths as meaning channels. Identify signature strengths (e.g., curiosity → "learning hour," appreciation of beauty → "daily savor walk," kindness → "check-in buddy"). The qualitative evidence indicates that strengths scaffold both routine and contribution, making-meaning practices more intrinsically rewarding and sustainable (Peterson & Seligman, 2004; Russo-Netzer & Littman-Ovadia, 2019).

6 Embed purpose in systems of care. In residential or community programs, schedule purpose-rich roles (welcome host, library curator, garden steward), add legacy interviews, and institutionalize "impact briefings" that show whom residents help. Such designs align with findings that structured activity and visible usefulness reduce the sense of being "outside the game" and replace vacuum with value (Rowe & Kahn, 1997; Russo-Netzer & Littman-Ovadia, 2019).

7 Attend to culture and voice. Meaning and resources vary with culture, history, and cohort; elicit personal definitions of "aging well" and tailor pathways accordingly (e.g., faith communities as key anchors; narrative traditions as legacy vehicles). The evidence reviewed here underscores the importance of **bottom-up** listening to older adults' own meaning language when planning interventions.

Overall, aging and elderly care benefit when clinical and community practices treat meaning as a daily design problem rather than a trait. By coupling gerontological insight with logotherapy's three pathways, and by borrowing directly from older adults' lived strategies, care teams can transform routines, relationships, and attitudes into reliable conduits of purpose, belonging, and dignity in late life (Frankl, 1959; Ryff, 1995; Carstensen et al., 1999; Russo-Netzer & Littman-Ovadia, 2019).

71 Palliative care

Palliative care is internationally defined as *active, holistic care* for people with serious illness that seeks to enhance quality of life by addressing physical, psychological, social, and spiritual sources of suffering—an orientation increasingly framed as an ethical responsibility of people-centered health systems (Radbruch et al., 2020; World Health Organization [WHO], 2020). This remit dovetails with logotherapy's core claim that even under severe constraints persons retain the freedom to realize meaning via creative contributions, experiential receptivity, and chosen attitudes toward the unavoidable (Frankl, 1959). Within palliative contexts, existential distress and demoralization are prevalent and often entwined with diminished meaning; they can contribute to complex presentations such as the *wish to hasten death*, underscoring the clinical salience of meaning-oriented care (Martins et al., 2024; Rodríguez-Prat et al., 2024).

Over the past decade and a half, a robust evidence base has emerged for Meaning-Centered Psychotherapy (MCP)—an intervention explicitly derived from logotherapy. Randomized and controlled trials demonstrate that both group and individual MCP improve spiritual well-being, sense of meaning, and overall quality of life while reducing existential despair compared with supportive therapy or usual care (Breitbart et al., 2015; Breitbart et al., 2018). Complementary existential interventions, most notably Dignity Therapy, a structured life-review and legacy process, have shown promise for improving dignity-related outcomes, quality of life, meaning, and psychological distress, including depression and anxiety, although effects vary across studies, baseline distress levels, and study design (Cuevas et al., 2021; Haneef & Abdullah, 2024; Martínez et al., 2017; Vuksanovic et al., 2017). Taken together, these data position meaning-oriented psychotherapy as a validated pillar of psychosocial palliative care alongside symptom control and family support (Breitbart et al., 2015; Radbruch et al., 2020).

Practice: evidence-informed applications

Meaning-centered assessment integrated with routine care. Screen early for existential symptoms (loss of meaning, demoralization, hopelessness) alongside pain and mood. Use "logo-hooks"—recurring metaphors, legacy concerns, peak affects—to elicit *what still matters* and to map Frankl's three pathways into the care plan (e.g., *creative*: small acts of contribution; *experiential*: moments of beauty/connection; *attitudinal*: a stance toward fatigue or uncertainty) (Frankl, 1959; Radbruch et al., 2020; WHO, 2020).

Deliver structured MCP modules when feasible. For patients with adequate stamina, brief MCP protocols (typically 7–8 sessions) cultivate sources of meaning—legacy, creativity, love, courage—articulate a personal "for-the-sake-of" statement, and connect daily efforts to valued beneficiaries; expect gains in spiritual well-being and meaning with downstream benefits for distress (Breitbart et al., 2015; Breitbart et al., 2018).

Offer Dignity Therapy for legacy and identity needs. A structured interview yields a legacy document capturing values, lessons, and hopes for loved ones; sharing it can bolster generativity and acceptance and, in several studies, reduce depression—particularly among those with elevated baseline distress (Martínez et al., 2016; Cuevas et al., 2021; Vuksanovic et al., 2017; Haneef et al., 2024).

Address the wish to hasten death with a meaning-informed lens. When expressed, explore remediable contributors (pain, demoralization, loss of purpose, social disconnection) and pair optimal symptom control with rapid-cycle meaning practices (micro-acts of contribution, brief connection rituals, stance sentences) and family-inclusive conversations about mattering; qualitative syntheses indicate this wish is multifactorial and closely intertwined with existential suffering (Rodríguez-Prat et al., 2024; Martins et al., 2024).

Embed meaning in interprofessional routines. Use short "impact briefings" (who benefited from today's efforts), family-facing legacy moments (recordings, letters), and collaborations with spiritual care to surface values and communities—operationalizing the consensus call for spiritual care as part of standard palliative practice (Radbruch et al., 2020; WHO, 2020).

Match intervention to energy and readiness. For patients with limited stamina, deploy ultra-brief MCP-informed exercises: a 5-minute "sources of meaning" check-in; a single "for-the-sake-of" sentence to read before treatments; one legacy note to a loved one; one attitudinal phrase for predictable distress (Breitbart et al., 2015; Martínez et al., 2016).

In sum, contemporary palliative care explicitly recognizes spiritual and existential suffering as part of its remit. Meaning-centered approaches, grounded in logotherapy and validated in randomized trials, provide practical, brief, and scalable methods to restore purpose, connection, and dignity at the end of life, complementing symptom control and family support to improve quality of life for patients and those who care for them (Breitbart et al., 2015; Martínez et al., 2016; Radbruch et al., 2020; WHO, 2020).

72 Online and digital applications

The digital transformation of health and counseling services has opened new avenues for the delivery of existential and meaning-centered care. Digital delivery refers to the use of online platforms and technological tools to provide therapeutic interventions synchronously (e.g., video-based teletherapy) or asynchronously (e.g., mobile apps, text-based interventions, digital modules). While traditional logotherapy emphasizes authentic human encounter, its core principles—creative contribution, experiential receptivity, and attitudinal choice—can be effectively translated into digital modalities without loss of existential depth (Frankl, 1959). The shift toward online and mobile interventions is also driven by the need for accessibility, scalability, and inclusivity, especially for individuals who face barriers to in-person therapy due to illness, geography, or stigma (Benavides-Vaello et al., 2013; Wind et al., 2020).

Digital applications of meaning-centered care manifest across several modalities. Teletherapy allows clinicians to deliver logotherapy and meaning-centered psychotherapy (MCP) via secure video conferencing, maintaining therapeutic presence while reducing logistical barriers. Mobile health (mHealth) interventions provide daily prompts, journaling exercises, and brief "meaning reps"—short reflective practices that operationalize creative, experiential, and attitudinal pathways. For example, a recent randomized controlled trial demonstrated that WhatsApp-based logotherapy significantly reduced depression, hopelessness, and suicidal ideation in patients with major depressive disorder, highlighting the clinical viability of asynchronous micro-interventions (Shaygan et al., 2023). Similarly, an online mixed-methods study of group logotherapy for dementia caregivers found reduced caregiver burden and qualitative increases in hope and meaning, suggesting that existential group processes may be adaptable to digital spaces (Yang et al., 2024).

Evidence from meaning-centered psychotherapy further illustrates the adaptability of existential interventions to online platforms. MCP, originally developed for patients with advanced cancer, has been successfully piloted in virtual formats, showing improvements in spiritual well-being and reductions in existential distress (Breitbart et al., 2015; Applebaum et al., 2024). Dignity Therapy, another logotherapy-aligned intervention focused on legacy and generativity, has also been adapted for remote delivery. A recent pilot study of virtual Dignity Therapy for patients with advanced cancer found the intervention feasible and acceptable, with participants reporting satisfaction and perceived benefits, although larger controlled studies are needed to establish efficacy (Weng et al., 2025). These developments are consistent with a broader evidence base showing that digitally adapted meaning-centered interventions can improve quality of life, increase meaning in life, and reduce symptoms of depression and anxiety across diverse populations (Vos et al., 2015; van der Spek et al., 2017; Vos & Vitali, 2018).

Beyond clinical contexts, digital education and self-guided programs expand the reach of logotherapy to broader audiences. Meaning-centered curricula delivered via e-learning platforms enable students and employees to engage in structured reflection, values clarification, and purpose exploration exercises. Interactive platforms can incorporate **logo-hooks** (e.g., recurring metaphors, emotionally salient memories) and translate them into weekly commitments, while dashboards provide real-time feedback on progress in coherence, purpose, and mattering. Such tools align with the broader movement toward digital mental health interventions, which show promise for increasing access and scalability, while also requiring careful attention to engagement, evidence quality, privacy, and equity (Moshe et al., 2021; Philippe et al., 2022).

At the same time, digital delivery raises important challenges. Maintaining existential depth and **authentic presence** in online encounters requires careful design to avoid superficiality. Privacy, data protection, and digital literacy barriers must be addressed to ensure equitable access (Wind et al., 2020). Moreover, cultural adaptation is critical: what constitutes meaningful engagement varies across cultural and spiritual traditions, necessitating flexible digital platforms that allow for personalization. In practice, digital logotherapy should be viewed not as a replacement for in-person presence, but as an **extension of Frankl's principle of freedom within constraint**: by harnessing technology, clinicians can offer individuals new ways of accessing meaning even when face-to-face encounters are limited. This aligns with logotherapy's existential stance that meaning is always possible—sometimes discovered in new, unconventional forms when circumstances impose limitations.

Part 4

Professional considerations

73 Ethical framework

Logotherapy touches the client's core commitments, and often their deepest vulnerabilities. Hence, ethical practice is not a procedural formality; it is the protective structure that makes authentic exploration possible. Ethics in logotherapy can be framed as a continual commitment to *humility (limits), clarity (informed consent), fidelity (confidentiality and boundaries), and responsibility (beneficence without value-imposition).*

Professional competence, scope of practice, and referral

Ethical logotherapeutic work begins with professional humility: knowing what one is qualified to do, and recognizing when consultation, supervision, or referral is necessary to protect the client's welfare (Wise, 2008; APA, 2017). Historically, logotherapy was first articulated in relation to "neurotic" suffering and existential frustration, and later developed into a broader clinical approach that can be integrated across settings and populations (Schulenberg et al., 2008). Even so, the ethical principle remains constant: logotherapists should not diagnose, treat, or intervene beyond their formal competence, training, and licensure/authorization, unless they are specifically qualified through recognized education and supervised training (APA, 2017; Wise, 2008). When a client's needs exceed the therapist's scope of practice, ethical responsibility requires timely consultation/supervision and/or referral to services better suited to the client's condition (APA, 2017).

DOI: 10.4324/9781003624417-4

Initial evaluation and informed consent

Ethically responsible practice starts with a structured intake meeting that combines relational attunement with clinical evaluation. The therapist clarifies the client's presenting concerns, expectations, and goals, reviews relevant history (including psychiatric history when relevant), and considers whether logotherapy is best offered as a primary approach, an adjunctive intervention, or within coordinated care (APA, 2017; Schulenberg et al., 2008). Informed consent should be explicit, understandable, and revisited as therapy deepens. Consistent with professional ethics, the logotherapist should explain: professional identity and qualifications (including limits of practice), the rationale and aims of meaning-centered work, core methods likely to be used, what the process may look like, the client's role in it, foreseeable benefits and limitations, and confidentiality (APA, 2017; ACA, 2014).

Fit, readiness, and when logotherapy should be primary vs. adjunctive

A key ethical question concerns *fit*: is the reason for seeking therapy relatively focused (e.g., meaning disruption, values conflict, vocational purpose), or diffuse and multi-domain with significant clinical complexity? As logotherapy is often used integratively, ethical decision-making frequently involves determining when meaning-centered methods should be primary versus adjunctive within a broader, evidence-informed plan (Schulenberg et al., 2008). Fit also includes readiness. Meaning-centered work is typically most effective when clients can participate actively in reflective exploration and collaborate on realistic goals, while the therapist calibrates depth, pacing, and intensity to the client's capacities, distress level, and context (Schulenberg et al., 2008; Szabó & Baji, 2025).

Confidentiality, consultation, and responsible information-sharing

Confidentiality is foundational: therapy depends on the client's trust that personal information will be protected. The logotherapist should explain how confidentiality works in practice, including record handling and the use of consultation/supervision. At the same time, ethical codes recognize that confidentiality has limits, particularly when there is a serious risk of harm or when disclosure is legally required. These limits should be communicated clearly early in the relationship and applied cautiously and proportionately. When clinically helpful, coordination with other professionals should follow "minimum necessary" sharing, relevance to care, and informed consent, typically written consent. If the client refuses consent and the therapist believes coordination is essential for safety or effective care, this should be discussed transparently and ethically, with careful consideration of next steps (ACA, 2014).

Responsibility, autonomy, and "meaning without imposition"

The clinician's ethical mandate includes beneficence and nonmaleficence: promoting well-being, reducing suffering, and avoiding harm (APA, 2017). In logotherapy, this mandate has a distinctive edge: the therapist must never turn "meaning" into prescription. Ethical logotherapy protects the client's autonomy by supporting discovery rather than directing the client toward the therapist's values, ideology, or preferred hierarchy of "what matters" (Chanouha et al., 2026; Szabó & Baji, 2025). This is particularly important when working with responsibility. Logotherapy emphasizes responsibility as an existential capacity, yet ethical practice differentiates between (a) areas where agency can realistically be exercised and (b) areas shaped by unavoidable constraints, so that the client's freedom is strengthened without moralizing or blame (Chanouha et al., 2026; Schulenberg et al., 2008).

Ethical dimensions distinctive to logotherapy

Logotherapy is practiced in multiple professional fields (psychotherapy, counseling, medicine, nursing, education, leadership). Therefore, logotherapists are ethically bound first by the codes of their primary profession (e.g., American Psychological Association or American Counseling Association), within which logotherapeutic principles are applied. Within the logotherapy community itself, quality and accountability are also addressed through training and accreditation structures. Conceptually, it can be helpful to frame logotherapy as moving on two ethical "gears":

- **Synthesis (supportive/organizing work):** illuminating values, strengthening meaning, and orienting clients toward purposeful engagement. On this level, logotherapy often integrates well with other care systems (e.g., medical, psychiatric, rehabilitative), supporting coherence rather than fragmentation.
- **Analysis (existential-exploratory work):** examining assumptions and confronting existential givens (e.g., guilt, suffering, death, freedom). Because this can be emotionally demanding, ethical practice requires careful pacing, attention to the client's resources, and continuous consent and collaboration. Finally while logotherapy does not operate under a single universal "modality-specific" ethics code, its foundational commitments carry direct ethical implications: the will to meaning, the unconditional meaningfulness of life, and freedom of will. These principles invite a consistent ethical posture: respect autonomy, avoid value-imposition, calibrate responsibility with compassion, and uphold dignity even in suffering.

74 Therapist's presence and authenticity

Meaning-centered work is shaped not only by the questions a therapist asks, but by the quality of the therapist's *accompaniment* while those questions unfold. In logotherapy, clients often wrestle with freedom and responsibility, with suffering, loss, and mortality—realities that can narrow attention, amplify fear, and tempt both client and therapist into premature certainty. In such contexts, the therapist's **authentic presence** is not a stylistic preference; it functions as a core therapeutic condition that supports agency and meaning-making under uncertainty.

At its heart, logotherapy begins with the **encounter**—a human meeting in which the client is not reduced to symptoms, and the therapist does not hide behind technique. Presence refers to the therapist's capacity to be psychologically available: attentive, emotionally grounded, and genuinely engaged with the client's lived world in the here-and-now (Geller & Greenberg, 2002). This emphasis is not merely philosophical. Across orientations, the **working alliance** shows a consistent, moderate association with psychotherapy outcomes (Flückiger et al., 2018), underscoring that the relationship—how we meet the client—reliably matters for change. Logotherapy adds a distinctive nuance: the alliance is not only a vehicle for symptom reduction; it becomes a **container for existential choice**. Within a steady relational field, clients are more able to approach questions they might otherwise avoid—*What is being asked of me now? What do I want to stand for?*—without feeling pushed, judged, or taken over.

Authenticity as an ethical stance

Authenticity in this context is not a license for spontaneity, self-expression, or "being personal." Rather, it is a disciplined congruence that communicates honesty, respect, and steadiness—while protecting the client's freedom. This is an ethical matter as much as a relational one: meaning is always value-laden, and therefore logotherapists must remain vigilant not to impose their worldview under the banner of "meaning." The therapist's authenticity serves the client's **freedom of will** precisely by *not* recruiting the client into the therapist's values, and by keeping the therapeutic space oriented toward the client's conscience and self-definition. This is also the context in which therapist self-disclosure must be handled with particular care. The research suggests that the impact of self-disclosure depends strongly on timing, intent, and—most importantly—the client's experience of the disclosure (Knox, 2003). In logotherapy, the guiding question is simple and ethically clarifying: *Does this disclosure widen the client's freedom and meaning-making—or does it narrow it by shifting attention toward the therapist?* Authenticity is expressed most reliably not through what the therapist reveals, but through how the therapist remains present, transparent, and trustworthy.

Presence as modeling: meaning-seeking and courage

Logotherapy does not ask people to "think positively." It invites them to recognize a residual freedom: the capacity to take a stand toward fate and to respond to life with responsibility. In this sense, the therapist inevitably models something—often more through presence than through instruction. A therapist who can stay grounded in the face of suffering models that suffering can be approached without collapse; a therapist who resists coercion models that responsibility can be invited without moral pressure; and a therapist who tolerates ambiguity models that meaningful action can proceed without perfect certainty. Authentic presence tends to model three logotherapeutic stances:

1 *Meaning-orientation (rather than fixation on symptom or self)*: A present therapist repeatedly helps the client's attention move from self-preoccupation toward values, tasks, and relationships that call the person beyond themselves—an alignment consistent with logotherapy's emphasis on self-transcendence and meaning-directed action (Schulenberg et al., 2008).
2 *Courage to face existential givens:* When clients touch guilt, suffering, loss, or death anxiety, presence is the therapist's capacity not to flee into technique, reassurance, or intellectualization. The therapist's steadiness communicates, often without words: *This can be faced* (Krug, 2009).
3 *Dignity in uncertainty:* Many clients long for certainty ("Tell me what to do"). Logotherapy respects this longing while refusing coercion. Presence models a mature stance: we can act responsibly without perfect clarity; we can choose a direction without pretending to control life.

Even within the alliance literature, evidence suggests that therapists vary meaningfully in their capacity to build alliances that support outcomes; therapist effects can be substantial (Del Re et al., 2012). This finding strengthens a central implication for logotherapy: presence is not merely a personality trait—it is a professional practice, cultivated intentionally through training, self-observation, supervision, and ethical discipline. The deeper the existential stakes in the client's life, the more the therapist's inner stance becomes part of the clinical instrument.

Because logotherapy engages themes such as conscience, freedom, guilt, suffering, and mortality, ethical practice requires sustained reflexivity and professional development (Wise, 2008). These capacities safeguard the client—and protect logotherapy itself from drifting into moralizing, rescuing, or value-imposition.

1 **Self-awareness**—noticing one's own thoughts, emotions, and impulses as they arise, and how these may shape clinical judgment (Wise, 2008).
2 *Logotherapeutic relevance:* This is how we prevent "meaning" from becoming projection. When the therapist notices an internal push ("I want the client to choose X"), self-awareness creates a pause in which humility and ethics can return—making room again for the client's freedom.
3 **Relational reflexivity**—monitoring what emerges within the therapeutic relationship and ensuring it serves the client's process rather than the therapist's needs (Wise, 2008).
4 *Logotherapeutic relevance:* Meaning work can evoke powerful responses in therapists—admiration, urgency, protectiveness, impatience, even moral distress. Relational reflexivity helps the therapist metabolize these reactions (often in supervision) so the session remains the client's space rather than the therapist's agenda.
5 **Boundary sensitivity** — maintaining clear professional boundaries and revisiting them over time, prioritizing the client's best interests (APA, 2017; ACA, 2014).
6 *Logotherapeutic relevance:* Logotherapy can feel deeply personal and "life-guiding." Boundaries ensure that depth does not slide into dependency, role confusion, or subtle coercion—and that the client's autonomy remains protected even in intimate existential work.

75 Resonance and attunement

Resonance in psychotherapy refers to the therapist's disciplined capacity to attune—moment by moment—to the client's unique inner world, and to respond in ways that deepen understanding while protecting autonomy. This attunement is expressed not only in what the therapist says, but in pacing, tone, and the ability to stay regulated and curious in the face of suffering and uncertainty.

A robust body of research shows a consistent association between the working alliance and therapeutic improvement (Flückiger et al., 2018), and suggests that therapists differ meaningfully in their capacity to build alliances that support change (Del Re et al., 2012). Attunement is one of the central ways the alliance becomes *felt* rather than merely agreed upon. From an ethical standpoint, attunement is also a form of competence. It is part of the therapist's obligation to offer care that is responsive to the client's needs, context, and limits, and to avoid interventions that are driven more by the therapist's urgency than by the client's readiness (APA, 2017; Wise, 2008).

A useful way to think about resonance is as *mutual responsiveness without loss of separateness.* The client "speaks," the therapist is affected, and responds in a way that helps the client recognize their own experience more clearly. Resonance is therefore not agreement, and it is not fusion. It is the felt sense that *the client's inner world has landed somewhere real*—and that the therapist is staying close enough to understand, while remaining distinct enough to think. This idea has strong developmental roots. Stern and colleagues described "affect attunement" as the caregiver's capacity to resonate with the infant's feeling state (often through rhythm, intensity, and timing rather than identical emotion), creating the early foundations of being known (Stern et al., 1985). Tronick's mutual regulation model similarly emphasizes that regulation is fundamentally dyadic: we learn emotional stability through cycles of attunement, misattunement, and repair (e.g., Tronick & Beeghly, 2011). Psychotherapy often becomes a new regulatory context in which the client's nervous system—and meaning system—can reorganize through a different kind of relationship: one where experience is met, named, and held with dignity.

Contemporary relational neuroscience has added language to what clinicians have long sensed: that much of attunement occurs beneath words—in prosody, pacing, micro-shifts of affect, and the therapist's capacity to remain regulated while the client is not.

Schore's work, for example, frames psychotherapy as deeply shaped by right-hemisphere processes involved in emotion regulation and implicit relational knowing, and highlights attunement and right-brain-to-right-brain communication as core mechanisms of change in affective treatments and attachment-informed psychotherapy (Schore & Fosha, 2009; Schore, 2022). Experiential relational approaches describe this as dyadic regulation: the client's capacity to feel and integrate emotion expands when intense affect can be held within an empathically attuned relationship (Fosha, 2001). This is highly compatible with logotherapy's insistence that we do not bypass suffering with slogans. Instead, we help the person face reality with support, so that freedom and responsibility remain accessible rather than collapsing under overwhelm.

The logotherapeutic nuance: attunement to meaning, conscience, and uniqueness

Logotherapy adds something distinctive to the concept of attunement. It is not only attunement to affect; it is also attunement to meaning—to the values a client is protecting, the responsibilities they feel called to, and the unique shape of their conscience and life situation. This includes listening for:

- **Value signals**: what the client mourns, defends, envies, fears losing, or feels guilty about (often clues to what matters).
- **Freedom signals**: the places where the client experiences "no choice," and the tiny places where choice still exists.
- **Responsibility signals**: burdens the client carries that are life-giving versus burdens that are crushing or imposed.
- **Uniqueness signals**: the person's unrepeatable roles, relationships, and tasks—what cannot be delegated or replaced.

Crucially, meaning-attunement is not meaning-imposition. The therapist's responsibility is to track the client's moral language and existential posture *with precision*—and then to ask questions that widen freedom rather than prescribe conclusions. This is where attunement becomes an ethical practice: it protects the client's autonomy while supporting deeper responsibility (APA, 2017).

Misattunement and repair: where resonance becomes trustworthy

Attunement is never perfect. In fact, the trustworthiness of the therapeutic relationship often depends less on continuous harmony and more on the capacity for **repair** after inevitable miscoordination. In logotherapy, repair has an additional layer: it models *responsible relationship.* When the therapist notices they missed something, moved too fast, moralized inadvertently, or offered an interpretation that felt constraining, repair is not just technique—it is lived ethics. It communicates: *freedom is real here; your experience matters here; we can correct course together.* Micro-practices for logotherapeutic attunement could involve *tracking rhythm before content*: noticing the client's tempo, intensity, and shifts in energy, and match pace before you offer ideas—an applied form of affect attunement (Stern et al., 1985). It could also involve gently *verbalizing meaning-gaps*, such as for example: "Part of you wants relief; another part wants to stay faithful to something important," as well as *concluding meaning-explorations with agency* by restoring choice. For example: "Given all of this, what feels like the next responsible step *for you*, even a small one?"

76 Societal and collective responsibilities of logotherapy

The societal horizon of logotherapy is already present in Frankl's own vision. Reflecting on the future of psychotherapy in the aftermath of World War II, Frankl expressed the hope that Vienna—the birthplace of psychiatric healing—might also become "the birthplace of a new psychotherapy: a psychotherapy that is aware of its social role, especially in times of inner and outer distress, and of its responsibility toward a world awaiting both spiritual and material rehabilitation" (Frankl, 1955). This statement situates logotherapy not only as a framework for individual healing and resilience, but also as an ethical and cultural response to collective suffering. Its core tenets—freedom of will, the will to meaning, and the unconditional meaningfulness of life—therefore extend beyond the private sphere, inviting persons, communities, and institutions alike to ask: *What is being asked of us now, together?*

From this perspective, meaning is not merely a solitary achievement, but also a relational and communal reality, discovered through commitments, values, and responsibilities that bind the individual to others and to the world. Contemporary commentators have accordingly described logotherapy as an "education to responsibility," emphasizing that responsibility extends beyond personal functioning toward the wider ecosystems in which human life unfolds. At the collective level, this shifts the unit of analysis. Logotherapy asks not only how individuals endure suffering, but how communities preserve dignity and agency under threat; how societies sustain their will to meaning amid systemic crisis; and how responsibility, central to Frankl's anthropology, extends beyond personal choice to obligations toward one another, future generations, and the conditions of life itself.

One of the most powerful, though still underdeveloped, applications of logotherapy lies in the domain of collective trauma. Frankl's work emerged from the aftermath of one of history's most devastating collective catastrophes, and logotherapeutic principles have repeatedly been adapted to contexts marked by displacement, loss, war, and large-scale adversity. A growing body of literature discusses logotherapy and meaning-centered approaches among populations facing migration-related distress, including work on immigrant mental health and meaning-oriented intervention. Frankl's concept of *noö-dynamics*—the constructive tension between present reality and a meaning potential—can also be expanded beyond the individual to illuminate collective life. Communities affected by shared trauma often inhabit an intensified gap between what is and what ought to be: the loss of safety, the collapse of shared narratives, the fracture of trust, and the longing for repair. Under such conditions, the presence or absence of shared purpose can shape whether a community moves toward paralysis or mobilization. When extended to communal life, this principle becomes a template for recovery: communities often heal not only by processing trauma, but by transforming it into meaningful contribution through memorial projects, mutual aid networks, social rebuilding, intergenerational storytelling, and initiatives that restore dignity to those most harmed. In such contexts, meaning-making is not only reflective but generative: it organizes grief into responsibility and turns survival into a moral project of repair.

Frankl argued that each era faces its own form of "collective neurosis." When existential emptiness emerges at scale, it may be expressed through social fragmentation, erosion of trust, polarization, and a diminished sense of shared purpose. A logotherapeutic lens thus highlights a central tension of modern life: societies may offer an abundance of stimulation and consumption while simultaneously frustrating the deeply human need for purpose, contribution, and belonging. From this standpoint, social suffering cannot be addressed by individual therapy alone. Social structures and cultural narratives may either support or obstruct meaning-making. Systems that reduce persons to economic units, privilege consumption over contribution, or erode communal bonds may intensify collective meaninglessness, creating conditions in which the will to meaning is persistently thwarted.

A logotherapy-informed approach to social distress therefore emphasizes three intertwined dimensions:

Structures and narratives: Social conditions can enable or constrain meaning at scale (belonging, dignity, opportunity for contribution, moral language).

Meaning is dialogical: Purposes are discovered through relationship and shared commitments, not merely through private insight.

Responsibility extends outward: Freedom gains ethical depth only when paired with responsibility for the consequences of our choices, particularly for those most vulnerable.

Toward a collective logotherapy: implications and future directions

Expanding logotherapy beyond the individual to encompass collective responsibilities is not a departure from Frankl's vision; it is a continuation of it. The core insight—that human beings retain a capacity for meaning even amid suffering—applies as powerfully to communities as to persons. Yet realizing this potential requires intentional development of collective practices, institutions, and professional roles. Several principles can guide the development of collective applications:

Work simultaneously at individual and systemic levels. Personal meaning-making is crucial, but must be paired with efforts to shift the social conditions that produce chronic trauma and meaninglessness.

Attend to power and justice. Without acknowledging structural barriers, logotherapy risks individualizing what is systemic. Collective meaning-making must therefore integrate insights from community psychology, social work, public health, and social ethics.

Cultivate shared purposes that transcend self-interest. Communities organized around mutual care, justice, cultural preservation, environmental stewardship, and civic responsibility often show stronger resilience than atomized individuals.

Foster "collective self-transcendence." A community's capacity to orient itself toward goods larger than immediate self-protection—concern for the wellbeing of all, including future generations and the more-than-human world—can become a cornerstone of collective healing.

Develop culturally responsive practices. Collective logotherapy must be adaptable to diverse traditions, narratives, and moral languages.The path forward includes building and evaluating practices such as community meaning-making circles, collective grief and remembrance work, meaning-centered approaches to social organizing, and educational initiatives that cultivate not only individual resilience but collective capacity for meaningful response. In such efforts, logotherapy contributes a distinctive ethic: not denial of suffering, and not facile optimism, but the courageous affirmation that even amid collective tragedy, meaning remains possible, responsibility remains real, and human beings retain a capacity for transcendence and transformation.

77 Situational freedom and positive anxiety in the logotherapeutic process

> Anxiety brings Dasein [existence] face to face with its Being free for the authenticity of its Being.
>
> Martin Heidegger

In logotherapy, meaning is not an abstract idea but a lived, concrete task—one that comes into sharp focus when life confronts the person with uncertainty, limitation, and suffering (Frankl, 1986). In that sense, meaning-oriented work is inseparable from the client's encounter with freedom and responsibility, and with the felt tremor that often accompanies that encounter: existential anxiety. The Existential Authenticity (EA) framework articulates this link with particular clarity, proposing that anxiety, freedom, and meaning are inseparable: anxiety dismantles the taken-for-granted, freedom appears in the moment of uncertainty, and meaning provides the compass that guides authentic existence (Davidov & Russo-Netzer, 2022). Within this integrated view, situational freedom is not a philosophical add-on, but a therapeutic threshold: the moment in which the client recognizes that their current way of interpreting themselves and their life is one possibility among others (Davidov & Russo-Netzer, 2022). This recognition is usually accompanied by anxiety—not only as a distress signal or a symptom, but as the very felt experience of freedom: the experiential sign that the person has stepped out of rigid patterns and into possibility (Davidov & Russo-Netzer, 2022; Russo-Netzer, 2025). Because old structures loosen, freedom can be lived as existential anxiety: for a moment, the person experiences "no map," no stable script, and is confronted more directly with existential concerns (e.g., helplessness, guilt, worthlessness, separateness)—precisely in the in-between space where change becomes possible (Davidov & Russo-Netzer, 2022).

Essentially, situational freedom is the dimension of intervention in which the client manages to step outside the taken-for-granted and realize that the meanings they attribute to life circumstances are not inevitable facts but interpretations—and therefore, potentially revisable (Davidov & Russo-Netzer, 2022). In this spirit, anxiety can be reframed not only as distress to reduce, but also as a signal that something alive is trying to emerge: an "awakening to possibilities" rather than a danger scenario (Russo-Netzer, 2025; Russo-Netzer & Davidov, 2020). As illustrated in the figure below, anxiety can be appraised either as threat (triggering fight/flight/freeze) or as an existential signal that opens situational freedom and possibility.

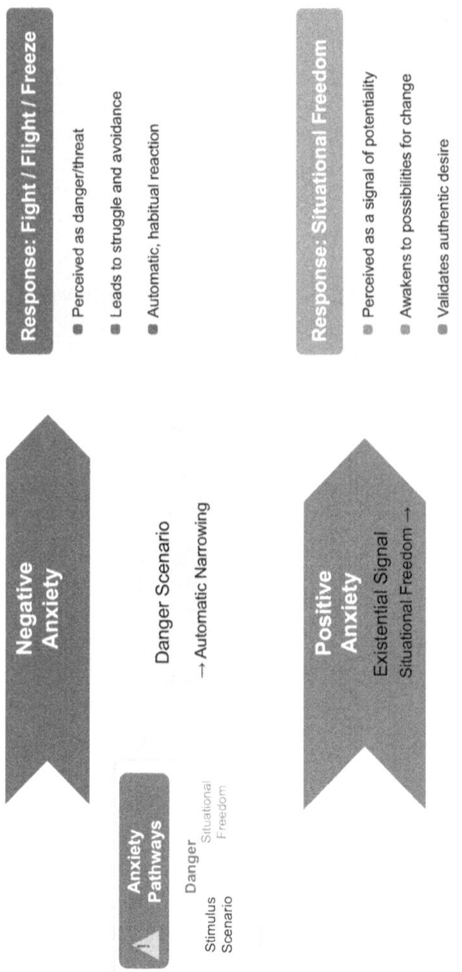

Figure 4.1 Existential Authenticity (EA) Framework

The aim is to support clients in recognizing moments of anxiety as invitations to endure groundlessness and to re-interpret dread as an opportunity—opening the door to more adaptive ways of engaging the same conditions that initially provoked anxiety (Russo-Netzer, 2025; Davidov & Russo-Netzer, 2022). A practical logotherapeutic assessment question here would be not only "What are the symptoms?" but also "What existential concern is being signaled here, and what coping strategy is being used?" (Davidov & Russo-Netzer, 2022). This groundwork is integrated as part of the logotherapeutic process, broadly following three dimensions:

1 *Taken-for-granted*: exploring the client's lifeworld and the existential concerns underlying distress (i.e., death/helplessness; meaninglessness/worthlessness; freedom/guilt; isolation/rejection) (Davidov & Russo-Netzer, 2022). From this view, the therapist listens for the client's dominant existential concern, their habitual defenses (avoidance, suppression, overcompensation), and the "trigger" contexts (situational/relational) where anxiety spikes (Davidov & Russo-Netzer, 2022). This assessment prepares the ground for a careful transition into situational freedom, because the goal is not to push the client into possibility faster than they can metabolize.
2 *Situational freedom*: stepping outside rigid interpretations and meeting anxiety as freedom (Davidov & Russo-Netzer, 2022; Russo-Netzer, 2025). The therapeutic task in this phase is subtle: to create conditions where the client can tolerate the freedom–anxiety experience without fleeing back into rigid certainty (Davidov & Russo-Netzer, 2022). Possible methods include moderated exposure to anxiety—initially building tolerance, and later cultivating compassion toward the anxious experience—transforming the relationship with anxiety from hostile to embracing (Davidov & Russo-Netzer, 2022; Russo-Netzer, 2025). This is also where positive anxiety becomes clinically actionable: the client learns to stay with the discomfort long enough for a new interpretation to emerge—one that can support mindful

openness, ambiguity tolerance, and the recognition of situational freedom (Russo-Netzer, 2025).

3 *Intentionality and meaning*: directing freedom toward values and commitments, because without meaning, freedom collapses into paralysis; without freedom, meaning becomes conformity; without anxiety, there is no opening to transformation (Davidov & Russo-Netzer, 2022). The therapeutic challenge here is to transform the anxiety–freedom experience into a compass for meaningful living (Davidov & Russo-Netzer, 2022). Once the client ceases to relate to anxiety defensively, the energy invested in self-protection can be redirected into commitment, creativity, and responsibility (Davidov & Russo-Netzer, 2022; Russo-Netzer, 2025). Here, logotherapeutic techniques become especially potent—not as disconnected "tools," but as ways of sustaining meaning-orientation, such as Dereflection (countering hyper-reflection by shifting attention outward toward tasks and relationships that embody meaning), Paradoxical intention (disrupting anticipatory anxiety loops by inviting a deliberate exaggeration of the feared behavior, loosening its hold), and Attitudinal modification (transforming unavoidable suffering into testimony of resilience, affirming life even in its tragic aspects) (Frankl, 1986; Davidov & Russo-Netzer, 2022).This sequence is especially useful as an organizing clinical principle because it prevents two common drifts: reducing logotherapy to "meaning talk" while the client is still flooded by unprocessed fear, and reducing therapy to regulation-only strategies that inadvertently strengthen avoidance, leaving existential anxiety untouched (Russo-Netzer, 2025; Davidov & Russo-Netzer, 2022). From a logotherapeutic perspective, thus, the question is rarely "How do we eliminate anxiety?" and more often, "What is life asking of you *through* this anxiety—and how can you respond with freedom, responsibility, and meaning?" When therapy helps clients endure the groundlessness of uncertainty and recognize anxiety as a gateway to situational freedom, it opens the space where meaning is not imposed but *discovered*—and where freedom is not feared but guided.

78 Boundaries of meaning exploration

Because meaning exploration is central to logotherapy, its boundaries must be handled with particular care. Meaning is inherently value-laden, and clinical work can easily drift from evocation to direction—from helping clients discover what matters to them to implying what should matter. As Schulenberg et al. (2008) note, logotherapy's stance is fundamentally elicitive—Socratic rather than prescriptive. Yet the language of meaning, responsibility, and conscience can become ethically hazardous when delivered as though the clinician holds an implicit answer key.

An ethically attuned logotherapeutic exploration widens freedom: it clarifies options, supports agency, and strengthens the client's capacity to take a stance that feels self-respecting and values-congruent (Schulenberg et al., 2008). It becomes ethically problematic when it narrows freedom—through subtle pressure, moralizing, premature conclusions, or "inspiration" that functions like coercion. In logotherapy, boundary crossings often happen not through overt misconduct but through directionality disguised as depth: the client begins to feel that meaning must look a certain way, or that "responsibility" is being used to push a particular life decision.

Where meaning exploration becomes intrusive or misattuned in logotherapy

The ethically problematic forms of meaning work are often recognizable by their clinical texture – that is, the client feels smaller, more pressured, or less free. Common patterns include:

1 *Value imposition through "meaning language*: The language of meaning and values often carries implicit moral rankings, such as worthy/unworthy, mature/immature, responsible/irresponsible, meaning exploration can inadvertently become a vehicle for value imposition. The counseling ethics literature explicitly addresses this risk and proposes ethical bracketing as a corrective strategy for value-based conflicts (Kocet & Herlihy, 2014). McWhorter (2019) further clarifies bracketing

as a clinical discipline: intentionally setting aside one's private values in-session so they do not steer the client's choices under the guise of professional guidance. In meaning-centered work, this is not "optional sensitivity"—it is a core boundary practice.

2 *Premature existential deepening*: Logotherapy often moves toward ultimate concerns, but meaning questions can become intrusive when they outpace the client's stability, capacity, or developmental readiness. The boundary issue is not whether existential themes are "important," but whether the exploration is paced so that the client remains agentic rather than flooded, ashamed, or compliant. In practical terms, the therapist's responsibility is to titrate depth and preserve psychological safety without abandoning the Franklian commitment to freedom and responsibility (Schulenberg et al., 2008).

3 *Responsibility that slips into blame:* Logotherapy's emphasis on responsibility is ethically sound when it identifies where freedom truly remains; it becomes ethically unsafe when responsibility is implicitly assigned where it does not belong—particularly in the wake of trauma, coercion, or structural oppression. The "boundary skill" here is discrimination: inviting the client to claim agency where possible while explicitly removing illegitimate burden where choice has been constrained. In logotherapy, this is a central safeguard against moralizing—especially when therapists themselves hold strong convictions about duty, calling, or "what a meaningful life should look like."

4 *Meaning as bypass* (purpose replacing emotion): Meaning exploration becomes misattuned when it functions as a shortcut around grief, rage, terror, or despair—moving too quickly from pain to "lesson," from loss to "growth." This pattern has been conceptualized in the clinical literature as spiritual bypassing—the use of spiritual or existential meaning frameworks to avoid painful psychological material (Picciotto, Fox, & Neto, 2018). For logotherapy, the ethical lesson is sequencing: meaning should emerge as integration—often through sustained emotional contact—rather than as an escape hatch from feeling.

5 *Therapist self-disclosure that recruits the client:* Meaning talk often invites therapist sharing, yet self-disclosure in meaning-centered work carries a specific boundary risk: the client may experience the therapist's values as a template to adopt. Knox and Hill (2003) show that the effects of therapist self-disclosure depend heavily on timing, intent, and how the client experiences it. In logotherapy, the decision rule is especially strict: disclosure is ethical only when it clearly serves the client's process and expands (rather than narrows) the client's freedom to arrive at their own meanings.

In light of these boundary risks, the following safeguards can help logotherapists preserve the depth of meaning exploration while preventing drift into directive, intrusive, or value-imposing practice:

- *Ethical bracketing as an ongoing discipline*: Notice when personal values, preferences, or "preferred outcomes" become activated (e.g., "I want them to choose X"), intentionally bracket them, and return to client-led inquiry (Kocet & Herlihy, 2014; McWhorter, 2019).
- *A sustained curious, nonjudgmental Socratic stance*: Shape questions to elicit lived meanings rather than to evaluate, correct, or steer the client toward an implied "right" interpretation (Schulenberg et al., 2008).
- *Anti-bypass sequencing: emotion first, meaning as integration:* When affect is intense, stay with the emotional reality before translating experience into meaning; allow meaning to emerge through contact with grief, fear, anger, or shame rather than as a shortcut around them (Picciotto et al., 2018).
- *Disclosure hygiene: minimal, purposeful, and impact-checked*: Use therapist self-disclosure sparingly and briefly, only with a clear clinical rationale, and explicitly check how the client experiences it—especially in value-laden conversations (Knox & Hill, 2003).

Ultimately, the ethical boundary in meaning work is measured not by how profound the conversation sounds, but by what it does to the client's freedom. When meaning exploration expands inner space—clarifying values, strengthening agency, and supporting responsibility without blame—it remains faithful to logotherapy's spirit. When it tightens into pressure, moralizing, recruitment into the therapist's worldview, or bypass of emotional reality, the work has crossed its boundary. The safeguards above help maintain a distinctively logotherapeutic ethic: to accompany clients toward meaning without commandeering it, and to invite responsibility without coercion—so that dignity, autonomy, and genuine self-transcendence can remain within reach, even in the midst of suffering.

79 Research methods

Viktor Frankl's logotherapy initially emerged from clinical observation and existential philosophy rather than systematic empirical research. Frankl developed his meaning-centered approach through decades of clinical practice, beginning in interwar Vienna and continuing through his harrowing experiences in Nazi concentration camps and subsequent therapeutic work. While Frankl offered compelling theoretical frameworks and vivid case illustrations, the systematic empirical investigation of logotherapy's principles and effectiveness developed more slowly. This gap between rich theoretical foundations and rigorous empirical validation has shaped logotherapy research over the past six decades, creating both challenges and opportunities for contemporary researchers seeking to establish logotherapy's evidence base.

The empirical study of logotherapy began in earnest with the development of quantifiable measures of meaning in life, particularly the Purpose in Life (PIL) Test by Crumbaugh and Maholick (1964), which operationalized Frankl's concepts for research purposes. Since then, logotherapy research has evolved considerably, embracing diverse methodological approaches including quantitative experimental designs, qualitative phenomenological investigations, and mixed-methods studies that integrate multiple perspectives. Contemporary logotherapy research reflects broader trends in psychological science toward methodological pluralism, recognizing that different research questions require different methodological approaches and that triangulation across methods strengthens conclusions. Understanding the methodological landscape of logotherapy research—its strengths, limitations, and evolving best practices—proves essential for researchers seeking to contribute rigorous evidence and for practitioners evaluating research to inform their clinical work.

Survey research examining correlates of meaning in life constitutes a substantial portion of logotherapy's empirical base. *Cross-sectional studies* assess participants at single time points, examining relationships between meaning and other variables including well-being, psychopathology, personality, values, and demographic characteristics. These studies have established that meaning in life correlates positively with life satisfaction, happiness, psychological well-being, and adaptive coping, while associating negatively with depression, anxiety, hopelessness, and suicidal ideation (Steger et al., 2006). *Longitudinal studies* follow participants across multiple time points, enabling examination of temporal precedence and dynamic relationships between variables. Research tracking meaning and well-being over extended periods has demonstrated that meaning in life predicts subsequent well-being levels even controlling for baseline well-being, supporting logotherapy's proposition that meaning constitutes a fundamental determinant of psychological health rather than merely its consequence. Longitudinal designs also permit examination of meaning development across the lifespan, stability versus change in meaning over time, and contextual factors that facilitate or impede meaning-making processes. Survey research proves particularly valuable for establishing population norms, examining meaning across diverse demographic groups, investigating cultural variations, and identifying risk and protective factors associated with meaning presence or absence.

Phenomenological research methods prove particularly well-suited to logotherapy given shared philosophical foundations in existential phenomenology. These approaches aim to understand phenomena from participants' lived experience perspectives, bracketing researchers' preconceptions to access essential meanings. Interpretative phenomenological analysis (IPA), descriptive phenomenology, and hermeneutic phenomenology each offer systematic procedures for capturing the texture of subjective experience while maintaining methodological rigor. For example, research exploring Alcoholics Anonymous members' experiences of aging with long-term recovery employed IPA methodology, explicitly framed within Frankl's logotherapy. The study utilized in-depth semi-structured interviews to access participants' meaning-making processes, conducting systematic analysis to identify convergent and divergent themes across cases. IPA's commitment to idiographic analysis—detailed examination of each individual case before identifying patterns—aligns well with logotherapy's emphasis on unique individual meaning. The approach revealed how participants constructed meaning from both their recovery experience and aging process, demonstrating resilience through existential reframing of life challenges. Similarly, research examining the psychological impact of logotherapy on women with breast cancer employed qualitative content analysis. Investigators conducted in-depth semi-structured interviews three months post-intervention with 15 women who completed logotherapy, plus interviews with healthcare professionals and family members to gain multiple perspectives. The analysis identified themes related to hope, perceived emotional well-being, meaning-making processes, and life expectancy perceptions, providing rich understanding of how logotherapy influenced participants' experiences that quantitative measures alone could not capture (Garcia-Alandete et al., 2025).

Phenomenological research contributes essential insights to logotherapy by elucidating meaning-making processes, capturing existential experiences in participants' own terms, and generating theory grounded in lived experience. The approach proves particularly valuable for understudied populations, novel phenomena, and exploratory research where existing conceptual frameworks may not adequately capture relevant experiences. Phenomenological findings inform intervention development by revealing how participants actually experience meaning and meaninglessness, what facilitates or impedes meaning discovery, and how therapeutic processes unfold from clients' perspectives. Rigor in phenomenological research requires explicit attention to trustworthiness criteria: credibility (confidence in findings' truth value), transferability (applicability to other contexts), dependability (stability over time and conditions), and confirmability (ensuring conclusions derive from data rather than researcher bias). Strategies for establishing trustworthiness include prolonged engagement, persistent observation, triangulation across data sources or investigators, member checking with participants, thick description enabling readers to assess transferability, and reflexive journaling documenting researcher assumptions and interpretive processes.

Narrative research methods examine how individuals construct meaning through storytelling, analyzing the content, structure, and function of personal narratives. Given logotherapy's emphasis on biographical meaning—discovering purpose through reflecting on one's life story—narrative approaches offer natural methodological alignment. These methods range from structured life story interviews to analysis of naturally occurring narratives in clinical or naturalistic contexts. Research examining meaning-making among female victims of temporary marriage in Indonesia employed narrative methodology within a mixed-methods framework. In-depth interviews explored participants' experiences and pursuit of meaningful life following trauma, analyzing how they constructed narratives that reframed suffering as opportunities for growth and meaning. The study demonstrated how logotherapy's emphasis on attitudinal values—finding meaning through one's stance toward unavoidable suffering—manifested in participants' narrative reconstructions of traumatic experiences into sources of wisdom and purpose. Narrative methods prove particularly valuable for examining meaning across the lifespan, understanding how individuals integrate disparate life experiences into coherent wholes, and investigating cultural variations in meaning construction. The approach illuminates temporal dimensions of meaning: how past experiences inform present purpose, how anticipated futures shape current meaning, and how people revise life stories in light of new experiences or changed circumstances. Methodological considerations in narrative research include decisions about data collection (structured versus open-ended interviews, oral versus written narratives), analytic strategies (thematic analysis, structural analysis, performance analysis), and attention to co-construction of narratives between interviewer and participant. Narrative researchers must also consider whose stories get told, whose perspectives privilege certain interpretations, and how power dynamics shape narrative construction and interpretation.

Mixed methods research integrates quantitative and qualitative approaches within single studies, leveraging the complementary strengths of each tradition while offsetting their respective limitations. These designs prove particularly valuable for logotherapy research given the complexity of meaning-related phenomena that resist capture through any single methodological lens. Mixed methods studies in logotherapy typically combine quantitative outcome measurement with qualitative exploration of processes, experiences, and contextual factors that explain quantitative results.

Concurrent mixed methods designs collect quantitative and qualitative data simultaneously or during the same general timeframe, then integrate findings during interpretation. These designs prove efficient and enable examination of the same phenomena from multiple perspectives. Research on temporary marriage victims in Indonesia employed concurrent methodology, collecting both quantitative meaning scale data and qualitative interview data, then integrating results to provide comprehensive understanding of meaning levels and meaning-making processes.

Concurrent designs face integration challenges since quantitative and qualitative data differ fundamentally in nature and analytic approaches. Researchers must explicitly plan integration strategies: developing joint displays that present quantitative and qualitative findings side by side for comparison; conducting data transformation where qualitative themes are quantified or quantitative variables are qualitized into categorical themes; or narrative integration that weaves together findings from both strands. Effective integration demonstrates how quantitative and qualitative results complement, expand, or occasionally contradict each other, leading to meta-inferences that transcend what either method alone could provide.

Systematic reviews and meta-analyses synthesize existing research to provide comprehensive assessment of evidence on specific questions. These secondary research methods prove essential for evidence-based practice, identifying knowledge gaps, and informing future research directions. Both quantitative meta-analysis and qualitative evidence synthesis contribute to understanding logotherapy's empirical status.

Current limitations

Logotherapy research faces several methodological challenges that future work must address. Intervention standardization remains limited: what exactly constitutes logotherapy varies considerably across studies in theoretical fidelity, specific techniques employed, session frequency and duration, and therapist training. This heterogeneity, while reflecting logotherapy's flexibility, complicates interpretation and replication. Developing manualized protocols with defined core components while allowing principled adaptation would strengthen research rigor without sacrificing clinical responsiveness. Geographical concentration presents another concern. Research disproportionately originates from Western, educated, industrialized, rich, and democratic (WEIRD) contexts, with notable concentrations in Europe, North America, and Iran. While some cross-cultural research exists, systematic investigation across diverse cultural contexts remains insufficient. Given that meaning-making processes likely reflect cultural values and worldviews, establishing logotherapy's cross-cultural validity requires intentional global collaboration.

Outcome measurement heterogeneity creates challenges for synthesis and comparison. Studies employ diverse measures of meaning, well-being, psychopathology, and other outcomes, sometimes with questionable psychometric properties in studied populations. Establishing a core outcome set—a minimum collection of measures all studies should include—would facilitate comparison while allowing additional outcomes addressing specific research questions. Such core outcomes should include validated meaning measures, relevant symptom assessments, and functional outcomes important to stakeholders including clients, families, and service systems.

Research on mechanisms remains underdeveloped. While studies demonstrate that logotherapy produces beneficial outcomes, understanding how and why it works receives less attention. Mediational analyses examining whether meaning changes explain symptom improvements, moderation analyses identifying for whom logotherapy works best, and process research linking specific techniques to specific outcomes would strengthen theoretical understanding and optimize intervention delivery. Several methodological innovations offer promise for advancing logotherapy research. Digital delivery platforms enable intervention scaling while facilitating research through automated data collection, real-time ecological momentary assessment, and remote participant access. Studies examining mobile-based and online logotherapy demonstrate feasibility while raising questions about mechanisms and optimal implementation that future research must address.

Network analysis methods offer novel approaches for examining meaning-related constructs. Rather than assuming meaning, well-being, and psychopathology represent latent variables with observable indicators, network models conceptualize psychological phenomena as complex systems of mutually reinforcing elements. Network analysis could illuminate how specific meaning sources relate to particular well-being dimensions, identify central nodes in meaning networks that maximally influence overall meaning, and examine how meaning networks differ across populations or change following intervention.

Machine learning approaches might identify complex patterns in large datasets that traditional statistical methods miss. For instance, random forests or support vector machines could identify combinations of demographic, clinical, and contextual variables that predict treatment response, enabling personalized intervention matching. Natural language processing could analyze therapy session transcripts or written narratives to quantify meaning-making processes, identify linguistic markers associated with meaning presence, or track meaning development over time.

Participatory research approaches involving stakeholders, including clients, families, community members, and practitioners—in research design, implementation, and interpretation could enhance research relevance, cultural validity, and impact. Such approaches align well with logotherapy's emphasis on individual meaning and contextual sensitivity while addressing power imbalances in traditional researcher-participant relationships.

In sum, research methodology in logotherapy has evolved considerably since Crumbaugh and Maholick's pioneering work quantifying Frankl's concepts. Contemporary logotherapy research embraces methodological pluralism, recognizing that different questions require different approaches and that triangulation across methods strengthens understanding. Quantitative experimental designs establish efficacy and examine outcomes; qualitative investigations illuminate processes and lived experiences; mixed methods integrate complementary perspectives; and systematic reviews synthesize evidence to guide practice and identify research gaps.

Yet significant methodological challenges remain. Intervention standardization, outcome measurement consistency, geographical diversity, mechanism investigation, and research-practice translation all require continued attention. Emerging methodological innovations—digital platforms, network analysis, machine learning, participatory approaches—offer promising directions while raising new questions about validity, interpretation, and application.

80 Meaning scales

What makes life worth living? Once posed primarily in the language of philosophy and existential thought, this question has increasingly been translated into the language of psychological science. Over the past six decades, researchers have developed psychometric instruments to operationalize and assess meaning in life—allowing meaning to be studied systematically, compared across individuals and cultures, and examined in relation to mental health, resilience, well-being, and human flourishing (Frankl, 1969, 2006; Steger et al., 2006). A key turning point came with the publication of the Purpose in Life Test by James Crumbaugh and Leonard Maholick, which marked an early attempt to bring Frankl's insights into empirical assessment and clinical research (Crumbaugh & Maholick, 1964). From that moment onward, meaning was no longer only a guiding therapeutic concept; it became a measurable construct, one that could be tracked over time, linked to outcomes, and used to evaluate interventions. The stakes of this measurement enterprise extend far beyond academic curiosity. In clinical and applied settings, reliable meaning measures can help practitioners identify existential distress that may otherwise remain unspoken, differentiate between the presence of meaning and the search for meaning, monitor change during therapy, and inform the tailoring of meaning-centered interventions to clients' needs and contexts (Steger et al., 2006; Schulenberg et al., 2011).

Yet measuring meaning poses distinctive methodological and conceptual challenges. Unlike constructs such as working-memory capacity or reaction time, meaning is a subjective, phenomenologically layered experience that shifts across persons, cultures, and life stages. Meaning is not a single, uniform construct; it is a multidimensional phenomenon comprising related but distinguishable components, such as cognitive appraisals that life is coherent and matters, affective resonance and vitality, motivational commitment to valued aims, and an existential sense of significance and belonging. These facets may converge in some individuals and contexts, yet diverge in others, implying that different measurement strategies may be needed for different purposes. Accordingly, meaning measurement forces researchers to make explicit theoretical choices that shape both instrument design and interpretation: Is meaning best treated as a unitary construct or a multidimensional one? Should assessment target global meaning in life, or domain-specific meaning across work, relationships, spirituality, and community? Are the presence of meaning and the search for meaning opposite ends of a single continuum, or relatively independent dimensions that can co-occur? And how can standardized measures remain sensitive to culturally diverse meaning systems while still enabling valid comparisons across groups? These questions are not merely technical; they determine what a scale can legitimately claim to measure, and they set the boundaries of how findings should be generalized across populations.

The history of meaning measurement mirrors broader debates in psychological science about how abstract, existential constructs can be operationalized without losing their depth. Early behaviorist traditions were skeptical that subjective phenomena such as meaning could be studied rigorously, privileging observable behavior over inner experience. The cognitive revolution reopened the scientific legitimacy of mental life and created conceptual space for systematic investigation of meaning-related processes, yet the measurement problem remained: meaning is not directly observable, and its expression is shaped by language, culture, developmental stage, and context. Meaning is therefore not best understood as a single psychological variable that can be captured by one indicator. Rather, it is a multidimensional phenomenon that may include cognitive appraisals of coherence and mattering, affective resonance and vitality, motivational commitment to valued aims, and an existential sense of significance and belonging—components that may converge in some individuals and diverge in others. This complexity forces measurement developers to make explicit theoretical choices that directly shape what a scale can legitimately claim to assess and how its scores should be interpreted.

Central questions recur across the literature: Is meaning a unitary construct or a set of distinct dimensions? Should instruments assess global meaning in life or domain-specific meanings (e.g., work, relationships, spirituality, community)? Are the presence of meaning and the search for meaning opposite ends of a continuum or separable dimensions that may co-occur? How can standardized instruments remain sensitive to culturally diverse meaning systems while still enabling valid comparison across groups? These are not merely technical issues; they determine item content, factor structure, validity evidence, and the conclusions researchers and practitioners draw from the data. Despite these challenges, psychometric innovation has made meaning assessment increasingly sophisticated. The field has moved beyond single-score instruments toward multidimensional measures that distinguish key facets (including presence versus search), map diverse sources of meaning across life domains, assess meaning-making processes, capture the role of meaning in coping with adversity, and support developmental measurement across the lifespan. At the same time, contemporary work increasingly recognizes that a comprehensive understanding of meaning cannot rely on one method alone. Self-report questionnaires offer standardized comparisons and feasibility at scale, but they are complemented by qualitative phenomenological interviews that capture lived meaning content and process; narrative and idiographic methods that illuminate personal meaning structures; behavioral indicators that index meaning-directed action; and therapeutic process measures that evaluate meaning-work as it unfolds in clinical contexts. In this sense, mature meaning assessment increasingly reflects methodological pluralism rather than allegiance to a single measurement tradition.

The significance of valid meaning measurement extends beyond academic inquiry. Clinicians need reliable tools to detect existential distress that may remain unarticulated, to determine whether meaning-centered interventions are indicated, and to monitor therapeutic change over time. Researchers studying meaning in relation to mental and physical health, coping, resilience, and flourishing depend on psychometrically sound instruments for rigorous hypothesis testing and interpretable findings. Public health and community professionals developing meaning-promoting programs require measures that can demonstrate effectiveness and guide implementation. Educational institutions seeking to cultivate purpose and meaning benefit from developmentally appropriate tools that track meaning development across childhood, adolescence, and emerging adulthood. In all of these settings, the quality of measurement directly shapes both scientific understanding and practical application.

Meaning assessment instruments are most useful when they serve two aims simultaneously: conceptual clarity and evidence-informed selection for practice and research. Meaning measures gain their value when they are anchored in theory and interpreted with psychometric and contextual care. The evolution of meaning assessment reflects an ongoing effort to operationalize existential life-questions without reducing their complexity, while refining tools that are useful for both research and practice. Systematic measurement of meaning in life is commonly traced to James Crumbaugh and Leonard Maholick's development of the Purpose in Life Test (PIL) in the early 1960s, an effort explicitly motivated by clinical encounters with what Frankl described as the existential vacuum and by a desire to bring logotherapeutic insights into empirical study. The PIL represented a watershed in existential psychology: it demonstrated that meaning-related experience could be operationalized, assessed, and examined in relation to mental health outcomes and intervention processes. Consistent with the dominant psychometric paradigms of the time, early meaning measurement relied primarily on self-report formats and factor-analytic approaches. The PIL was initially framed in largely unidimensional terms, positioning respondents along a continuum from low purpose/emptiness to high purpose/fulfillment. Over subsequent decades, the PIL accumulated extensive use across diverse populations and contributed substantially to the field's early legitimacy, as scores showed patterned associations with psychological distress, well-being indicators, and theoretically related constructs. At the same time, intensive use also exposed limitations that propelled the next wave of development. Critics noted potential overlap between certain meaning items and distress content, raising questions about discriminant validity in some contexts. Factor-analytic findings were not always consistent across samples, suggesting that the underlying structure might be more complex than originally assumed. Importantly, early measures tended to emphasize the presence of meaning but offered less precision regarding meaning-seeking as an active motivational process—whether a person lacking meaning is searching for it, avoiding it, or experiencing demoralized resignation.

A major conceptual advance in the 1990s and early 2000s was the recognition that the presence of meaning and the search for meaning are not necessarily opposite ends of a single continuum, but may represent related yet separable dimensions. This distinction opened space for qualitatively different profiles with distinct implications for well-being and intervention: individuals may experience high meaning with little active searching, low meaning with active searching, high meaning alongside ongoing exploration, or low meaning accompanied by disengagement or avoidance. The Meaning in Life Questionnaire (MLQ) operationalized this bidimensional approach by assessing presence and search with separate subscales, enabling more nuanced research and clinically informative interpretation (Steger et al., 2006). Subsequent work has consistently shown that meaning presence tends to relate robustly to well-being, whereas meaning search is more context-sensitive—sometimes reflecting adaptive curiosity and growth, and in other cases reflecting distress-driven striving when meaning is threatened or absent (Steger et al., 2006; Park, 2010). These findings underscore a central interpretive principle: meaning scores gain validity when read within a coherent theoretical model and the person's context, rather than treated as uniformly "positive" or "negative."

In the 21st century, assessment expanded beyond global indices toward instruments that examine how meaning is organized and lived—including sources of meaning across life domains (e.g., relationships, spirituality, contribution, work), orientations toward meaning (e.g., self-focused versus self-transcendent), and approaches to meaning-making (e.g., traditional/authority-based, functional/goal-based, phenomenological/experiential). This expansion reflects a growing recognition that global meaning scores can conceal clinically important distinctions: two people may report similar overall meaning yet derive it from markedly different sources, prioritize different values, or rely on different meaning-making processes—differences that may shape coping, ethical functioning, relational patterns, and vulnerability under stress (Park, 2010; Vos, 2016; Wong, 2012). Alongside this conceptual broadening, measures have also become more population- and context-sensitive, with instruments tailored to trauma and adversity, serious illness, later life, and developmentally appropriate assessment for children and adolescents. Such specialization allows assessment to be clinically calibrated rather than relying solely on generic adult measures.

Recent developments further highlight that meaning is both stable and dynamic. Trait-like assessments remain useful for baseline profiles and between-person comparisons, yet newer methods increasingly examine within-person fluctuations in meaning across shorter time scales and real-world contexts through intensive longitudinal designs, including ecological momentary assessment. Parallel advances include narrative-based assessment and computational approaches to meaning-related language in personal texts. Collectively, these approaches reflect a shift from treating meaning as a static attribute toward conceptualizing it as an ongoing process that varies across time, context, and developmental transitions—an orientation that strengthens both theory and intervention research (Park, 2010; Shiffman et al., 2008).

The diversification of instruments has also supported assessment of meaning within specific psychological tasks and clinical contexts. Measures have been developed to evaluate meaning-making in coping with trauma and adversity (e.g., the Posttraumatic Growth Inventory), orientations toward mortality and death-related meaning (e.g., multidimensional measures of death attitudes), and competencies relevant to meaning-centered work in practice. Developmentally tailored tools for younger populations similarly reflect a broader trend: meaning is now assessed not only as an adult life-evaluation but as a developmental capacity shaped by relationships, identity formation, culture, and lived experience. The cumulative effect is a more differentiated measurement landscape, one that supports sharper clinical formulation and more targeted research questions.

At the methodological level, contemporary meaning assessment increasingly embraces pluralism. Quantitative self-report questionnaires remain indispensable for standardization, norms, and population-level inference. At the same time, qualitative phenomenological interviews capture idiographic depth about what meaning consists of for a given person and how it is constructed in context. Intensive repeated measurement captures temporal variability that retrospective trait measures miss, and narrative and language-based methods can identify meaning themes without relying exclusively on predefined item content. A mature measurement science of meaning therefore relies less on any single method and more on triangulation across approaches, matching method to the facet of meaning under investigation and the purpose of assessment.

Across these developments, two enduring challenges continue to shape the field. First, meaning measures necessarily embody theoretical assumptions—about dimensionality, universality versus cultural specificity, and the relationship between meaning and neighboring constructs such as purpose, coherence, value, and life satisfaction. Careful alignment between theory, measure, and interpretive frame remains essential. Second, cultural validity requires sustained attention. Meaning systems vary across cultural contexts; collectivistic societies may emphasize communal, relational, and duty-based meanings more strongly than individualistic models foregrounded in many Western-developed instruments. Ensuring that measures capture culturally resonant meaning structures—while maintaining psychometric integrity for comparison—remains an ongoing task for research and practice.

Taken together, the evolution of meaning measurement represents a substantial achievement: existential concerns have been translated into empirically tractable constructs without fully stripping them of their human depth. The most responsible use of meaning scales involves selecting tools that fit the assessment purpose and population, prioritizing psychometric quality and theoretical alignment, integrating multiple methods when feasible, and interpreting results within the person's cultural and developmental context. When used with such care, meaning measures support both scientific progress and applied impact—enabling clinicians, educators, and researchers to recognize existential distress, evaluate interventions, and better understand the processes through which people cultivate and sustain lives experienced as meaningful.

81 New directions in the study of meaning in life

Six decades of research have established meaning in life as a central pillar of psychological functioning and human flourishing. What began as philosophical reflection and clinical insight has developed into a robust empirical field, supported by integrative reviews and meta-analytic evidence showing that meaning is consistently associated with psychological well-being and adaptation, and is also linked to physical health outcomes and longevity (Park, 2010; King & Hicks, 2021; Czekierda et al., 2017; Cohen et al., 2016). Meta-analytic syntheses confirm that the presence of meaning reliably predicts life satisfaction, positive affect, adaptive coping, and reduced psychological distress across diverse populations and cultural contexts (Steger, 2012; Vos & Vitali, 2018). The field has therefore moved beyond the question of whether meaning matters. The more pressing questions now concern how meaning develops, through which mechanisms it exerts its influence, how it fluctuates across time and culture, and how it can be cultivated responsibly and effectively through intervention.

The presence–search distinction

One of the most generative advances in contemporary meaning research has been the distinction between the presence of meaning and the search for meaning as related but separable dimensions (Steger et al., 2006). Rather than representing opposite ends of a continuum, presence and search can coexist in multiple configurations, each with distinct psychological implications. Presence of meaning—experiencing life as purposeful, coherent, and significant—shows robust and consistent associations with well-being, resilience, optimism, and lower depression and anxiety across cultures (Steger et al., 2006; Park, 2010). Longitudinal research suggests that meaning presence predicts future well-being above baseline levels, indicating more than simple co-occurrence (Steger et al., 2009). Search for meaning, by contrast, exhibits context-dependent patterns. In individuals experiencing meaning deficits, search often correlates with rumination, distress, and existential uncertainty. However, when accompanied by adequate meaning presence, search may reflect growth-oriented exploration, curiosity, and deepening engagement (Steger et al., 2008a). These nuanced patterns underscore a crucial interpretive principle: meaning-related variables cannot be treated as uniformly positive or negative. Their psychological function depends on configuration, context, and developmental stage.

Mechanisms linking meaning to well-being

Research increasingly examines how meaning influences psychological and physical outcomes. Several pathways have empirical support, though their relative contributions remain under investigation. First, meaning appears to facilitate adaptive coping. Individuals high in meaning are more likely to engage in problem-focused coping, constructive reappraisal, and post-traumatic growth following adversity (Park, 2010; Park & George, 2013). Meaning buffers stress reactivity and supports resilience in the face of loss and trauma. Second, meaning strengthens motivation and goal persistence. Experiencing life as meaningful enhances commitment to valued aims, sustained effort under difficulty, and alignment between behavior and values—processes central to self-determination and eudaimonic well-being (Ryan & Deci, 2017). Third, meaning is deeply intertwined with social connection. Individuals reporting high meaning tend to experience stronger relational bonds, greater perceived social support, and enhanced prosocial engagement (Lambert et al., 2010). Evidence suggests bidirectional influence: relationships generate meaning, and meaning motivates relational investment. Emerging research also links meaning to physical health through potential biological pathways, including stress-regulation mechanisms and inflammatory processes, though causal evidence remains preliminary (Hill & Turiano, 2014). Collectively, these findings suggest that meaning functions as a regulatory meta-resource—shaping cognition, emotion, motivation, and social engagement in ways that promote adaptation.

Sources, types, and approaches to meaning

The field has moved beyond global indices toward examining what provides meaning and how individuals relate to it. Research identifies diverse sources, including relationships, spirituality, achievement, contribution, generativity, and self-transcendence (Wong, 2012; Schnell, 2009). Importantly, not all sources relate equally to well-being. Socially oriented and self-transcendent meanings tend to show stronger positive associations than purely materialistic or hedonistic orientations (Schnell, 2009). Meaning-making approaches also vary. Some individuals rely primarily on externally prescribed traditions; others construct meaning through rational planning; still others engage meaning phenomenologically through lived experience and reflective discernment (Vos, 2016). These approaches differ in cultural prevalence and psychological outcomes, highlighting that meaning is not merely a content variable but also a process variable.

Developmental research indicates that meaning evolves across the lifespan. Adolescence and emerging adulthood involve exploration and identity-based meaning construction. Midlife often emphasizes generativity and contribution, while later life may foreground legacy, integration, and acceptance (McAdams & de St. Aubin, 1992; Steger et al., 2009). Individual trajectories vary considerably, shaped by personality, social resources, and life events. Cross-cultural research reveals both universality and variation. The drive for meaning appears widespread, and its positive association with well-being generalizes across cultures (Steger et al., 2008b). However, meaning content and structure vary: individualistic contexts emphasize autonomy and achievement, whereas collectivistic cultures foreground relational harmony, duty, and communal responsibility (Markus & Kitayama, 1991). Interestingly, the typically negative correlation between presence and search observed in Western samples is weaker or even positive in some Asian samples, suggesting cultural differences in how meaning-seeking is understood and valued (Steger et al., 2008b). These findings caution against assuming cultural neutrality in measurement or theory.

Despite progress, several foundational challenges remain, including:

Causality and Mechanisms. Much of the evidence remains correlational. Intensive longitudinal designs and experimental manipulations are needed to clarify temporal ordering and mediating pathways (Park, 2010). Reciprocal feedback loops between meaning and well-being likely exist, but their dynamics remain poorly specified.

The Search Paradox. The dual nature of meaning search—adaptive exploration versus distressed striving—requires finer differentiation, possibly distinguishing qualitatively different types of search.

Temporal Dynamics. Meaning exhibits both trait-like stability and state-like fluctuation. Ecological momentary assessment reveals day-to-day variation, yet the implications of such fluctuations for long-term well-being are not fully understood.

Cultural Validity. Greater inclusion of non-WEIRD populations and development of culturally grounded instruments are essential. Measurement invariance does not guarantee conceptual equivalence; indigenous frameworks may enrich or challenge existing models.

Conceptual Integration. Clarifying meaning's relationship with purpose, mattering, coherence, values, and eudaimonic well-being remains an important theoretical task (Martela & Steger, 2016; Ryan & Deci, 2017).

In sum, meaning research now stands on firm empirical ground while facing intellectually demanding next steps. The field has demonstrated that meaning can be measured, that it predicts critical outcomes, that it operates across cultures and developmental stages, and that it can be enhanced through intervention. Yet advancing the science of meaning requires methodological rigor, conceptual clarity, cross-cultural humility, and translational sensitivity. Robust findings warrant application; unresolved questions demand careful investigation. By integrating longitudinal designs, multi-method assessment, cross-cultural collaboration, and mechanism-focused experimentation, meaning science can deepen its explanatory power while preserving the existential richness that first motivated its study. Such progress holds not only theoretical significance but practical consequence: a more precise understanding of meaning enhances our capacity to recognize existential distress, design effective interventions, and support lives experienced as coherent, purposeful, and significant.

82 Logotherapy in integrative practice

In contemporary psychotherapeutic work, logotherapy is often practiced most faithfully not as a "stand-alone school," but as an integrative orientation—a way of seeing the person and organizing the therapeutic encounter. Its classical assumptions already invite integration: Frankl's non-reductionism positions the human being as simultaneously biological, psychological, and noetic/spiritual, with each dimension real and clinically relevant, yet nonsufficient on its own (Frankl, 1970; Lukas, 1998). Within this view, symptoms are not treated merely as malfunctions to be eliminated, but also as signals that invite a broader existential reading—one that includes meaning, conscience, responsibility, and the person's capacity to take a stand toward fate (Russo-Netzer & Vos, 2026). This is precisely why logotherapy can function as an integrative "spine" for practice: it supports the therapist in working competently with evidence-based methods for distress reduction, while also keeping the deeper question alive: *What is life asking of this person now, and how might they respond in a way that is responsible, value-consistent, and meaning-aligned?* In many treatments, change begins with stabilizing symptoms and restoring functioning; logotherapy does not oppose this. Rather, it adds a distinctive clinical aim: helping the client move from being determined by circumstances to becoming an active partner in meaning discovery, even under constraint (Ameli, 2016; Frankl, 1970).

A helpful way to conceptualize integration here is "both/and" sequencing. In many cases, clients first need support with regulation, safety, and cognitive flexibility before they can approach existential concerns without becoming overwhelmed. Logotherapy, at its best, does not spiritualize suffering or rush toward "meaning talk." It attends to the person's readiness, defenses, and resources so that meaning exploration remains invitational rather than invasive (Yalom, 2011). At the same time, logotherapy prevents the opposite drift: a purely technical focus that inadvertently narrows therapy to symptom management alone, leaving the client's existential vacuum, value conflict, or loss of direction untouched (Frankl, 1970; Schulenberg et al., 2008).

Integration with CBT and REBT is one of the most natural bridges, because both traditions care about how interpretations shape experience, yet they often differ in what they treat as "primary." Early behavioral traditions sometimes regarded existential meaning as peripheral; this has shifted substantially, and meaning is increasingly recognized as clinically relevant in second- and third-wave CBT developments (DiGiuseppe et al., 2013; Heidenreich et al., 2021; Russo-Netzer & Vos, 2026; Van Bruggen et al., 2013). From a logotherapeutic perspective, CBT contributes powerful tools for reducing secondary disturbance—rumination, harsh self-evaluation, catastrophic thinking—processes that can constrict the person's freedom and make meaning-detection difficult (Beck et al., 1979; Russo-Netzer & Vos, 2026). Logotherapy, in turn, protects CBT from becoming overly functionalistic by widening the clinical lens: *What existential condition is the client facing (mortal guilt)? What meanings are threatened or possible? What resources and power dynamics shape the person's options?* This synergy is captured well by integrative models that explicitly combine rationality and meaning. For example, integrative logotherapy/REBT helps clients examine the rationality and helpfulness of beliefs about meaning—challenging unrealistic or coercive internal philosophies ("If I cannot succeed, my life is worthless") while supporting self-transcendence and values-based direction (Russo-Netzer & Ameli, 2021; Russo-Netzer & Vos, 2026). In practice, CBT techniques (e.g., behavioral experiments, cognitive restructuring, exposure, skills training) can be positioned as servants of freedom: they help expand the person's behavioral repertoire so the person can actually live in accordance with values, rather than merely endorsing them in insight (Beck et al., 1979).

Schema therapy and recovery-oriented cognitive therapy offer additional integrative openings because they already attend to needs, aspirations, and meaningful activity. When logotherapy is integrated here, schema work is not only about reducing maladaptive patterns, but also about freeing the person to explore meanings not previously available to them, especially meanings constrained by early life adaptations and ontological core schemas (Beck et al., 2020; ; Ottens & Hanna, 1998; Russo-Netzer & Vos, 2026; Young et al., 2003).

Integration with psychodynamic and psychoanalytic traditions can be equally robust, though it requires careful translation of language. Psychodynamic work highlights how meaning is shaped by conscious and unconscious forces, internalized relationships, conflict, defense, and longing, often expressed through repetitive relational patterns and through central life domains such as love, work, and relatedness (Freud, 1958b; McWilliams, 2004; Shedler, 2010). Psychoanalytic and psychodynamic approaches may help uncover obstacles that block desire, choice, and creative engagement, and clarifies how real and imagined relationships shape values, goals, inhibitions, and the felt sense of freedom (McWilliams, 2004; Shedler, 2010) . Integration becomes especially meaningful when logotherapy provides the existential horizon and psychodynamic work provides the depth psychology of constraints. Put simply: psychodynamics can illuminate why freedom feels dangerous (e.g., guilt, loyalty binds, fear of separation), while logotherapy supports clients in making responsible choices in the present, even when doing so entails the emotional pain of separation, loss, or individuation (Frankl, 1970; Yalom, 1980). This integration also carries ethical advantages. Because logotherapy works explicitly with values and responsibility, it is important to ensure that meaning-oriented dialogue remains invitational rather than prescriptive. Psychodynamic reflexivity can support this stance by helping clinicians notice when value language begins to function defensively, becomes shaped by compliance needs, or echoes familiar authority dynamics within the therapeutic relationship (McWilliams, 2004). Conversely, logotherapy can help psychodynamic exploration remain clinically anchored by linking insight to the client's present life: What might be the next meaningful step, even a modest one, that expresses the person's values within real constraints? Evidence that psychodynamic psychotherapy is effective and can yield enduring gains further supports the clinical legitimacy of this integrative bridge (Shedler, 2010).

Logotherapy aligns naturally with **narrative therapy**, because meaning is lived through story: coherence, identity, and future direction are carried in the narratives people inhabit and revise. Meaning-centered therapies frequently incorporate narrative interventions, such as life review, legacy work, re-authoring, especially in contexts of illness, loss, and transition (Breitbart & Poppito, 2014; MacKinnon et al., 2013, 2014; Russo-Netzer & Vos, 2026). Narrative therapy's classic emphasis on externalizing problems and thickening preferred stories (White & Epston, 1990) pairs well with logotherapy's emphasis on self-distancing and attitudinal freedom: the person is not identical with symptoms, history, or diagnosis; they can relate to experience, take a stand, and choose a direction (Frankl, 1970; White & Epston, 1990). In integrative practice, narrative methods become logotherapeutically potent when the therapist attends not only to plot and identity statements (e.g., "I am broken"), but also to the client's latent meaning potentials. Specifically, the therapist listens for openings related to Frankl's three pathways to meaning: creative values (contribution and purposeful action), experiential values (love, connection, and encounter), and attitudinal values (the stance one takes toward unavoidable suffering). The clinical aim is not to reframe suffering into an artificially uplifting storyline, but to co-construct a narrative that is both truthful and dignifying, one that holds the reality of tragedy while restoring agency, responsibility, and the client's capacity for self-transcendence. This often involves identifying what remained intact and human in the person even under dehumanizing conditions (Frankl, 1970; Russo-Netzer & Vos, 2026).

Integration with **mindfulness-based therapies and Acceptance and Commitment Therapy (ACT)** has become increasingly prominent, reflecting a strong conceptual and clinical fit. Mindfulness practices cultivate capacities that meaning-centered work often requires: presence, decentering, tolerance of ambiguity, and the ability to remain with pain without immediate avoidance. Formal mindfulness stabilizes attention and acceptance, while informal mindfulness embeds these capacities into daily life, transforming ordinary moments into opportunities for value realization. Empirically, mindfulness is associated with meaning, and mindfulness training can increase meaning through mechanisms such as decentering and authentic self-awareness (Chu & Mak, 2020). MBCT explicitly integrates mindfulness with cognitive therapy principles (Segal et al., 2002), and existential therapies have long shared phenomenological attention to lived experience, making MBCT a natural partner for logotherapy's here-and-now encounter. ACT provides a particularly strong bridge because it already centers acceptance, present-moment contact, and committed action guided by values. ACT practitioners vary widely in how systematically they explore values and meaning, and the valuing process can be operationalized more narrowly relative to the broader meaning-in-life literature (Matheus Rahal & Caserta Gon, 2020; Reilly et al., 2019; Barney et al., 2019; Russo-Netzer & Vos, 2026). Here, logotherapy offers something distinctive: it deepens "values work" into responsibility education—a dialogue with conscience, uniqueness, and concrete tasks that call the person beyond self-preoccupation (Lukas, 1998; Schulenberg et al., 2008).

Across these integrations, several clinical principles help preserve coherence. First, case formulation can remain logotherapeutic even when methods vary: the therapist can formulate the client's difficulties along multiple dimensions—symptom patterns and maintaining processes (CBT), relational themes and defenses (psychodynamic), dominant identity stories (narrative) and cognitive fusion (ACT), and attentional habits (mindfulness), while also naming the meaning-centered questions that organize the work: *Where is freedom constricted? What responsibility is emerging? What meaning potentials are blocked, threatened, or waiting?* (Frankl, 1970; Hill, 2018; Russo-Netzer & Vos, 2026).

Second, method selection can be guided by readiness and the ethics of pacing. When anxiety is flooding, dereflection, mindfulness grounding, or skills building may be the compassionate first move, not because meaning is irrelevant, but because the person needs enough inner space to hear it. When cognition is rigid, CBT/REBT can restore flexibility so the client can entertain alternative meanings without collapse. When shame and relational fear dominate, psychodynamic attunement to transference/countertransference and attachment needs can make meaning exploration safer rather than prematurely exposing. When identity is shattered by trauma or illness, narrative reconstruction and legacy work can restore coherence and direction (Breitbart & Poppito, 2014; Russo-Netzer & Vos, 2026).

Third, integration is strengthened when we explicitly hold both common factors and specific factors. The alliance, therapist responsiveness, and shared purpose reliably matter across treatments; and at the same time, techniques matter when they are used with integrity and fit (Norcross & Goldfried, 2019; Wampold & Imel, 2015). Logotherapy adds a particular "common factor" emphasis of its own: the therapist as a human presence who models responsible freedom and meaning-orientation, without coercion. Yalom's view of the therapist–client relationship similarly underscores the relationship itself as a living model of meaningful engagement; this emphasis is strengthened when therapists remain aware of their own meaning assumptions and existential anxieties (Hill, 2018; Yalom, 2011).

In sum, logotherapy in integrative practice is not a loose eclecticism. It is an ethically grounded, person-centered stance that protects the dignity of the client as a meaning-seeking being—while welcoming the best of other traditions. CBT can help clients think and act more flexibly; psychodynamic work can reveal the relational and unconscious knots that make freedom feel impossible; narrative therapy can restore coherence and authorship; mindfulness-based approaches can cultivate the capacity to stay present with pain without avoidance; ACT can translate values into committed action. Logotherapy weaves these into a single clinical promise: even under constraint, something remains free—our stance, our responsibility, and our possibility of meaning (Frankl, 1970).

83 Working with religious beliefs

For many clients, religious and spiritual traditions are central meaning structures that organize identity and provide an overarching orientation to life. In this sense, religious and spiritual frameworks often function as foundational meaning systems, shaping how people interpret suffering and hope, define responsibility, and experience belonging. C. S. Lewis's striking claim that "God whispers to us in our pleasures" but "shouts in our pain: it is His megaphone to rouse a deaf world... it removes the veil; it plants the flag of truth within the fortress of the rebel soul" vividly captures why religious beliefs and spiritual interpretations often become especially salient in times of suffering (Lewis, 1940/2001, pp. 91, 93). Pain, within this view, is not merely an experience to be endured, but a condition that may strip away illusion, intensify existential awareness, and confront the person with questions of truth, dependence, responsibility, and transcendence. Across cultures, religious and spiritual frameworks can therefore serve as major psychological resources, offering coherence, practices of coping, and communities of support, while also becoming sites of struggle, doubt, or moral conflict that carry clinical significance (Abu-Raiya & Pargament, 2015; Exline et al., 2014; Koenig, 2012; Pargament et al., 1998). Within logotherapy, this calls for a stance of ethical openness and disciplined humility: the therapist seeks to understand the client's sacred worldview as part of the person's meaning horizon, while safeguarding freedom of conscience and avoiding any drift toward prescriptive or coercive value-guidance (Frankl, 1970; Russo-Netzer & Vos, 2026).

Frankl distinguished psychotherapy's clinical aims from religion's ultimate commitments: therapy seeks psychological relief and functioning, while religion speaks to transcendence and salvation (Frankl, 1970). Logotherapy remains open to the spiritual dimension without claiming theological authority, safeguarding freedom of conscience and the client's autonomy in defining an ultimate horizon of meaning (Lukas, 2000; Russo-Netzer & Vos, 2026). This boundary is an ethical safeguard, ensuring meaning-centered work remains invitational rather than prescriptive (APA, 2017). It helps the logotherapist avoid two common drifts:

(a) *proselytizing* (subtly steering the client toward the therapist's faith or metaphysics), and (b) *spiritual reductionism* (treating religion as "just a defense" or "just a symptom," thereby dismissing the client's deepest sources of meaning and belonging). Instead, the therapist's task is to translate logotherapeutic questions into the client's own sacred vocabulary: *What is life asking of you here? What kind of person are you being called to become? What responsibility is yours, and what is not?*

In this context, a culturally responsive logotherapeutic practice begins with an assessment stance that is curious, collaborative, and non-evaluative. Practically, this often involves taking a brief spiritual history that maps the client's religious/spiritual background; current practices and community ties; images of God/the sacred; sources of comfort and hope; sources of fear, shame, or guilt; experiences of exclusion, spiritual abuse, or moral injury; and the ways faith shapes decisions about suffering, healing, family roles, and identity (Lucchetti et al., 2013; Pargament, 2007). When relevant, therapists can also draw on culturally oriented assessment frameworks that help situate meaning within the client's own explanatory model and sociocultural context rather than importing the therapist's assumptions (American Psychiatric Association, 2013). Because religious/spiritual struggles are robustly linked with psychological distress across diverse settings, it can be clinically important to name and normalize such struggles without pathologizing them. In Pargament's terms, spiritual struggle often reflects disruptions in the person's relationship with what they perceive as sacred, experienced as tension, conflict, doubt, anger, or moral pain (Pargament, 2007). Empirically, the Religious and Spiritual Struggles Scale (RSS) identifies multiple domains of struggle (e.g., divine, demonic, interpersonal, moral, doubt, and ultimate meaning), offering a nuanced map of how faith can become a site of suffering as well as a potential resource (Exline et al., 2014). Related findings suggest that these struggles are relatively common and are associated with, and may prospectively predict, poorer mental and physical health outcomes, underscoring their clinical relevance (Grubbs et al., 2016). In logotherapy, such struggles can be explored as noö-dynamics: tensions between current lived reality and the meaning demands of conscience, values, and community expectations—tensions that may deepen the person's faith and responsibility, or conversely amplify fragmentation, depending on how they are held, metabolized, and translated into action (Frankl, 1970; Pargament, 2007).

Working with religious beliefs also requires careful attention to culture and context. In many collectivistic contexts, meaning is not primarily centered on individual self-actualization but on family continuity, communal responsibility, and relational harmony; accordingly, "choice" and "freedom" may be lived through obligations and interdependence rather than through autonomy alone (Markus & Kitayama, 1991). This has direct clinical implications: interventions that emphasize autonomy and individual preference may be experienced as misattuned, or even ethically problematic, when a client's moral world is primarily organized around duty, kinship obligations, and communal care. For clients from Indigenous communities and other historically traumatized groups, meaning-making may be inseparable from community, land, ancestors, and collective memory. Contemporary scholarship cautions that approaches that ignore historical trauma, or that reduce suffering to decontextualized "individual coping," can unintentionally replicate harm (Kirmayer et al., 2014). A culturally humble integration therefore invites partnership with community resources when appropriate, ongoing consultation and supervision, and a disciplined awareness of power, history, and systemic constraints, so that logotherapy's emphasis on dignity and responsibility is expressed in a way that is both ethically sound and culturally resonant (Hook et al., 2013; Kirmayer et al., 2014).

Practically, logotherapists may use the three pathways to meaning (creative, experiential, attitudinal) to explore religion in a grounded way—without collapsing it into abstraction. *Creative values* may appear as service, volunteering, vocational calling, or repair (charity/acts of compassion). *Experiential values* may be expressed through prayer, ritual, sacred music, nature, Sabbath rest, pilgrimage, or moments of encounter that restore belonging. *Attitudinal values* become central when suffering is unavoidable: the client's stance toward illness, loss, infertility, disability, or moral injury, often shaped by theological interpretations. At this juncture, ethical practice requires particular sensitivity and careful pacing. The therapist should avoid instrumentalizing the client's faith in ways that encourage premature acceptance, enforced endurance, or unprocessed forgiveness. Rather, the logotherapist supports a process of discernment, helping the client identify elements within their tradition that genuinely foster dignity, responsibility, compassion, and growth, while also examining interpretations that may be shaped by fear, trauma, coercion, or internalized shame.

Because religious belief can be both protective and painful, many cases benefit from explicitly differentiating *supportive faith* from *harmful faith-interpretations.* A supportive faith stance usually expands the person's humanity: it nurtures compassion, accountability without humiliation, belonging without erasure, hope without denial. Harmful interpretations typically constrict the person's humanity: rigid moral perfectionism, fear-based images of God, spiritualized blame ("I'm suffering because I'm bad"), or enforced silence about grief and anger. Research on religious coping underscores this duality, showing that *positive religious coping* (e.g., benevolent religious reappraisal, spiritual support) often relates to better adjustment, whereas *negative religious coping* (e.g., spiritual discontent, punishing God reappraisals) is often associated with distress. In logotherapy, the ethical aim is not to judge the client's theology, but to protect the client's dignity and freedom by examining the *consequences* of an interpretation: Does it enlarge agency and responsibility, or collapse the person into fear, shame, and passivity?

Professional ethics also requires explicit competence and sustained respect for diversity. Ethical codes emphasize that clinicians should practice within the boundaries of their competence, avoid harm, respect client dignity and autonomy, and refrain from discrimination—principles that become especially salient when working with religion and spirituality, particularly when therapist and client differ in faith, observance, or worldview (APA, 2017; ACA, 2014). In practice, this entails clarity about professional role and limits (the clinician is not acting as clergy or a religious authority), ongoing consultation or supervision when the client's religious context is unfamiliar or complex, and, when appropriate and requested by the client, thoughtful collaboration with faith leaders or community resources (APA, 2017; ACA, 2014). Such collaboration should remain client-led and consent-based, with explicit agreement regarding purpose, information-sharing, and confidentiality. Equally important is boundary maintenance: spiritual language can be therapeutically meaningful, yet it must not drift into directive "life-guidance," moral persuasion, or implicit coercion; the clinician's task is to support the client's discernment and freedom of conscience, not to prescribe an ultimate stance (Frankl, 1970; Pargament, 2007). Finally, a phenomenological sensibility can train attention to what is already present in lived experience, including forms of sacredness embedded in ordinary life. This is not naïveté, but disciplined receptivity: an attentional stance that helps clients recover sensitivity to value, gratitude, and encounter.

In sum, ethically grounded logotherapeutic work with religious beliefs avoids two equal risks: treating faith as irrelevant on the one hand, and stepping into a moral or spiritual authority role on the other. Instead, it offers a culturally responsive, autonomy-affirming encounter that takes the client's religious world seriously as a lived source of meaning, while also remaining attentive to places where religious interpretations intensify shame, fear, or coercion. At its best, this work protects freedom of conscience, honors dignity, and supports discernment, helping clients translate what they hold sacred into concrete, responsible choices within real-life constraints. In this way, the therapist returns consistently to the logotherapeutic center: meaning discovered rather than imposed, and responsibility enacted with humility, clarity, and compassion.

84 Gender and diversity issues

While Frankl's conceptualization of meaning addresses fundamental dimensions of human existence, its contemporary application requires sustained attention to gender, diversity, and cultural context. Meaning is not pursued in a social vacuum; rather, it is constituted, negotiated, and enacted within historically situated lives shaped by identity, social location, and relational worlds. Accordingly, the search for meaning may be differentially structured by gender identity, sexual orientation, race and ethnicity, disability, socioeconomic conditions, and culture, as well as by the intersection of these positions. In addition, systems of oppression—including sexism, racism, transphobia, and ableism—may substantially constrain access to recognition, safety, opportunity, and belonging, thereby shaping the conditions under which meaning can be discovered and lived. A contemporary logotherapeutic framework should therefore avoid both reductionism and abstraction: it must neither reduce persons to social categories nor treat existential freedom as if it were exercised under uniform conditions. The clinical and ethical task is to preserve logotherapy's core commitments to freedom, responsibility, and self-transcendence while engaging, with conceptual and cultural humility, the complex realities of clients' intersecting identities and structural constraints.

These concerns have become increasingly salient as logotherapy has expanded beyond its European intellectual and clinical origins into diverse cultural and social contexts. This broader reach requires careful examination of how meaning-making is itself culturally mediated, how gender and sexuality shape existential experience, and how marginalization and privilege influence the conditions under which purpose can be pursued, recognized, and sustained. An inclusive contemporary logotherapy therefore benefits from engagement with feminist philosophy, multicultural psychology, queer theory, critical race scholarship, and intersectionality frameworks—not to replace Frankl's framework, but to refine its application in contexts marked by power differentials and social inequality. The present discussion positions logotherapy as a particularly relevant framework for gender- and diversity-informed practice, precisely because it centers the person's capacity for meaning, agency, and self-transcendence even under constraint. It examines how logotherapeutic concepts—freedom of will, responsibility, and meaning-as-response—intersect with gendered patterns of meaning-making, the existential realities of LGBTQ+ individuals, cross-cultural variation in meaning construction, and the cumulative effects of intersecting marginalized identities. The aim is not to dilute logotherapy's core commitments, but to strengthen their clinical and ethical application: to articulate how freedom and responsibility can be upheld without abstraction, and how self-transcendence can be supported without bypassing the structural conditions and lived experiences that shape what is possible, safe, and recognizable as "meaning" in a given context.

Traditional psychological theories, including many existential and humanistic approaches, have been critiqued for centering male experience as normative while marginalizing or pathologizing women's experiences. Feminist scholars in psychology have documented how theories developed primarily by and about men often fail to account for gendered socialization, power imbalances, and the specific constraints women face in male-dominated societies. While logotherapy's emphasis on meaning-making and self-transcendence possesses inherent appeal across genders, its contemporary clinical use is strengthened when these commitments are interpreted in relation to gendered social realities rather than presumed to operate under neutral conditions. Women's search for meaning often unfolds within contexts of systemic gender inequality. Feminist therapy, which emerged in the 1960s alongside logotherapy's international expansion, emphasizes that personal struggles cannot be divorced from social, cultural, and political contexts that shape women's lives. Where women face restricted educational opportunities, occupational discrimination, wage gaps, disproportionate caregiving burdens, and vulnerability to gender-based violence, the terrain of meaning-making differs fundamentally from that available to men. Logotherapy's concept of creative values—finding meaning through work and achievement—takes on different significance when women encounter glass ceilings, workplace harassment, and societal devaluation of traditionally feminine contributions. Similarly, the notion of experiential values—meaning derived through relationships and love—must be examined critically when cultural scripts pressure women toward self-sacrifice, emotional labor, and subordination of their own needs.

Feminist approaches to therapy emphasize several principles highly compatible with logotherapy yet requiring explicit integration. First, the personal is political: individual suffering often reflects broader systems of oppression rather than merely personal failing. When women in therapy struggle with feelings of inadequacy, emptiness, or lack of purpose, these experiences may stem from societal structures that limit women's possibilities for self-actualization. A feminist logotherapy would help clients recognize systemic constraints while simultaneously affirming their freedom and responsibility within those constraints—a delicate balance between validating external barriers and empowering internal agency.

Second, feminist therapy insists on egalitarian therapeutic relationships that demystify the therapeutic process and position clients as experts on their own experience. This resonates powerfully with logotherapy's phenomenological stance—that individuals possess unique, unrepeatable perspectives on their lives' meaning. Yet gender dynamics in therapy require active attention: male therapists working with female clients must remain vigilant about not reproducing patriarchal patterns of male authority and female deference. Female therapists working with male clients can model relational equality while helping men examine restrictive masculinity scripts that may constrain their meaning-making. Across therapeutic relationships, gender-sensitive logotherapy requires attention to how socialization shapes clients' lived relationship to freedom, choice, responsibility, and authenticity.

Third, gender-sensitive logotherapy must recognize diverse gender identities beyond the binary. Transgender, non-binary, and gender-diverse individuals face unique existential challenges related to authenticity, embodiment, and social recognition. For transgender clients, the search for meaning often involves profound questions about the relationship between inner identity and external expression, between individual truth and social acceptance. Logotherapy's emphasis on authentic existence and the courage to stand by one's convictions despite social pressure proves particularly relevant. Yet therapists must approach gender identity not as a problem requiring resolution but as a site of meaning-making deserving affirmation and support. Gender transition itself can be understood as an act of existential courage, choosing to live authentically despite societal resistance, economic risks, and potential loss of relationships.

Research on gender and meaning suggests both shared and gender-patterned processes. For example, in a large cross-cultural study of the three dimensions of meaning (coherence, purpose, and mattering), men scored higher than women on coherence, women scored higher than men on mattering, and no gender difference emerged for purpose (Russo-Netzer et al., 2023). Women's meaning-making is often strongly anchored in relational domains—including close relationships, caregiving, and community connection—particularly in the domain of social significance/mattering (e.g., Bonhag & Froese, 2022; Marshall et al., 2010; Schieman & Taylor, 2001). A gender-informed logotherapeutic approach would therefore honor relational and caregiving sources of meaning without allowing them to become prescriptive or restrictive. It would affirm meaning found through motherhood, caregiving, and connection, while equally supporting meaning pursued through professional contribution, creative expression, leadership, activism, or any other value-congruent path a woman chooses.

Similarly, men face gender-specific constraints on meaning-making. Traditional masculinity norms discourage emotional vulnerability, help-seeking, and the acknowledgment of existential anxiety—all of which may interfere with authentic engagement with logotherapeutic processes. Men socialized to value power, control, and stoic self-reliance may struggle with logotherapy's emphasis on accepting life's inherent limitations and finding meaning even in unavoidable suffering. Gender-sensitive work with men involves creating space for emotional expression and vulnerability while helping them examine how restrictive masculinity scripts may limit their capacity for meaningful relationships, self-transcendence, and authentic existence.

Sexual orientation, LGBTQ+ identity, and existential meaning

Lesbian, gay, bisexual, transgender, queer, and other sexual and gender minority (LGBTQ+) individuals face distinctive existential challenges that make logotherapy's insights particularly relevant while demanding culturally competent application. The process of discovering, accepting, and expressing one's authentic sexual orientation or gender identity constitutes a profound existential journey involving core Franklian themes: freedom and responsibility, authentic versus inauthentic existence, the courage to stand by one's truth despite social pressure, and the search for meaning amid suffering and marginalization.

Research consistently shows elevated rates of depression, anxiety, substance use, and suicidality among LGBTQ+ populations relative to heterosexual and cisgender populations, with disparities attributable primarily to minority stress rather than to LGBTQ+ identity itself (Frost & Meyer, 2023; Meyer, 2003; Moagi et al., 2021). Minority stress theory clarifies how stigma, discrimination, victimization, concealment, and internalized stigma create chronic stress burdens that shape mental health and well-being (Meyer, 2003). Accordingly, for LGBTQ+ individuals, meaning-making often unfolds within contexts of family rejection, social exclusion, religious non-affirmation, violence, and heteronormative or cisnormative erasure. This context makes logotherapy particularly relevant, when applied in an affirming and culturally competent manner. Existential and humanistic approaches share core commitments with LGBTQ+-affirmative therapy, including authenticity, agency, personal growth, and the courage to live truthfully under social pressure (APA, 2015; Nakamura et al., 2022). These themes align closely with logotherapy's emphasis on freedom, responsibility, and self-transcendence, provided they are not used to minimize structural inequities or minority stress.

Logotherapy offers several resources for this work. Self-transcendence can help clients move from identity under threat toward identity-in-relation-to-values, commitments, and contribution. Rather than remaining confined to defensive self-focus, LGBTQ+ clients may discover meaning through community-building, advocacy, creativity, caregiving, spiritual life, or professional contribution. Relatedly, research suggests that existential well-being and social support are associated with better self-esteem and lower conflict regarding sexual orientation (Yakushko et al., 2005). Attitudinal values may also be especially relevant in the context of discrimination and marginalization. Logotherapy can support clients in identifying meaningful responses to unjust suffering, such as solidarity, advocacy, creativity, or spiritual resilience, while maintaining a critical ethical boundary.

Isolation and loneliness warrant special attention in LGBTQ+-affirming logotherapy. Many sexual and gender minority clients experience social isolation due to rejection, concealment, or limited access to affirming communities. Research indicates that connectedness functions as an important protective factor, particularly for LGBTQ+ youth and young adults (Garcia et al., 2020; Ryan et al., 2009). In logotherapeutic terms, this supports work on both social belonging (e.g., chosen family, community ties) and existential isolation (the irreducible aloneness of human existence), without collapsing one into the other.

Spirituality is another clinically important domain. Many LGBTQ+ individuals experience conflict between identity and non-affirming religious traditions, which can precipitate crises of meaning. Research suggests a differentiated pattern: rejecting religious environments are linked to poorer outcomes, whereas spirituality, distinguished from punitive or exclusionary religious contexts, may serve as a source of resilience, coherence, and meaning (Barnes & Meyer, 2012; McCann et al., 2020). Logotherapy can be especially useful here because its spiritual orientation is not tied to a single doctrine, allowing therapists to support clients in reconstructing meaning, conscience, and transcendence without imposing either religiosity or secularism.

Intersectionality and meaning-centered practice

Applying intersectionality to logotherapy requires moving beyond single-axis accounts of identity and distress. A client's search for meaning may be shaped simultaneously by race, gender, sexuality, class, disability, migration status, and other social locations, each of which influences access to safety, recognition, and opportunity (Crenshaw, 1989, 1991). An intersectionally informed logotherapeutic approach therefore does not weaken agency; it situates agency within real conditions of power and constraint.

The ADDRESSING framework (Hays, 2016)—a clinical heuristic for attending to major sociocultural identity dimensions (e.g., age, disability, religion/spirituality, ethnicity, socioeconomic status, sexual orientation, Indigenous heritage, national origin, and gender)—provides a useful structure for intersectionally informed logotherapeutic assessment and dialogue. Used in a logotherapeutic spirit, it broadens phenomenological inquiry rather than replacing it: Which identities are most salient now? Where is the client encountering privilege or marginalization? How do these experiences affect what feels meaningful, possible, or costly?

This approach is also supported by psychotherapy research. Meta-analytic evidence suggests that client-perceived multicultural competence is associated with psychotherapy process and outcome variables (Tao et al., 2015), and recent reviews indicate ongoing gaps in LGBTQ+-specific knowledge and training among mental health practitioners (e.g., Cruciani et al., 2024). For logotherapy, this means that cultural humility, identity responsiveness, and intersectional awareness should be treated as core clinical competencies rather than optional supplements.

Several principles follow for intersectionally informed logotherapy: avoid assumptions based on identity categories; privilege client expertise regarding lived experience; attend explicitly to power and therapeutic hierarchy; connect personal suffering to structural conditions without erasing agency; and foster empowerment by recognizing strengths, resistance, and community-based resources alongside constraint. These principles strengthen logotherapy's ethical commitments by clarifying the difference between invitation and imposition, responsibility and blame, and freedom and abstraction. Finally, intersectional practice requires attention to access and equity. Marginalized communities often face barriers to care, including cost, stigma, language obstacles, provider shortages, and mistrust of mental health systems (Dahlhamer et al., 2016; Moagi et al., 2021). Inclusive implementation of logotherapy across diverse populations depends not only on conceptual refinement, but also on practical efforts to improve accessibility, foster affirming care environments, and strengthen culturally responsive training.

Frankl's insights into meaning remain deeply relevant in contemporary clinical work, but their full force is realized only when logotherapy is practiced with explicit attention to gender, culture, diversity, and power. Meaning is never pursued in abstraction: it is discovered within embodied, socially located, and historically shaped lives. A clinically rigorous logotherapy therefore attends to the ways identity, marginalization, privilege, and cultural context shape both the constraints people face and the possibilities available to them. Far from reducing logotherapy's scope, this orientation sharpens its central commitments—freedom, responsibility, self-transcendence, and dignity—by grounding them in the realities through which clients actually live. In practice, this requires cultural humility, disciplined listening, and ongoing reflexivity, so that meaning-centered work expands rather than narrows the client's freedom. When approached in this way, logotherapy is not only preserved; it becomes more clinically vital for the diverse worlds in which people seek meaning today.

85 The logotherapist's self-care through meaning

Logotherapy is practiced through presence. The therapist's most central "instrument" is not only technique, but the capacity to remain human—open, receptive, ethically grounded, and self-connected. In such work, depletion and burnout are often an outcome of sustained emotional labor and responsibility under conditions of high demand (Edú-Valsania et al., 2022; Maslach & Jackson, 1981). In psychotherapy specifically, contemporary syntheses describe burnout as shaped by chronic emotional exposure, high relational responsibility, and the felt weight of outcomes, often accompanied by withdrawal, reduced social engagement, and a narrowing of empathic capacity (Vivolo et al., 2024). Contemporary literature also describes compassion fatigue, secondary traumatic stress, and moral distress as pressures that can erode empathy, meaning, and professional vitality (Bride, 2007; Epstein & Hamric, 2009; Figley, 1995).

From the standpoint of Conservation of Resources (COR) theory, psychological strain escalates when resource loss outpaces resource gain, creating "loss spirals," while well-being strengthens through "gain spirals" that restore capacity and expand resilience (Hobfoll, 1989; Hobfoll et al., 2018). Meaning can function as a high-order resource, supporting coherence, motivation, self-regulation, and value-guided action (Chen & Russo-Netzer, 2025). In healthcare contexts, recent research links meaning in life with lower burnout and better psychological functioning, suggesting that meaning is not merely philosophical, but operationally protective (Van Simaeys et al., 2025). Meaning, thus, can function as a "resource caravan passageway," supporting replenishment, protecting against loss spirals, and enabling gain spirals (Hobfoll, 1989; Hobfoll et al., 2018). In line with this resource-based perspective, evidence from physicians suggests that *meaning salience*—the day-to-day awareness that one's life is meaningful—is associated with less burnout and fatigue and with greater well-being (Hooker et al., 2020). This provides an important bridge for logotherapists: the aim is not merely to *possess* meaning as an abstract life belief, but to sustain ongoing contact with meaning in real time, especially under pressure. From a logotherapeutic standpoint, burnout is therefore not only an accumulation of stressors; it often reflects a gradual thinning of existential contact—with values, freedom, responsibility, and the lived sense of "why." In this sense, burnout can be understood as closely related to a loss of existential meaning, resonating with Frankl's notion of the existential vacuum and the consequences of prolonged value-disconnection (Riethof & Bob, 2019). Accordingly, logotherapy conceptualizes the therapist's restoration not primarily as relaxation or "time off," but as a deliberate reconnection to values and purpose as a renewable psychological resource.

The three pathways of meaning as therapist resource restoration

Frankl's triad can be translated into a clinician-facing restoration model with three complementary aims: *(1) restoring agency, (2) restoring connection,* and *(3) restoring inner freedom.* Each pathway replenishes a different "slice" of the therapist's depleted system by returning the clinician to a lived sense of meaning—through what they *do*, what they *receive*, and how they *choose to stand* (Frankl, 1984).

1) *Creative values: restoring agency:* Creative values express meaning through work, service, and responsibility (Frankl, 1984). For the therapist, this pathway supports renewal through what they give, not through over-giving, but through value-aligned contribution that re-establishes professional authorship. In practice, creative values become most sustainable when translated into small, repeatable micro-interventions that generate a sense of efficacy and "gain" amid ongoing demand.

One simple practice is the *Minimum Viable Meaningful Act:* before the first session or after the last, intentionally choose one micro-act that expresses the therapist you aspire to be, such as drafting one carefully crafted Socratic question, identifying a deeply held value you want to embody today, or selecting one client-centered intention to carry into the room. A guiding prompt might be: *"What is one small act that embodies the therapist I want to be today?"* A second practice is creating a brief *Meaning Portfolio*: a weekly record of (a) one moment of courage you witnessed, (b) one boundary you upheld, and (c) one therapeutic decision you feel proud of. This functions as existential consolidation: it helps the clinician register meaningful contribution and strengthens awareness of "gain spirals," rather than allowing depletion to dominate perception. Finally, therapists can practice *boundary-as-meaning* by framing one boundary as a value commitment rather than a self-protective withdrawal—for example: *"I protect my presence so my work remains human."* When boundaries are articulated as meaning-consistent choices, they are more likely to be upheld without guilt, and they become part of the clinician's ethical and restorative practice.

2) *Experiential values: restoring connection:* Experiential values locate meaning in encounter: through being touched by life, rather than through what one produces or achieves (Frankl, 1984). For therapists, this pathway restores resources through what they receive: love, beauty, awe, community, nature, spiritual life, and genuine human connection. In clinical terms, experiential meaning directly counteracts two common burnout processes, depersonalization and emotional numbing, by reopening contact with life, relationship, and felt aliveness.

Experiential values are most sustainable when practiced as brief, intentional micro-moments of reception. One simple practice is a *daily "human moment" record*: at the end of the workday, document (in one sentence) a moment that moved you—something you witnessed in a client's courage, vulnerability, humor, or humanity. This trains attention toward meaningful encounter and helps preserve emotional availability in the face of repeated exposure to distress.

A second practice is *meaning-oriented reflective journaling*, using prompts that reconnect the clinician to lived engagement rather than performance: *"Where did I feel most alive in my work this week?" "Where did I lose myself?" "What value am I returning to next week?"* These questions shift the focus from outcomes to presence, and from self-critique to value-guided reorientation. Finally, therapists can create a *Meaning Nourishment Map*, comprised of four short lists titled *People, Places, Practices, and Spirit/Awe.* Every two weeks, select one item from each list to intentionally weave into daily life (e.g., a brief walk in a specific place, a short call with a nourishing person, a small aesthetic ritual, or a spiritual/awe practice). This makes experiential meaning concrete and plan-able, ensuring that the therapist's inner life is regularly replenished through contact, beauty, and belonging.

3) *Attitudinal values: restoring inner freedom under constraint:* Attitudinal values become most salient when the situation cannot be changed, yet one can still choose one's response (Frankl, 1984). For therapists, this pathway is especially vital because clinical outcomes are often only partially controllable. When a client deteriorates, drops out, or progress unfolds slowly despite best efforts, the therapist's remaining freedom is *stance*: the position they choose in the face of limitation, uncertainty, and suffering. In logotherapy, this is the preservation of inner freedom and moral coherence when external control is constrained.

A practical way to cultivate attitudinal values is through *Self-Socratic dialogue.* The therapist may select a challenging moment and ask: *What was in my control? What was not? What is my precise responsibility here? What stance do I want to represent as a clinician?* This process restores freedom by re-differentiating responsibility from omnipotence, reducing guilt-driven over-responsibility and strengthening grounded commitment. A complementary practice is a *meaning-centered reframing of "failure."* If a client deteriorates or disengages, logotherapy invites a stance that can hold tragedy without self-erasure: *"I grieve, I learn, and I remain committed to human presence."* This reframing does not deny loss; rather, it protects the clinician's identity and values from collapsing into self-blame, and it preserves the capacity to continue practicing with dignity and compassion.

A sustainable integrative protocol: the Meaning Restoration Cycle (MRC)

To translate the three pathways into a routine clinicians can sustain, a simple weekly cycle can be implemented: (a) *Scan:* Rate from 0 to 10 your current sense of agency (creative), connection (experiential), inner freedom (attitudinal); (b) *Select:* choose the lowest domain as the week's focus; (c) *Micro-commitment:* one action only and one daily two-minute ritual; (d) *Close the loop:* end-of-week reflection: *"What restored me, even slightly?"* This operationalizes meaning salience: the goal is not simply endorsing meaning as a belief, but maintaining lived contact with meaning in real time—an orientation that has been linked to lower burnout in physicians (Hooker et al., 2020). A brief meaning-based check-in can itself function as a micro-intervention: even one weekly question, such as *"Where did I experience meaning in my work this week?"* trains attention toward gain spirals and supports ongoing restoration.

86 Therapist self-reflection as practice

Logotherapy is grounded in the premise that human beings are oriented toward meaning, and that psychotherapy is most effective when it helps a person clarify values, assume responsibility, and exercise inner freedom in concrete life choices (Frankl, 1984; George & Park, 2016). From this perspective, therapist professionalism includes an ongoing capacity to discern meaning within the clinical encounter, especially when sessions become morally complex, emotionally charged, or existentially ambiguous. Therapist self-reflection is therefore best understood not as private reflection but as an ongoing professional practice: a disciplined effort to refine language, examine stance, and sustain alignment between clinical action and ethical commitments. In the broader psychotherapy training literature, structured reflective practices are increasingly viewed as mechanisms that strengthen therapist competence, self-awareness, and clinical decision-making over time (Bennett-Levy & Finlay-Jones, 2018; Bennett-Levy, 2019; Collard et al., 2024).

A logotherapeutic reflective practice is not an invitation to endless self-analysis. Its aim is practical and ethical: to cultivate self-distancing (the ability to step back from immediate impulses), noetic awareness (sensitivity to meaning, values, **and** responsibility), and a habit of translating insight into choice (Frankl, 1984). Put simply, reflective practice helps the therapist repeatedly answer three professional questions: *What is happening in me? What is happening in this encounter? What is the most responsible next step?*

Reflective practice triad: writing, mindfulness, and life review

Therapist self-reflection becomes clinically potent when it is translated into repeatable personal practices that sharpen discernment and protect ethical clarity in the moment of care. Three practices are especially useful within a logotherapeutic frame: reflective writing (to clarify and consolidate meaning-oriented clinical thinking), mindfulness (to strengthen freedom-in-the-moment), and life review (to integrate vocational identity and moral coherence across time).

1) *Reflective writing as personal calibration:* Reflective writing functions as a "slow-motion replay" of practice: it externalizes tacit processes, such as micro-decisions, language choices, and emotional signals that might otherwise remain implicit. In the health professions literature, reflective writing has been associated with empathy-related outcomes and with deeper emotional processing, supporting its role as a developmental tool rather than a purely expressive activity (Chen & Forbes, 2014). Reflective writing supports capacities of discernment (distinguishing what is central from what is noise), ethical precision (naming responsibility without slipping into over-responsibility), language sensitivity (noticing how wording opens or closes meaning), and countertransference awareness (recognizing how inner reactions shape interventions). Practically, these capacities can be cultivated through brief, repeatable micro-practices.

2) *Mindfulness as training for freedom-in-the-moment:* Within logotherapy, mindfulness is most useful when framed as attention training in the service of freedom: the capacity to notice internal impulses without being governed by them, and to respond in ways

that remain consistent with one's values. A randomized controlled trial evaluating a mindfulness- and compassion-based intervention for psychotherapists reported improvements in therapists' mindfulness skills and self-reported empathy, with additional analyses incorporating patient-related variables (Garrote-Caparrós et al., 2023). Such mindfulness-based personal practice supports several clinically relevant capacities: non-reactivity (the space between impulse and intervention), affect tolerance (staying present with suffering without shutting down), attunement (listening for values beneath content), and ethical steadiness (returning to responsibility rather than performance).

In practice, these capacities can be cultivated through brief, repeatable micro-practices embedded around sessions. For example, a 30-second noetic pause before entering the room—one breath in and out, silently: "I meet a person, not a problem"—helps establish dignity and encounter as the ground of the work. A 60-second post-session pause can then consolidate learning and reduce cumulative carryover: "What am I still holding?" and "What do I carry forward as learning—and what do I place down?" Used consistently, these small practices support sustained clarity and presence across the day.

3) *Life review as vocational integration and moral coherence:* Life review is a structured form of autobiographical reflection aimed at integration: revisiting significant life events to consolidate identity, meaning, and continuity. It has been conceptualized as an interpretive and evaluative process, beyond simple reminiscence, and is widely linked in the literature to meaning-making, coping, and narrative coherence across the lifespan (Butler, 1963; Westerhof & Bohlmeijer, 2014). In an RCT of life review, improvement in personal meaning was found to mediate effects on depressive symptoms, supporting meaning as a plausible mechanism of change (Westerhof et al., 2010).

For therapists, a professional life review can serve as a form of vocation consolidation, strengthening the ethical and existential "throughline" that holds practice steady across years, inevitable disappointments, and shifting systems. Life review practices help support capacities of moral coherence (what one will and will not do in the name of helping), humility with responsibility (owning one's role without omnipotence), resilient vocation (why one practices even when outcomes are mixed), and narrative clarity (how one's story shapes listening and boundaries).

Practically, a monthly practice can be structured as follows: create a timeline of five turning points: what called you into helping work; a moment of doubt or helplessness; a moment when you learned something true about suffering; a moment of quiet integrity; and a moment when a boundary protected your humanity. For each turning point, write briefly: What value became clearer here? What stance do I want to embody because of this? Used consistently, this practice helps anchor professional identity in values and responsibility and supports ethical steadiness over time.

87 Language and dialogue in logotherapy

In logotherapy, language is never merely a vehicle for content; it is part of the intervention itself. The words a person uses to describe their life—"*I failed,*" "*I'm trapped,*" "*nothing matters,*" "*I'm broken*"—do not only report experience; they actively *organize* experience, shaping what feels possible, unacceptable, or meaningful. Because logotherapy works at the level of meaning, freedom, and responsibility, linguistic sensitivity becomes a core professional responsibility: the clinician must listen for how language narrows or opens the client's world, how metaphors carry hidden assumptions, and how dialogue can either invite ethical agency or unintentionally pressure it (Frankl, 1959; Lukas, 1998).

A central logotherapeutic insight is that "meaning" itself is a linguistic bridge between *semantic meaning* (what words signify) and *existential meaning* (what life asks of the person). Across languages, the term "meaning" tends to straddle both domains and can therefore serve as a clinical doorway: when clients speak about what something "means," they are often already near questions of value, intention, and transcendence, even if they do not name them explicitly (Russo-Netzer & Mishani-Uval, 2022). The framing of shared features of meaning—especially transcendence (the movement beyond the thing itself), and the role of context and intention—maps naturally onto Frankl's understanding of self-transcendence: the human capacity to orient beyond the self toward a person to love, a task to fulfill, or a stance to choose (Frankl, 1969/ 1988). In practice, this invites a disciplined double listening: *What does the client's language denote?* and *what does it disclose about what matters—what calls them—what they long for, fear, or feel responsible to?*

Metaphor is especially important here because metaphors function as "compressed philosophies." When a client says, "My anxiety is a monster," "I'm carrying a stone," or "I'm drowning," they are not only describing distress; they are presenting an implicit theory of the self and of agency: monsters must be fought, stones must be carried, drowning requires rescue. Contemporary work in cognitive linguistics has shown that metaphor is one of the mind's primary ways of structuring lived reality (Lakoff & Johnson, 1980). For logotherapy, this matters ethically: metaphors can either imprison a client in inevitability or re-open situational freedom. A clinician might gently explore: "When you say *drowning*—what counts as *air* for you?" or "If this is a *stone*—what has it demanded of you, and what would it mean to set it down for a moment?" The point is not to "replace" the client's metaphor with the therapist's preferred one, but to help the client hear their own language, test whether it serves life, and, when appropriate, discover alternative meanings that preserve truth while restoring freedom (Frankl, 1959, 2006; Russo-Netzer & Mishani-Uval, 2022).

This is where Socratic dialogue becomes more than a technique; it becomes an ethical stance. Frankl's Socratic method aims to evoke, not impose—to draw out the client's conscience, values, and possibilities without turning therapy into persuasion (Frankl, 1969, 1988; Lukas, 1998). The logotherapist therefore treats questions as moral instruments: questions can dignify or humiliate; open or corner; clarify or coerce. Professional responsibility means crafting questions that (a) remain faithful to the client's lived world, (b) respect the client's freedom of conscience, and (c) invite responsibility in a way that is proportional to the client's capacities and constraints. In practice, Socratic dialogue often moves in three interwoven directions: clarifying meaning ("What does this loss *mean* to you?"), clarifying freedom ("Where is there still a margin of choice—however small?"), and clarifying responsibility ("What is life asking of you now, given what cannot be changed?") (Frankl, 1959, 2006; Schulenberg et al., 2008).

Because language can be sharp, logotherapy also requires careful boundary-keeping in meaning exploration. Questions about purpose, conscience, guilt, and the "right" response can easily slide into moralizing if phrased carelessly or delivered too quickly. The ethical difference is often subtle but decisive: *"You should take responsibility"* is pressure; *"Where do you feel responsibility calling you, and what makes that hard right now?"* is inquiry. This is one reason that reflective practice matters: clinicians must monitor when their own value language is becoming directive, when "meaning talk" is being used to bypass emotion, or when existential language is inadvertently shaming a client who is still flooded, traumatized, or psychologically constrained (Wise, 2008; Kocet & Herlihy, 2014). The clinician's role is not to win an argument for meaning, but to protect a space where meaning can be discovered with integrity.

Logotherapy's classic techniques can also be understood as *linguistic interventions* that reorganize attention and possibility. Dereflection is partly an ethical redirection of the "pronoun economy" of distress—from relentless "I, me, my symptoms" toward "you, we, task, value, other"—without denying pain (Frankl, 1969, 1988; Lukas, 1998). Paradoxical intention works, in part, by changing the language of fear: it disrupts catastrophic prediction and rigid self-instructions by introducing deliberate, humorous, non-catastrophic phrasing that loosens anticipatory anxiety (Frankl, 1959, 2006). Even attitudinal modification—Frankl's work with unavoidable suffering—depends on language that can hold tragedy without collapsing into nihilism or sentimental inspiration. Here, the therapist's words must be both honest and existentially accurate: acknowledging what is irreparable while still inviting the question of stance, witness, and human dignity (Frankl, 1959, 2006; Vos et al., 2015).

Finally, meaning-centered language must be culturally and spiritually literate. Words like *freedom, choice, calling, conscience,* and even *meaning* do not land the same way in every cultural world. Meaning is always shaped by convention and context, not only by private experience (Russo-Netzer & Mishani-Uval, 2022). In some cultural contexts, "freedom" is primarily experienced through relational obligation and communal care rather than individual autonomy; in others, spiritual language may be central to how suffering is organized, while for some clients it may be loaded with exclusion or moral injury. The therapist's responsibility is therefore to *translate without imposing*: to let the client's own "meaning language" lead, to ask what a word means *for them*, and to avoid importing an ideological template—whether secular or religious—into the client's existential horizon (APA, 2017; Pargament, 2007).

In sum, logotherapy treats language as a doorway into the human spirit: not because words are magical, but because words reveal where a person is bound, and where they are still free. When the therapist listens with semantic precision and existential care, metaphors become maps, questions become ethical instruments, and dialogue becomes a space where meaning can be discovered rather than prescribed. In that kind of encounter, language does what logotherapy hopes for: it restores the person to agency, responsibility, and dignity, within the real constraints of life (Frankl, 1959, 2006; Lukas, 1998; Russo-Netzer & Mishani-Uval, 2022).

88 Building a logotherapy practice

A well-grounded logotherapy practice is built at the intersection of clinical competence, ethical discipline, and meaning-centered formulation. Its task is not simply to speak about meaning, but to help clients discern and enact meaning under real conditions of fear, loss, conflict, and uncertainty. This requires a form of practice that can work with suffering without pathologizing the human condition, invite responsibility without moralizing, and protect freedom of conscience while translating existential insight into livable clinical steps.

At its foundation is a clear professional identity. Logotherapy is an existential approach that understands the person as capable of taking a stance toward conditions and of discovering meaning through values, conscience, responsibility, and self-transcendence (Frankl, 1984; George & Park, 2016). In practice, this identity is best held in partnership with the clinician's primary professional 'home'—psychology, counseling, psychiatry, social work, nursing, chaplaincy, coaching, or education. A mature logotherapy practice does not compete with one's base discipline; it deepens it by adding an explicit meaning lens to assessment, case formulation, intervention, and ethical decision-making.

Logotherapy-informed coaching

Logotherapy-informed coaching is a natural extension of meaning work when the client's primary task is existential-developmental rather than clinical treatment: clarifying direction, strengthening agency, rebuilding responsibility, and translating values into action. In this context, the central question is not only, "What do you want to achieve?" but also, "For the sake of what?"—that is, what meaning is asking to be lived here, in these circumstances?

The coaching stance must remain explicitly client-owned and non-coercive. It may invite responsibility, but it cannot impose a moral agenda; it may clarify values, but it cannot prescribe them; it may support commitment, but it must avoid "should-talk" and covert persuasion, especially when clients are uncertain or vulnerable (Frankl, 1970). Because meaning-centered coaching often resembles therapeutic dialogue in tone and depth, ethical practice depends on sharp boundaries and explicit contracting.

A logotherapy-informed coaching practice should therefore clearly define what it is and is not, and identify indicators for referral or shared care. At minimum, this includes: (a) naming the focus of coaching (e.g., goals, direction, decision-making, habits, leadership, relationship commitments), (b) clarifying limits (coaching is not treatment for mental disorders, trauma destabilization, acute risk, or severe functional impairment), and (c) establishing a referral pathway when clinical care is indicated. Within these boundaries, coaching can help clients formulate goals as responsibility-in-action under real constraints. Three micro-practices are especially useful:

- *Socratic deepening (from outcome to meaning):* A client says, "I want a promotion." The coach explores: "What would that make possible that matters to you?" "Which value would it serve?" "If it does not happen, what would still be worth living and enacting?" The aim is to reformulate goals as meaning-anchored directions with behavioral steps.

- *Dereflection for performance/self-monitoring loops:* When attention collapses inward ("Am I good enough?" "Did I fail?"), the coach redirects attention toward task, relationship, and contribution ("What does this situation require?" "Who benefits if you show up differently?"). The aim is not to deny emotion, but to restore contact with life beyond self-evaluation.
- *Constraint-aware responsibility framing:* Goals are clarified in a way that acknowledges circumstances rather than bypassing them, preserving both realism and agency.

In organizational coaching, an additional ethical layer is introduced when a sponsor (the organization) is involved. Here, confidentiality boundaries and reporting agreements should be clarified in advance, and meaning work must be protected from becoming a tool of coercion. A logotherapy-informed stance is especially valuable in these settings: responsibility is invited, not imposed; conscience is respected; and dignity remains non-negotiable even when performance is a central concern.

Building professional competence in logotherapy

Because logotherapy is used across professions and settings, the most ethically defensible approach is to treat logotherapy competence as an additional specialization built through structured study, supervised application, and continuing development. Meaning work is not only conceptual; it is relational, technical, and ethically demanding. Established training pathways reflect this by requiring supervised practice and applied hours as part of credentialing (e.g., VFIL pathways and related institute standards). In practical terms, building competence means operationalizing it:

- *Scope clarity:* Which populations and presentations are you trained to treat? When is referral or shared care needed?
- *Supervision and consultation:* Meaning work can evoke moral distress, value countertransference, and the clinician's own

existential assumptions. Supervision is part of ethical containment, not an optional support.

- *Continuing education and calibration:* Evidence, ethical guidance, and cultural knowledge evolve. A logotherapy practice must remain a learning practice.

A logotherapy practice is strongest when it is explicit about role, limits, and process. Professional ethics codes across disciplines converge on competence, nonmaleficence, dignity, autonomy, and non-discrimination—principles that become especially salient when work includes values, conscience, spirituality, suffering, or mortality (APA, 2017; ACA, 2014).

Logotherapy's distinctive ethical vulnerability is also its distinctive strength: it works directly with meaning and responsibility. The safeguard is not to dilute these themes, but to practice them with discernment. Clinicians protect freedom of conscience by avoiding covert persuasion, "should-talk," and value imposition, especially when clients are highly suggestible due to grief, fear, dependency, or crisis. Meaning exploration remains ethically sound when it is invitational, dialogical, and client-owned: clarifying values rather than prescribing them; widening possibilities rather than narrowing them; helping the client answer life's questions rather than replacing the client's answer with the clinician's preferred one (Frankl, 1970). Ethical clarity also depends on practical infrastructure: informed consent, privacy protections, record keeping, consultation policies, telehealth boundaries, and referral pathways.

Meaning-centered formulation in a contemporary practice

A logotherapeutic formulation typically asks:

- Where is freedom experienced as constricted—by fear, avoidance, shame, trauma, or circumstance?
- What responsibility is realistically available now (situated responsibility, not idealized responsibility)?
- What meaning potentials are blocked, threatened, or waiting—through creative, experiential, and attitudinal values?

- Where is hyper-reflection or self-absorption narrowing the person's field, and where might dereflection restore contact with life beyond the symptom?

This formulation does not replace symptom-based formulation; it complements it. The aim is not to choose between symptom relief and meaning, but to keep symptom work in service of a larger task: restoring agency and orientation toward a meaningful life.

A sustainable logotherapy practice translates existential principles into a reliable clinical pathway:

- *Intake and assessment:* In addition to symptom and risk assessment, explore current sources of meaning and meaning threats, value conflicts, conscience language, belonging, and the client's stance toward loss, guilt, fate, and uncertainty.
- *Contracting and informed consent:* Clarify what meaning-centered work is and is not, what techniques may be used (e.g., Socratic dialogue, dereflection, paradoxical intention when appropriate), and how value/spiritual differences will be handled ethically (APA, 2017; ACA, 2014).
- *Pacing and readiness:* Meaning exploration has an ethics of pacing. Stabilization, grounding, alliance work, and behavioral/cognitive flexibility are often what make meaning work possible—not alternatives to it.
- *Ongoing process:* Return regularly to orienting questions: What is the task of this moment? What is still free? What responsibility is realistic? What is a meaningful next step under these constraints?
- *Ending and continuity:* Termination includes meaning consolidation—not only symptom change, but shifts in stance, commitments, relationships, and self-transcendence, and how the client will continue meaning-directed action beyond therapy.

Finally, a sustainable practice requires that the therapist's work is supported by supervision and peer community, protected from over-responsibility, and grounded in ongoing learning. In an era of burnout, the logotherapist's credibility is not perfection but ethical steadiness: showing, in small and consistent ways, that even under pressure something remains free—one's stance, one's responsibility, and one's capacity to respond humanly. A well-built logotherapy practice is therefore neither rigidly "pure" nor loosely eclectic. It is principle-centered and clinically flexible: anchored in the dignity of the person, disciplined by ethics and competence, responsive to context and culture, and oriented toward the central promise of logotherapy, helping people discover and enact meaning not as an abstract ideal, but as the next livable task.

89 Research on meaning-centered practices

Over the past two decades, meaning-centered psychotherapy has shifted from a primarily conceptual-clinical tradition to an increasingly testable set of interventions evaluated in clinical trials and meta-analyses. Across outcome studies and evidence syntheses, a consistent pattern emerges: when interventions explicitly cultivate meaning (e.g., through values clarification, responsibility-in-action, narrative integration, and stance-taking under constraint), participants tend to show improvements in existential well-being and, often, reductions in distress and improvements in quality of life. Large-scale syntheses generally support the promise of meaning-oriented therapies while highlighting heterogeneity. For example, a meta-analysis of existential therapies found that meaning-centered approaches showed comparatively stronger effects on perceived meaning and moderate effects on psychological outcomes, whereas several other existential therapy variants showed smaller or non-significant effects in the included trials (Vos et al., 2015). A broader meta-analysis focused specifically on meaning-centered therapies reported improvements in quality of life and reductions in psychological stress, and—importantly—meta-regression results indicated that increases in meaning predicted decreases in stress, aligning with the field's proposed mechanism of change (Vos et al., 2015; Vos & Vitali, 2018).

Overal, the literature highlights a recurring methodological and clinical reality: meaning-centered interventions are not a single uniform treatment, but a family of practices that share a meaning-oriented clinical logic while differing in delivery format, population, dose, and emphasis. In practical terms, the evidence base supports two conclusions at once: (a) meaning-centered work is broadly promising across contexts, and (b) clinicians and researchers must attend carefully to *what exactly was delivered*, and what mechanisms of change are plausible in each setting (Vos & Vitali, 2018). The empirical literature can be organized into two complementary categories: *(1) Manualized meaning-centered psychotherapies* (structured session-by-session protocols, often tested in trials), and *(2) Meaning-centered practices* (repeatable exercises that can be integrated into broader therapy, groups, or community interventions).

In terms of the first category, *manualized meaning-centered psychotherapies*, one of the most developed research lines comes from meaning-centered psychotherapy in psycho-oncology, which adapts logotherapy-informed principles into brief individual and group protocols intended to support spiritual well-being and meaning in patients facing advanced illness. The protocolized form, often delivered in groups, was designed to help patients sustain or enhance meaning, peace, and purpose even under existential threat (Breitbart et al., 2010). Meaning-centered protocols have also been adapted for cancer survivorship. In a randomized controlled trial, meaning-centered group psychotherapy for cancer survivors was evaluated against supportive group psychotherapy and care-as-usual, with findings supporting its efficacy for improving personal meaning and related outcomes (van der Spek et al., 2017). A longer-term follow-up study further examined sustained effects over time, supporting the view that meaning-centered group work can produce benefits that are not purely immediate "symptom shifts," but changes in meaning-related functioning (Holtmaat et al., 2020). These protocols tend to operationalize *meaning literacy*: helping clients name sources of meaning (relationships, creativity, legacy, values, stance), *narrative integration:* connecting life story, identity, and responsibility into a coherent "throughline," *existential coping:* strengthening the capacity to live with uncertainty, limitation, and mortality while remaining value-guided, and *legacy and contribution*: translating meaning into concrete acts that preserve dignity and continuity.

Alongside manualized protocols, the literature includes studies *of logotherapy and meaning practices applied in different populations and formats*. These include repeatable exercises that can be embedded within broader therapies, groups, coaching, health care, or community interventions. This strand includes structured life review and reminiscence programs linked to meaning-making and psychological outcomes (Westerhof et al., 2010), as well as creative and non-verbal practices (e.g., photography-based meaning work) designed to access meaning and values affirmation (e.g., Russo-Netzer, 2021; Russo-Netzer & Atad, 2025; Russo-Netzer & Vos, 2026; Steger et al., 2014). A recent development include technology-mediated delivery. Emerging studies suggest that meaning-centered work can be adapted beyond traditional in-person formats, provided core existential mechanisms remain intact. For example, a study of mobile-based logotherapy delivered via WhatsApp for major depressive disorder reported reductions in depression- and hopelessness-related outcomes, supporting feasibility and potential impact while underscoring the ongoing need for fidelity-focused evaluation (Shaygan et al., 2023).

Taken together, the intervention literature supports a coherent proposition: meaning can be cultivated through structured practices, and doing so is associated with improvements in existential well-being and, often, psychological distress and quality of life. At the same time, variability across "meaning-centered" labels is not simply a weakness; it is a signal that meaning-centered work is highly translatable, but must be described precisely, implemented with conceptual integrity, and tested with designs that illuminate both outcomes and mechanisms (Vos & Vitali, 2018). Across reviews and trials, several priorities recur: stronger active comparators and longer follow-up to clarify durability and specificity (Sun et al., 2024); clearer articulation of intervention components and fidelity procedures to reduce interpretive ambiguity (Vos, 2018; Vos & Vitali, 2018); broader populations and delivery contexts (including caregivers and digital pathways) to strengthen generalizability (Shaygan et al., 2023); and more mechanism-focused designs that test how meaning changes, not only whether distress declines (Westerhof et al., 2010).

The task for contemporary logotherapy, therefore, is twofold: to continue strengthening the evidence base through rigorous trials and mechanism studies, and to translate validated meaning-centered practices into formats that meet modern clinical realities including groups, telehealth, and scalable community interventions, without losing the existential core.

Part 5

Contemporary developments and future directions

90 Cross-cultural adaptations

Logotherapy addresses questions that arise across many human lives - how one responds to suffering, what one feels responsible for, and what one considers worth living for. Yet these questions are lived within culturally shaped moral worlds, relational expectations, spiritual traditions, and social realities that influence how suffering, dignity, hope, and responsibility are understood and expressed (Bernal et al., 1995; Frankl, 1984; Markus & Kitayama, 1991). For this reason, cross-cultural work is integral to logotherapy practice.

This task begins with a distinction that is central to contemporary cross-cultural practice: the distinction between existential core and cultural carriers. What remains relatively stable in logotherapy are its central commitments -human dignity, freedom-as-stance under constraint, responsibility, conscience, and self-transcendence. What requires translation are the forms through which these commitments are lived and communicated: idioms of distress, relational norms, symbols and metaphors, spiritual frameworks, and culturally legitimate pathways to meaning (Bernal et al., 1995; Frankl, 1984). In practice, the therapist's task is not to import a fixed model of "meaning" into a new context, but to help meaning-work become clinically intelligible within the client's own cultural world.

This is especially important because much of the formal evidence base for meaning-centered therapies has been developed primarily in Western settings, and reviews have repeatedly noted the need for broader cultural validation and clearer specification

DOI: 10.4324/9781003624417-5

of intervention components and delivery conditions (Vos & Vitali, 2018). The implication is methodological as well as clinical: logotherapists should avoid assuming that an intervention "travels" unchanged across contexts. Cross-cultural practice requires careful adaptation, explicit documentation of what is delivered, and ongoing evaluation of fit and outcome (Henrich et al., 2010; Vos & Vitali, 2018).

A culturally responsive logotherapy therefore involves more than using culturally familiar examples. In psychotherapy science, this is described as cultural adaptation: modifying language, metaphors, goals, and methods so that the intervention fits the client's cultural ecology without losing the mechanisms that make it effective (Bernal et al., 1995; Day et al., 2023). Applied to logotherapy, this means preserving the existential logic of the approach while translating its clinical expression. The aim is not cultural relativism (in which the core disappears) and not rigid fidelity (in which the client's world is ignored), but a disciplined integration of both.

Several domains are especially important in this adaptation work: First, concepts of selfhood and personhood differ across cultural contexts. Many Western clinical models assume an autonomous, bounded self organized around individual choice and self-definition. In many other contexts, identity is experienced more relationally or interdependently, with obligations to family, community, and tradition carrying primary moral weight (Markus & Kitayama, 1991). In such contexts, logotherapy's emphasis on responsibility and unique meaning may need reframing, not as solitary self-assertion, but as meaning enacted through relational commitments, communal roles, and forms of contribution that preserve both belonging and dignity.

Second, the meaning of freedom must be handled with precision. Frankl's account of freedom remains one of logotherapy's defining contributions, but its clinical application can become distorted if existential freedom is conflated with social opportunity. Across contexts marked by poverty, displacement, political repression, rigid hierarchy, or collective trauma, logotherapists must be able to affirm freedom-as-stance without minimizing real external constraints. This distinction helps preserve agency while avoiding moralizing or victim-blaming.

Third, communication norms shape how meaning-oriented dialogue can be conducted. Norms of emotional expression, self-disclosure, authority, and indirectness vary substantially across cultures. A Socratic dialogue style that feels collaborative in one context may feel intrusive, disrespectful, or overly abstract in another. Culturally responsive logotherapy therefore treats technique as adaptable in form while stable in purpose: the goal remains meaning clarification, but the route may shift through story, proverb, poetry, sacred text, silence, or relationally framed questioning (Bernal et al., 1995).

Fourth, spirituality and religion often function as central meaning frameworks and require nuanced handling across cultures. Frankl's approach is open to spirituality but not tied to a single doctrine. In cross-cultural practice, this flexibility is an asset, but only if therapists refrain from translating all spiritual worlds into a single existential vocabulary. Different traditions organize suffering, obligation, transcendence, and hope in different ways. The task is not to impose a logotherapeutic grammar onto the client's worldview, but to work within the client's moral and spiritual language while preserving the core orientation to meaning, dignity, and response.

These adaptation tasks are best supported not by a stance of cultural "mastery," but by cultural humility: a disciplined posture of openness, self-reflection, and accountability to the client's lived meaning-world (Hook et al., 2013). This is especially important in meaning-focused work, where therapists can unintentionally import culturally specific assumptions about the "good life," proper expressions of freedom, or preferred forms of responsibility unless these are made explicit and explored in context. Cross-cultural logotherapy becomes clinically strong when it combines fidelity to existential principles with humility about their cultural expression.

A concise, culturally attuned assessment can keep logotherapy anchored in the client's lived moral ecology rather than in demographic labels or imported assumptions. Useful entry points include:

- *Sources:* Where does life most reliably feel worth living?
- *Obligations:* What responsibilities are non-negotiable in your world?

- *Boundaries:* What would feel disloyal, dishonorable, or spiritually unsafe?
- *Idioms of suffering:* How is suffering spoken about—or not spoken about—in your family/community?
- *Hope carriers:* What supports endurance here (e.g., faith, family, duty, service, ritual, learning, community)?

This form of inquiry helps clarify how meaning is organized in the client's context and reduces the risk of imposing culturally narrow assumptions about "purpose," "autonomy," or self-expression (Chiu & Hong, 2007).

Socratic dialogue can also be adapted without losing its function. In cross-cultural logotherapy, this may involve entering through culturally resonant carriers (story, proverb, poetry, sacred text), using permission-based depth ("May we explore what this means in your tradition?"), and framing questions relationally when appropriate ("Who needs to be considered in this decision in your world?"). These are not cosmetic changes; they are clinically meaningful adjustments that protect both therapeutic alliance and conceptual precision.

Work with immigrants and refugees illustrates this integration clearly. Meaning-centered approaches may be especially relevant in contexts of displacement, loss, acculturation stress, and identity rupture. At the same time, effective application requires attention to the full ecology of the person's experience—pre-migration trauma, migration hardship, and post-migration realities such as discrimination, language barriers, economic precarity, and cultural alienation. Here, logotherapy is most useful when it is practiced as context-aware meaning work rather than as abstract existential interpretation.

In sum, cross-cultural logotherapy is best understood as both a fidelity task and an ethics task: fidelity to logotherapy's existential logic, and ethical responsibility to meet the client within the cultural world that gives life coherence, obligation, and worth. When adaptation is explicit—what remains stable, what is translated, and how fit is monitored—the work becomes more precise, more respectful, and more clinically effective across diverse contexts (Bernal et al., 1995; Day et al., 2023; Hook et al., 2013; Russo-Netzer & Mayseless, 2021).

91 Digital age challenges

Digital life has altered the *tempo* and *texture* of everyday existence. Many people now live inside environments that are continuously "on": constant availability, rapid task-switching, and an intensive stream of information and demands. What changes clinically is not only stress load, but the *existential ecology* in which meaning is discovered: when time is experienced as compressed and attention is repeatedly fragmented, it becomes harder to sustain reflective space, clarify values, and maintain a coherent narrative of "what I am responsible for and why." This condition resonates with broader analyses of late modernity that emphasize acceleration, contingency, and a weakening of stable life structures—features that can undermine comprehensibility and deepen alienation (Rosa, 2013; Bauman, 2000). From a logotherapeutic perspective, these shifts matter because meaning is not only an idea a person endorses; it is a lived orientation enacted through freedom, responsibility, and self-transcendence (Frankl, 1984). The digital condition can subtly compromise the very capacities through which meaning becomes *experienced*, particularly the noetic "space" for self-distancing, conscience, and stance-taking. Logotherapy therefore approaches digital challenges with a distinctive aim: not rejecting technology, but restoring the human ability to choose one's stance and commitments within it.

Attention erosion and "noetic shrinkage": Many digital environments are built around interruption and rapid novelty. This often presents as diminished sustained attention, restless mental switching, and reduced tolerance for silence and inward listening. The deeper risk, in logotherapeutic language, is noetic shrinkage: when the inner space needed for value-clarification and stance-taking becomes harder to access. Importantly, emerging causal evidence suggests that reducing constant mobile internet connectivity can improve sustained attention and indicators of well-being, supporting the clinical intuition that perpetual connection may carry psychological costs (Castelo et al., 2025).

Technostress and the moral economy of "always available": Beyond workload, digital work creates a specific strain commonly described as *technostress*—stress arising from technology-related overload, invasion into private time, complexity, uncertainty, and insecurity. Recent reviews summarize consistent links between technostress dynamics and employee well-being, while emphasizing the need for both organizational and individual interventions (Kumar, 2024). These dimensions are often framed as "techno-overload," "techno-invasion," "techno-complexity," "techno-uncertainty," and related pressures (Tarafdar et al., 2007, 2015).

From a logotherapeutic standpoint, technostress frequently contains a meaning conflict—confusion between responsibility and omnipotence. Clients can begin to equate worth with speed, responsiveness, and output, which quietly erodes dignity and inner freedom.

AI, outsourcing of judgment, and threats to authorship: As AI tools spread across education, work, and healthcare, a subtle psychological shift can occur: people may begin to outsource judgment, interpretation, and even identity work ("tell me what to do," "tell me what fits me," "tell me who I am"). This is not inherently harmful—tools can support functioning—but it can reduce the felt experience of *authorship* if the person stops practicing choice. From a logotherapeutic standpoint, a central point is that AI can support action, but it cannot carry responsibility. Responsibility remains a human task, rooted in the noetic dimension—the person's capacity to step back, discern what matters, and choose a stance and commitments, especially under conditions of uncertainty.

Datafication and performance pressure: Another characteristic of contemporary technological culture is *datafication*: the steady conversion of life into measurable indicators (productivity metrics, performance dashboards, quantified routines). Constant quantification can create the illusion that what matters most is what can be measured. For some clients, this becomes an existential trap: life turns into performance management. In late modern contexts where stable narratives weaken and individuals are pushed toward self-constructed guidelines, metrics can become a substitute for meaning rather than a support for it (Bauman, 2000; Rosa, 2013). From a logotherapeutic standpoint, a central point is that dignity is not metric-based. Meaning requires re-anchoring worth in values and commitments that are not reducible to performance indicators.

Misinformation, "false certainty," and epistemic humility: Generative systems can produce persuasive narratives that feel certain even when they are inaccurate. This can amplify confusion, anxiety, or rigid interpretations. Recent reporting and professional discussion highlight the need for caution regarding the reliability and psychological risks of unregulated "self-service" mental health uses of generative AI, particularly when these tools are treated as replacements for professional judgment and relational care (World Health Organization, 2025). From a logotherapeutic standpoint, a central point is that meaning-work requires epistemic humility—the capacity to live with uncertainty while choosing responsible steps. False certainty often functions as an attempt to escape existential tension rather than to meet it.

Overall, a logotherapeutic approach to digital challenges avoids two opposite errors: (a) romanticizing the past ("technology ruined everything"), or (b) surrendering agency ("this is just the world now"). Instead, it treats digital life as a context in which freedom and responsibility must be practiced with greater precision. The clinical emphasis is on restoring: noetic space (a pause in which stance is possible), authorship (language of choice and commitment), dignity beyond metrics, and self-transcendence (re-orienting life toward values, relationships, and contribution). These are not abstract ideals; they are the psychological capacities through which meaning becomes livable in a high-intensity technological culture.

92 Meaning and the creative arts

Meaning is not only something people analyze or explain; it is also something they encounter, feel, and live through, often before it can be fully put into words. In this sense, Jyoti Arora's observation that "when all else seems lost and steeped in hopelessness, the magic of creativity can still keep you going" captures a vital dimension of the creative arts: their capacity to sustain the human spirit when ordinary language, certainty, or control begin to fail. In everyday life, the creative arts provide one of the most natural languages of meaning. They shape experience into image, sound, movement, story, and symbol, making inner life perceivable, shareable, and, crucially, more bearable. Art can hold ambiguity without forcing premature closure, and it can carry emotional and existential depth without requiring immediate conceptual clarity. In this sense, the arts are not merely expressive; they are meaning-forming practices that help people sense coherence, value, and direction in the midst of complexity (Frankl, 1985a; Russo-Netzer & Shor, 2026).

Logotherapy approaches meaning as a *lived orientation* enacted through the noetic dimension—self-distancing, conscience, responsibility, and self-transcendence (Frankl, 1985b). Creative activity can mobilize these capacities directly. First, artistic form creates self-distancing without disengagement: when experience is given shape (e.g., a photograph, a sketch, a stanza, a melody), the person gains a slight inner "space" from which they can relate to what is happening rather than being submerged by it. Second, the arts often carry values implicitly—beauty, truthfulness, fidelity, dignity, compassion—so that conscience and value-clarification can emerge through symbol and process rather than through debate. Third, the arts readily evoke self-transcendence: a creative act is frequently oriented toward witness, offering, contribution, or communion, moving the person beyond self-absorption and toward relationship, purpose, and service (Frankl, 1985a). This perspective is complemented by broader evidence syntheses in arts and health, which link arts engagement with psychosocial benefits relevant to well-being and resilience, including emotion regulation, social connection, and quality of life (Fancourt & Finn, 2019; Stuckey & Nobel, 2010).

Arts-based work becomes logotherapy-aligned when it is organized around responsibility-in-action, not around symptom reduction or aesthetic performance. The guiding questions are existential and ethical: *What is life asking of me here? What value is trying to become real? Where is freedom still available—even if only as stance? What would a dignified response look like now?* (Frankl, 1985a). Framed in this way, the arts contribute several functions that map cleanly onto logotherapeutic principles. First, the arts enable *externalization without reduction*. An image, poem, or movement can hold complexity without forcing immediate explanation; this protects dignity and prevents premature closure. Second, the artwork can create a "third space" for encounter: it stands between the person and the listener, allowing difficult material to be approached more safely while preserving authorship (Moon, 2009; Schaverien, 2000). Third, the arts cultivate *phenomenological precision*: they naturally invite description before interpretation—what is present, what stands out, what is the felt tone—an ethos that aligns with logotherapy's respect for the person's lived meaning-world (Russo-Netzer & Shor, 2026). Fourth, creative revision supports *agency and re-authorship*. Editing, collage, rewriting, re-scoring, or re-framing embodies the possibility of changing one's relationship to experience without denying reality—an enacted stance rather than a purely cognitive maneuver. Finally, the arts often deepen *relational meaning*: meaning consolidates when it is witnessed and received. Shared creative processes can cultivate recognition, belonging, and communal validation. For example, photography can become an intentional practice of presence and meaning-making: the act of "framing" is treated as a noetic move, selecting what matters, noticing what calls, and holding reality with both honesty and choice (Russo-Netzer & Shor, 2026). Such method can also be used to discern and align with sources of meaning in life, using images, metaphors, and creative reflections can anchor values and intentions in daily life in concrete, culturally resonant ways (Russo-Netzer, 2021; Steger et al., 2013). Along these lines, a logotherapy-consistent micro-application, which can be woven into everyday life, may involve a person takes, or selects, one photo that represents a lived value or a moment of self-transcendence, titles it with a single phrase, and answers one question in one sentence: *"What does this image ask me to remain faithful to?"* This keeps the practice explicitly noetic: the photograph is not the goal; it is the carrier of commitment. Another possible mini-practice is *"metaphor-to-commitment":* choose one line, image, or motif that stays with you; name the value it carries; then translate it into one concrete act within 48 hours. The goal is the conversion of experience into responsibility-in-action—exactly the logotherapeutic move.

Overall, arts-based modalities contribute several therapeutic functions that are especially relevant to logotherapy:

- *Externalization without reduction:* an image, poem, melody, or movement can hold complexity without forcing immediate explanation. This protects dignity and prevents premature closure.
- *A "third space" for encounter:* the artwork stands between therapist and client, making it safer to approach difficult material while preserving the client's authorship (Moon, 2009).
- *Phenomenological precision:* arts invite description before interpretation—an ethos that fits logotherapy's respect for the person's lived meaning, concrete experience, and irreducible uniqueness.
- *Agency and re-authorship:* creative revision (editing, collage, rewriting, re-scoring) embodies the possibility of "reframing" without denial: an enacted stance rather than a forced cognitive maneuver.
- *Relational meaning:* sharing art in a group can create recognition and belonging—meaning deepens when it is witnessed and held within a responsive community.

93 Meaning and synchronicity awareness

> Synchronicity is an ever present reality for those who have eyes to see.
> (Jung, 1955, p. 34)

Have you ever experienced an unexplained coincidence that had a special meaning for you? That signified something special? A coincidence which helped you make an important decision you had to make? What was the meaning/role of the experience for you? What is your main takeaway from this experience?

Synchronistic moments often arrive as brief disruptions of the ordinary—unexpected alignments that feel personally resonant, even if they cannot be explained in straightforward causal terms. In this spirit, a logotherapeutic lens treats such moments not as proofs to be defended or dismissed, but as *invitations*: openings that sharpen perception of what one is living through, what one is being asked to take responsibility for, and which values are seeking expression now (Frankl, 1985a).

Experiences of "meaningful coincidence" are common in everyday life: a song on the radio that seems to answer an inner question, an unexpected message at a precise moment, a dream followed by a strikingly aligned event, an unexpected sign on the street that resonates with a private struggle, or thinking of someone and then receiving a call. Such experiences are often described as emotionally evocative, timely, and accompanied by a felt sense that "this matters." From a logotherapeutic standpoint, the clinical relevance is not whether the event can be explained causally, but how the person relates to it: does it become a doorway into values, responsibility, and a more coherent orientation, or does it become fuel for anxiety, rumination, and over-interpretation (Frankl, 1985a; Russo-Netzer & Icekson, 2020). This focus fits a foundational assumption in logotherapy: meaning (logos) is not reducible to logic or intellectual certainty. What guides a person is often not deductive proof, but an existential responsiveness towhat conscience discloses as the "right" direction in the midst of contingency, suffering, or transition (Frankl, 1985b). In that spirit, synchronistic experiences can be understood as heightened moments of meaning salience: occasions that intensify attention, evoke affect, and invite narrative integration. They may become particularly salient during periods of change, grief, moral strain, or uncertainty, when the need for coherence is strong and the person is listening more sharply for what life is asking of them (Russo-Netzer & Icekson, 2020, 2023).

The first systematic articulation of "meaningful coincidence" in psychological literature is associated with Jung's formulation of *synchronicity* as an acausal meaningful coincidence—an experienced connection between an inner event (e.g., thought, internal event occurring in a strikingly resonant way) (Jung, 1951, 1969). Over time, the concept gained cultural influence and clinical interest, particularly within Jungian and related psychodynamic approaches, where case-based writings suggested that synchronicity experiences may coincide with insight and therapeutic movement (Main, 2011; Hocoy, 2012). For many years, however, empirical research remained relatively sparse and was concentrated mainly in psychotherapy and career-development writing, leaving key questions about prevalence, mechanisms, and boundary conditions insufficiently addressed (Cho et al., 2009; Guindon & Hanna, 2002).

A contemporary contribution of the recent empirical line of work in this area is the shift from treating synchronicity primarily as a metaphysical claim to treating it as a psychologically describable *meaning process*, one that can be studied in everyday life as lived experience and examined with measurement and model-testing. A phenomenological exploration of synchronicity awareness described a dynamic process composed of three interlocking building blocks: *Receptiveness, Exceptional Encounter* (or Emotion-Evoking Experience), and *Meaning-Detecting* (REM) model (Russo-Netzer & Icekson, 2020). The first component, *Receptiveness (R),* is not passive suggestibility. It is a readiness characterized by heightened attention and openness to both inner cues (e.g., feelings, images, bodily signals, intuitive knowing) and outer cues (e.g., environmental details, conversations, texts, music, encounters), often accompanied by a deliberate stance of curiosity and an intention to pay attention rather than move through life on autopilot (Russo-Netzer & Icekson, 2020). In the qualitative descriptions, receptiveness often included sensory attunement and a felt "readiness to receive" in which the person becomes more capable of noticing subtle invitations in the world without forcing them (Russo-Netzer & Icekson, 2020). This resonates with logotherapy's idea that meaning is frequently disclosed through *responsible attention* to the concrete demands of a situation—what Frankl called the question life asks of the person—rather than through abstract speculation (Frankl, 1984). Conceptually, receptiveness also overlaps with psychological constructs such as openness to experience, tolerance for ambiguity, and forms of mindful receptive attention that increase sensitivity to what is present and unexpected (Bishop et al., 2004; Brown & Ryan, 2003; Russo-Netzer & Icekson, 2020).

The second component, *Exceptional Encounter / Emotion-Evoking Experience (E)*, refers to the moment the coincidence emerges as extraordinary: an unlikely event that aligns with an inner concern, question, or state and is experienced as emotionally charged, memorable, and timely. Across accounts, three features repeatedly appeared: (a) proper timing (the sense that it happened "exactly when needed"), (b) remarkability/memorability (its improbability or vividness), and (c) emotional intensity (surprise, awe, relief, fear, tenderness, or deep resonance) (Russo-Netzer & Icekson, 2020). From a logotherapeutic perspective, the specific event or experience matters less as proof of an external order and more as an existential interruption that re-opens the person's capacity for wonder, self-distancing, and stance-taking. In other words, the encounter creates psychological space in which the person can respond, ethically and meaningfully, rather than simply react.

The third component, *Meaning-Detecting (M)*, is the integrative act that makes the experience therapeutically and existentially consequential. It involves linking the event to one's life narrative and value-world, deriving a sense of coherence, validation, or direction that can inform responsible action (Russo-Netzer & Icekson, 2020). Crucially, meaning-detecting is the interpretive work of answering: *What might this invite? What does it illuminate about what matters? What commitment does it strengthen?* When integrated well, participants described outcomes such as positive emotion, increased coherence, strengthened self-direction, and a renewed sense of purpose (Russo-Netzer & Icekson, 2020). This is also where logotherapy's emphasis on responsibility becomes decisive: meaning is not "found" as a magical label; it is *realized* through the stance one chooses and the values one embodies in response (Frankl, 1984).

Empirically, the REM framework was operationalized through the development and validation of the Synchronicity Awareness and Meaning-Detecting (SAMD) Scale, which captures two related but distinct dimensions: (1) *Synchronicity Awareness (SA)*—the tendency to notice and report meaningful coincidences, and (2) *Meaning-Detecting (MD)*—the tendency to interpret and integrate such events in a personally significant way (Russo-Netzer & Icekson, 2023). Across multiple community samples and real-life monitoring designs, most participants report at least one synchronicity-type experience, suggesting that "meaningful coincidences" are not rare anomalies but part of ordinary lived experience (Russo-Netzer & Icekson, 2023; Rosenstreich et al., 2024; Rominger et al., 2024).

Crucially, the REM findings imply that the psychological leverage point is not the coincidence itself, but the *meaning-making sequence* around it. SA reflects the moment of noticing—when attention flags an event as potentially significant, whereas MD reflects the next step: the person actively *weaves* the event into a broader narrative of coherence, direction, or value. In this sense, the model highlights an interpretive pathway: searching for meaning predicts greater synchronicity awareness; awareness predicts meaning-detecting; and meaning-detecting, in turn, predicts optimism and presence of meaning, which then relate to life satisfaction (Russo-Netzer & Icekson, 2023). This emphasis on interpretation is precisely what makes the topic clinically relevant, and what calls for clinical care. Because MD involves attributing meaning under uncertainty, it can function as a healthy integrative capacity, but it can also become vulnerable to rigidity when a person is distressed, overwhelmed, or craving certainty. Unregulated explanatory models of coincidences, especially when adopted uncritically or held as conclusive proof, may, in some individuals or contexts, contribute to paranoid or magical thinking styles (Beitman et al., 2010). Logotherapy offers an ethical anchor here: meaning is not tested by intensity alone, but by conscience, responsibility, and whether an interpretation enlarges dignity and life-affirming commitment rather than narrowing reality into fear-driven certainty (Frankl, 1984). Meaning-centered work, thus, is vulnerable to two opposite errors: Dismissal ("it's just random; don't talk about it"), which can undermine or invalidate clients' lived experience and foreclose meaning, and over-affirmation ("it's definitely a sign; follow it"), which can slide into therapist-imposed interpretation and inflate certainty.

Practically, this stance helps keep meaning-making both psychologically healthy and reality-based, without humiliation or dismissal. The therapist (and client) can hold the experience with openness while also applying ethical-discernment questions such as: *Does this interpretation expand freedom or narrow it? Does it increase dignity—for me and for others—or does it feed fear, suspicion, or compulsion? Does it lead to value-consistent action, or to endless checking and looping? Can I hold this as a possibility rather than a verdict?* When these questions guide the process, synchronicity becomes less about grasping for certainty and more about cultivating responsible responsiveness—an invitation toward meaning that remains anchored in conscience and in the world.

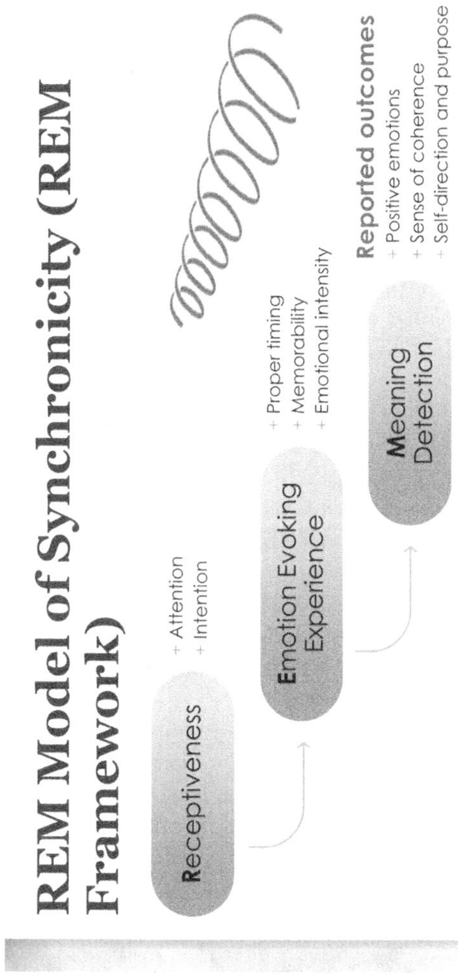

Figure 5.1 REM model

94 Meaning developments in positive psychology

Positive psychology and logotherapy meet at a shared center: meaning awareness as a core psychological capacity that supports both flourishing and coping. Yet each field contributes something distinct. Positive psychology has increasingly refined meaning into measurable components and testable mechanisms, while logotherapy offers an irreplaceable clinical stance: meaning is not merely useful; it is answered through freedom, responsibility, and conscience (Frankl, 1969, 1984). Early positive psychology, often described as the "first wave," emphasized strengths, positive emotion, and life satisfaction as a corrective to deficit-focused models (Martin Seligman & Mihaly Csikszentmihalyi, 2000). As the field matured, two pressures pushed meaning to the foreground. First, researchers increasingly recognized that happiness and meaning somewhat overlap but are not identical: what predicts feeling good "right now" is not always what makes life feel coherent, significant, and worth living across time (Baumeister et al., 2013). Second, critiques from within positive psychology highlighted the need for a more contextual, dialectical view, one that can hold suffering, limitation, and existential vulnerability without treating them as mere "noise" around positivity (Lomas & Ivtzan, 2016; McNulty & Fincham, 2012; Wong, 2011). These developments align naturally with logotherapy's starting point: the human person is not reducible to affect, performance, or symptom counts. Meaning is a central dimension of human existence that is relevant both for striving and for coping, especially under uncertainty (Frankl, 1969; Batthyány & Russo-Netzer, 2014).

One reason meaning research advanced quickly is conceptual sharpening. A widely used synthesis distinguishes three interrelated facets of meaning in life: coherence (life makes sense), purpose (life has direction), and significance/mattering (life matters) (Martela & Steger, 2016). Logotherapy resonates strongly with these distinctions, but adds an important safeguard: meaning is not only a cognitive structure (coherence) or a motivational direction (purpose). It is also a moral–existential stance—how a person relates to values, responsibility, and the concrete "call" of a situation (Frankl, 1969, 1985). This is precisely where logotherapy can function as a hermeneutic bridge between existential and positive psychology: it integrates creative and experiential pathways to meaning with the attitudinal stance toward suffering and limitation, while retaining an optimistic, future-oriented view of life's unconditional meaningfulness (Batthyány & Russo-Netzer, 2014).

In parallel, researchers clarified the difference between meaning in life (a relatively stable sense that one's life is coherent, purposeful, and significant) and meaning-making (the processes by which people interpret events, revise beliefs, and restore or deepen coherence after disruption) (Park, 2010). This distinction is an especially strong bridge to logotherapy: Frankl's approach is not only about identifying sources of meaning, but also about helping clients respond to the demands of the situation—particularly when life disrupts prior assumptions (Frankl, 1969). Another major refinement was distinguishing presence of meaning from search for meaning, most prominently operationalized in the Meaning in Life Questionnaire (Steger et al., 2006).

Meta-analytic evidence points to a consistent, theoretically important pattern: presence of meaning tends to relate to lower psychological distress, while search for meaning tends to relate to higher distress, yet with meaningful moderation by culture/region and by the type of distress indicators examined (He et al., 2023; Steger et al., 2006). Logotherapy helps translate this nuance into an immediate clinical stance. "Search" can reflect healthy existential inquiry, but it can also reflect disorientation, threat, or value-conflict. The clinical task is not to stop searching, but to help transform searching into responsible discovery—a movement from circular rumination ("Why is this happening?") to answerable orientation ("What is being asked of me now?") (Frankl, 1969; Batthyány & Russo-Netzer, 2014). In other words, positive psychology helped clarify the constructs; logotherapy clarifies the existential direction of the work.

A major contemporary shift is that meaning is now treated not only as an individual difference variable, but as a core domain of flourishing at population scale. The Global Flourishing Study is a large longitudinal panel study of 200,000+ participants across 22 countries, designed to examine the distribution and determinants of flourishing, explicitly including meaning and purpose as central domains (VanderWeele et al., 2025). At the same time, cross-cultural work also warns against simplistic universals. Meaning is pursued and expressed under cultural variability, through different life narratives, value hierarchies, religious/secular frames, and social expectations (He et al., 2023; Park, 2010). Logotherapy aligns well with this cultural humility because it does not prescribe one content of meaning; it invites a person-centered discovery grounded in the concrete situation and the person's responsibility within it (Frankl, 1969). Positive psychology's intervention tradition helped meaning science move from description to application. Across health psychology and psycho-oncology, meaning-centered approaches have been tested in controlled designs, with systematic reviews and meta-analyses suggesting benefits for quality of life and existential distress in specific populations (e.g., meaning-centered interventions in cancer contexts) (Wang et al., 2025). For logotherapy, the key contribution is not merely "meaning interventions work," but *when and why* they work. The accumulating evidence suggests that meaning-supportive interventions are most credible when they avoid forced positivity and instead support values clarification, agency and contribution, connection and belonging, and an attitude toward unavoidable suffering that protects dignity rather than denying pain (Frankl, 1969; Park, 2010). This is also where logotherapy complements positive psychology: it offers a disciplined framework that can hold suffering without collapsing into either nihilism ("nothing matters") or premature uplift ("everything happens for a reason").

As meaning became a pillar in flourishing models, an understandable risk emerged: meaning can be treated instrumentally, as a technique for improving well-being metrics, rather than as a dimension of truthfulness, responsibility, and integrity. The concern is not that positive psychology intends this, but that in applied settings meaning talk can slide into performance language ("find meaning so you can function better") and lose existential depth (Batthyány & Russo-Netzer, 2014). Logotherapy offers a corrective criterion: meaning is evaluated not by intensity of conviction, but by whether it enlarges freedom and responsibility, whether it leads toward value-consistent action, dignity, and self-transcendence (Frankl, 1969). This safeguard is clinically practical. When meaning is used defensively, as a way to bypass grief, uncertainty, or moral complexity, clients may feel pressured to "sound meaningful" rather than to live truthfully.

In sum, positive psychology has strengthened meaning research through conceptual refinement (coherence–purpose–significance), improved measurement (presence vs. search), mechanistic models of meaning-making under stress, large-scale cross-cultural evidence that positions meaning and purpose as core domains of flourishing, and a growing base of intervention trials (He et al., 2023; Martela & Steger, 2016; Steger et al., 2006; Park, 2010; VanderWeele et al., 2025; Wang et al., 2024). Logotherapy complements these advances by safeguarding meaning's existential depth and ethical direction: meaning is not merely a predictor of well-being but a response to life's call, shaped by conscience, responsibility, and self-transcendence (Batthyány & Russo-Netzer, 2014; Frankl, 1969). Together, they offer a fuller map—one that is empirically grounded and clinically answerable, helping clients move from asking why life hurts to discerning what is asked of them now and how to respond with dignity.

95 Meaning and the senses

> I who am blind can give one hint to those who see: Use your eyes as if tomorrow you would be stricken blind… Hear the music of voices, the song of a bird, the mighty strains of an orchestra, as if you would be stricken deaf tomorrow. Touch each object as if tomorrow your tactile sense would fail. Smell the perfume of flowers, taste with relish each morsel, as if tomorrow you could never smell and taste again. Make the most of every sense; glory in the beauty which the world in all the facets of pleasure reveals to you.
>
> (Keller, 1933, p. 42)

Keller's words point to a deep-seated truth: what is constantly available becomes psychologically invisible. Ralph Waldo Emerson made a similar observation with his image of the stars—if they appeared only once in a thousand years, people would gather in wonder, but because they appear nightly, we stop seeing them

(Emerson, 1836). Everyday perception is shaped by habituation and adaptation: attention withdraws, emotional intensity fades, and the extraordinary becomes "ordinary" over time (Wilson & Gilbert, 2008). In clinical work, this matters because meaning rarely vanishes outright. More often, *access* to meaning becomes constrained. Under chronic stress, burnout, grief, or emotional numbing, clients may still *know* what matters—family, contribution, faith, values—yet feel disconnected from it in daily life. They can speak with insight and coherence while describing their days as flat, rushed, or distant.

In such moments, the most direct route back to meaning is not always another interpretation. A meaning-centered approach understands such dullness as a natural byproduct of adaptation and overload, and invites a gentle return to awareness through renewed attention. Often, it is a return to the *sensorium*—to what can be seen, heard, smelled, touched, and tasted—because sensory experience restores immediacy, evokes self-defining memories, and reawakens value-salience in a way that abstract reflection alone sometimes cannot. Put simply: the senses carry the person's lived world in ways the abstract mind does not always access.

Logotherapy insists that meaning is *discovered*, not manufactured, and that discovery occurs within concrete life: in love and encounter, in work and contribution, in conscience and responsibility, and in the stance one chooses toward unavoidable suffering (Frankl, 1969, 2006). Sensory presence supports a logotherapeutic stance because it returns the person to the situation *as it is*, not the situation as theorized, defended against, or prematurely reframed. This "return" is also empirically grounded. Sensory and situational cues can evoke personally significant autobiographical memories with unusual vividness and emotional force, often spontaneously and without deliberate effort (Berntsen & Hall, 2004; Herz, 2004; Willander & Larsson, 2006). The smell of a childhood dish, the sound of a familiar song, the texture of a blanket, or the taste of a holiday food can bypass overworked cognition and reactivate emotionally laden, self-defining material, restoring continuity ("this is me"), value salience ("this matters"), and relational anchoring ("I belong to someone/something").

Two sensory pathways are especially well documented: *Olfaction (smell):* Odor-evoked autobiographical memories are often experienced as especially vivid and affectively potent; they can also skew earlier in the life span compared to other cues (Herz, 2004; Larsson et al., 2014; Willander & Larsson, 2006). Also, *music (sound)*-evoked memories reliably connect to identity, nostalgia, and emotional uplift (Belfi & Jakubowski, 2021; Krumhansl & Zupnick, 2013). Together, these findings support a clinically important implication: sensory cues can "open" emotionally laden self-material when verbal exploration remains flat, defended, or cognitively overtaxed.

This view dovetails with embodied accounts of cognition, which argue that thought is not detached computation but is grounded in perceptual and bodily systems (Barsalou, 2008). It also aligns with models of interoception and subjective feeling, emphasizing that what we experience as "feeling" is inseparable from how the body represents and updates internal states (Craig, 2009). Clinically, this helps explain a familiar pattern: when clients are emotionally numb, cognitively overloaded, or stuck in circular rumination, sensory routes may remain accessible even when purely verbal routes are depleted. Sensory-based work can therefore function as a pragmatic bridge—from constricted meaning access back to lived contact, and from abstract reflection back to values that are *felt*, remembered, and answerable in the concrete situation.

A recent brief randomized controlled trial illustrates this potential. In a one-week intervention, participants recalled a personally meaningful memory anchored in a dominant sensory experience (e.g., smell, taste, sound), reflected on its emotional and value-based dimensions, and then engaged in a related sensory activity. Compared with controls, the intervention group showed increases in subjective well-being, self-insight, prioritizing meaning, and hope, alongside reductions in psychological distress; qualitative findings pointed to strengthened self-continuity, clarified values, and deeper emotional connection (Russo-Netzer & Atad, 2025).

Two implications are especially relevant for logotherapy: Sensory cues can reopen access to meaningful, self-defining material when meaning feels distant. Furthermore, meaning consolidates through enactment, when reflection is translated into value-congruent action (Sheldon & Elliot, 1999; Lyubomirsky & Layous, 2013). In logotherapeutic terms, the senses do not *supply* meaning, and they do not replace dialogue. Rather, they can reopen the space of freedom in which meaning becomes *hearable* again, so that the person can discern what the situation is asking and respond with responsibility, conscience, and self-transcendence.

A substantial body of research suggests that autobiographical memory supports meaning-making by helping us interpret the present, anticipate the future, and preserve self-continuity across time (Prebble et al., 2013; McAdams, 2001; McAdams & McLean, 2013). This continuity aligns with dominant models of meaning in life, which describe meaning as comprising *coherence* (life makes sense), *purpose* (life has direction), and *significance/mattering* (life matters) (Martela & Steger, 2016). Crucially, autobiographical memory does not operate only through deliberate reflection. Many personally significant memories are retrieved involuntarily, triggered by sensory cues—smells, tastes, sounds, textures—often with heightened vividness and emotion (Berntsen & Hall, 2004; Schlagman & Kvavilashvili, 2008). This is the empirical backbone of what is often called the "Proust effect": sensory cues can evoke memories that feel immediate, embodied, and emotionally potent.

Logotherapy's three pathways: revisited through the senses

Frankl's pathways to meaning—*creative values* (what we give), *experiential values* (what we receive and encounter), and *attitudinal values* (the stance we take toward unavoidable suffering)—can be deepened through sensory awareness (Frankl, 1969, 2006).

- *Experiential values (encounter and presence).* The senses are a doorway to encounter: beauty, nature, music, another person's voice, a child's hand, a sacred moment. Sensory attentiveness can restore presence and reverence—especially when life has become hurried, automated, or emotionally muted.
- *Creative values (contribution through the body).* Sensory experience can inspire concrete acts of giving: cooking a family

recipe, repairing an object with care, crafting, playing music, gardening. The body becomes a vehicle for contribution.

- *Attitudinal values (dignity under limitation).* When circumstances cannot be changed, sensory grounding can support a dignified stance: breathing with awareness, noticing one stable sensory anchor, allowing grief to be felt without collapse, and choosing one value-consistent step even in pain. This is not forced positivity; it is disciplined presence—freedom within constraint.

In this sense, sensory work can become a concrete route toward Frankl's central claim: meaning is not merely found; it is answered—in attention, in conscience, and in responsible action. More specifically, a logotherapeutic–sensory approach can be organized into four movements:

1 *Attune:* Invite the client to notice: *"What is one sensory moment this week that touched you—even slightly?"* This restores contact with lived reality and counters existential numbness.
2 *Evoke (sensory memory as portal)*: Identify a sensory cue (smell, taste, sound, sight, touch) that carries resonance: *"What does this sensation bring back?"*
3 *Interpret (meaning cues in the memory):* Explore the memory not as material for analysis alone, but as a site of values and selfhood: *"What mattered here? What did you love? What were you protecting? What does this reveal about who you are?"*. This is meaning-making in an integrative sense (Park, 2010).
4 *Enact (translation into value-consistent action):* Help the client take one small step that embodies the value now: reconnect, contribute, repair, create, commit. Meaning stabilizes when it moves from insight to responsible action (Sheldon & Elliot, 1999). This sequence preserves logotherapy's core safeguard: the therapist does not impose meaning; the therapist supports the client in discerning what the situation is asking—and in responding.

Alongside the potential benefits of sensory-focused interventions, several key considerations warrant attention. *First, trauma sensitivity*: sensory cues can evoke distressing memories; therefore, work with titration, choice, and grounding, and build safety before inviting evocative recall. *Second, avoid sentimental bypass:* the aim is to contact what matters truthfully and translate it into responsible action. *Third, cultural humility is essential:* sensory meaning is culturally shaped, asfood, touch norms, sacred sounds, and rituals vary widely across cultures. Invite the client's world rather than importing your own.

Sensory-anchored meaning memory exercise (adapted from Russo-Netzer & Atad, 2025)

Step 1—Choose a meaningful sensory memory: Recall a meaningful memory from any period of your life that involves one dominant sense (taste, smell, sight, hearing, or touch). *Example:* "The smell of my grandmother's orange cake during Friday family dinner when I was 10."

Step 2—Write the memory in detail: Who was there? What were you doing? Where did it happen? What did you feel in your body? What were you thinking? What made this memory meaningful to you?

Step 3—Identify "meaning cues": Look for the hidden carriers of meaning in your story: What value is present (e.g., love, belonging, courage, faith, learning, care, responsibility)? What need is being met (connection, contribution, dignity, growth)? What does this memory reveal about who you are at your best?

Step 4—Translate into a small value-consistent action: Choose one concrete action this week that embodies the same value through the same sense:

- *Smell:* bake/cook something meaningful; visit a place with a familiar scent.
- *Hearing:* listen to a personally significant song; call someone whose voice matters.
- *Taste:* prepare a recipe connected to identity or family.
- *Touch:* hold an object linked to love; do a grounding tactile ritual.
- *Sight:* revisit meaningful photos; take a "meaning walk" noticing beauty.
- Step 5—Close with a logotherapeutic question: "What is being asked of me now—and what is one small responsible step I can take?"

Brief applications for practice

1 *"Three-sense check-in":* Name one sound, one sight, and one tactile sensation you noticed today that felt even slightly meaningful.
2 *Meaning-cue journaling (weekly):* Record one sensory moment and identify the value it carried (connection, contribution, dignity, beauty, faith, growth).
3 *Micro-encounters (experiential values):* Prescribe brief encounters with beauty, nature, art, music, or relationship, then ask: *"What did this awaken in you?"*
4 *Attitudinal practice under limitation:* When change is impossible, choose one sensory anchor (breath, touch, sound) to support a dignified stance and a responsible next step.

In sum, the senses remind us that meaning is not only a conclusion we reach—it is often an invitation we *feel*. Sensory moments can reopen access to self-defining memories, clarify values, restore self-continuity, and move clients from abstraction to enactment. For logotherapy, this is the essential direction: meaning is not a feeling to chase, but a response to life's questions, shaped by freedom, responsibility, conscience, and self-transcendence. Sensory awareness, when held ethically, becomes one more way to help clients answer that call—in the body, in daily life, and in the concrete situation that is asking something of them now.

96 Meaning and character strengths

In day-to-day psychotherapeutic work, "meaning" can feel too broad to hold, especially when a client arrives in an existential vacuum, burned out, anxious, or emotionally numb. In such moments, one of the most useful moves is to translate the existential question ("What is worth living for now?") into a language of capability and agency, by shifting the focus to character strengths. Character strengths can be understood as *capacities through which meaning becomes livable*—stable yet developable dispositions that shape how people notice possibilities, respond to difficulty, and translate values into action (Peterson & Seligman, 2004).

Essentially, meaning and strengths are best seen as *mutually illuminating*: Meaning gives strengths direction, and strengths give meaning a reliable pathway into daily choices, relationships, and commitments. From a logotherapeutic perspective, this integration is not an "add-on" but a natural extension of core principles—human freedom, responsibility, conscience, and self-transcendence (Frankl, 1969, 1984). When strengths are explicitly linked to meaning, they become more than traits; they become instruments of agency in the service of what matters. Conversely, when meaning is explored through strengths, it becomes less abstract and less moralistic—more operational, practiceable, and sustainable over time.

What are character strengths?

The VIA framework (Values in Action) describes 24 character strengths—positive, morally valued capacities that appear across cultures and can be recognized in thoughts, feelings, motivations, and behaviors (Peterson & Seligman, 2004). Strengths are not "talents" (which are often innate and performance-based) and not merely "skills" (which can be learned without reflecting who a person is becoming). Rather, strengths are qualities of character: patterns of action and perception that often feel authentic, energizing, and identity-congruent when expressed well (see Appendix). Several features make strengths especially useful in psychotherapy:

1. They are observable (in stories, patterns, relational moves, choices).
2. They are developable (clients can learn to use them more intentionally).
3. They can be ethically anchored (strengths can be guided by conscience and responsibility).
4. They translate values into behavior (bridging insight to enactment).

Importantly, strengths are not "always good" in every form. Like any human capacity, they can be expressed too little, too much, or in a way mismatched to context—an idea often described as a "golden mean" in strengths use (Niemiec, 2019).

Why strengths language helps meaning work

Logotherapy insists that the "why" is not imposed, but rather discovered through dialogue that respects the person's uniqueness and concrete life situation. Yet discovery alone is rarely sufficient for durable change. People also need a workable "how"—psychological resources that allow them to live their insights. Character strengths can operationalize this movement from insight to enactment. At the same time, both meaning language and strengths language can be misused. Strengths talk can turn into moral pressure ("Be grateful"), and meaning talk can turn into spiritual bypass ("Everything happens for a reason"). A logotherapeutic-strengths approach is most ethical when it holds existential authenticity at the center, using strengths to support truthful engagement with life, not to deny it (Park, 2010). In practice, this means using strengths to help clients face reality with more freedom, responsibility, and capacity to choose their stance.

A helpful bridge between existential theory and empirical research is the growing consensus that meaning in life includes at least three interrelated facets: Coherence/comprehension (life makes sense), Purpose (life is directed by valued aims), and Significance/mattering (life has inherent value; one's existence counts) (George & Park, 2016; Martela & Steger, 2016). This tripartite framing resonates strongly with logotherapy's view of meaning as something motivating enough to organize life around, and valuable enough to justify effort and sacrifice even under constraint (Frankl, 1969). Large-scale findings increasingly support the intuition that strengths and meaning are deeply interwoven. In a mixed-methods study with 23,641 participants across more than 100 countries, the 24 VIA strengths were assessed alongside these three facets of meaning. All strengths showed positive associations with meaning, and multivariate models suggested that different strengths may be especially relevant to different facets (Russo-Netzer, Tarrasch, & Niemiec, 2023). This is clinically important: not all meaning needs are the same, and strengths can be matched to the kind of meaning a person is missing or seeking. At the level of overall pattern, certain strengths often stand out as strongly connected to meaning—particularly hope, spirituality, gratitude, zest, curiosity, and love—echoing broader findings linking these strengths to well-being and positive functioning (Park, Peterson, & Seligman, 2004; Schutte & Malouff, 2019). Yet the most clinically useful insight is *differentiation*: meaning work becomes more precise when we ask, "Which facet is fragile here?" and "Which strengths offer the most leverage right now?"

The qualitative component of the same study underscores this matching logic: For *coherence*, participants often named relational and integrative strengths such as love, kindness, and perspective. For *purpose*, strengths like perseverance, self-regulation, and hope were frequently highlighted. For *significance/mattering*, strengths such as spirituality, appreciation of beauty, gratitude, and love were commonly named (Russo-Netzer et al., 2023). These patterns do not prescribe a one-size-fits-all formula, but rather offer clinicians a powerful guiding question:

Which facet of meaning is most threatened, and which strengths can restore movement?

Strength identification becomes transformative when it moves beyond labeling and becomes shared discovery. A rigorous, clinically grounded approach often integrates three lenses:

1 *Self-report and structured assessment*: The VIA inventory offers a shared vocabulary and can help clients notice capacities they have normalized, minimized, or forgotten (Peterson & Seligman, 2004).
2 *Narrative strengths-spotting:* Logotherapy has always been narrative in spirit: a person's life is treated as a text containing implicit values and commitments. Strengths emerge in recurring patterns of choice: *Where do you reliably show courage?, What do you protect across time?, When do you become most alive?, What do you refuse to abandon—even in hardship?.* This lens is essential for clients who struggle to "name" strengths but can recognize them in action.
3 *Relational and situational observation*: Strengths are context-sensitive. Some clients possess strengths they rarely deploy because the environment punishes them, trauma has narrowed their repertoire, or a strength is expressed in a distorted form. Observation, inside and outside the session, helps differentiate a true absence from an underused capacity.

A distinct logotherapeutic refinement is to treat strengths not merely as performance advantages but as ethical-existential capacities. The question is not only *"What are you good at?"* but also: *"Who are you becoming when you use this—and what are you serving?"* This protects strengths work from drifting into self-optimization detached from conscience and values. Strengths have a golden-mean quality: expressed too little, they are absent; expressed too much, they can become harmful; expressed without discernment, they can become mismatched to the moment (Niemiec, 2019). For example: Honesty can become harshness, prudence can become avoidance, perseverance can become rigidity, kindness can become self-erasure.

A strengths-and-meaning formulation therefore asks two parallel questions:

1 *Which strengths are relevant to meaning here?*
2 *How are those strengths currently being used—and are they serving the client's deepest values and real-life demands?*

This is also where ethical care matters: strengths should never be used as a tool to invalidate pain. In a logotherapeutic stance, strengths support the capacity to face reality and choose one's stance within it, not to pretend reality is different. Strengths are offered as universal categories, but their expression is shaped by culture, community norms, context, and lived history. Meaning is always personal and situated. A clinically mature integration holds both truths at once: shared human capacities and singular human lives. This is crucial for preventing strengths work from becoming culturally tone-deaf or morally coercive. The goal is not to produce an "ideal" person, but to help a real person reclaim freedom and responsibility within their actual circumstances.

A synergistic integration between logotherapy and character strengths becomes most powerful when we keep the logotherapeutic core in view: meaning is not a feeling to chase—it is a response to life's questions, shaped by freedom, responsibility, conscience, and self-transcendence (Frankl, 1969, 1984). In this sense, strengths do not replace meaning; they carry it. In other words, meaning provides direction: what matters, what is worthy, while strengths provide capacity: how I can enact that call in concrete choices.

When clients are stuck in meaninglessness, they often do not only lack answers; they lack *movement*. Strengths offer a pathway from existential reflection to lived response: small, repeated acts of agency that gradually reconstitute coherence, rebuild purpose, and restore a sense of mattering. Finally, this integration aligns naturally with Frankl's classic pathways to meaning: *creative values* (what we give), *experiential values* (what we receive and encounter), and *attitudinal values* (the stance we take toward unavoidable suffering). Strengths can be viewed as the psychological "muscles" that help clients realize each pathway: strengths that support contribution and commitment (creative), strengths that deepen relationship and presence (experiential), and strengths that enable courageous and dignified stance (attitudinal). In this way, character strengths become not merely descriptive vocabulary, but practical instruments for self-transcendence, helping clients live meaning as an embodied, ethically anchored, and culturally grounded practice.

97 Environmental crisis and meaning

The accelerating environmental crisis—climate change, biodiversity loss, ecosystem degradation, and the destabilization of familiar seasons and landscapes—confronts people with more than lifestyle adjustments. It confronts them with existential questions: *What kind of world am I living in? What kind of future is possible?* The crisis touches identity, belonging, moral orientation, responsibility, and the continuity of life stories across generations. Environmental disruption amplifies collective experiences of vulnerability and loss, but it can also awaken questions of conscience, responsibility, and self-transcendence—central coordinates in logotherapy.

Contemporary existential-phenomenological scholarship has begun to conceptualize *environmental anxiety* not simply as pathology, but as an intelligible response to a real situation—an "attunement" to ecological instability that can reshape hope, identity, and meaning. *Eco-anxiety/climate anxiety* is commonly used as an umbrella term for worry, dread, and cognitive-emotional strain related to climate change and environmental degradation. Measurement tools have been developed to capture its dimensions, including impairment and rumination (Clayton &

Karazsia, 2020). Large-scale research suggests this distress is widespread, especially among youth. For example, a landmark global survey of young people reported high levels of climate-related worry and strong feelings of being let down by societal responses (Hickman et al., 2021). Importantly, climate anxiety can be adaptive or impairing. In some people it is linked to motivation and engagement; in others it is associated with functional difficulties ("eco-paralysis"), including interference with daily life (Heeren et al., 2022).

Alongside anxiety, many experience *ecological grief*—grief tied to experienced or anticipated ecological losses (loss of species, landscapes, livelihoods, or culturally meaningful places). Cunsolo and Ellis (2018) argue that ecological grief can be a natural mental health response to climate-related loss, especially among communities with close ties to place and land. A related construct is *solastalgia*—distress associated with environmental change impacting one's home environment, capturing the pain of "homesickness while still at home" (Albrecht et al., 2007). A comprehensive narrative review synthesizes these climate-related emotions and emphasizes a crucial point: negative emotions can correlate with suffering, yet they can also serve constructive roles, such as motivating care, meaning-focused coping, and collective engagement (Ojala et al., 2021).

Applied to the environmental crisis, logotherapy begins by taking climate-related emotions seriously. Fear, grief, anger, and moral pain are often proportionate responses to genuine existential threat, not signs of personal weakness. Several Franklian concepts offer a particularly relevant lens. *Existential frustration* captures the distress that arises when the will to meaning meets obstacles that feel immovable or overwhelming. *Existential vacuum* describes the drift into numbness, cynicism, disengagement, or "nothing matters" reactions when trust in institutions, future narratives, or shared moral horizons erodes. Finally, climate disruption can activate Frankl's *tragic triad—pain, guilt, and death*: pain through loss and instability; guilt through feelings of complicity, privilege, or inaction; and death through heightened awareness of mortality, extinction, and irreversibility (Frankl, 1969, 1985).

At the same time, environmental harms are deeply entangled with political, economic, and historical structures; many people suffer consequences they did not create. A logotherapeutic approach can hold both truths at once: it acknowledges the systemic roots of this distress rather than placing the burden on the individual, while still affirming that the person retains freedom to take a stance and to respond within their sphere of responsibility. This is where "hope" becomes clinically and ethically complex. In environmental contexts, hope is often polarized, either demanded as positivity or dismissed as delusion. Existential-phenomenological work offers a more refined distinction between *naïve hope* (which can function as emotional bypass or denial) and *radical/courageous hope*—hope that faces reality, tolerates uncertainty, and still commits to values and action. Logotherapy aligns naturally with this mature hope: Frankl emphasized the possibility of *meaningful response*—the capacity to answer life's questions with responsibility and self-transcendence even amid tragedy.

Reframed through Frankl's pathways to meaning, the environmental crisis can awaken multiple meaning responses. Along the *creative pathway*, many experience a renewed longing to contribute, through restoration projects, advocacy, education, sustainable innovation, mutual aid, intergenerational mentoring, or community resilience work. Research suggests that climate anxiety can co-exist with pro-environmental behavior and activism, even as it may also relate to lower well-being—highlighting the importance of supporting *sustainable engagement* rather than burnout-driven urgency (Ogunbode et al., 2022). Along the *experiential pathway*, meaning is often found through encounter, with nature, beauty, love, relationship, spirituality, and reverence. Environmental disruption can threaten these experiences through the loss of familiar landscapes and ecological rhythms, yet it can also intensify them by heightening preciousness and deepening relationality with the more-than-human world. Indigenous and relational perspectives emphasize reciprocity, responsibility, and kinship with land and community, an orientation that resonates with Frankl's insistence that meaning is discovered in relationship and responsibility rather than self-absorption (Whyte, 2017). Finally, the *attitudinal pathway* becomes crucial where aspects of ecological damage are already irreversible and adaptation and mourning are unavoidable. Attitudinal meaning here is not resignation, but a dignified, truthful stance: grieving what is lost, honoring love for place, refusing numbness, and choosing value-consistent action even under constraint. Ecological grief, in this sense, can be understood as evidence of attachment and care, not simply distress to eliminate (Cunsolo & Ellis, 2018).

Environmental loss can also shatter basic assumptions about safety, continuity, and justice. Meaning reconstruction work in grief therapy therefore offers clinically useful questions that translate well to ecological grief (Neimeyer, 2015), including sense-making ("How do I make sense of what is happening? What story can hold this?"), identity reconstruction ("Who am I in light of this loss, and who am I becoming?"), belief accommodation ("Which cherished beliefs are strained, revised, or transformed by this reality?"), and relational validation ("Who can witness this with me without minimizing it?"). These questions become especially powerful when paired with Frankl's central safeguard: meaning is not invented as a slogan; it is discerned—in values, conscience, relationship, and responsibility.

In sum, environmental disruption confronts people with the limits of control, and simultaneously with a profound invitation: to choose who we will be within a changing world. Logotherapy does not offer comfort through denial. It offers a disciplined, compassionate stance: to face reality, to mourn honestly, to discern conscience, and to respond with responsibility and self-transcendence. In this sense, meaning is not a private achievement, but a relational, ethical response to life's questions, now asked on a planetary scale.

98 Social media and meaning

In contemporary digital life, social media has increasingly become a meaning environment: a space in which people seek belonging, recognition, identity, and a sense of value. As Frankl observed, "The meaning of human existence is based upon its irreversible quality. An individual's responsibility in life must therefore be understood in terms of temporality and singularity." This perspective is especially relevant to social media, where the pressure for constant visibility can obscure the singular and unrepeatable character of human life. It reminds us that meaning is grounded not in endless display or repetition, but in the unrepeatable character of a person's life, choices, and response to what each moment asks. Social media, by contrast, offers built-in and immediate "meaning platforms"—likes, comments, shares, follower counts, and views—that translate attention into visible metrics. These can function as public, quantifiable signals of social acknowledgment in ways that everyday offline life rarely provides with such speed or consistency. When the longing to matter meets a system that measures attention numerically, it becomes easy to confuse visibility with value and validation with meaning. From a logotherapeutic perspective, this reflects a collision between enduring human needs—to belong, to matter, and to contribute—and a contemporary ecosystem designed to maximize engagement. Much of what draws people to social media can thus be understood as an attempt to answer existential needs, sometimes in adaptive ways and sometimes in ways that gradually externalize the person's inner compass.

A useful starting point is the dual-motive model, according to which people are drawn to social networking sites primarily for *belonging* and *self-presentation* (Nadkarni & Hofmann, 2012). These motives map closely onto the need to belong, a fundamental drive for stable, caring bonds and social inclusion (Baumeister & Leary, 1995). In practice, social media can serve these needs through several distinct affordances. It enables belonging at scale by expanding access to communities and ongoing ties that may not be available locally (Ellison et al., 2007). It provides recognition and mattering cues through rapid feedback, such as likes and comments, which may function as potent social-reward signals and strengthen perceived social significance (Sherman et al., 2016; Flett, 2018). It also offers *narrative identity tools* through which people curate and communicate their life stories, values, and affiliations (McAdams & McLean, 2013; Zhao et al., 2008), while creating micro-contribution opportunities that allow users to share resources, mentor, advocate, create, and provide support in ways that may feel purposeful and socially impactful (Burke et al., 2010).

From the perspective of *Self-Determination Theory*, these platforms may support core psychological needs—especially relatedness, and at times competence and autonomy, when engagement is intentional, reciprocal, and values-consistent (Ryan & Deci, 2000). Yet the same platforms can also frustrate these needs when use becomes pressured, performative, or comparison-driven, shifting the person from authentic participation to self-monitoring and strategic impression management (Nadkarni & Hofmann, 2012; Zhao et al., 2008). Thus, social media can become a genuine arena for meaning, but it can also become a marketplace in which the self is continuously appraised.

Social media is rich in *meaning signals*—attention, praise, likes—that often correlate with connection and belonging, but *meaning sources* are deeper anchors: values, commitments, responsibility, contribution, and conscience (Frankl, 1969, 1985). When meaning signals become the primary "barometer," a person's sense of worth and direction can become contingent *("If I'm noticed, I matter; if I'm ignored, I disappear")*. Here the psychology of *mattering* is especially relevant: humans need to feel significant, yet significance is not the same as performance or visibility (Flett, 2018, 2022; Rosenberg & McCullough, 1981). In Franklian terms, the risk is not social media per se, but a gradual shift from self-transcendence, living toward values beyond the self, to self-absorption, in which the self is treated as an object evaluated by others. The guiding question therefore changes from *"How do I look?"* to Frankl's deeper prompt: *"What is life asking of me—here and now?"* (Frankl, 1969, 1985).

When visibility becomes a stand-in for value, the person's inner compass is gradually outsourced to external metrics. What begins as a search for connection can shift into restless self-monitoring—an anxious effort to secure belonging through signals that are immediate yet unstable. In logotherapeutic terms, the problem is not *needing* recognition (a deeply human need), but becoming *dependent* on recognition as the primary "evidence" that one matters (Baumeister & Leary, 1995; Flett, 2018). This dynamic helps explain why FoMO, compulsive checking, and perpetual "meaning search" can intensify at the expense of "meaning presence." Meaning in life research often distinguishes between *presence of meaning* (a grounded sense that life is coherent and worthwhile) and *search for meaning* (the felt sense that something is missing and must be found) (Steger et al., 2006). Under attention-economy conditions, the person may remain in search mode—scanning, comparing, refreshing—while presence becomes harder to access (Steger et al., 2006).

Social media can shift from a resource into a risk not through one single factor, but through a cluster of interacting mechanisms that gradually reshape attention, self-evaluation, and the person's "meaning economy." A central pathway involves *social comparison*. Comparison is a natural feature of social life and a basic process of self-evaluation (Festinger, 1954), yet on social media it becomes intensified by the continuous availability of curated "highlight reels" and by algorithmic amplification of salient, idealized content. Over time, upward comparison can narrow the self's criteria for worth toward externally rewarded traits, such as appearance, popularity, status, productivity, leaving less room for quieter but deeper values such as integrity, care, service, and wisdom (Festinger, 1954; Verduyn et al., 2017). In logotherapeutic terms, this narrowing can gradually shift the person from value-guided self-transcendence to a more evaluative, performative stance toward the self. Closely related is the role of *FoMO (fear of missing out)*—the fear that others are having rewarding experiences without us—which can lock attention into scanning, checking, and "just-in-case" monitoring (Przybylski et al., 2013). FoMO often carries an implicit existential threat to belonging and significance, which makes it especially potent as a driver of compulsive checking (Baumeister & Leary, 1995; Przybylski et al., 2013). Meaning-in-life research adds an important nuance here: FoMO has been linked to higher search for meaning and lower presence of meaning, with maladaptive use tendencies (e.g., Social Networks Use Disorder tendencies) helping explain this association (Steger et al., 2006; Montag et al., 2023). This pattern is logotherapeutically meaningful: the person remains in "search mode" ("something is missing"), while the grounded experience of meaning presence becomes harder to access and sustain.

A third mechanism concerns what Frankl described as the *existential vacuum*—numbness, boredom, cynicism, or the feeling that "nothing really matters" when values and responsibility lose their lived immediacy (Frankl, 1969, 1985). In digital life, this may appear as high stimulation with low nourishment: endless consumption, rapid emotional shifts, and constant novelty that does not consolidate into significance. The person stays occupied, yet not inwardly met. From a meaning-centered standpoint, the risk is not stimulation itself, but the replacement of value-consistent participation with passive absorption that temporarily soothes while quietly thinning the sense of purpose (Frankl, 1969; Ryan & Deci, 2000). This is why the form of engagement matters. Evidence suggests that *passive use* (scrolling and monitoring without reciprocal interaction) is more consistently linked to reduced well-being than *active, relational use,* although findings remain nuanced and context-dependent (Verduyn et al., 2015, 2017). This aligns with meaning theory: meaning tends to grow where there is participation, relationship, contribution, and agency, not merely exposure (Frankl, 1969; Verduyn et al., 2017). What looks like "social connection" on the surface can, in practice, function as social surveillance and self-evaluation, especially when one's attention is repeatedly recruited into comparison and metric tracking.

Finally, the broader literature points to an important caution: average associations between digital technology use and well-being are often small, yet this overall picture conceals substantial heterogeneity, by individual vulnerabilities, developmental stage, motives for use, and specific patterns of engagement (Orben & Przybylski, 2019; Valkenburg, 2022). The same platform can support one person's vocation, creativity, and community, while amplifying another person's emptiness, self-doubt, and dependence on external validation. The clinical task, therefore, is not to demonize the medium, but to clarify when a person's use supports *meaning sources* (values, relationships, contribution, conscience) and when it increasingly substitutes them with unstable *meaning signals* (Frankl, 1969, 1985; Steger et al., 2006). A complementary nuance underscores this complexity: social media may simultaneously reduce existential isolation (feeling unseen or unrecognized) while increasing emotional loneliness (missing others), depending on how one engages with it (Helm et al., 2022).

These dynamics suggest that the key question is not whether social media is "harmful," but *when and how* it shifts people from meaning sources to meaning signals. Logotherapy's enduring strength is precisely its capacity to distinguish what is meaningful from what is merely stimulating, soothing, or status-affirming (Frankl, 1969, 1985). Accordingly, a logotherapeutic approach to social media is best framed as *meaning discernment*: helping clients (or students) reclaim freedom, responsibility, and self-transcendence within a digital reality that powerfully shapes attention and self-evaluation (Frankl, 1969; Kross et al., 2021). Several practical elements can organize the implementation of such a framework.

A helpful first step is to map the person's "*meaning economy*"—the implicit exchange between what social media gives and what it costs. Therapists can begin with concrete questions such as: *What do you go online for—connection, escape, inspiration, validation, purpose, boredom? What does it give you immediately, and what does it cost you later (energy, self-respect, time, relationships, sleep)? Which numbers affect your mood most, and what story do you tell yourself when they go up or down? When do you feel most grounded in what matters, online or offline, and what conditions make meaning presence more available?* These questions can clarify whether the platform is serving values or gradually substituting for them.

From there, core interventions can be adapted to the digital context without moralizing or overcorrecting. One central move is *de-reflection* from the "self-as-performance" loop. When attention becomes fixated on how one is perceived, logotherapy invites a gentle pivot outward, toward a task, a person, or a value. The aim is not to shame the need for validation, but to reduce its tyranny by strengthening value-organized action and self-transcendence (Frankl, 1969). Another possible intervention is *Socratic dialogue* that helps translate approval-seeking into value-clarity, with questions such as: *What does a "like" symbolize for you—belonging, worth, safety, love, significance? If that need were met in a truer way, what would change? What would you keep doing even if nobody applauded?* Such questions invite the client back to conscience and responsibility rather than contingent appraisal.

A third element involves *meaning-based boundaries*, where freedom is practiced concretely through small, value-aligned choices: using time windows rather than endless access; entering with purpose (*I'm here to connect/learn/serve—then I leave*); and reducing triggers that recruit comparison or compulsive checking. Experimental evidence suggests that, for some people, limiting social media use can improve well-being, supporting the practicality of brief boundary experiments as a clinical tool rather than a moral prescription (Hunt et al., 2018). Finally, a meaning-centered approach consistently replaces *meaning signals* with *meaning actions*. When someone is stuck in meaning search, the intervention is often not "think harder," but "live one step": one real conversation, one act of contribution, one encounter with beauty without documentation. In Franklian terms, this converts restless searching into responsible enactment; in motivational terms, it supports autonomy and internalization by aligning behavior with values rather than external metrics (Frankl, 1969; Ryan & Deci, 2000).

In sum, social media powerfully amplifies the human longing to belong and to matter. It can support meaning when it becomes a tool for learning, community, contribution, and genuine encounter (Cuong et al., 2025; Helm et al., 2022). It can undermine meaning when it turns the self into a product and replaces inner conscience with external metrics, intensifying comparison, FoMO loops, and existential emptiness (Przybylski et al., 2013; Montag et al., 2023). Logotherapy offers a balanced alternative to both demonizing and idealizing social media: it helps people reclaim freedom within constraint, re-anchor identity in values, and convert restless searching into responsible, self-transcendent action, online and offline (Frankl, 1969, 1985).

99 Future challenges

As logotherapy's evidence base and practice expand, the field is gaining momentum, supported by a broader empirical literature on meaning in life, widening applications across clinical and community settings, and growing interest from adjacent disciplines. With this growth comes a decisive question: *how can logotherapy be delivered competently, ethically, and at scale, without losing its phenomenological depth and its commitment to the uniqueness of personal meaning?* As the evidence base matures, the field's next developmental step is *translation:* moving from promising findings and foundational principles to sustainable, context-sensitive practice in real-world systems. Yet translation does not happen by intention alone; it requires an evidence-informed account of how an approach can take root in everyday care. This is where implementation research becomes indispensable. It examines the strategies and contextual conditions that enable evidence-informed interventions to be adopted, delivered with quality, and sustained over time in routine settings (Damschroder et al., 2009; Proctor et al., 2011). For logotherapy, this turns into three closely related lines of inquiry: feasibility across settings (schools, hospitals, community programs, low-resource contexts), competence-building through training and supervision, and organizational fit—the conditions that allow logotherapy to take root and remain part of routine care over time.

A second future challenge concerns *training standards*—not because logotherapy lacks training traditions, but because growth intensifies the need for clearer articulation, shared benchmarks, and scalable pathways. Logotherapy's clinical stance requires disciplined presence, careful Socratic dialogue, ethical sensitivity, and the capacity to help clients discern meaning without imposing it. As the field expands across settings, it becomes increasingly valuable to clarify and align core competencies, including meaning-focused assessment, dereflection, values clarification without moralizing, existential risk formulation, and the cultivation of responsibility and self-transcendence. In practice, this calls for strengthening training and supervision in ways that keep logotherapy's core commitments—dignity, freedom, responsibility, and self-transcendence—alive in everyday therapeutic work across diverse contexts.

This connects to a third, closely related task: ensuring that logotherapy remains both *faithful and transferable* as it travels across cultures, communities, and systems. The field has long navigated the balance between conceptual clarity and clinical responsiveness; the challenge ahead is to sustain that balance under conditions of wider dissemination. In implementation terms, this is the familiar tension between fidelity and adaptation, best approached not as an either–or, but as thoughtful stewardship of what must remain stable in principle, alongside responsible adaptation in form.

A fourth challenge, and opportunity, concerns *technology*. Digital environments increasingly shape attention, identity formation, belonging, and vulnerability, and AI systems are entering health care and mental health ecosystems with unprecedented speed. For logotherapy, the question is not whether digital tools will be used, but how to integrate them in ways that safeguard dignity, responsibility, and genuine encounter. Logotherapy reminds digital mental health that persons are not data points; that suffering is not merely a symptom cluster; and that meaning cannot be outsourced to an algorithm. At best, technology may support access and continuity, such as screening, psychoeducation, guided exercises, follow-up, and self-monitoring that strengthens accountability. Yet logotherapy's core "instrument" remains the human capacity for conscience, responsibility, and self-transcendence.

Finally, the future of logotherapy will require more explicit engagement with *collective realities*. Contemporary meaning crises are frequently embedded in social, economic, and political structures: displacement, war, poverty, discrimination, ecological disruption, and institutional distrust. The field's challenge is to hold two truths at once: people may not be responsible for the conditions they inherit, and yet they retain the freedom to take a stance and to respond within their sphere of responsibility. In this sense, logotherapy's future invites meaning-centered thinking not just for individuals in therapy, but for institutions, communities, and cultures seeking moral direction under pressure. The task is thus both scientific and ethical: to strengthen logotherapy's evidence and delivery without flattening its spirit; to widen access without diluting depth; and to carry its central claim into the realities of the twenty-first century, that meaning is discovered in the concrete demands of life and answered through responsible, self-transcendent action.

100 The continuing relevance of logotherapy

The continuing relevance of logotherapy is aptly captured in Theodore Roszak's observation that the central question facing human beings is not merely "How shall we know?" but "How shall we live?" This shift—from knowledge alone to lived responsibility—helps explain why logotherapy remains urgently relevant today. The modern world offers unprecedented information, choice, and connectivity, yet many people experience increasing disorientation: rising loneliness, pervasive uncertainty, and a fragile sense of belonging. Against this backdrop, logotherapy offers a broader frame. The issue is not only distress that requires relief, but also a threatened sense of meaning—coherence, purpose, and mattering—that calls for restoration.

Uncertainty is no longer episodic; for many, it has become structural. The *World Uncertainty Index* shows pronounced global spikes during major crises. In its GDP-weighted global series, uncertainty reached its highest recorded level in the third quarter of 2025, approximately twice the size of the spike observed during the first quarter of 2020, at the onset of the COVID-19 pandemic (Ahir et al., 2026). Uncertainty is psychologically destabilizing because it undermines core assumptions about safety, trustworthy institutions, a predictable future, and basic fairness, often pushing people to oscillate between anxious control and numbing resignation. Logotherapy offers a third posture: it does not promise control, but invites response.

A second defining feature of contemporary life is social disconnection. The World Health Organization Commission on Social Connection reported in 2025 that 1 in 6 people worldwide is affected by loneliness, with significant consequences for health and well-being, and estimates linking loneliness to more than 871,000 deaths annually (World Health Organization, 2025). Beyond these direct health consequences, chronic disconnection also helps illuminate a broader pattern often discussed as "deaths of despair," a term used to describe rising mortality associated with suicide, substance-related causes, and alcohol-related disease, typically in contexts marked by social and economic strain, eroding institutions, and weakened community ties (Beseran et al., 2022; Case & Deaton, 2015; Case & Deaton, 2020). From a logotherapeutic perspective, this linkage is conceptually significant: when belonging and mattering are repeatedly threatened, distress is not only symptomatic; it often reflects a deeper crisis of orientation and responsibility. This underscores why meaning-centered work must address not only individual coping, but also the relational and communal conditions that sustain a life worth living.

People do not heal meaningfully by obsessively monitoring the self; they heal by being claimed by something beyond the self—love, responsibility, creative contribution, and service. In this sense, meaning is not solely an intrapsychic state; it is co-constructed through relational contexts and enacted through ethical commitment. It emerges in the space between persons, communities, and commitments. This is why logotherapy remains relevant in a world shaped by pandemics, war, polarization, ecological disruption, artificial intelligence, and digital acceleration. These forces can erode the shared moral horizons that help communities cohere. They can also generate moral pain and grief over losses, anger in the face of injustice, guilt about complicity, and fear about the future. Logotherapy does not dismiss these experiences, but understands them as signals that something deeply valued is at stake. Its enduring relevance lies precisely in this: it reminds us that even when the world becomes fractured, accelerated, and uncertain, human beings remain capable of answering life with freedom, responsibility, and meaning.

A forward-looking vision: meaning as a collective capacity

The most pressing challenges facing contemporary societies—mass loneliness, institutional mistrust, climate-related grief, the fragmenting effects of digital culture— are not merely social or political in nature. They are, fundamentally, challenges to meaning. They erode the conditions under which individuals and communities sustain coherence, purpose, and a sense of significance; and they unfold not in isolation but structurally, at scale. It is precisely here that logotherapy's conceptual resources remain vital: not as a therapeutic modality, but as a framework capable of articulating, without collapsing into ideology, a shared language for collective resilience and ethical direction.

Looking forward, the field faces a defining question: not only how individuals find meaning under adversity, but how societies create and sustain the conditions that make meaning widely accessible. This calls for meaning-centered thinking across domains—in educational systems that cultivate inner purpose alongside academic achievement; in healthcare settings that recognize existential suffering as a clinical concern; in workplaces and civic institutions that treat belonging and significance as foundational rather than incidental goods. Frankl wrote from the ruins of the 20th century with the conviction that meaning could be found even there. To carry that conviction forward—critically, creatively, and collectively—is perhaps the most urgent task the field now faces. A life worth living, it turns out, is never only a personal achievement. It is, at its deepest, a shared one.

Appendix A

Accredited Logotherapy and Existential Analysis Training Institutes (Viktor Frankl Institute Vienna Directory)

This appendix provides a reader-friendly entry point to accredited institutes and initiatives affiliated with the International Association of Logotherapy and Existential Analysis (IALEA) at the Viktor Frankl Institute Vienna. Because institutional details (contacts, addresses, and program offerings) may change over time, readers are encouraged to consult the official directory for the most current information.

Official directory (Viktor Frankl Institute Vienna): https://www.viktorfrankl.org/institutes_wwE.html

Accreditation information: https://www.viktorfrankl.org/accreditationENG.html

Note. The complete country-by-country directory (including additional accredited institutes and initiatives worldwide) is maintained on the Viktor Frankl Institute Vienna website.

The 24 VIA character strengths (for Chapter 96)

Wisdom and Knowledge

1 **Creativity** – generating novel and useful ideas or approaches.
2 **Curiosity** – interest, exploration, openness to experience.
3 **Judgment / Open-mindedness** – examining evidence fairly; flexible thinking.
4 **Love of learning** – enjoying mastery and acquiring knowledge.
5 **Perspective** – offering wise counsel; seeing the big picture.

Courage

6 **Bravery** – acting despite fear; standing up for what is right.
7 **Perseverance** – finishing what one starts; sustained effort.
8 **Honesty** – authenticity, integrity, speaking truthfully.
9 **Zest** – vitality, aliveness, energetic engagement with life.

Humanity

10 **Love** – valuing close relationships; warmth and attachment.
11 **Kindness** – generosity, care, doing good for others.
12 **Social intelligence** – awareness of emotions, motives, and relational dynamics.

Justice

13 **Teamwork** – loyalty, collaboration, being a good group member.

14. **Fairness** – treating people equally; giving everyone a chance.
15 **Leadership** – organizing, motivating, and facilitating group goals.

Temperance

16 **Forgiveness** – letting go of resentment; offering second chances.
17 **Humility** – letting achievements speak; not seeking the spotlight.
18 **Prudence** – caution, wise decision-making, foresight.
19 **Self-regulation** – managing impulses, emotions, and habits.

Transcendence

20 **Appreciation of beauty and excellence** – awe; elevating attention to what is beautiful or skillful.
21 **Gratitude** – noticing and appreciating the good.
22 **Hope** – expecting the best while working toward it.
23 **Humor** – playfulness; bringing lightness and connection.
24 **Spirituality** – connection to the sacred/ultimate; meaning in a larger context.

Appendix C

Prioritizing Meaning Scale (Russo-Netzer, 2018)

Using the scale below, please select a response from 1 to 9:
In my everyday life…

1	2	3	4	5	6	7	8	9
Disagree strongly	Disagree mostly	Disagree somewhat	Disagree slightly	Neither disagree or agree	Agree slightly	Agree somewhat	Agree mostly	Agree strongly

1. I prefer to engage in activities which are related to the sense of meaning in my life	1	2	3	4	5	6	7	8	9
2. I devote as much time as I can to activities that have great meaning for me	1	2	3	4	5	6	7	8	9
3. The manner in which I organize my day reflects values that are meaningful to me	1	2	3	4	5	6	7	8	9
4. My major decisions in life (e.g., the job I choose, where I choose to live) are influenced by how much I might experience meaning as a result	1	2	3	4	5	6	7	8	9
5. I admire people who make their decisions based on the meaning they will gain	1	2	3	4	5	6	7	8	9

6. One of the main considerations in my choice whether to do something is the sense of meaning it will bring me	1	2	3	4	5	6	7	8	9
7. In my day-to-day life, I choose to do things in accordance with my life's purpose	1	2	3	4	5	6	7	8	9
8. I choose and prefer activities which stimulate a sense of value and meaning	1	2	3	4	5	6	7	8	9
9. The consideration which guides the priority I give to activities is the extent to which I will be able to be involved in things that are meaningful and make a difference in the world	1	2	3	4	5	6	7	8	9
10. I structure my day to be involved in things that are meaningful and valuable to me	1	2	3	4	5	6	7	8	9
11. The activities I choose to be involved with reflect who I really am	1	2	3	4	5	6	7	8	9
12. I choose to include in my life activities that are meaningful to me, even if they often require effort	1	2	3	4	5	6	7	8	9

Bibliography

Abdollahzadeh, H., Mahmoodi, H., & Aghajani, S. (2024). The effectiveness of logotherapy on the sense of energy and spiritual self-esteem of the elderly living in nursing homes. *Aging Psychology*, 9(4), 343–359. doi:10.22126/jap.2024.9587.1729

Abu-Raiya, H., & Pargament, K. I. (2015). Religious coping among diverse religions: Commonalities and divergences. *Psychology of Religion and Spirituality*, 7(1), 24–33. doi:10.1037/a0037652

Ahir, H., Bloom, N., & Furceri, D. (2026). *World Uncertainty Index (WUI) dataset (Updated January* 4, 2026).

Aiello-Puchol, A., & García-Alandete, J. (2025). A systematic review on the effects of logotherapy and meaning-centered therapy on psychological and existential symptoms in women with breast and gynecological cancer. *Supportive Care in Cancer*, 33, Article 465. doi:10.1007/s00520-025-09519-1

Al-Ghafri, B. R., Al-Sinawi, H., Al-Harrasi, A. M., Al-Saidi, Y., Al-Mahrezi, A., Al-Ghusaini, Z. B. R., Al-Zeedy, K. B. R., & Chan, M. F. (2024). Effects of life-story review on quality of life, depression, and life satisfaction in older adults in Oman: A randomized controlled study. *BMC Geriatrics*, 24(1), Article 530. doi:10.1186/s12877-024-05133-8

Albrecht, G., Sartore, G. M., Connor, L., Higginbotham, N., Freeman, S., Kelly, B., Stain, H., Tonna, A., & Pollard, G. (2007). Solastalgia: The distress caused by environmental change. *Australasian Psychiatry*, 15(Suppl. 1), S95–S98. doi:10.1080/10398560701701288

Allan, B. A., Batz-Barbarich, C., Sterling, H. M., & Tay, L. (2019). Outcomes of meaningful work: A meta-analysis. *Journal of Management Studies*, 56(3), 500–528. doi:10.1111/joms.12406

Ameli, M. (2016). Integrating logotherapy with cognitive behavior therapy: A worthy challenge. In A. Batthyány (Ed.), *Logotherapy and existential analysis: Proceedings of the Viktor Frankl Institute Vienna* (Vol. 1, pp. 197–217). Springer International Publishing.

American Counseling Association. (2014). *ACA code of ethics.* Author.

American Psychiatric Association. (2013). *Diagnostic and statistical manual of mental disorders* (5th ed.). doi:10.1176/appi.books.9780890425596

American Psychiatric Association (APA). (2022). *Diagnostic and statistical manual of mental disorders* (5th ed., text rev.; DSM-5-TR). American Psychiatric Publishing.

American Psychiatric Association (APA). (2023). *The American Psychiatric Association practice guideline for the treatment of patients with eating disorders* (4th ed.). American Psychiatric Association Publishing. doi:10.1176/appi.books.9780890424865

American Psychological Association (APA). (2015). Guidelines for psychological practice with transgender and gender nonconforming people. *American Psychologist*, 70(9), 832–864. doi:10.1037/a0039906

American Psychological Association (APA). (2017). *Ethical principles of psychologists and code of conduct (2002*, amended effective June 1, 2010, and January 1, 2017). Author.

American Psychological Association. Guideline Development Panel for the Treatment of PTSD in Adults. (2019). Summary of the clinical practice guideline for the treatment of posttraumatic stress disorder (PTSD) in adults. *American Psychologist*, 74(5), 596–607. doi:10.1037/amp0000473

Ariza-Mateos, A., Calvache-Mateo, A., Bravo-Esteban, E., García-Conesa, S., & Rueda-Ruiz, C. (2019). Benefits of graded exposure in patients with chronic nonspecific low back pain: A randomized controlled trial. *Pain Medicine.*

Arnold, K. A., Turner, N., Barling, J., Kelloway, E. K., & McKee, M. C. (2007). Transformational leadership and psychological well-being: The mediating role of meaningful work. *Journal of Occupational Health Psychology*, 12(3), 193–203. doi:10.1037/1076-8998.12.3.193

AshaRani, P. V., Wang, P., Roystonn, K., Vaingankar, J. A., Lee, E. S., & Subramaniam, M. (2022). Purpose in life in older adults: A systematic review on conceptualization, measures, and determinants. *International Journal of Environmental Research and Public Health*, 19(10), 5860. doi:10.3390/ijerph19105860

Assor, A. (2018). The striving to develop an authentic inner compass as a key component of adolescents' need for autonomy: Parental antecedents and effects on identity, well-being, and resilience. In B. Soenens, M. Vansteenkiste, & S. Van Petegem (Eds.), *Autonomy in adolescent development: Toward conceptual clarity* (pp. 119–144). Psychology Press. doi:10.4324/9781315636511-6

Atwood, M. E., & Friedman, A. (2020). A systematic review of enhanced cognitive behavioral therapy (CBT-E) for eating disorders . *International Journal of Eating Disorders*, 53(3), 311–330. doi:10.1002/eat.23206

Baker, T. B., Piper, M. E., McCarthy, D. E., Majeskie, M. R., & Fiore, M. C. (2004). Addiction motivation reformulated: An affective processing model of negative reinforcement. *Psychological Review*, 111(1), 33–51. doi:10.1037/0033-295X.111.1.33

Barnes, D. M., & Meyer, I. H. (2012). Religious affiliation, internalized homophobia, and mental health in lesbians, gay men, and bisexuals. *American Journal of Orthopsychiatry*, 82(4), 505–515. doi:10.1111/j.1939-0025.2012.01185.x

Barney, J. L., Lillis, J., Haynos, A. F., Forman, E. M., & Juarascio, A. S. (2019). Assessing the valuing process in Acceptance and Commitment Therapy: Experts' review of the current status and recommendations for future directions. *Journal of Contextual Behavioral Science*, 12, 225–233. doi:10.1016/j.jcbs.2018.08.002

Barsalou, L. W. (2008). Grounded cognition. *Annual Review of Psychology*, 59, 617–645. doi:10.1146/annurev.psych.59.103006.093639

Bartels, D. M., & Urminsky, O. (2011). On intertemporal selfishness: How the perceived instability of identity underlies impatient consumption. *Journal of Consumer Research*, 38(1), 182–198. doi:10.1086/658339

Batthyány, A., & Russo-Netzer, P. (2014). Psychologies of meaning. In A. Batthyány & P. Russo-Netzer (Eds.), *Meaning in positive and existential psychology* (pp. 3–24). Springer. doi:10.1007/978-1-4939-0308-5_1

Bauer, J. J., & McAdams, D. P. (2010). Eudaimonic growth: Narrative growth goals predict increases in ego development and subjective well-being three years later. *Developmental Psychology*, 46(4), 761–772. doi:10.1037/a0019654

Bauman, Z. (2000). *Liquid modernity*. Polity Press.

Baumeister, R. F., & Leary, M. R. (1995). The need to belong: Desire for interpersonal attachments as a fundamental human motivation. *Psychological Bulletin*, 117(3), 497–529. doi:10.1037/0033-2909.117.3.497

Baumeister, R. F., Kellerman, G., Reece, A., Ruscio, A. M., & Sjåstad, H. (2024). Pragmatic prospection: Theory, research, and practice. In A. J. Elliot (Ed.), *Advances in motivation science* (Vol. 11, pp. 1–38). Elsevier. doi:10.1016/bs.adms.2024.03.005

Baumeister, R. F., Vohs, K. D., Aaker, J. L., & Garbinsky, E. N. (2013). Some key differences between a happy life and a meaningful life. *The Journal of Positive Psychology*, 8(6), 505–516. doi:10.1080/17439760.2013.830764

Beck, A. T., Rush, A. J., Shaw, B. F., & Emery, G. (1979). *Cognitive therapy of depression*. Guilford Press.

Beck, A. T., Grant, P., Inverso, E., Brinen, A. P., & Perivoliotis, D. (2020). *Recovery-oriented cognitive therapy for serious mental health conditions*. Guilford Press.

Beitman, B. D., Celebi, E., & Coleman, S. L. (2010). Synchronicity and healing. In D. A. Monti & B. D. Beitman (Eds.), *Integrative psychiatry* (pp. 445–483). Oxford University Press.

Belfi, A. M., & Jakubowski, K. (2021). Music and autobiographical memory. *Music & Science*, 4, 20592043211047123. doi:10.1177/20592043211047123

Bennett-Levy, J. (2019). Why therapists should walk the talk: The theoretical and empirical case for personal practice in therapist training and professional development. *Journal of Behavior Therapy and Experimental Psychiatry*, 62, 133–145. doi:10.1016/j.jbtep.2018.08.004

Bennett-Levy, J., & Finlay-Jones, A. (2018). The role of personal practice in therapist skill development: A model to guide therapists, educators, supervisors and researchers. *Cognitive Behaviour Therapy*, 47(3), 185–205. doi:10.1080/16506073.2018.1434678

Bernal, G., Bonilla, J., & Bellido, C. (1995). Ecological validity and cultural sensitivity for outcome research: Issues for the cultural adaptation and development of psychosocial treatments with Hispanics. *Journal of Abnormal Child Psychology*, 23(1), 67–82. doi:10.1007/BF01447045

Berntsen, D., & Hall, N. M. (2004). The episodic nature of involuntary autobiographical memories. *Memory & Cognition*, 32(5), 789–803. doi:10.3758/BF03195869

Beseran, E., Pericàs, J. M., Cash-Gibson, L., Ventura-Cots, M., Pollack Porter, K. M., & Benach, J. (2022). Deaths of despair: A scoping review on the social determinants of drug overdose, alcohol-related liver disease and suicide. *International Journal of Environmental Research and Public Health*, 19(19), 12395. doi:10.3390/ijerph191912395

Biesta, G. (2010). *Good education in an age of measurement: Ethics, politics, democracy*. Paradigm Publishers.

Bishop, S. R., Lau, M., Shapiro, S., Carlson, L., Anderson, N. D., Carmody, J., Segal, Z. V., Abbey, S., Speca, M., Velting, D., & Devins, G. (2004). Mindfulness: A proposed operational definition. *Clinical Psychology: Science and Practice*, 11 (3), 230–241.

Blustein, D. L., Kenny, M. E., Autin, K. L., & Duffy, R. D. (2023). Understanding decent work and meaningful work. *Annual Review of Organizational Psychology and Organizational Behavior*, 10, 289–314. doi:10.1146/annurev-orgpsych-031921-024847

Bojanowska, A., Kaczmarek, Ł. D., Urbańska, B., & Puchalska, M. (2022). Acting on values: A novel intervention enhancing hedonic and eudaimonic well-being. *Journal of Happiness Studies*, 23, 3889–3908. doi:10.1007/s10902-022-00585-4

Bonhag, R., & Froese, P. (2022). Sources of mattering for women and men: Gender differences and similarities in feelings of social significance. *Sociological Perspectives*, 65(4), 745–764. doi:10.1177/07311214211057119.

Boreham, I. D., & Schutte, N. S. (2023). The relationship between purpose in life and depression and anxiety: A meta-analysis. *Journal of Clinical Psychology*, 79(12), 2736–2767. doi:10.1002/jclp.23576

Boyle, P. A., Barnes, L. L., Buchman, A. S., & Bennett, D. A. (2009). Purpose in life is associated with mortality among community-dwelling older persons. *Psychosomatic Medicine*, 71(5), 574–579. doi:10.1097/PSY.0b013e3181a5a7c0

Brassai, L., Piko, B. F., & Steger, M. F. (2012). Existential attitudes and Eastern European adolescents' problem and health behaviors: Highlighting the role of the search for meaning in life. *The Psychological Record*, 62, 719–734. doi:10.1007/BF03395831

Breitbart, W. S., & Poppito, S. R. (2014). *Meaning-centered group psychotherapy for patients with advanced cancer: A treatment manual.* Oxford University Press.

Breitbart, W., Pessin, H., Rosenfeld, , Applebaum, A. J.B., Lichtenthal, W. G., Li, Y., Saracino, R. M., Marziliano, A. M., Masterson, M., Tobias, K., & Fenn, N. (2018). Individual meaning-centered psychotherapy for the treatment of psychological and existential distress: A randomized controlled trial in patients with advanced cancer. *Cancer*, 124(15), 3231–3239. doi:10.1002/cncr.31539

Breitbart, W., Poppito, S., Rosenfeld, B., Vickers, A. J., Li, Y., Abbey, J., Olden, M., Pessin, H., Lichtenthal, W., Sjoberg, D., Cassileth, B. R., & others. (2010). Meaning-centered group psychotherapy for patients with advanced cancer: A pilot randomized controlled trial. *Psycho-Oncology*, 19(1), 21–28. doi:10.1002/pon.1556

Breitbart, W., Rosenfeld, B., Pessin, H., Applebaum, A., Kulikowski, J., & Lichtenthal, W. G. (2015). Meaning-centered group psychotherapy: An effective intervention for improving psychological well-being in patients with advanced cancer. *Journal of Clinical Oncology*, 33(7), 749–754. doi:10.1200/JCO.2014.57.2198

Breitbart, W., Rosenfeld, B., Pessin, H., Applebaum, A., Kulikowski, J., Lichtenthal, W. G., … (2012). Individual meaning-centered psychotherapy for the treatment of psychological and existential distress: A randomized controlled trial in patients with advanced cancer. *Journal of Clinical Oncology*, 30(12), 1304–1309. doi:10.1200/JCO.2011.36.2517

Brewin, C. R. (2025). Key concepts, methods, findings, and questions about traumatic memories. *Journal of Traumatic Stress*, 38(5), 771–780. doi:10.1002/jts.23164

Bride, B. E. (2007). Prevalence of secondary traumatic stress among social workers. *Social Work*, 52(1), 63–70.

Bronk, K. C. (2011). The role of purpose in life in healthy identity formation: A grounded model. *New Directions for Youth Development*, 2011(132), 31–44. doi:10.1002/yd.426

Bronk, K. C. (2014). *Purpose in life: A critical component of optimal youth development*. Springer. doi:10.1007/978-94-007-7491-9

Brown, K. W., & Ryan, R. M. (2003). The benefits of being present: Mindfulness and its role in psychological well-being. *Journal of Personality and Social Psychology*, 84(4), 822–848.

Bruner, J. S. (1990). *Acts of meaning*. Harvard University Press.

Bryant, R. A., Kenny, L., Joscelyne, A., Rawson, N., Maccallum, F., Cahill, C., Hopwood, S., Aderka, I. M., & Nickerson, A. (2014). Treating prolonged grief disorder: A randomized clinical trial. *JAMA Psychiatry*, 71(12), 1332–1339. doi:10.1001/jamapsychiatry.2014.1600

Buchholz, J. L., Blakey, S. M., Abramowitz, J. S., Reuman, L., & Riemann, B. C. (2022). Expectancy violation during exposure therapy: A pilot randomized controlled trial. *Journal of Behavioral and Cognitive Therapy*, 32(1), 13–24. doi:10.1016/j.jbct.2021.12.004

Burke, M., Marlow, C., & Lento, T. (2010). *Social network activity and social well-being*. In *Proceedings of the SIGCHI Conference on Human Factors in Computing Systems* (pp. 1909–1912). ACM.

Burrow, A. L., & Hill, P. L. (2011). Purpose as a form of identity capital for positive youth adjustment. *Developmental Psychology*, 47(4), 1196–1206. doi:10.1037/a0023818

Butler, R. N. (1963). The life review: An interpretation of reminiscence in the aged. *Psychiatry*, 26(1), 65–76. doi:10.1080/00332747.1963.11023339

Calhoun, L. G., & Tedeschi, R. G. (2014). The foundations of posttraumatic growth: An expanded framework. In L. G. Calhoun & R. G. Tedeschi (Eds.), *Handbook of posttraumatic growth: Research and practice* (pp. 3–23). Routledge.

Campbell, J. (1949). *The hero with a thousand faces.* Pantheon Books.
Carton, A. M. (2018). "I'm not mopping the floors, I'm putting a man on the moon": How leaders enhance the meaningfulness of work by changing the meaning of work. *Administrative Science Quarterly*, 63(2), 323–369. doi:10.1177/0001839217713748.
Case, A., & Deaton, A. (2015). Rising morbidity and mortality in midlife among white non-Hispanic Americans in the 21st century. *Proceedings of the National Academy of Sciences of the United States of America*, 112(49), 15078–15083. doi:10.1073/pnas.1518393112
Case, A., & Deaton, A. (2020). *Deaths of despair and the future of capitalism.* Princeton University Press.
Castelo, N., Kushlev, K., Ward, A. F., Esterman, M., & Reiner, P. B. (2025). Blocking mobile internet on smartphones improves sustained attention, mental health, and subjective well-being. *PNAS Nexus*, 4(2), pgaf017. doi:10.1093/pnasnexus/pgaf017
Chanouha, N., Chassevent, A., Macnamara, E. F., Schaa, K., Thoeny, R., & Tansey, J. (2026). Exploring the principles of logotherapy in genetic counseling: Enhancing decision-making, adaptation, and justice. *Journal of Genetic Counseling*, 35(1), e70165. doi:10.1002/jgc4.70165
Chen, I., & Forbes, C. (2014). Reflective writing and its impact on empathy in medical education: Systematic review. *Journal of Educational Evaluation for Health Professions*, 11, Article 20. doi:10.3352/jeehp.2014.11.20
Chen, S., & Russo-Netzer, P. (2025). The power of "why": Meaning as a key resource in the workplace. *Innovations in Management*, 17, 43–56. [Hebrew]
Chen, S., Westman, M., & Hobfoll, S. E. (2015). The commerce and crossover of resources: Resource conservation in the service of resilience. *Stress and Health*, 31(2), 95–105. doi:10.1002/smi.2574
Chiu, C.-Y., & Hong, Y.-Y. (2007). *Social psychology of culture.* Psychology Press.
Cho, L. Y., Miller, L. J., Hrastar, M. G., Sutton, N. A., & Younes, J. P. (2009). Synchronicity awareness intervention: An open trial. *Teachers College Record*, 111(12), 2786–2799. doi:10.1177/016146810911101205
Chochinov, H. M., Kristjanson, L. J., Breitbart, W., McClement, S., Hack, T. F., Hassard, T., & Harlos, M. (2011). Effect of dignity therapy on distress and end-of-life experience in terminally ill patients: A randomized controlled trial. *The Lancet Oncology*, 12(8), 753–762. doi:10.1016/S1470-2045(11)70153-X
Choy, Y., Fyer, A. J., & Lipsitz, J. D. (2007). Treatment of specific phobia in adults. *Clinical Psychology Review*, 27(3), 266–286. doi:10.1016/j.cpr.2006.10.002

Chu, S. T. W., & Mak, W. W. S. (2020). How mindfulness enhances meaning in life: A meta-analysis of correlational studies and randomized controlled trials. *Mindfulness*, 11, 177–193. doi:10.1007/s12671-019-01258-9

Clark, D. A., & Beck, A. T. (2010). *Cognitive therapy of anxiety disorders: Science and practice*. Guilford Press.

Clarke, D. M., & Kissane, D. W. (2002). Demoralization: Its phenomenology and importance. *Australian & New Zealand Journal of Psychiatry*, 36(6), 733–742. doi:10.1046/j.1440-1614.2002.01086.x

Clayton, S., & Karazsia, B. T. (2020). Development and validation of a measure of climate change anxiety. *Journal of Environmental Psychology*, 69, 101434. doi:10.1016/j.jenvp.2020.101434

Cloud, W., & Granfield, R. (2008). Conceptualizing recovery capital: Expansion of a theoretical construct. *Substance Use & Misuse*, 43(12–13), 1971–1986. doi:10.1080/10826080802289762

Cohen, G. L., & Garcia, J. (2008). Identity, belonging, and achievement: A model, interventions, implications. *Current Directions in Psychological Science*, 17(6), 365–369. doi:10.1111/j.1467-8721.2008.00607.x

Cohen, R., Bavishi, C., & Rozanski, A. (2016). Purpose in life and its relationship to all-cause mortality and cardiovascular events: A meta-analysis. *Psychosomatic Medicine*, 78(2), 122–133. doi:10.1097/PSY.0000000000000274

Collard, J. (2024). Use of self-practice/self-reflection (SP/SR) exercises for competency-based training and assessment in CBT. *The Cognitive Behaviour Therapist*, 17, e1. doi:10.1017/S1754470X23000375

Copeland, A., Jones, A., & Field, M. (2020). The association between meaning in life and harmful drinking is mediated by individual differences in self-control and alcohol value. *Addictive Behaviors Reports*, 11, Article 100258. doi:10.1016/j.abrep.2020.100258

Cornelius-White, J. H. D., Watson, S. M., Kanamori, Y., & Cornelius-White, A. J. (2025). Logotherapy for depressive symptoms: A meta-analysis of passive and active control studies. *Journal of Humanistic Counseling*, 64(2), 130–142. doi:10.1002/johc.12237

Craig, A. D. (2009). How do you feel—now? The anterior insula and human awareness. *Nature Reviews Neuroscience*, 10(1), 59–70. doi:10.1038/nrn2555

Craske, M. G., Treanor, M., Conway, C. C., Zbozinek, T., & Vervliet, B. (2014). Maximizing exposure therapy: An inhibitory learning approach. *Behaviour Research and Therapy*, 58, 10–23. doi:10.1016/j.brat.2014.04.006

Craske, M. G., Treanor, M., Zbozinek, T. D., & Vervliet, B. (2022). Optimizing exposure therapy with an inhibitory retrieval approach and the OptEx Nexus. *Behaviour Research and Therapy*, 152, 104069. doi:10.1016/j.brat.2022.104069

Crego, A., Yela, J. R., Gómez-Martínez, M. Á., & Karim, A. A. (2020). The contribution of meaningfulness and mindfulness to psychological well-being and mental health: A structural equation model. *Journal of Happiness Studies*, 21(8), 2827–2850. doi:10.1007/s10902-019-00201-y

Crego, A., Yela, J. R., Gómez-Martínez, M. Á., Riesco-Matías, P., & Petisco-Rodríguez, C. (2021). Relationships between mindfulness, purpose in life, happiness, anxiety, and depression: Testing a mediation model in a sample of women. *International Journal of Environmental Research and Public Health*, 18(3), Article 925. doi:10.3390/ijerph18030925

Crenshaw, K. (1989). Demarginalizing the intersection of race and sex: A Black feminist critique of antidiscrimination doctrine, feminist theory and antiracist politics. *University of Chicago Legal Forum*, 1989(1), 139–167.

Crenshaw, K. (1991). Mapping the margins: Intersectionality, identity politics, and violence against women of color. *Stanford Law Review*, 43 (6), 1241–1299. doi:10.2307/1229039.

Creswell, J. D., Welch, W. T., Taylor, S. E., Sherman, D. K., Gruenewald, T. L., & Mann, T. (2005). Affirmation of personal values buffers neuroendocrine and psychological stress responses. *Psychological Science*, 16(11), 846–851. doi:10.1111/j.1467-9280.2005.01624.x

Critcher, C. R., & Dunning, D. (2015). Self-affirmations provide a broader perspective on self-threat. *Personality and Social Psychology Bulletin*, 41(1), 3–18. doi:10.1177/0146167214554956

Cruciani, G., Quintigliano, M., Mezzalira, S., Scandurra, C., & Carone, N. (2024). Attitudes and knowledge of mental health practitioners towards LGBTQ+ patients: A mixed-method systematic review. *Clinical Psychology Review*, 113, Article 102488. doi:10.1016/j.cpr.2024.102488

Crumbaugh, J. C., & Maholick, L. T. (1964). An experimental study in existentialism: The psychometric approach to Frankl's concept of noogenic neurosis. *Journal of Clinical Psychology*, 20(2), 200–207.

Csikszentmihalyi, M. (1990). *Flow: The psychology of optimal experience*. Harper & Row.

Csikszentmihalyi, M. (1997). *Finding flow: The psychology of engagement with everyday life*. Basic Books.

Cuevas, P. E., Davidson, P., Mejilla, J., & Rodney, T. (2021). Dignity therapy for end-of-life care patients: A literature review. *Journal of Patient Experience*, *8*, Article 2374373521996951. doi:10.1177/2374373521996951

Cunsolo, A., & Ellis, N. R. (2018). Ecological grief as a mental health response to climate change-related loss. *Nature Climate Change*, 8(4), 275–281. doi:10.1038/s41558-018-0092-2

Cuong, N., Piko, B., & Tuong, N. (2025). The role of social media in constructing meaning in life: A structural equation modeling analysis. *i-com*, 24(2), 327–340. doi:10.1515/icom-2024-0060

Czekierda, K., Banik, A., Park, C. L., & Luszczynska, A. (2017). Meaning in life and physical health: Systematic review and meta-analysis. *Health Psychology Review*, 11(4), 387–418. doi:10.1080/17437199.2017.1327325

de Mille, A. (1991). *Martha: The life and work of Martha Graham*. Random House.

Dahlhamer, J. M., Galinsky, A. M., Joestl, S. S., & Ward, B. W. (2016). Barriers to health care among adults identifying as sexual minorities: A US national study. *American Journal of Public Health*, 106(6), 1116–1122. doi:10.2105/AJPH.2016.303049

Damon, W. (2008). *The path to purpose: How young people find their calling in life*. The Free Press.

Damschroder, L. J., Aron, D. C., Keith, R. E., Kirsh, S. R., Alexander, J. A., & Lowery, J. C. (2009). Fostering implementation of health services research findings into practice: A consolidated framework for advancing implementation science. *Implementation Science*, 4, 50. doi:10.1186/1748-5908-4-50.

Davidov, J., & Russo-Netzer, P. (2022). *Existential authenticity: Theory and practice*. Palgrave Macmillan.

Day, S., Laver, K., Jeon, Y.-H., Radford, K., & Low, L.-F. (2023). Frameworks for cultural adaptation of psychosocial interventions: A systematic review with narrative synthesis. *Dementia*, 22(8), 1921–1949. doi:10.1177/14713012231192360

Deci, E. L., & Ryan, R. M. (2000). The "what" and "why" of goal pursuits: Human needs and the self-determination of behavior. *Psychological Inquiry*, 11(4), 227–268. doi:10.1207/S15327965PLI1104_01

de Figueiredo, J. M. (1993). Depression and demoralization: Phenomenologic differences and research perspectives. *Comprehensive Psychiatry*, 34(5), 308–311. doi:10.1016/0010-440X(93)90016-W

Del Re, A. C., Flückiger, C., Horvath, A. O., Symonds, D., & Wampold, B. E. (2012). Therapist effects in the therapeutic alliance–outcome relationship: A restricted-maximum likelihood meta-analysis. *Clinical Psychology Review*, 32(7), 642–649.

Dezutter, J., Luyckx, K., & Wachholtz, A. (2015). Meaning in life in chronic pain patients over time: Associations with pain experience and psychological well-being. *Journal of Behavioral Medicine*, 38(2), 384–396. doi:10.1007/s10865-014-9614-1

DiGiuseppe, R. A., Doyle, K. A., Dryden, W., & Backx, W. (2013). *A practitioner's guide to rational-emotive behavior therapy* (3rd ed.). Oxford University Press. doi:10.1093/med:psych/9780199743049.001.0001

Dugas, M. J., Gagnon, F., Ladouceur, R., & Freeston, M. H. (1998). Generalized anxiety disorder: A preliminary test of a conceptual model. *Behaviour Research and Therapy*, 36(2), 215–226. doi:10.1016/S0005-7967(97)00070–00073

Earnshaw, V. A., Mousavi, M., Qiu, X., & Fox, A. B. (2025). Mental illness and substance use disorder stigma: Mapping pathways between structures and individuals to accelerate research and intervention. *Annual Review of Clinical Psychology*, 21, 85–111. doi:10.1146/annurev-clinpsy-081423-023228

Edú-Valsania, S., Laguía, A., & Moriano, J. A. (2022). Burnout: A review of theory and measurement. *International Journal of Environmental Research and Public Health*, 19(3), 1780.

Ehlers, A., & Clark, D. M. (2000). A cognitive model of posttraumatic stress disorder. *Behaviour Research and Therapy*, 38(4), 319–345. doi:10.1016/S0005-7967(99)00123–0

Eisma, M. C. (2023). Prolonged grief disorder in ICD-11 and DSM-5-TR: Challenges and controversies. *Australian & New Zealand Journal of Psychiatry*, 57(7), 944–951. doi:10.1177/00048674231154206.

Ellison, N. B., Steinfield, C., & Lampe, C. (2007). The benefits of Facebook "friends": Social capital and college students' use of online social network sites. *Journal of Computer-Mediated Communication*, 12(4), 1143–1168.

Emerson, R. W. (1836). *Nature*. James Munroe and Company.

Epstein, E. G., & Hamric, A. B. (2009). Moral distress, moral residue, and the crescendo effect. *The Journal of Clinical Ethics*, 20(4), 330–342.

Erikson, E. H. (1968). *Identity: Youth and crisis*. W. W. Norton.

Ernzen, F. I. (1990). Frankl's Mountain Range Exercise: A logotherapy activity for small groups. *The International Forum for Logotherapy*, 13, 133–134.

Ersner-Hershfield, H., Garton, M. T., Ballard, K., Samanez-Larkin, G. R., & Knutson, B. (2009). Don't stop thinking about tomorrow: Individual differences in future self-continuity account for saving. *Judgment and Decision Making*, 4(4), 280–286. doi:10.1017/S1930297500003855

Everitt, B. J., & Robbins, T. W. (2016). Drug addiction: Updating actions to habits to compulsions ten years on. *Annual Review of Psychology*, 67, 23–50. doi:10.1146/annurev-psych-122414-033457

Exline, J. J., Pargament, K. I., Grubbs, J. B., & Yali, A. M. (2014). The Religious and Spiritual Struggles Scale: Development and initial validation. *Psychology of Religion and Spirituality*, 6(3), 208–222. doi:10.1037/a0036465

Fabry, J. B. (1988). *Guideposts to meaning: Discovering what really matters*. New Harbinger Publications.

Fabry, J. B. (1994). *The pursuit of meaning: Viktor Frankl, logotherapy, and life* (New rev. ed.). Institute of Logotherapy Press.

Fairburn, C. G., Cooper, Z., & Shafran, R. (2003). Cognitive behaviour therapy for eating disorders: A "transdiagnostic" theory and treatment. *Behaviour Research and Therapy*, 41(5), 509–528. doi:10.1016/S0005-7967(02)00088–00088

Fancourt, D., & Finn, S. (2019). *What is the evidence on the role of the arts in improving health and well-being? A scoping review*. WHO Regional Office for Europe. (Health Evidence Network synthesis report 67).

Farhoudian, A., Razaghi, E., Hooshyari, Z., Noroozi, A., Pilevari, A., Mokri, A., Mohammadi, M. R., & Malekinejad, M. (2022). Barriers and facilitators to substance use disorder treatment: An overview of systematic reviews. *Substance Abuse: Research and Treatment*, 16, 11782218221118462. doi:10.1177/11782218221118462

Festinger, L. (1954). A theory of social comparison processes. *Human Relations*, 7(2), 117–140. doi:10.1177/001872675400700202

Figley, C. R. (1995). *Compassion fatigue: Coping with secondary traumatic stress disorder in those who treat the traumatized*. Brunner/Mazel.

Fischer, I. C., Smidt, A. M., Nugent, N. R., & Lechner, W. V. (2020). The association between meaning in life and posttraumatic stress symptoms: A systematic review and meta-analysis. *Journal of Affective Disorders*, 277, 1024–1037. doi:10.1016/j.jad.2020.08.063

Fisher, W. R. (1987). *Human communication as narration: Toward a philosophy of reason, value, and action*. University of South Carolina Press.

Flett, G. L. (2018). *The psychology of mattering: Understanding the human need to be significant*. Academic Press.

Flett, G. L. (2022). An introduction, review, and conceptual analysis of mattering as an essential construct and an essential way of life. *Journal of Psychoeducational Assessment*, 40(1), 3–36. doi:10.1177/07342829211057640

Flückiger, C., Del Re, A. C., Wampold, B. E., & Horvath, A. O. (2018). The alliance in adult psychotherapy: A meta-analytic synthesis. *Psychotherapy: Theory, Research, Practice, Training*, 55(4), 316–340. doi:10.1037/pst0000172

Fosha, D. (2001). The dyadic regulation of affect. *Journal of Clinical Psychology*, 57(2), 227–242. doi:10.1002/1097-4679(200102)57:2%3C227::AID-JCLP8%3E3.0.CO;2-1

Frankl, V. E. (1924). Zur mimischen Bejahung und Verneinung. *Internationale Zeitschrift für Psychoanalyse*, 10, 437–438.
Frankl, V. E. (1946/2006) *Man's search for meaning* (I. Lasch, Trans.). Beacon Press.
Frankl, V. E. (1955). *The doctor and the soul: An introduction to logotherapy* (R. Winston & C. Winston, Trans.). Alfred A. Knopf. (Original work published 1946.)
Frankl, V. E. (1959). *Man's search for meaning*. Beacon Press.
Frankl, V. E. (1962). Psychiatry and man's quest for meaning. *Journal of Religion and Health*, 1(2), 93–103. doi:10.1007/BF01532076
Frankl, V. E. (1963). *Man's search for meaning: An introduction to logotherapy*. Washington Square Press.
Frankl, V. E. (1967). *Psychotherapy and existentialism: Selected papers on logotherapy*. Washington Square Press.
Frankl, V. E. (1969). *The will to meaning: Foundations and applications of logotherapy*. New American Library.
Frankl, V. E. (1970). *The will to meaning: Foundations and applications of logotherapy*. New American Library.
Frankl, V. E. (1978). *The unheard cry for meaning: Psychotherapy and humanism*. Simon & Schuster.
Frankl, V. E. (1984). *Man's search for meaning* (Rev. ed.). Washington Square Press.
Frankl, V. E. (1985a). *Man's search for meaning* (Rev. ed.). Washington Square Press.
Frankl, V. E. (1985b). *The unheard cry for meaning: Psychotherapy and humanism*. Washington Square Press.
Frankl, V. E. (1986). *The doctor and the soul: From psychotherapy to logotherapy* (3rd expanded ed.; R. Winston & C. Winston, Trans.). Vintage Books (Original work published 1946.)
Frankl, V. E. (1988). *The will to meaning: Foundations and applications of logotherapy* (Expanded ed.). Meridian.
Frankl, V. E. (2006). *Man's search for meaning* (I. Lasch, Trans.). Beacon Press. (Original work published 1946.)
Frankl, V. E. (2010). *The feeling of meaninglessness: A challenge to psychotherapy and philosophy* (A. Batthyány, Ed.; A. Tallon, Intro. Ed.). Marquette University Press.
Fredrickson, B. L. (1998). What good are positive emotions? *Review of General Psychology*, 2(3), 300–319. doi:10.1037/1089-2680.2.3.300
Fredrickson, B. L. (2001). The role of positive emotions in positive psychology: The broaden-and-build theory of positive emotions. *American Psychologist*, 56(3), 218–226. doi:10.1037/0003-066X.56.3.218

Freud, S. (1958). Formulations on the two principles of mental functioning. In J. Strachey (Ed. & Trans.), *The standard edition of the complete psychological works of Sigmund Freud* (Vol. 12, pp. 213–226). Hogarth Press. (Original work published 1911.)

Freud, S. (1958). Remembering, repeating and working-through: Further recommendations on the technique of psycho-analysis II. In J. Strachey (Ed. & Trans.), *The standard edition of the complete psychological works of Sigmund Freud* (Vol. 12, pp. 145–156). Hogarth Press. (Original work published 1914.)

Freud, S. (1961). *Beyond the pleasure principle* (J. Strachey, Trans.). W. W. Norton. (Original work published 1920.)

Freud, S. (2006). *Interpreting dreams* (J. A. Underwood, Trans.; A. Phillips, Ed.). Penguin Books. (Original work published 1900)

Frost, D. M., & Meyer, I. H. (2023). Minority stress theory: Application, critique, and continued relevance. *Current Opinion in Psychology*, 51, Article 101579. doi:10.1016/j.copsyc.2023.101579

Garcia, J., & Cohen, G. L. (2013). A social psychological approach to educational intervention. In E. Shafir (Ed.), *The behavioral foundations of public policy* (pp. 329–347). Princeton University Press.

Garcia, J., Vargas, N., Clark, J. L., Magaña Álvarez, M., Nelons, D. A., & Parker, R. G. (2020). Social isolation and connectedness as determinants of well-being: Global evidence mapping focused on LGBTQ youth. *Global Public Health*, 15(4), 497–519. doi:10.1080/17441692.2019.1682028

García-Alandete, J. (2024). The place of religiosity and spirituality in Frankl's logotherapy: Distinguishing salvific and hygienic objectives. *Journal of Religion and Health*, 63(1), 6–30. doi:10.1007/s10943-023-01760-4

Garcia-Alandete, J., Pérez, S., & Marco, J. H. (2025). Exploring the psychological impact of logotherapy on hope, meaning, and perceived life expectancy in women with breast cancer: A qualitative study. *Healthcare*, 13(1), 42–58.

Garland, E. L., Farb, N. A., Goldin, P. R., & Fredrickson, B. L. (2015). Mindfulness broadens awareness and builds eudaimonic meaning: A process model of mindful positive emotion regulation. *Psychological Inquiry*, 26(4), 293–314. doi:10.1080/1047840X.2015.1064294

Garrote-Caparros, E., Lecuona, O., Bellosta-Batalla, M., Moya-Albiol, L., & Cebolla, A. (2023). Efficacy of a mindfulness and compassion-based intervention in psychotherapists and their patients: Empathy, symptomatology, and mechanisms of change in a randomized controlled trial. *Psychotherapy*, 60(2), 182–193. doi:10.1037/pst0000467

Geller, S. M., & Greenberg, L. S. (2002). Therapeutic presence: Therapists' experience of presence in the psychotherapy encounter. *Person-Centered & Experiential Psychotherapies*, 1, 71–86. doi:10.1080/14779757.2002.9688279

George, L. S., & Park, C. L. (2016). Meaning in life as comprehension, purpose, and mattering: Toward integration and new research questions. *Review of General Psychology*, 20(3), 205–220. doi:10.1037/gpr0000077

Gollwitzer, P. M. (1999). Implementation intentions: Strong effects of simple plans. *American Psychologist*, 54(7), 493–503. doi:10.1037/0003-066X.54.7.493

Graber, A. V. (2004). *Viktor Frankl's logotherapy: Method of choice in ecumenical pastoral psychology.* Wyndham Hall Press.

Grassi, L., & Nanni, M. G. (2016). Demoralization syndrome: New insights in psychosocial cancer care. *Cancer*, 122(14), 2130–2133. doi:10.1002/cncr.30022

Grubbs, J. B., Wilt, J., Stauner, N., Exline, J. J., & Pargament, K. I. (2016). Self, struggle, and soul: Linking personality, self-concept, and religious/spiritual struggle. *Personality and Individual Differences*, 101, 144–152. doi:10.1016/j.paid.2016.05.365

Grupe, D. W., & Nitschke, J. B. (2013). *Uncertainty and anticipation in anxiety: An integrated neurobiological and psychological perspective.* Nature Reviews Neuroscience, 14(7), 488–501. doi:10.1038/nrn3524.

Guindon, M. H., & Hanna, F. J. (2002). Coincidence, happenstance, serendipity, fate, or the hand of God: Case studies in synchronicity. *The Career Development Quarterly*, 50, 195–208. doi:10.1002/J.2161-0045.2002.TB00894.X

Haber, D. (2006). Life review: Implementation, theory, research, and therapy. *The International Journal of Aging and Human Development*, 63(2), 153–171. doi:10.2190/DA9G-RHK5-N9JP-T6CC

Habermas, T., & Bluck, S. (2000). Getting a life: The emergence of the life story in adolescence. *Psychological Bulletin*, 126(5), 748–769. doi:10.1037/0033-2909.126.5.748

Haneef, S. H., & Abdullah, M. (2024). Effects of dignity therapy for palliative care patients and family caregivers: A systematic review. *Cureus*, 16(9), Article e70431. doi:10.7759/cureus.70431

Hays, P. A. (2016). *Addressing cultural complexities in practice: Assessment, diagnosis, and therapy* (3rd ed.). American Psychological Association.

He, X.-X., Wang, X.-Q., Steger, M. F., Ji, L.-J., Jing, K., Liu, M., & Ye, B. (2023). Meaning in life and psychological distress: A meta-analysis. *Journal of Research in Personality*, 104, 104381. doi:10.1016/j.jrp.2023.104381

Heeren, A., Mouguiama-Daouda, C., & Contreras, A. (2022). On climate anxiety and the threat it may pose to daily life functioning and adaptation to climate change. *Climatic Change*, 173, Article 10. doi:10.1007/s10584-022-03402-2

Heidenreich, T., Noyon, A., Worrell, M., & Menzies, R. (2021). Existential approaches and cognitive behavior therapy: Challenges and potential. *International Journal of Cognitive Therapy*, 14, 209–234. doi:10.1007/s41811-020-00096-1

Heine, S. J., Proulx, T., & Vohs, K. D. (2006). The meaning maintenance model: On the coherence of social motivations. *Personality and Social Psychology Review*, 10(2), 88–110. doi:10.1207/s15327957pspr1002_1

Helgeson, V. S., Reynolds, K. A., & Tomich, P. L. (2006). A meta-analytic review of benefit finding and growth. *Journal of Consulting and Clinical Psychology*, 74(5), 797–816. doi:10.1037/0022-006X.74.5.797

Helm, P. J., Jimenez, T., Galgali, M. S., Edwards, M. E., Vail, K. E., III, & Arndt, J. (2022). Divergent effects of social media use on meaning in life via loneliness and existential isolation during the coronavirus pandemic. *Journal of Social and Personal Relationships*, 39(6), 1768–1793.

Henrich, J., Heine, S. J., & Norenzayan, A. (2010). The weirdest people in the world? *Behavioral and Brain Sciences*, 33(2–3), 61–83. doi:10.1017/S0140525X0999152X

Henrion, R. (2002). Alcohol use disorders: Alcohol dependence. *The International Forum for Logotherapy*, 25, 30–38.

Hershfield, H. E., & Bartels, D. M. (2018). The future self. In G. Oettingen, A. T. Sevincer, & P. M. Gollwitzer (Eds.), *The psychology of thinking about the future* (pp. 89–109). Guilford Press.

Herz, R. S. (2004). A naturalistic analysis of autobiographical memories triggered by olfactory, visual and auditory stimuli. *Chemical Senses*, 29 (3), 217–224. doi:10.1093/chemse/bjh025

Hickman, C., Marks, E., Pihkala, P., Clayton, S., Lewandowski, R. E., Mayall, E. E., Wray, B., Mellor, C., & van Susteren, L. (2021). Climate anxiety in children and young people and their beliefs about government responses to climate change: A global survey. *The Lancet Planetary Health*, 5(12), e863–e873doi:10.1016/S2542-5196(21)00278–00273

Hill, C. E. (2018). *Meaning in life: A therapist's guide*. American Psychological Association.

Hill, C. E., & Knox, S. (2010). The use of dreams in modern psychotherapy. *International Review of Neurobiology*, 92, 291–317. doi:10.1016/S0074-7742(10)92013-8

Hill, P. L., & Turiano, N. A. (2014). Purpose in life as a predictor of mortality across adulthood. *Psychological Science*, 25(7), 1482–1486. doi:10.1177/0956797614531799.

Hobfoll, S. E. (1989). Conservation of resources: A new attempt at conceptualizing stress. *American Psychologist*, 44(3), 513–524. doi:10.1037/0003-066X.44.3.513

Hobfoll, S. E., Halbesleben, J., Neveu, J.-P., & Westman, M. (2018). Conservation of resources in the organizational context: The reality of resources and their consequences. *Annual Review of Organizational Psychology and Organizational Behavior*, 5, 103–128. doi:10.1146/annurev-orgpsych-032117-104640

Hocoy, D. (2012). Sixty years later: The enduring allure of synchronicity. *Journal of Humanistic Psychology*, 52, 467–478. doi:10.1177/0022167812436427

Hodgkinson, G. P., Sadler-Smith, E., Burke, L. A., Claxton, G., & Sparrow, P. R. (2009). Intuition in organisations: Some implications for strategic management. *Long Range Planning*, 42(3), 277–297. doi:10.1016/j.lrp.2009.05.003

Hoffman, E. (1995). Victor Frankl at ninety: A voice for life. *America*, 172(9), 17–22.

Hoffman, L., & Vallejos, S. (2020). Existential shattering. In V. Zeigler-Hill & T. K. Shackelford (Eds.), *Encyclopedia of personality and individual differences*. Springer. doi:10.1007/978-3-319-24612-3_2965

Holmes, R. (1991). Alcoholics Anonymous as group logotherapy. *The International Forum for Logotherapy*, 14, 36–41.

Holtmaat, K., van der Spek, N., Lissenberg-Witte, B. I., Breitbart, W., Cuijpers, P., & Verdonck-de Leeuw, I. M. (2020). Long-term efficacy of meaning-centered group psychotherapy for cancer survivors: 2-year follow-up results of a randomized controlled trial. *Psycho-Oncology*, 29 (4), 711–718. doi:10.1002/pon.5323

Hong, E. K., Zhang, Y., & Sedikides, C. (2024). Future self-continuity promotes meaning in life through authenticity. *Journal of Research in Personality*, 109, Article 104463. doi:10.1016/j.jrp.2024.104463

Honka, A. M., Helander, E., Pavel, M., Jimison, H., Mustonen, P., Korhonen, I., & Ermes, M. (2019). Exploring associations between the self-reported values, well-being, and health behaviors of Finnish citizens: Cross-sectional analysis of more than 100,000 web-survey responses. *JMIR Mental Health*, 6(4), e12170. doi:10.2196/12170

Hook, J. N., Davis, D. E., Owen, J., Worthington, E. L., Jr., & Utsey, S. O. (2013). Cultural humility: Measuring openness to culturally diverse clients. *Journal of Counseling Psychology*, 60(3), 353–366. doi:10.1037/a0032595.

Hooker, S. A., Post, R. E., & Sherman, M. D. (2020). Awareness of meaning in life is protective against burnout among family physicians: A CERA study. *Family Medicine*, 52(1), 11–16. doi:10.22454/FamMed.2019.562297

Humer, E., Kisler, I.-M., Bach, D., Schimbock, W., Pieh, C., & Probst, T. (2025). Effect of a group logotherapeutic program for older adults on mental health indicators. *Journal of Humanistic Counseling*, 64(1), 68–90. doi:10.1002/johc.12216

Hunt, M. G., Marx, R., Lipson, C., & Young, J. (2018). No more FOMO: Limiting social media decreases loneliness and depression. *Journal of Social and Clinical Psychology*, 37(10), 751–768. doi:10.1521/jscp.2018.37.10.751

Janoff-Bulman, R. (1992). *Shattered assumptions: Towards a new psychology of trauma*. Free Press.

Jansson-Fröjmark, M., Alfonsson, S., Bohman, B., Rozental, A., & Norell-Clarke, A. (2022). Paradoxical intention for insomnia: A systematic review and meta-analysis. *Journal of Sleep Research*, 31(2), e13464. doi:10.1111/jsr.13464

Jung, C. G. (1951). On synchronicity. In H. Read, M. Fordham, G. Adler, & W. McGuire (Eds.), *The collected works of C. G. Jung: Vol. 8. The structure and dynamics of the psyche* (R. F. C. Hull, Trans., 2nd ed.). Princeton University Press.

Jung, C. G. (1955). Synchronicity: An acausal connecting principle. In C. G. Jung & W. Pauli, *The interpretation of nature and the psyche* (R. F. C. Hull, Trans., pp. 1–146). Pantheon Books. (Original work published 1952.)

Jung, C. G. (1969). Synchronicity: An acausal connecting principle. In H. Read, M. Fordham, G. Adler, & W. McGuire (Eds.), *The collected works of C. G. Jung: Vol. 8. The structure and dynamics of the psyche* (R. F. C. Hull, Trans., 2nd ed., pp. 417–531). Princeton University Press.

Kabat-Zinn, J. (1990). *Full catastrophe living: Using the wisdom of your body and mind to face stress, pain, and illness*. Delacorte.

Kashdan, T. B., Rottenberg, J., Goodman, F. R., Disabato, D. J., & Begovic, E. (2015). Lumping and splitting in the study of meaning in life: Thoughts on surfing, surgery, scents, and sermons. *Psychological Inquiry*, 26(4), 336–342. doi:10.1080/1047840X.2015.1073659

Keller, H. (1933). Three days to see. *The Atlantic Monthly*, 151(1), 35–42.

Kelly, J. F., Humphreys, K., & Ferri, M. (2020). Alcoholics Anonymous and other 12-step programs for alcohol use disorder. *Cochrane Database of Systematic Reviews*, 2020(3), Article CD012880. doi:10.1002/14651858.CD012880.pub2

Khalsa, S. S., Craske, M. G., Li, W., Vangala, S., Strober, M., & Feusner, J. D. (2015). Altered interoceptive awareness in anorexia nervosa: Effects of meal anticipation, consumption, and bodily arousal. *International Journal of Eating Disorders*, 48(7), 889–897. doi:10.1002/eat.22387

Khantzian, E. J. (1997). The self-medication hypothesis of substance use disorders: A reconsideration and recent applications. *Harvard Review of Psychiatry*, 4(5), 231–244. doi:10.3109/10673229709030550

Khantzian, E. J. (2013). Addiction as a self-regulation disorder and the role of self-medication. *Addiction*, 108(4), 668–669. doi:10.1111/add.12004

Khantzian, E. J. (2021). Commentary: It is not about supply, it is about demand: Why the self-medication hypotheses is still so important. *The American Journal on Addictions*, 30(4), 301–304. doi:10.1111/ajad.13111

Kim, E. S., Delaney, S. W., & Kubzansky, L. D. (2020). Sense of purpose in life and likelihood of future illicit drug misuse and prescription medication misuse. *Psychosomatic Medicine*, 82(7), 715–721. doi:10.1097/PSY.0000000000000842

Kirmayer, L. J., Gone, J. P., & Moses, J. (2014). Rethinking historical trauma. *Transcultural Psychiatry*, 51(3), 299–319. doi:10.1177/1363461514536358

King, L. A., & Hicks, J. A. (2021). The science of meaning in life. *Annual Review of Psychology*, 72, 561–584. doi:10.1146/annurev-psych-072420-122921

Kissane, D. W., Clarke, D. M., & Street, A. F. (2001). Demoralization syndrome: A relevant psychiatric diagnosis for palliative care. *Journal of Palliative Care*, 17(1), 12–21. doi:10.1177/082585970101700103

Kissane, D. W., Wein, S., Love, A., Lee, X. Q., Kee, P. L., & Clarke, D. M. (2004). The Demoralization Scale: A report of its development and preliminary validation. *Journal of Palliative Care*, 20(4), 269–276. doi:10.1177/082585970402000402

Klass, D., Silverman, P. R., & Nickman, S. (Eds.). (1996). *Continuing bonds: New understandings of grief.* Taylor & Francis. doi:10.4324/9781315800790

Kleim, B., & Ehlers, A. (2009). Evidence for a curvilinear relationship between posttraumatic growth and posttrauma depression and PTSD in assault survivors. *Journal of Traumatic Stress*, 22(1), 45–52. doi:10.1002/jts.20378

Klingberg, H., Jr. (2001). *When life calls out to us: The love and lifework of Viktor and Elly Frankl*. Doubleday.

Knox, S., & Hill, C. E. (2003). Therapist self-disclosure: Research-based suggestions for practitioners. *Journal of Clinical Psychology*, 59(5), 529–539. doi:10.1002/jclp.10157

Kocet, M. M., & Herlihy, B. J. (2014). Addressing value-based conflicts within the counseling relationship: A decision-making model. *Journal of Counseling & Development*, 92(2), 180–186.

Koenig, H. G. (2012). Religion, spirituality, and health: The research and clinical implications. *ISRN Psychiatry*, 2012, Article 278730. doi:10.5402/2012/278730

Koizumi, M., Ito, H., Kaneko, Y., & Motohashi, Y. (2008). Effect of having a sense of purpose in life on the risk of death from cardiovascular diseases. *Journal of Epidemiology*, 18(5), 191–196. doi:10.2188/jea.JE2007388

Koltko-Rivera, M. E. (2006). Rediscovering the later version of Maslow's hierarchy of needs: Self-transcendence and opportunities for theory, research, and unification. *Review of General Psychology*, 10(4), 302–317. doi:10.1037/1089-2680.10.4.302

Komischke-Konnerup, K. B., Zachariae, R., Boelen, P. A., Marello, M. M., & O'Connor, M. (2024). Grief-focused cognitive behavioral therapies for prolonged grief symptoms: A systematic review and meta-analysis. *Journal of Consulting and Clinical Psychology*, 92(4), 236–248. doi:10.1037/ccp0000884

Kono, S., & Walker, G. (2020). Theorizing the interpersonal aspect of ikigai ('life worth living') among Japanese university students: A mixed-methods approach. *International Journal of Wellbeing*, 10(2), 101–123. doi:10.5502/ijw.v10i2.979

Koob, G. F., & Schulkin, J. (2019). Addiction and stress: An allostatic view. *Neuroscience & Biobehavioral Reviews*, 106, 245–262. doi:10.1016/j.neubiorev.2018.09.008

Koole, S. L., Smeets, K., van Knippenberg, A., & Dijksterhuis, A. (1999). The cessation of rumination through self-affirmation. *Journal of Personality and Social Psychology*, 77(1), 111–125. doi:10.1037/0022-3514.77.1.111

Kross, E., Verduyn, P., Sheppes, G., Costello, C. K., Jonides, J., & Ybarra, O. (2021). Social media and well-being: Pitfalls, progress, and next steps. *Trends in Cognitive Sciences*, 25(1), 55–66. doi:10.1016/j.tics.2020.10.005.

Krug, O. T. (2009). James Bugental and Irvin Yalom: Two masters of existential therapy cultivate presence in the therapeutic encounter. *Journal of Humanistic Psychology*, 49, 329–354. doi:10.1177/0022167809334001

Kruglanski, A. W., & Raviv, D. (2025). *The quest for significance: Harnessing the need that makes the world go round*. Routledge. doi:10.4324/9781003410706

Krumhansl, C. L., & Zupnick, J. A. (2013). Cascading reminiscence bumps in popular music. *Psychological Science*, 24(10), 2057–2068. doi:10.1177/0956797613486486

Kübler-Ross, E. (Ed.). (1975). *Death: The final stage of growth*. Prentice-Hall.

Kumano, M. (2018). On the concept of well-being in Japan: Feeling shiawase as hedonic well-being and feeling ikigai as eudaimonic well-being. *Applied Research in Quality of Life*, 13(2), 419–433. doi:10.1007/s11482-017-9532-9

Kumar, P. S. (2024). Technostress: A comprehensive literature review on dimensions, impacts, and management strategies. *Computers in Human Behavior Reports*, 16, 100475. doi:10.1016/j.chbr.2024.100475

Lachman, M. E. (2015). Mind the gap in the middle: A call to study midlife. *Research in Human Development*, 12(3–4), 327–334. doi:10.1080/15427609.2015.1068048

Lakoff, G., & Johnson, M. (1980). *Metaphors we live by*. University of Chicago Press.

Lambert, N. M., Stillman, T. F., Baumeister, R. F., Fincham, F. D., Hicks, J. A., & Graham, S. M. (2010). Family as a salient source of meaning in young adulthood. *Journal of Positive Psychology*, 5(5), 367–376. doi:10.1080/17439760.2010.516616

Lantz, J. (1992). Using Frankl's concepts with post-traumatic stress disorder clients. *Journal of Contemporary Psychotherapy*, 22(1), 13–22. doi:10.1007/BF00944318

Lantz, J. (1998). Viktor Frankl and interactional group therapy. *Journal of Religion and Health*, 37(2), 93–104. doi:10.1023/A:1022922713843

Larsson, M., Willander, J., Karlsson, K., & Arshamian, A. (2014). Olfactory LOVER: Behavioral and neural correlates of autobiographical odor memory. *Frontiers in Psychology*, 5, 312. doi:10.3389/fpsyg.2014.00312

Lassiter, J. M., Saleh, L. D., Grov, C., Starks, T. J., Ventuneac, A., & Parsons, J. T. (2019). Spirituality and multiple dimensions of religion are associated with mental health in gay and bisexual men: Results from the One Thousand Strong Cohort. *Psychology of Religion and Spirituality*, 11(4), 408–416. doi:10.1037/rel0000146

Lee, M.-A., & Kawachi, I. (2019). The keys to happiness: Associations between personal values regarding core life domains and happiness in South Korea. *PLOS ONE*, 14(1), Article e0209821. doi:10.1371/journal.pone.0209821

Levinson, J. I. (2002). Dr. Jerry L. Long—In memoriam. *The International Forum for Logotherapy*, 25, 118–124.

Lewis, C. S. (2001). *The problem of pain.* HarperOne. (Original work published 1940.)

Lindsay, E. K., & Creswell, J. D. (2017). Mechanisms of mindfulness training: Monitor and Acceptance Theory (MAT). *Clinical Psychology Review*, 51, 48–59. doi:10.1016/j.cpr.2016.10.011

Lips-Wiersma, M., & Morris, L. (2009). Discriminating between "meaningful work" and the "management of meaning". *Journal of Business Ethics*, 88(3), 491–511. doi:10.1007/s10551-009-0118-9

Lomas, T., & Ivtzan, I. (2016). Second wave positive psychology: Exploring the positive–negative dialectics of wellbeing. *Journal of Happiness Studies*, 17, 1753–1768. doi:10.1007/s10902-015-9668-y

Long, J. L., Jr. (1995). The quest for meaning in the twenty-first century. *The International Forum for Logotherapy*, 18, 60–62.

Lucchetti, G., Bassi, R. M., & Lucchetti, A. L. G. (2013). Taking spiritual history in clinical practice: A systematic review of instruments. *Explore: The Journal of Science and Healing*, 9(3), 159–170. doi:10.1016/j.explore.2013.02.004

Lukas, E. (1979/1995). The four steps of logotherapy. In J. B. Fabry, R. P. Bulka, & W. S. Sahakian (Eds.), *Finding meaning in life: Logotherapy* (pp. 95–103). Jason Aronson.

Lukas, E. (1998). *Logotherapy textbook: Theory and practice of Viktor E. Frankl's logotherapy.* Liberty Press.

Lukas, E. (2000). *Meaning-centered psychotherapy.* Liberty Press.

Lukas, E. (2020). *Logotherapy: Principles and methods.* Elisabeth-Lukas-Archiv gGmbH.

Lyubomirsky, S., & Layous, K. (2013). How do simple positive activities increase well-being? *Current Directions in Psychological Science*, 22(1), 57–62. doi:10.1177/0963721412469809.

Maercker, A. (2002). Life-review technique in the treatment of PTSD in elderly patients: Rationale and three single case studies. *Journal of Clinical Geropsychology*, 8, 239–249. doi:10.1023/A:1015952429199

MacKinnon, C. J., Milman, E., Smith, N. G., Henry, M., Berish, M., Copeland, L. S., Körner, A., Chochinov, H. M., & Cohen, S. R. (2013). Means to meaning in cancer-related bereavement: Identifying clinical implications for counseling psychologists. *The Counseling Psychologist*, 41(2), 216–239. doi:10.1177/0011000012459969

MacKinnon, C. J., Smith, N. G., Henry, M., Berish, M., Milman, E., Körner, A., Copeland, L. S., Chochinov, H. M., & Cohen, S. R. (2014). Meaning-based group counseling for bereavement: Bridging theory with emerging trends in intervention research. *Death Studies*, 38 (3), 137–144. doi:10.1080/07481187.2012.738768

Main, R. (2011). Synchronicity and the limits of re-enchantment. *International Journal of Jungian Studies*, 3(2), 144–158. doi:10.1080/19409052.2011.592723.

Manco, N., & Hamby, S. (2021). A meta-analytic review of interventions that promote meaning in life. *American Journal of Health Promotion*, 35(6), 866–873. doi:10.1177/0890117121995736

Marco, J. H., Martinez-Micó, A., García-Alandete, J., Guillén, V., Grimaldos, J., Pérez, S., & Quero, S. (2024). A systematic review of the effectiveness of meaning-centred psychotherapies in depressed participants. *Clinical Psychology & Psychotherapy*, 31(1), e2936. doi:10.1002/cpp.2936.

Markus, H. R., & Kitayama, S. (1991). Culture and the self: Implications for cognition, emotion, and motivation. *Psychological Review*, 98(2), 224–253. doi:10.1037/0033-295X.98.2.224.

Markus, H., & Nurius, P. (1986). Possible selves. *American Psychologist*, 41(9), 954–969. doi:10.1037/0003-066X.41.9.954.

Marshall, S. K., Liu, Y., Wu, A., Berzonsky, M., & Adams, G. R. (2010). Perceived mattering to parents and friends for university students: A longitudinal study. *Journal of Adolescence*, 33(3), 367–375. doi:10.1016/j.adolescence.2009.09.003.

Marshall, M., & Marshall, E. (2012). *Logotherapy revisited: Review of the tenets of Viktor E. Frankl's logotherapy*. Ottawa Institute of Logotherapy.

Martela, F., & Steger, M. F. (2016). The three meanings of meaning in life: Distinguishing coherence, purpose, and significance. *The Journal of Positive Psychology*, 11(5), 531–545. doi:10.1080/17439760.2015.1137623

Martin-Cuellar, A. (2018). Self-reflexivity through journaling: An imperative process for the practicing clinician. *The William & Mary Educational Review*, 5(1), Article 11.

Martin, R. A., MacKinnon, S., Johnson, J., & Rohsenow, D. J. (2011). Purpose in life predicts treatment outcome among adult cocaine abusers in treatment. *Journal of Substance Abuse Treatment*, 40(2), 183–188. doi:10.1016/j.jsat.2010.10.002

Martínez, M., Arantzamendi, M., Belar, A., Carrasco, J. M., Carvajal, A., Rullán, M., & Centeno, C. (2017). "Dignity therapy," a promising intervention in palliative care: A comprehensive systematic literature review. *Palliative Medicine*, 31(6), 492–509. doi:10.1177/0269216316665562

Martins, H., Silva, R. S., Bragança, J., Romeiro, J., & Caldeira, S. (2024). Spiritual distress, hopelessness, and depression in palliative care: Simultaneous concept analysis. *Healthcare*, 12(10), Article 960. doi:10.3390/healthcare12100960

Maslach, C., & Jackson, S. E. (1981). The measurement of experienced burnout. *Journal of Occupational Behavior*, 2(2), 99–113.

Matheus Rahal, M. A., & Caserta Gon, M. (2020). Values-based work in Acceptance and Commitment Therapy: A systematic review of utility and accessibility of values assessment tools. *International Journal of Psychology and Psychological Therapy*, 20(3), 267–287.

McAdams, D. P. (2001). The psychology of life stories. *Review of General Psychology*, 5(2), 100–122. doi:10.1037/1089-2680.5.2.100

McAdams, D. P. (2011). Narrative identity. In S. J. Schwartz, K. Luyckx, & V. L. Vignoles (Eds.), *Handbook of identity theory and research* (pp. 99–115). Springer. doi:10.1007/978-1-4419-7988-9_5

McAdams, D. P. (2019). “First we invented stories, then they changed us”: The evolution of narrative identity. *Evolutionary Studies in Imaginative Culture*, 3(1), 1–18. doi:10.26613/esic.3.1.110

McAdams, D. P., & de St. Aubin, E. (1992). A theory of generativity and its assessment through self-report, behavioral acts, and narrative themes in autobiography. *Journal of Personality and Social Psychology*, 62(6), 1003–1015. doi:10.1037/0022-3514.62.6.1003

McAdams, D. P., & McLean, K. C. (2013). Narrative identity. *Current Directions in Psychological Science*, 22(3), 233–238. doi:10.1177/0963721413475622

McCann, E., Donohue, G., & Timmins, F. (2020). An exploration of the relationship between spirituality, religion and mental health among youth who identify as LGBT+: A systematic literature review. *Journal of Religion and Health*, 59(2), 828–844. doi:10.1007/s10943-020-00989-7

McLean, K. C., & Pasupathi, M. (2012). Processes of identity development: Where I am and how I got there. *Identity: An International Journal of Theory and Research*, 12(1), 8–28. doi:10.1080/15283488.2011.dispatch

McWhorter, M. R. (2019). Balancing value bracketing with the integration of moral values in psychotherapy: Evaluation of a clinical practice from the perspective of Catholic moral theology. *The Linacre Quarterly*, 86(2–3), 207–224. doi:10.1177/0024363919856810

McWilliams, N. (2004). *Psychoanalytic psychotherapy: A practitioner's guide*. Guilford Press.

McNulty, J. K., & Fincham, F. D. (2012). Beyond positive psychology? Toward a contextual view of psychological processes and well-being. *American Psychologist*, 67(2), 101–110. doi:10.1037/a0024572

Meyer, I. H. (2003). Prejudice, social stress, and mental health in lesbian, gay, and bisexual populations: Conceptual issues and research evidence. *Psychological Bulletin*, 129(5), 674–697. doi:10.1037/0033-2909.129.5.674

Mihandoust, S., Radfar, M., & Soleymani, M. (2021). Effectiveness of group logotherapy on meaning in life in mothers of children with autism spectrum disorder: A randomized clinical trial. *Journal of Advances in Medical and Biomedical Research*, 29(132), 54–62. doi:10.30699/jambs.29.132.54

Miller, W. R., & Rollnick, S. (2013). *Motivational interviewing: Helping people change* (3rd ed.). Guilford Press.

Milne, S., Lomax, C., & Freeston, M. H. (2019). A review of the relationship between intolerance of uncertainty and threat appraisal in anxiety. *The Cognitive Behaviour Therapist*, 12, e38. doi:10.1017/S1754470X19000230

Moagi, M. M., van der Wath, A. E., Jiyane, P. M., & Rikhotso, R. S. (2021). Mental health challenges of lesbian, gay, bisexual and transgender people: An integrated literature review. *Health SA Gesondheid*, 26, a1487. doi:10.4102/hsag.v26i0.1487

Moustakas, C. E. (1996). *Existential psychotherapy and the interpretation of dreams.* Jason Aronson.

Montag, C., Müller, M., Pontes, H. M., & Elhai, J. D. (2023). On fear of missing out, social networks use disorder tendencies and meaning in life. *BMC Psychology*, 11, 358. doi:10.1186/s40359-023-01342-9

Moon, B. L. (2009). *Existential art therapy: The canvas mirror* (3rd ed.). Charles C Thomas Publisher.

Moshe, I., Terhorst, Y., Philippi, P., Domhardt, M., Cuijpers, P., Cristea, I. A., Pulkki-Råback, L., Baumeister, H., & Sander, L. B. (2021). Digital interventions for the treatment of depression: A meta-analytic review. *Psychological Bulletin*, 147(8), 749–786. doi:10.1037/bul0000334

Musich, S., Wang, S. S., Kraemer, S., Hawkins, K., & Wicker, E. (2018). Purpose in life and positive health outcomes among older adults. *Population Health Management*, 21(2), 139–147. doi:10.1089/pop.2017.0063

Nadkarni, A., & Hofmann, S. G. (2012). *Why do people use Facebook?* Personality and Individual Differences, 52(3), 243–249. doi:10.1016/j.paid.2011.11.007.

Nakamura, N., Dispenza, F., Abreu, R. L., Ollen, E. W., Pantalone, D. W., Canillas, G., Gormley, B., & Vencill, J. A. (2022). The APA guidelines for psychological practice with sexual minority persons: An executive summary of the 2021 revision. *American Psychologist*, 77(8), 953–962. doi:10.1037/amp0000939

Napier, A. D., Slemp, G. R., & Vella-Brodrick, D. A. (2024). Life crafting and self-determination: An intervention to help emerging adults create an authentic and meaningful life. *Emerging Adulthood*, 12(4), 629–647. doi:10.1177/21676968241252196

National Institute for Health and Care Excellence. (2020). *Eating disorders: Recognition and treatment (NICE guideline NG69) (Updated 16 December 2020)*. (Original work published 2017.)

Neimeyer, R. A. (2019). Meaning reconstruction in bereavement: Development of a research program. *Death Studies*, 43(2), 79–91. doi:10.1080/07481187.2018.1456620

Neimeyer, R. A. (Ed.). (2015). *Techniques of grief therapy: Assessment and intervention*. Routledge.

Niemiec, R. M. (2019). Finding the golden mean: The overuse, underuse, and optimal use of character strengths. *Counselling Psychology Quarterly*, 32(3–4), 453–471. doi:10.1080/09515070.2019.1617674

Noddings, N. (2003). *Happiness and education*. Cambridge University Press.

Norcross, J. C., & Goldfried, M. R. (Eds.). (2019). *Handbook of psychotherapy integration* (3rd ed.). Oxford University Press.

OECD. (2023). *Health at a glance 2023: OECD indicators*. OECD Publishing. doi:10.1787/7a7afb35-en

Ogunbode, C. A., Doran, R., Hanss, D., Ojala, M., Salmela-Aro, K., van den Broek, K. L., Bhullar, N., Aquino, S., Marot, T., Schermer, J. A., Wlodarczyk, A., Aruta, J. J. B. R., & others. (2022). Climate anxiety, wellbeing and pro-environmental action: Correlates of negative emotional responses to climate change in 32 countries. *Journal of Environmental Psychology*, 84, 101887.

Ojala, M., Cunsolo, A., Ogunbode, C. A., & Middleton, J. (2021). Anxiety, worry, and grief in a time of environmental and climate crisis: A narrative review. *Annual Review of Environment and Resources*, 46, 35–58. doi:10.1146/annurev-environ-012220-022716

Oprea, B. T., Barzin, L., Virgă, D., Iliescu, D., & Rusu, A. (2019). Effectiveness of job crafting interventions: A meta-analysis and utility analysis. *European Journal of Work and Organizational Psychology*, 28(6), 723–741. doi:10.1080/1359432X.2019.1646786

Orben, A., & Przybylski, A. K. (2019). The association between adolescent well-being and digital technology use. *Nature Human Behaviour*, 3 (2), 173–182. doi:10.1038/s41562-018-0506-1.

Ostafin, B. D., & Feyel, N. (2019). The effects of a brief meaning in life intervention on the incentive salience of alcohol. *Addictive Behaviors*, 90, 107–111. doi:10.1016/j.addbeh.2018.10.035

Ottens, A. J., & Hanna, F. J. (1998). Cognitive and existential therapies: Toward an integration. *Psychotherapy: Theory, Research, Practice, Training*, 35(3), 312–324. doi:10.1037/h0087832

Pargament, K. I. (2007). *Spiritually integrated psychotherapy: Understanding and addressing the sacred*. Guilford Press.

Pargament, K. I., Smith, B. W., Koenig, H. G., & Perez, L. (1998). Patterns of positive and negative religious coping with major life stressors. *Journal for the Scientific Study of Religion*, 37(4), 710–724. doi:10.2307/1388152

Park, C. L. (2010). Making sense of the meaning literature: An integrative review of meaning making and its effects on adjustment to stressful life events. *Psychological Bulletin*, 136(2), 257–301. doi:10.1037/a0018301

Park, C. L. (2022). Meaning making following trauma. *Frontiers in Psychology*, 13, 844891. doi:10.3389/fpsyg.2022.844891

Park, C. L., & George, L. S. (2013). Assessing meaning and meaning making in the context of stressful life events: Measurement tools and approaches. *The Journal of Positive Psychology*, 8(6), 483–504. doi:10.1080/17439760.2013.830762

Park, N., Peterson, C., & Seligman, M. E. P. (2004). Strengths of character and well-being. *Journal of Social and Clinical Psychology*, 23(5), 603–619. doi:10.1521/jscp.23.5.603.50748

Pattakos, A. (2004). *Prisoners of our thoughts: Viktor Frankl's principles at work*. Berrett-Koehler Publishers.

Pepperdine, E., Lomax, C., & Freeston, M. H. (2018). Disentangling intolerance of uncertainty and threat appraisal in everyday situations. *Journal of Anxiety Disorders*, 57, 31–38. doi:10.1016/j.janxdis.2018.04.002

Pesant, N., & Zadra, A. (2004). Working with dreams in therapy: What do we know and what should we do? *Clinical Psychology Review*, 24(5), 489–512. doi:10.1016/j.cpr.2004.05.002

Peterson, C., & Seligman, M. E. P. (2004). *Character strengths and virtues: A handbook and classification*. American Psychological Association; Oxford University Press.

Philippe, T. J., Sikder, N., Jackson, A., Koblanski, M. E., Liow, E., Pilarinos, A., & Vasarhelyi, K. (2022). Digital health interventions for delivery of mental health care: Systematic and comprehensive meta-review. *JMIR Mental Health*, 9(5), Article e35159. doi:10.2196/35159

Piaget, J. (1952). *The origins of intelligence in children* (M. Cook, Trans.). International Universities Press.

Picciotto, G., Fox, J., & Neto, F. (2018). A phenomenology of spiritual bypass: Causes, consequences, and implications. *Journal of Spirituality in Mental Health*, 20(4), 333–354. doi:10.1080/19349637.2017.1417756

Prebble, S. C., Addis, D. R., & Tippett, L. J. (2013). Autobiographical memory and sense of self. *Psychological Bulletin*, 139(4), 815–840. doi:10.1037/a0030146

Proctor, E., Silmere, H., Raghavan, R., Hovmand, P., Aarons, G., Bunger, A., Griffey, R., & Hensley, M. (2011). Outcomes for implementation research: Conceptual distinctions, measurement challenges, and research agenda. *Administration and Policy in Mental Health and Mental Health Services Research*, 38(2), 65–76. doi:10.1007/s10488-010-0319-7

Przybylski, A. K., Murayama, K., DeHaan, C. R., & Gladwell, V. (2013). Motivational, emotional, and behavioral correlates of fear of missing out. *Computers in Human Behavior*, 29(4), 1841–1848. doi:10.1016/j.chb.2013.02.014

Radbruch, L., De Lima, L., Knaul, F., Wenk, R., Ali, Z., Bhatnaghar, S., Blanchard, C., Bruera, E., Buitrago, R., Burla, C., Callaway, M., Munyoro, E. C., Centeno, C., Cleary, J., Connor, S., Davaasuren, O., Downing, J., Foley, K., Goh, C., … Pastrana, T. (2020). Redefining palliative care—A new consensus-based definition. *Journal of Pain and Symptom Management*, 60(4), 754–764. doi:10.1016/j.jpainsymman.2020.04.027

Raja, S. N., Carr, D. B., Cohen, M., Finnerup, N. B., Flor, H., Gibson, S., Keefe, F. J., Mogil, J. S., Ringkamp, M., Sluka, K. A., Song, X.-J., Stevens, B., Sullivan, M. D., Tutelman, P. R., Ushida, T., & Vader, K. (2020). The revised International Association for the Study of Pain definition of pain: Concepts, challenges, and compromises. *Pain*, 161(9), 1976–1982.

Ravari, A., Mirzaei, T., Hosieni, F., & Hassanshahi, E. (2021). Comparison of the effects of cognitive therapy and logotherapy on Iranian elderly people's general health. *International Journal of Community Based Nursing and Midwifery*, 9(4), 289–299. doi:10.30476/IJCBNM.2021.88217.1497

Reber, R. (2019). Making school meaningful: Linking psychology of education to meaning in life. *Educational Review*, 71(4), 445–465. doi:10.1080/00131911.2018.1428177

Reilly, E. D., Farchione, T. J., Macy, A. S., & Jacobson, N. C. (2019). A systematic review of values measures in Acceptance and Commitment Therapy research. *Journal of Contextual Behavioral Science*, 12, 290–304. doi:10.1016/j.jcbs.2018.10.004

Reveley, J. (2015). Foucauldian critique of positive education and related self-technologies: Some problems and new directions. *Open Review of Educational Research*, 2(1), 78–93. doi:10.1080/23265507.2014.996768

Riethof, N., & Bob, P. (2019). Burnout syndrome and logotherapy: Logotherapy as a useful conceptual framework for explanation and prevention of burnout. *Frontiers in Psychiatry*, 10, 382.

Robatmili, S., Sohrabi, F., Shahrak, M. A., Talepasand, S., Nokani, M., & Hasani, M. (2015). The effect of group logotherapy on meaning in life and depression levels of Iranian students. *International Journal for the Advancement of Counselling*, 37(1), 54–62. doi:10.1007/s10447-014-9225-0

Robinson, T. E., & Berridge, K. C. (1993). The neural basis of drug craving: An incentive-sensitization theory of addiction. *Brain Research Reviews*, 18(3), 247–291. doi:10.1016/0165-0173(93)90013-P

Robinson, T. E., & Berridge, K. C. (2025). The incentive-sensitization theory of addiction 30 years on. *Annual Review of Psychology*, 76, 29–58. doi:10.1146/annurev-psych-011624-024031

Rodríguez-Prat, A., Pergolizzi, D., Crespo, I., Julià-Torras, J., Balaguer, A., Kremeike, K., Voltz, R., & Monforte-Royo, C. (2024). The wish to hasten death in patients with life-limiting conditions: A systematic overview. *Journal of Pain and Symptom Management*, 68(2), e91–e115. doi:10.1016/j.jpainsymman.2024.04.023

Rogers, B. A., Chicas, H., Kelly, J. M., Kubin, E., Christian, M. S., Kachanoff, F. J., Berger, J., Puryear, C., McAdams, D. P., & Gray, K. (2023). Seeing your life story as a Hero's Journey increases meaning in life. *Journal of Personality and Social Psychology*, 125(4), 752–778. doi:10.1037/pspa0000341

Rominger, C., Fink, A., & Perchtold-Stefan, C. M. (2024). Experiencing more meaningful coincidences is associated with more real-life creativity? Insights from three empirical studies. *PLoS ONE*, 19(5), e0300121. doi:10.1371/journal.pone.0300121

Rosa, H. (2013). *Social acceleration: A new theory of modernity* (J. Trejo-Mathys, Trans.). Columbia University Press.

Rosenberg, M., & McCullough, B. C. (1981). Mattering: Inferred significance and mental health among adolescents. In R. Simmons (Ed.), *Research in community mental health* (Vol. 2, pp. 163–182). JAI Press.

Rosenstreich, E., Russo-Netzer, P., & Icekson, T. (2024). Beyond coincidence: An investigation of the interplay between synchronicity awareness and the mindful state. *PLoS ONE*, 19(10), e0307443.

Rowe, J. W., & Kahn, R. L. (1997). Successful aging. *The Gerontologist*, 37(4), 433–440. doi:10.1093/geront/37.4.433

Russo-Netzer, P. (2019). Prioritizing meaning as a pathway to meaning in life and well-being. *Journal of Happiness Studies*, 20(6), 1863–1891. doi:10.1007/s10902-018-0031-y

Russo-Netzer, P. (2021). Preliminary exploration of creative expressions of ikigai. In D. Fido & Y. Kotera (Eds.), *Ikigai: Towards a psychological understanding of a life worth living* (pp. 49–71). Concurrent Disorders Society Publishing.

Russo-Netzer, P. (2023). Recalibrating the compass in a changing world: Education for meaning and meaningful education. *Journal of Constructivist Psychology*, 36(2), 168–184. doi:10.1080/10720537.2022.2068708

Russo-Netzer, P. (2025). Positive anxiety: Existential authenticity as a pathway to well-being. *The Journal of Positive Psychology*, 20(5), 823–833. doi:10.1080/17439760.2025.2498128

Russo-Netzer, P., & Ameli, M. (2021). Optimal sense-making and resilience in times of pandemic: Integrating rationality and meaning in psychotherapy. *Frontiers in Psychology*, 12, Article 645926. doi:10.3389/fpsyg.2021.645926

Russo-Netzer, P., & Atad, O. I. (2024). Activating values intervention: An integrative pathway to well-being. *Frontiers in Psychology*, 15, Article 1375237. doi:10.3389/fpsyg

Russo-Netzer, P., & Atad, O. I. (2025). Embodied meaning-making: A sensory-based intervention to foster psychological well-being. *The Journal of Positive Psychology*. Advance online publication. doi:10.1080/17439760.2025.2601574

Russo-Netzer, P., & Davidov, J. (2020). Transformative life experience as a glimpse into potentiality. *Journal of Humanistic Psychology*. Advance online publication. doi:10.1177/0022167820937487

Russo-Netzer, P., & Icekson, T. (2020). Engaging with life: Synchronicity experiences as a pathway to meaning in life and personal growth. *Current Psychology*. Advance online publication. doi:10.1007/s12144-019-00595-1

Russo-Netzer, P., & Icekson, T. (2023). An underexplored pathway to life satisfaction: The development and validation of the synchronicity awareness and meaning-detecting scale. *Frontiers in Psychology*, 13, 1053296. doi:10.3389/fpsyg.2022.1053296

Russo-Netzer, P., & Littman-Ovadia, H. (2019). "Something to live for": Experiences, resources, and personal strengths in late adulthood. *Frontiers in Psychology*, 10, Article 2452. doi:10.3389/fpsyg.2019.02452

Russo-Netzer, P., & Mayseless, O. (2021). Meaning in life at the crossroads of personal processes and cultural crisis. In O. Mayseless & P. Russo-Netzer (Eds.), *Finding meaning: An existential quest in postmodern Israel*. Oxford University Press.

Russo-Netzer, P., & Mishani-Uval, Y. (2022). Reflections on meaning in language and life. *The International Forum for Logotherapy: Journal of Search for Meaning*, 45(1), 47–55.

Russo-Netzer, P., & Shor, D. (2026). Shifting focus: A journey to existential wellness through the camera's lens. In D. Laird, E. Maisel, & A. Cantú (Eds.), *Existential wellness: Human-centered approaches as alternatives to the medical model* (pp. 494–521). Ethics International Press.

Russo-Netzer, P., & Shoshani, A. (2020). Authentic inner compass, well-being, and prioritization of positivity and meaning among adolescents.

Personality and Individual Differences, 167, Article 110248. doi:10.1016/j.paid.2020.110248

Russo-Netzer, P., Tarrasch, R., & Niemiec, R. M. (2023). A meaningful synergy: The integration of character strengths and the three types of meaning in life. *Social Sciences*, 12(9), 494. doi:10.3390/socsci12090494

Russo-Netzer, P., & Vos, J. (2026). Meaning interventions: Working with meaning in life in psychological therapies. In L. Hoffman, L. X. Vallejos, D. Hocoy, P. Tummala-Narra, & E. DeRobertis (Eds.), *APA handbook of humanistic and existential psychology: Vol. 2. Clinical and social applications* (pp. 175–206). American Psychological Association. doi:10.1037/0000432-009

Russo-Netzer, P., Niemiec, R. M., & Tarrasch, R. (2023). Developmental, genderial and cross-cultural aspects of meaning. *Journal of Happiness Studies*. Advance online publication. doi:10.1007/s10902-023-00693-9

Ryan, C., Huebner, D., Diaz, R. M., & Sanchez, J. (2009). Family rejection as a predictor of negative health outcomes in White and Latino lesbian, gay, and bisexual young adults. *Pediatrics*, 123(1), 346–352. doi:10.1542/peds.2007-3524

Ryan, R. M., & Deci, E. L. (2000). Self-determination theory and the facilitation of intrinsic motivation, social development, and well-being. *American Psychologist*, 55(1), 68–78. doi:10.1037/0003-066X.55.1.68

Ryan, R. M., & Deci, E. L. (2017). *Self-determination theory: Basic psychological needs in motivation, development, and wellness*. Guilford Press.

Ryff, C. D., & Singer, B. H. (2008). Know thyself and become what you are: A eudaimonic approach to psychological well-being. *Journal of Happiness Studies*, 9(1), 13–39. doi:10.1007/s10902-006-9019-0

Sagiv, L., & Roccas, S. (2017). What personal values are and what they are not: Taking a cross-cultural perspective. In S. Roccas & L. Sagiv (Eds.), *Values and behavior: Taking a cross-cultural perspective* (pp. 3–13). Springer. doi:10.1007/978-3-319-56352-7_1

Sagiv, L., Roccas, S., Cieciuch, J., & Schwartz, S. H. (2017). Personal values in human life. *Nature Human Behaviour*, 1(9), 630–639. doi:10.1038/s41562-017-0185-3

Salkovskis, P. M., Clark, D. M., Hackmann, A., Wells, A., & Gelder, M. G. (1999). An experimental investigation of the role of safety-seeking behaviours in the maintenance of panic disorder with agoraphobia. *Behaviour Research and Therapy*, 37(6), 559–574. doi:10.1016/S0005-7967(98)00153–00153

Schaverien, J. (2000). The triangular relationship and the aesthetic countertransference in analytical art psychotherapy. In A. Gilroy & G.

McNeilly (Eds.), *The changing shape of art therapy: New developments in theory and practice* (pp. 55–83). Jessica Kingsley Publishers.

Schieman, S., & Taylor, J. (2001). Statuses, roles, and the sense of mattering. *Sociological Perspectives*, 44(4), 469–484. doi:10.1525/sop.2001.44.4.469

Schlagman, S., & Kvavilashvili, L. (2008). Involuntary autobiographical memories in and outside the laboratory: How different are they from voluntary autobiographical memories? *Memory & Cognition*, 36(5), 920–932. doi:10.3758/MC.36.5.920

Schlossberg, N. K. (2011). The challenge of change: The transition model and its applications. *Journal of Employment Counseling*, 48(4), 159–162. doi:10.1002/j.2161-1920.2011.tb01102.x.

Schneider, K. J., Pierson, J. F., & Bugental, J. F. T. (Eds.). (2015). *The handbook of humanistic psychology: Theory, research, and practice* (2nd ed.). SAGE Publications.

Schnell, T. (2009). The Sources of Meaning and Meaning in Life Questionnaire (SoMe): Relations to demographics and well-being. *The Journal of Positive Psychology*, 4(6), 483–499. doi:10.1080/17439760903271074

Schore, A. N. (2009). Right-brain affect regulation: An essential mechanism of development, trauma, dissociation, and psychotherapy. In D. Fosha, D. J. Siegel, & M. F. Solomon (Eds.), *The healing power of emotion: Affective neuroscience, development & clinical practice* (pp. 112–144). W. W. Norton.

Schore, A. N. (2022). Right brain-to-right brain psychotherapy: Recent scientific and clinical advances. *Annals of General Psychiatry*, 21, Article 46. doi:10.1186/s12991-022-00420-3

Schulenberg, S. E. (2003). Use of logotherapy's Mountain Range Exercise with male adolescents with mental retardation/developmental disabilities and sexual behavior problems. *Journal of Contemporary Psychotherapy*, 33(3), 219–234. doi:10.1023/A:1023925720279

Schulenberg, S. E., Hutzell, R. R., Nassif, C., & Rogina, J. M. (2008). Logotherapy for clinical practice. *Psychotherapy: Theory, Research, Practice, Training*, 45(4), 447–463. doi:10.1037/a0014331.

Schulenberg, S. E., Strack, K. M., & Buchanan, E. M. (2011). The Meaning in Life Questionnaire: Psychometric properties with individuals with serious mental illness in an inpatient setting. *Journal of Clinical Psychology*, 67(12), 1210–1219. doi:10.1002/jclp.20841

Schutte, N. S., & Malouff, J. M. (2019). The impact of signature character strengths interventions: A meta-analysis. *Journal of Happiness Studies*, 20(4), 1179–1196. doi:10.1007/s10902-018-9990-2

Schutzeichel, F., Waldorp, L. J., Rot, M. A. H., Glashouwer, K. A., Frey, M. I., Wiers, R. W., & de Jong, P. J. (2024). Life meaning and feelings of ineffectiveness as transdiagnostic factors in eating disorder and comorbid internalizing symptomatology: A combined undirected and causal network approach. *Behaviour Research and Therapy*, 172, 104439. doi:10.1016/j.brat.2023.104439

Schwartz, S. H., Cieciuch, J., Vecchione, M., Davidov, E., Fischer, R., Beierlein, C., Ramos, A., Verkasalo, M., Lönnqvist, J.-E., Demirutku, K., Dirilen-Gumus, O., & Konty, M. (2012). Refining the theory of basic individual values. *Journal of Personality and Social Psychology*, 103(4), 663–688. doi:10.1037/a0029393

Schwartz, S. H., & Sortheix, F. M. (2018). Values and subjective well-being. In E. Diener, S. Oishi, & L. Tay (Eds.), *Handbook of well-being* (Noba Scholar Handbook series: Subjective well-being). DEF Publishers.

Sedikides, C., Slabu, L., Lenton, A., & Thomaes, S. (2017). State authenticity. *Current Directions in Psychological Science*, 26(6), 521–525. doi:10.1177/0963721417713296

Segal, Z. V., Williams, J. M. G., & Teasdale, J. D. (2002). *Mindfulness-based cognitive therapy for depression: A new approach to preventing relapse*. Guilford Press.

Seligman, M. E. P., Ernst, R. M., Gillham, J., Reivich, K., & Linkins, M. (2009). Positive education: Positive psychology and classroom interventions. *Oxford Review of Education*, 35(3), 293–311. doi:10.1080/03054980902934563

Seligman, M. E. P., Railton, P., Baumeister, R. F., & Sripada, C. (2013). Navigating into the future or driven by the past. *Perspectives on Psychological Science*, 8(2), 119–141. doi:10.1177/1745691612474317

Shapiro, S. L., Carlson, L. E., Astin, J. A., & Freedman, B. (2006). Mechanisms of mindfulness. *Journal of Clinical Psychology*, 62(3), 373–386. doi:10.1002/jclp.20237

Shapiro, S. L., Siegel, R. D., & Neff, K. D. (2018). Paradoxes of mindfulness. Mindfulness, 9(6), 1693–1701. doi:10.1007/s12671-018-0957-5

Shaygan, M., Hosseini, F. A., Shemiran, M., & Hedayati, A. (2023). The effect of mobile-based logotherapy on depression, hopelessness, and suicidal ideation in patients with major depressive disorder: A mixed-methods study. *Scientific Reports*, 13, Article 15828. doi:10.1038/s41598-023-43051-8

Shear, M. K., Frank, E., Houck, P. R., & Reynolds, C. F. (2005). Treatment of complicated grief: A randomized controlled trial. *JAMA*, 293 (21), 2601–2608. doi:10.1001/jama.293.21.2601

Shedler, J. (2010). The efficacy of psychodynamic psychotherapy. *American Psychologist*, 65(2), 98–109. doi:10.1037/a0018378

Sheldon, K. M. (2014). Becoming oneself: The central role of self-concordant goal selection. *Personality and Social Psychology Review*, 18 (4), 349–365. doi:10.1177/1088868314538549

Sheldon, K. M., & Elliot, A. J. (1999). Goal striving, need satisfaction, and longitudinal well-being: The self-concordance model. *Journal of Personality and Social Psychology*, 76(3), 482–497. doi:10.1037/0022-3514.76.3.482

Sheldon, K. M., & Krieger, L. S. (2014). Walking the talk: Value importance, value enactment, and well-being. *Motivation and Emotion*, 38(5), 609–619. doi:10.1007/s11031-014-9424-3

Sherman, D. K., & Cohen, G. L. (2006). The psychology of self-defense: Self-affirmation theory. *Advances in Experimental Social Psychology*, 38, 183–242. doi:10.1016/S0065-2601(06)38004-5

Sherman, L. E., Payton, A. A., Hernandez, L. M., Greenfield, P. M., & Dapretto, M. (2016). The power of the like in adolescence: Effects of peer influence on neural and behavioral responses to social media. *Psychological Science*, 27(7), 1027–1035.

Shiffman, S., Stone, A. A., & Hufford, M. R. (2008). Ecological momentary assessment. *Annual Review of Clinical Psychology*, 4, 1–32. doi:10.1146/annurev.clinpsy.3.022806.091415

Skinner, B. F. (1953). *Science and human behavior*. Macmillan.

Sone, T., Nakaya, N., Ohmori, K., Shimazu, T., Higashiguchi, M., Kakizaki, M., Kikuchi, N., Kuriyama, S., & Tsuji, I. (2008). Sense of life worth living (ikigai) and mortality in Japan: Ohsaki study. *Psychosomatic Medicine*, 70(6), 709–715. doi:10.1097/PSY.0b013e31817e7e64

Soenens, B., Vansteenkiste, M., Van Petegem, S., Beyers, W., & Ryan, R. (2017). How to solve the conundrum of adolescent autonomy?: on the importance of distinguishing between independence and volitional functioning. In *Autonomy in adolescent development* (pp. 1–32). Psychology Press.

Stanford Center on Longevity. (2022). *The new map of life: State of longevity*. Stanford University.

Stauber, B., & Walther, A. (Eds.). (2022). *Doing transitions in the life course: Processes and practices*. Springer.

Steger, M. F. (2012). Making meaning in life. *Psychological Inquiry*, 23(4), 381–385. doi:10.1080/1047840X.2012.720832

Steger, M. F., Dik, B. J., & Duffy, R. D. (2012). Measuring meaningful work: The Work and Meaning Inventory (WAMI). *Journal of Career Assessment*, 20(3), 322–337. doi:10.1177/1069072711436160

Steger, M. F., Frazier, P., Oishi, S., & Kaler, M. (2006). The Meaning in Life Questionnaire: Assessing the presence of and search for meaning in life. *Journal of Counseling Psychology*, 53(1), 80–93. doi:10.1037/0022-0167.53.1.80

Steger, M. F., Kashdan, T. B., Sullivan, B. A., & Lorentz, D. (2008a). Understanding the search for meaning in life: Personality, cognitive style, and the dynamic between seeking and experiencing meaning. *Journal of Personality*, 76(2), 199–228. doi:10.1111/j.1467-6494.2007.00484.x

Steger, M. F., Kawabata, Y., Shimai, S., & Otake, K. (2008b). The meaningful life in Japan and the United States: Levels and correlates of meaning in life. *Journal of Research in Personality*, 42(3), 660–678. doi:10.1016/j.jrp.2007.09.003

Steger, M. F., O'Donnell, M. B., & Morse, J. L. (2021). Helping students find their way to meaning: Meaning and purpose in education. In *The Palgrave handbook of positive education* (pp. 551–579). Springer International Publishing.

Steger, M. F., Oishi, S., & Kashdan, T. B. (2009). Meaning in life across the life span: Levels and correlates of meaning in life from emerging adulthood to older adulthood. *The Journal of Positive Psychology*, 4 (1), 43–52. doi:10.1080/17439760802303127

Steger, M. F., Shim, Y., Barenz, J., & Shin, J. Y. (2014). Through the windows of the soul: A pilot study using photography to enhance meaning in life. *Journal of Contextual Behavioral Science*, 3(1), 27–30. doi:10.1016/j.jcbs.2013.11.002

Steinberg, L., & Morris, A. S. (2001). Adolescent development. *Annual Review of Psychology*, 52, 83–110. doi:10.1146/annurev.psych.52.1.83

Stern, D. N., Hofer, L., Haft, W., & Dore, J. (1985). Affect attunement: The sharing of feeling states between mother and infant by means of inter-modal fluency. In T. M. Field & N. A. Fox (Eds.), *Social perception in infants* (pp. 249–268). Ablex.

Stroebe, M., & Schut, H. (1999). The dual process model of coping with bereavement: Rationale and description. *Death Studies*, 23(3), 197–224. doi:10.1080/074811899201046

Stroebe, M., & Schut, H. (2010). The dual process model of coping with bereavement: A decade on. *Omega: Journal of Death and Dying*, 61(4), 273–289. doi:10.2190/OM.61.4.b

Stuckey, H. L., & Nobel, J. (2010). The connection between art, healing, and public health: A review of current literature. *American Journal of Public Health*, 100(2), 254–263. doi:10.2105/AJPH.2008.156497

Sun, M., Tian, X., Peng, Y., Wang, Z., Lu, Y., & Xiao, W. (2024). Effects of meaning therapy on spirituality, psychological health, and quality of life in patients with cancer: A systematic review and meta-analysis of randomized controlled trials. *Asia-Pacific Journal of Oncology Nursing*, 11(4), 100388. doi:10.1016/j.apjon.2024.100388

Sutin, A. R., Luchetti, M., Stephan, Y., Karakose, S., & Terracciano, A. (2025). Purpose in life and depressive symptoms: An individual-participant meta-analysis of >500,000 participants across six world regions. *Journal of Affective Disorders*. doi:10.1016/j.jad.2025.120881

Szabó, K., & Nagyné Baji, I. (2025). The current status and applications of logotherapy and existential analysis: A narrative review. *Developments in Health Sciences*, 8, 82–100. doi:10.1556/2066.2025.00083

Tarafdar, M., Tu, Q., Ragu-Nathan, B. S., & Ragu-Nathan, T. S. (2007). The impact of technostress on role stress and productivity. *Journal of Management Information Systems*, 24(1), 301–328. doi:10.2753/MIS0742-1222240109

Tarafdar, M., Pullins, E. B., & Ragu-Nathan, T. S. (2015). Technostress: Negative effect on performance and possible mitigations. *Information Systems Journal*, 25(2), 103–132. doi:10.1111/isj.12042

Tagore, R. (1912). *Gitanjali (Song offerings): A collection of prose translations made by the author from the original Bengali* (W. B. Yeats, Intro.). The India Society.

Tao, K. W., Owen, J., Pace, B. T., & Imel, Z. E. (2015). A meta-analysis of multicultural competencies and psychotherapy process and outcome. *Journal of Counseling Psychology*, 62(3), 337–350. doi:10.1037/cou0000086

Tecuta, L., Tomba, E., Grandi, S., & Fava, G. A. (2015). Demoralization: A systematic review on its clinical characterization. *Psychological Medicine*, 45(4), 673–691. doi:10.1017/S0033291714001597.

Tedeschi, R. G., & Calhoun, L. G. (1996). The Posttraumatic Growth Inventory: Measuring the positive legacy of trauma. *Journal of Traumatic Stress*, 9(3), 455–471. doi:10.1002/jts.2490090305

Tedeschi, R. G., & Calhoun, L. G. (2004). Posttraumatic growth: Conceptual foundations and empirical evidence. *Psychological Inquiry*, 15 (1), 1–18. doi:10.1207/s15327965pli1501_01

Tessier, J., Joussemet, M., Kurdi, V., & Mageau, G. A. (2021). Adolescents "walking the talk": How value importance and enactment relate to well-being and risk-taking. *Motivation and Emotion*, 45, 249–264.

Treasure, J., & Schmidt, U. (2013). The cognitive-interpersonal maintenance model of anorexia nervosa revisited: A summary of the evidence for cognitive, socio-emotional and interpersonal predisposing and perpetuating factors. *Journal of Eating Disorders*, 1, Article 13. doi:10.1186/2050-2974-1-13

Treede, R.-D., Rief, W., Barke, A., Aziz, Q., Bennett, M. I., Benoliel, R., Cohen, M., Evers, S., Finnerup, N. B., First, M. B., Giamberardino, M. A., Kaasa, S., Kosek, E., Lavand'homme, P., Nicholas, M., Perrot, S., Scholz, J., Schug, S., Smith, B. H., Svensson, P., Vlaeyen, J. W. S., & Wang, S.-J. (2019). Chronic pain as a symptom or a disease: The IASP Classification of Chronic Pain for the International Classification of Diseases (ICD-11). *Pain*, 160(1), 19–27. doi:10.1097/j.pain.0000000000001384

Tronick, E., & Beeghly, M. (2011). Infants' meaning-making and the development of mental health problems. *American Psychologist*, 66(2), 107–119. doi: 10.1037/a0021631

Turner, V. (1969). *The ritual process: Structure and anti-structure.* Aldine.

Twenge, J. M. (2017). *iGen: Why today's super-connected kids are growing up less rebellious, more tolerant, less happy — and completely unprepared for adulthood.* Atria Books.

Twohig, M. P., & Levin, M. E. (2017). Acceptance and commitment therapy as a treatment for anxiety and depression: A review . *Psychiatric Clinics of North America*, 40(4), 751–770. doi:10.1016/j.psc.2017.08.009

U.S. Department of Veterans Affairs & U.S. Department of Defense. (2022). VA/DoD clinical practice guideline for the management of major depressive disorder (Version 4.0). Retrieved February 18, 2026, from https://www.healthquality.va.gov/guidelines/MH/mdd/VADODMDDCPGFinal508.pdf

Valkenburg, P. M. (2022). Social media use and its impact on adolescent mental health: An umbrella review of the evidence. *Current Opinion in Psychology*, 44, 58–68.

Vanhooren, S. (2019). Struggling with meaninglessness: A case study from an experiential–existential perspective. *Person-Centered & Experiential Psychotherapies*, 18(1), 1–21. doi:10.1080/14779757.2019.1572029

van Bruggen, V., Vos, J., Westerhof, G., Bohlmeijer, E. T., & Glas, G. (2013). Over de plaats van existentiële thema's in cognitieve gedragstherapie [About the place of existential themes in cognitive behavioral therapy]. *Tijdschrift voor Gedragstherapie en Cognitieve Therapie*, 2, 119–134.

van der Spek, N., Vos, J., van Uden-Kraan, C. F., Breitbart, W., Cuijpers, P., Holtmaat, K., Witte, B. I., Tollenaar, R. A. E. M., & Verdonck-de Leeuw, I. M. (2017). Efficacy of meaning-centered group psychotherapy for cancer survivors: A randomized controlled trial . *Psychological Medicine*, 47(11), 1990–2001. doi:10.1017/S0033291717000447 van Doornik, S. F. W., Glashouwer, K. A., Ostafin, B. D., & de Jong, P. J. (2024). The effects of a meaning-centered intervention on meaning in life and eating disorder symptoms in undergraduate women with high weight and shape concerns: A randomized controlled trial. *Behavior Therapy*, 55(1), 177–190. doi:10.1016/j.beth.2023.05.012

van Gennep, A. (1960). *The rites of passage* (M. B. Vizedom & G. L. Caffee, Trans.). University of Chicago Press. (Original work published 1909.)

Van Simaeys, H., Clays, E., Lechner, L., & Lauwerier, E. (2025). Exploring the role of meaning in life in relation to burn-out symptoms among early and mid-career nurses: A cross-sectional study. *Journal of Nursing Management*, 2025, 1205579. doi:10.1155/jonm/1205579.

VanderWeele, T. J., (2025). The Global Flourishing Study: Study profile and initial results on flourishing. *Nature Mental Health*. doi:10.1038/s44220-025-00423-5

van Zyl, L. E., Custers, N. C., Dik, B. J., van der Vaart, L., & Klibert, J. J. (2023). The holistic life-crafting model: A systematic literature review of meaning-making behaviors. *Frontiers in Psychology*, 14, 271188. doi:10.3389/fpsyg.2023.1271188

Verduyn, P., Lee, D. S., Park, J., Shablack, H., Orvell, A., Bayer, J., Ybarra, O., & Jonides, J. (2015). Passive Facebook usage undermines affective well-being: Experimental and longitudinal evidence. *Journal of Experimental Psychology: General*, 144(2), 480–488.

Verduyn, P., Ybarra, O., Résibois, M., Jonides, J., & Kross, E. (2017). Do social network sites enhance or undermine subjective well-being? *A critical review. Social Issues and Policy Review*, 11(1), 274–302. doi:10.1111/sipr.12033

Verschueren, M., Claes, L., Palmeroni, N., Raemen, L., Moons, P., Bruckers, L., Molenberghs, G., Dierckx, E., Schoevaerts, K., & Luyckx, K. (2024). Identity functioning in patients with an eating disorder: Developmental trajectories throughout treatment. *Nutrients*, 16 (5), 591. doi:10.3390/nu16050591

Vivolo, M., Owen, J., & Fisher, P. (2024). Psychological therapists' experiences of burnout: A qualitative systematic review and meta-synthesis. *Mental Health & Prevention*, 33, 200253. doi:10.1016/j.mhp.2022.200253

Vlaeyen, J. W. S., & Linton, S. J. (2012). Fear-avoidance model of chronic musculoskeletal pain: 12 years on. *Pain*, 153(6), 1144–1147. doi:10.1016/j.pain.2011.12.009

Vlaeyen, J. W. S., & Linton, S. J. (2000). Fear-avoidance and its consequences in chronic musculoskeletal pain: A state of the art. *Pain*, 85 (3), 317–332. doi:10.1016/S0304-3959(99)00242-0

Volkow, N. D., Koob, G. F., & McLellan, A. T. (2016). Neurobiologic advances from the brain disease model of addiction. *The New England Journal of Medicine*, 374(4), 363–371. doi:10.1056/NEJMra1511480

Vos, J. (2016). Working with meaning in life in mental health care: A systematic literature review of the practices and effectiveness of meaning-centred therapies. *Psychology and Psychotherapy: Theory, Research and Practice*, 89(1), 1–20. doi:10.1111/papt.12078.

Vos, J. (2018). *Meaning in life: An evidence-based handbook for practitioners*. Bloomsbury Publishing.

Vos, J., Craig, M., & Cooper, M. (2015). Existential therapies: A meta-analysis of their effects on psychological outcomes. *Journal of Consulting and Clinical Psychology*, 83(1), 115–128. doi:10.1037/a0037167.

Vos, J., & Vitali, D. (2018). The effects of psychological meaning-centered therapies on quality of life and psychological stress: A meta-analysis. *Palliative & Supportive Care*, 16(5), 608–632. doi:10.1017/S1478951517000931

Vuksanovic, D., Green, H. J., Dyck, M., & Morrissey, S. A. (2017). Dignity therapy and life review for palliative care patients: A randomized controlled trial. *Journal of Pain and Symptom Management*, 53(2), 162–170.e1. doi:10.1016/j.jpainsymman.2016.09.005

Walton, G. M., & Wilson, T. D. (2018). Wise interventions: Psychological remedies for social and personal problems. *Psychological Review*, 125 (5), 617–655. doi:10.1037/rev0000115

Wampold, B. E., & Imel, Z. E. (2015). *The great psychotherapy debate: The evidence for what makes psychotherapy work* (2nd ed.). Routledge.

Wang, Z., Xu, D., Yu, S., Liu, Y., Han, Y., Zhao, W., & Zhang, W. (2025). Effectiveness of meaning-centered interventions on existential distress and mental health outcomes in cancer survivors and their family caregivers: A systematic review and meta-analysis of randomized controlled trials. *Worldviews on Evidence-Based Nursing*, 22(1), e12752. doi:10.1111/wvn.12752

Watkins, L. E., Sprang, K. R., & Rothbaum, B. O. (2018). Treating PTSD: A review of evidence-based psychotherapy interventions. *Frontiers in Behavioral Neuroscience*, 12, 258. doi:10.3389/fnbeh.2018.00258

Watson, J. B. (1913). Psychology as the behaviorist views it. *Psychological Review*, 20(2), 158–177.

Wechsler, T. F., Kümpers, F., & Mühlberger, A. (2019). Inferiority or even superiority of virtual reality exposure therapy in phobias?—A systematic review and quantitative meta-analysis on randomized controlled trials comparing VR exposure to in vivo exposure. *Frontiers in Psychology*, 10, 1758. doi:10.3389/fpsyg.2019.01758

Wells, A., Clark, D. M., Salkovskis, P., Ludgate, J., Hackmann, A., & Gelder, M. (1995). Social phobia: The role of in-situation safety behaviors in maintaining anxiety and negative beliefs. *Behaviour Research and Therapy*, 33(4), 409–421.

Weng, J., Wild, E., Chesak, S., Rhee, L., Piderman, K. M., Santiago, A. L., Rinker, C. J., Felt, M., Fischer, K. M., Ingram, C., & Pachman, D. R. (2025). Feasibility and acceptability of virtual dignity therapy for palliative care patients with advanced cancer. *American Journal of Hospice and Palliative Medicine*. Advance online publication. doi:10.1177/10499091251361467

Westerhof, G. J., & Bohlmeijer, E. T. (2014). Celebrating fifty years of research and applications in reminiscence and life review: State of the art and new directions. *Journal of Aging Studies*, 29, 107–114. doi:10.1016/j.jaging.2014.02.003

Westerhof, G. J., Bohlmeijer, E. T., van Beljouw, I. M. J., & Pot, A. M. (2010). Improvement in personal meaning mediates the effects of a life review intervention on depressive symptoms in a randomized controlled trial. *The Gerontologist*, 50(4), 541–549. doi:10.1093/geront/gnp168

White, M., & Epston, D. (1990). *Narrative means to therapeutic ends*. W. W. Norton.

White, M. A., & Kern, M. L. (2018). Positive education: Learning and teaching for wellbeing and academic mastery. *International Journal of Wellbeing*, 8(1), 1–17. doi:10.5502/ijw.v8i1.588

Whitson, J. A., & Galinsky, A. D. (2008). Lacking control increases illusory pattern perception. *Science*, 322(5898), 115–117. doi:10.1126/science.1159845

Whyte, K. P. (2017). Indigenous climate change studies: Indigenizing futures, decolonizing the Anthropocene. *English Language Notes*, 55(1–2), 153–162.

Willander, J., & Larsson, M. (2006). Smell your way back to childhood: Autobiographical odor memory. *Psychological Science*, 17(3), 240–244. doi:10.1111/j.1467-9280.2006.01693.x

Williams, A. C. de C., Fisher, E., Hearn, L., & Eccleston, C. (2020). Psychological therapies for the management of chronic pain (excluding headache) in adults. *Cochrane Database of Systematic Reviews*, 2020 (8), CD007407. doi:10.1002/14651858.CD007407.pub4

Wilson, A. E., & Ross, M. (2001). From chump to champ: People's appraisals of their earlier and present selves. *Journal of Personality and Social Psychology*, 80(4), 572–584. doi:10.1037/0022-3514.80.4.572

Wilson, A. E., & Ross, M. (2003). The identity function of autobiographical memory: Time is on our side. *Memory*, 11(2), 137–149. doi:10.1080/741938210

Wilson, T. D., & Gilbert, D. T. (2008). Explaining away: A model of affective adaptation. *Perspectives on Psychological Science*, 3(5), 370–386. doi:10.1111/j.1745-6924.2008.00085.x

Wise, E. H. (2008). Dual relationships, professional integrity, and the therapist's responsibility. *Psychotherapy: Theory, Research, Practice, Training*, 45(4), 544–553.

Witkiewitz, K., & Marlatt, G. A. (2004). Relapse prevention for alcohol and drug problems: That was Zen, this is Tao. *American Psychologist*, 59(4), 224–235. doi:10.1037/0003-066X.59.4.224

Wittouck, C., Van Autreve, S., De Jaegere, E., Portzky, G., & van Heeringen, K. (2011). The prevention and treatment of complicated grief: A meta-analysis. *Clinical Psychology Review*, 31(1), 69–78. doi:10.1016/j.cpr.2010.09.005

Wolitzky-Taylor, K. B., Horowitz, J. D., Powers, M. B., & Telch, M. J. (2008). Psychological approaches in the treatment of specific phobias: A meta-analysis. *Clinical Psychology Review*, 28(6), 1021–1037. doi:10.1016/j.cpr.2008.02.007

Wong, P. T. P. (2011). Positive psychology 2.0: Towards a balanced interactive model of the good life. *Canadian Psychology*, 52(2), 69–81. doi:10.1037/a0022511.

Wong, P. T. P. (2012). *Toward a dual-systems model of what makes life worth living*. In P. T. P. Wong (Ed.), *The human quest for meaning: Theories, research, and applications* (2nd ed., pp. 3–22). Routledge.

Wong, P. T. P. (2016). Meaning-centered positive group intervention. In P. Russo-Netzer, S. E. Schulenberg, & A. Batthyány (Eds.), *Clinical perspectives on meaning: Positive and existential psychotherapy* (pp. 423–445). Springer. doi:10.1007/978-3-319-41397-6_21

Wong, P. T. P. (2023). Pioneer in research in existential positive psychology of suffering and global flourishing: Paul T. P. Wong. *Applied Research in Quality of Life*, 18, 2153–2157. doi:10.1007/s11482-023-10207-7

World Health Organization (WHO). (2020, August 5). *Palliative care*. https://www.who.int/news-room/fact-sheets/detail/palliative-care

World Health Organization (WHO). (2025, August 29). *Depressive disorder (depression)*. Retrieved February 18, 2026, from https://www.who.int/news-room/fact-sheets/detail/depression.

Wrzesniewski, A., & Dutton, J. E. (2001). Crafting a job: Revisioning employees as active crafters of their work. *Academy of Management Review*, 26(2), 179–201. doi:10.5465/amr.2001.4378011

Yakushko, O., Watson, M., & Thompson, S. (2005). Influence of social support, existential well-being, and stress over sexual orientation on self-esteem of gay, lesbian, and bisexual individuals. *International Journal for the Advancement of Counselling*, 27, 131–143. doi:10.1007/s10447-005-2259-6

Yalom, I. D. (2011). *The gift of therapy: An open letter to a new generation of therapists and their patients* (Rev. and updated ed.). Piatkus.

Yalom, I. D. (1980). *Existential psychotherapy.* Basic Books.

Yalom, I. D., & Leszcz, M. (2020). *The theory and practice of group psychotherapy* (6th ed.). Basic Books.

Yang, X., Zhang, P., Jing, S., Cheng, Y., & Cavaletto, A. (2024). Logotherapy-based interventions for Chinese family caregivers of older adults with dementia through online groups: A mixed-methods study. *Journal of Gerontological Social Work*, 67(7), 865–880. doi:10.1080/01634372.2024.2326689

Young, J. E., Klosko, J. S., & Weishaar, M. E. (2003). *Schema therapy: A practitioner's guide.* Guilford Press.

Zhao, S., Grasmuck, S., & Martin, J. (2008). Identity construction on Facebook: Digital empowerment in anchored relationships. *Computers in Human Behavior*, 24(5), 1816–1836.

Index

For Product Safety Concerns and Information please contact our EU representative GPSR@taylorandfrancis.com Taylor & Francis Verlag GmbH, Kaufingerstraße 24, 80331 München, Germany

Batch number: 10726001

Printed by Printforce, the Netherlands